OPIUM

Also by Martin Booth

Fiction
Hiroshima Joe
The Jade Pavilion
Black Chameleon
Dreaming of Samarkand
A Very Private Gentleman
The Humble Disciple
The Iron Tree
Toys of Glass
Adrift in the Oceans of Mercy

Non-fiction
Carpet Sahib – a life of Jim Corbett
The Triads
Rhino Road
The Dragon and the Pearl

Children's Books
War Dog

Edited books
The Book of Cats (with George MacBeth)

OPIUM

A History

MARTIN BOOTH

St. Martin's Press New York

A THOMAS DUNNE BOOK.
An imprint of St. Martin's Press.

OPIUM: A HISTORY. Copyright © 1996 by
Martin Booth. All rights reserved. Printed
in the United States of America. No part of
this book may be used or reproduced in
any manner whatsoever without written
permission except in the case of brief quo-
tations embodied in critical articles or
reviews. For information, address St.
Martin's Press, 175 Fifth Avenue, New
York, N.Y. 10010.

Library of Congress Cataloging-in-
Publication Data

Booth, Martin.
   Opium : a history / Martin
Booth.
      p.   cm.
   Originally published: London
Simon & Schuster Ltd., 1996.
   Includes bibliographical refer-
ences (p.   ) and index.
    ISBN 0-312-18643-6
    1. Opium habit—History. 2.
Opium trade—History.   I. Title.
HV5816.B66 1998   98-14851
615'.32335—cd21   CIP

First published in Great Britain by Simon
& Schuster Ltd.

First U.S. Edition: July 1998

10 9 8 7 6 5 4 3 2 1

Contents

Acknowledgements	ix
Foreword	xi
Chapter 1 – Raw Opium	1
Chapter 2 – The Discovery of Dreams	15
Chapter 3 – Pleasure-domes in Xanadu	35
Chapter 4 – Poverty, Potions and Poppy-heads	51
Chapter 5 – Heroic Substances	67
Chapter 6 – God's Own Medicine	81
Chapter 7 – The Fantasy Traders	103
Chapter 8 – The Government of Opium	139
Chapter 9 – Coolies and Conferences	175
Chapter 10 – Junkies and the Living Dead	191
Chapter 11 – DORA, Isabella and Olivia	211
Chapter 12 – Carpets, Condoms and Cats	227
Chapter 13 – Enter the Mobster	243
Chapter 14 – Soldiers and Secrets	255
Chapter 15 – Warlords, Barons and Laundrymen	293
Chapter 16 – Bacteria and The $1,000,000 Bathtub	339
Bibliography	355
Index	361

Opiate – an unlocked door in the prison of identity. It leads into the jail yard.

Ambrose Bierce: *The Devil's Dictionary*.

Everything one does in life, even love, occurs in an express train racing toward death. To smoke opium is to get out of the train while it is still moving. It is to concern oneself with something other than life or death.

Jean Cocteau.

Acknowledgements

I am indebted to a large number of people for their considerable assistance, support and encouragement in the researching and writing of this book. To the following I offer my heartfelt gratitude for, without them, the task could not have been completed: Dr Terry Boyce of the University of Hong Kong; Dr Ingrid Hook and the staff of the Department of Pharmacognosy, School of Pharmacy, Trinity College, Dublin; the librarian and staff of the University of Hong Kong Library; John Keep, H.M. Customs & Excise, London; A. Renouf, H.M. Customs & Excise, Jersey; J.L.S. Keesing, Royal Botanical Gardens, Kew; Dr Neil Bruce of the Institute of Biotechnology, Cambridge University; Dr Brigid Allen, the Archivist, Jesus College, Oxford; Jeffrey Robinson; Kevin Laurie of the Police Tactical Unit, Royal Hong Kong Police; William L. Ruzzamenti, Office of Congressional & Public Affairs, the US Department of Justice; Vera Savko of the Mayor's Office, St Petersburg; Roger Lewis of the Centre for HIV/AIDS and Drugs Studies, Edinburgh; Superintendent Clive Tricker and Sen. Insp. Ricky Fung Hing-nam of the Narcotics Bureau, Royal Hong Kong Police; Maureen Sheehan, the Poppy Advisory and Control Board, Tasmania; Dr Harry Payne and David Mercer of MacFarlan Smith, Ltd; the Intelligence Division of the US Drug Enforcement Administration; Cathay Pacific Airways; John Powell, Somerset County Libraries; Murray Pollinger, my literary agent and a large number of people in Britain, the USA, Hong

Kong, Thailand, Russia and Eastern Europe who operate at the barricades of the war against heroin and other drugs and who, for security reasons, must remain anonymous, but who have my considerable admiration.

Finally, my wife Helen whose considerable skill and research assistance, patience, forbearance and months before a computer monitor were utterly invaluable and without which this book would not have been written.

Foreword

In 1398, the following words were translated from the writings of John de Trevisa: 'Of popy comyth iuys that physycyens callyth Opium other Opion'. Approximately two years later, in Lanfrank's *Science of cirugie*, appeared the advice, 'It is not yuel to putte a litil opium to þe oile of þe rosis'. What the physicians used opium for, or what good it did when mixed with oil of roses, was not stated until Jerome of Brunswick published his *The noble experyence of the vertuous handyworke of surgeri*. Translated into English in 1525, it contained an early reference to opium as a medicinal drug: 'Whan the payne is grete, then it is nedefull to put therto a lytell Opium'.

Few nouns can be more evocative than opium. Derived from the ancient Greek for the sap of the poppy pod, it has moved a long way from its original innocent meaning. It simultaneously conjures up exotic images of murky drug dens filled with besotted addicts, white slavers and Fu Manchu-like fiends, maudlin and tubercular Romantic poets and, by association, alleyways across the cities of the world littered with discarded hypodermic needles, trained sniffer dogs going over airline baggage, haggard youths shooting up heroin in public lavatory cubicles, AIDS sufferers and prostitutes, mafiosi, drug barons riding in sleek limousines, machine-gun-toting smugglers, street-corner peddlers and Hollywood gangster movies.

To an addict, opium and its derivatives are the raw substance of

dreams, the means of escape from reality and temporary entry into
heaven – or at least another place apart from the here and now: it is
also slave-master, cruel mistress and possessive lover. For narcotics
agents, law enforcement or customs officers, opium is the source of
the evil by the hunting down of which they earn a salary and may
lose their life. To politicians and their secret service operatives, it
is the ideal substance of subversion and political instability. Those
dedicated to the eradication of drugs from society regard it as being
just as much their *raison d'être*, their quest, even their holy grail,
as it is the junkie's: they both search for it with a zealot's avidity.
For the racketeer, opium is a means to considerable wealth for a
comparatively low capital outlay. And there are those who find
it has other uses: poisoners kill with it and have done so since at
least Roman times; terrorists finance mayhem with it; urban crime
is fuelled by it; arms dealers use it as a form of currency and
governments are either blackmailed by it or employ it to corrupt
or to apply pressure to other administrations, nations or political
adversaries. Opium (in the form of heroin) accounts for an illicit
multi-national trade which is larger than that of many countries.

In short, society is undermined – some might say underpinned
– by opium.

Yet for all these detrimental aspects, opium has a benign side.
The economies of some countries depend upon it, the opium harvest being all that stands between social stability and political overthrow, well-being and disease or starvation. Many a Third World
peasant farmer regards opium as a steady, reliable, easily grown
and harvested cash crop. For the terminal cancer patient, opium
and its derivatives afford a blessed relief from the tortures and
indignities of pain. Even a passing headache can be eradicated by
an opiate bought over the counter of many a pharmacist's shop.

In other words, opium and its derivatives are all things to all
men and have been so for centuries.

The story of opium goes back well before the nineteenth century
invention of heroin, opium clippers riding the South China Sea,
the discovery of morphine, poets habituated to laudanum, the
rudimentary pharmacology of the Middle Ages and the political
machinations of ambitious Roman murderers. It has its origins in
the start of human society and its use almost certainly pre-dates
civilisation. In fact, there seems little doubt that opium was one of
the first medicinal substances known to mankind.

OPIUM

1

Raw Opium

The opium poppy is botanically classified as *Papaver somniferum*. The genus is named from the Greek noun for a poppy, the species from the Latin word meaning 'sleep inducing': it was Linnaeus, the father of botany, who first classified it in his book *Genera Plantarum* in 1753. Like many of his contemporaries, and generations before him, he was well aware of its capabilities.

The plant has a dubious history. Some horticulturists consider it evolved naturally, but there are others who claim it is a cultivor developed by century upon century of careful human cultivation. Another theory is that it is a naturally mutated plant which evolved because of a quirk of climate or altitude. This is not far-fetched for plants will take on atypical forms in unique conditions: the cannabis trees of Bhutan prove the point. No one can be certain.

Although there is no positive proof, it is thought *P. somniferum* may have evolved, or been generated, either from the wild poppy, *Papaver setigerum*, which contains small amounts of opium and which indigenously grows throughout the countries bordering the Mediterranean Sea, or from a poppy native to Asia Minor.

To many not specifically engaged in its cultivation, the poppy is either an ornamental flower with a delicate beauty or a simple, scarlet blossom growing wild in the cereal fields of Europe, an image for the blood spilled in the trenches of the First World War. In fact, it comes from a large botanical family of 28 genera and over 250 individual species, most of which grow in the temperate and sub-tropical regions of the Northern Hemisphere. Many popular varieties have been specifically cultivated: the bush and tree poppies, the Welsh poppy, the blue and Syrian tulip poppies, the alpine poppy, the sub-arctic Iceland poppy, the Californian poppy. Even the opium poppy itself may be found in borders and displays in well-kept gardens, albeit illegally in most countries. In its wild state, the poppy is a single bloom but double flowers and specialist blooms with serrated and fringed petals have also been bred in a multitude of colours: the most exquisite are two variations of the opium poppy, the Pink Chiffon and the Pæony-flowered Mixed. Several species, such as the Oriental poppy from Asia Minor, are perennials.

Of all these species, only *P. somniferum* and *P. bracteatum* produce opium in any significant amount, although the latter is not used at present as a commercial drug source but is sometimes grown as a decorative blossom from which a number of hybrids have derived.

Papaver somniferum is an annual with a growth cycle of approximately 120 days. It requires a rich, well-cultivated soil and, in the wild, is more likely to flourish in recently dug or ploughed ground, hence its presence in farm fields and, traditionally, by cart tracks and animal droves. The best growing climate is temperate, warm with low humidity and not too much rainfall during early growth. Ideally, although it will grow in clay or sandy clay, the best soil is a sandy loam which retains nutrients and moisture and is not too hard for the delicate early roots to penetrate. Both excessive and insufficient rainfall affect growth: too much moisture causes waterlogging and, if the soil is not properly drained, the plants will quickly die whilst dull, cloudy weather or excessive rain in days thirty to ninety of the growth period will reduce the opium-producing capabilities. Sunlight is especially important. The opium poppy is a 'long day' photo-responsive plant which means it will not produce blooms unless it has grown through a period of long days and short nights, preferably with direct sunlight at least twelve hours daily.

These requirements aside, the plant is easy to grow. It does not require irrigation unless it is in danger of drying out, demands no expensive fertilisers, has few pests or ailments and, therefore, requires no insecticides or fungicides.

The seeds (about the size of a pin-head) are naturally sown by the pod blowing in the breeze and shaking like a pepper-pot, the contents scattering. When deliberately set, they are either broadcast or dropped in rows of shallow holes made by a stick or dibber, the timing of the sowing depending heavily upon local seasonal and climatic conditions. About 500 grams of seed are sown to half a hectare. The seeds may range over a wide variety of colours from white through yellow to brown, grey or black, the coloration not being relevant to the eventual blossom. Other cash crops, such as beans, peas or tobacco, may be planted alongside the poppy: these do not hinder it and are usually only a means of obtaining a higher return from the same area of land.

The seeds germinate quickly in warm, moist conditions and, within six weeks, the plant is established by which time it vaguely resembles a young cabbage with glaucous, green leaves with a dull grey or bluish tint. By eight weeks, it reaches a height of about 60 centimetres and consists of a main stem the upper portion of which (the peduncle) bears no leaves or secondary stems. Below the peduncle, secondary stems (called tillers) may appear from leaf bases where they join the main stem. Apart from the peduncle, the stems are frequently covered with hairs.

As the plant matures, it grows to a height of between 90 and 150 centimetres, the leaves appearing alternately, those on the main stem being oblong, tooth-edged and between 10 and 40 centimetres long. The main stem and each tiller ends in a single flower bud. As these develop, the ends of the peduncle and tillers extend and bend over to form a distinctive hook shape, the young buds suspended upside down. However, as the buds mature the stems straighten, the main bud at the head of the peduncle pointing upwards. Within two days of becoming vertical, the sepals of the bud – which are the same colour as the leaves – open and the flower blooms. In ideal conditions, the main blossom appears around the ninetieth day from germination.

At first, it appears crumpled, like a butterfly emerging from its chrysalis, but the four petals quickly expand and smoothen, each marginally overlapping the other. Their colour may vary from plant to plant. Traditionally, opium poppies are white but they may just as readily be pink, crimson, weakly purple or a variegation of these with the colour darker at the petal base. Inside the flower is a ring of anthers on top of what will become the pod. Fertilisation is carried out by insects.

The flower is short-lived. In two to four days the petals drop, exposing a small, round pod the size of a large pea. This rapidly grows and may become ovoid or globular: when mature, it is the size of a small hen's egg with a diameter of between 5 and 7.5 centimetres. It is bluish green with a slightly waxy appearance, the top surrounded by a small crown from which the stigmas rise. Where the pod joins the peduncle is a ring of petal base scars.

The pod is made of an outer skin enclosing the wall of the ovary, which is made up of three layers, and cavities or segments separated by seed-producing walls. The seeds, of which one pod may produce over 1000, are reniform in shape with distinct reticulations. When mature, they are loose in the pod before dispersal through small holes which open just under the crown.

The opium poppy has two main products: one, the seeds, is quite innocuous whilst the other, opium, is infamously insidious.

The word 'opium' is misleading, implying the substance is a single chemical compound whereas it is an elaborate cocktail containing sugars, proteins, ammonia, latex, gums, plant wax, fats, sulphuric and lactic acids, water, meconic acid and a wide range of alkaloids. The significant parts are the alkaloids.

An alkaloid is a highly complex organic base (an alkali) with the common characteristic properties of containing nitrogen, of being basic and forming salts and water with acids, found in plants and having a characteristically bitter taste. Over fifty have been identified in opium, the most important being morphine (from which heroin can be made), noscapine, papaverine, codeine and thebaine. They appear partially or loosely chemically bonded to meconic acid, the presence of which can be used as a test to detect opium.

In its raw state, opium is the dried latex or juice of the seed pod which is also known as the capsule, bulb or poppy-head. It is an opaque, milky sap which, although found throughout the plant, concentrates the active ingredients in the pod.

Until recently, it was unknown how the poppy manufactured such a complex chemical as an alkaloid. It is now accepted that the substances are actually created in the lactifers (cells which produce the latex), possibly from the synthesis of albumen: the mechanism, however, is still undiscovered. Furthermore, opium is only produced during a ten-to-twelve-day period when the pod is ripening. Once it has reached maturity, the alkaloids are no longer made and are broken down in time.

Why the plant goes through such a process is unknown. Theories abound. One suggests the alkaloids are essential to the formation of the seeds. Another proposes they are a form of deterrent against animal pests. The most intriguing propounds that the plant has developed opium simply to ensure humans maintain it in cultivation, an elaborate and incredibly ingenious example of symbiosis.

Harvesting opium is an exhausting, back-breaking and labour-intensive process which can really only be done by hand and requires knowledge, experience and dexterity. Little changed for centuries, it is obtained by tapping the individual pods.

The harvest begins about two weeks after the petals have dropped. The opium farmer first examines the pod and erect crown. By now, the pod will have lost its grey-green colour and darkened. If the points of the crown are standing straight out or curving upwards, the pod is ready. Not all the pods in a field will mature at the same time so the farmer has to keep a close daily eye on his whole crop over a period of some weeks.

Today, the tapping tool is generally a specialised knife consisting of a set of three or four parallel steel or glass blades mounted on a handle. This is run vertically over two or three sides of the pod. If the blades cut too deeply into the pod wall, the opium will flow too quickly and drip to the earth where it will be lost. Furthermore, deep incisions will cause it to weep internally and injure the pod, cutting off production within the lactifers and preventing the seeds from developing. The pod will then shrivel and die. If the cuts are too shallow, the flow will be too slow and harden on the pod wall, sealing the cut like a scab. The ideal depth for a cut is 1–1.5 millimetres, achieved by setting the tapping knife blades.

The tapping (also known as scoring or lancing) is sometimes carried out in the late afternoon in the hope that the opium will ooze out overnight and coagulate slowly on the surface of the pod. If the tapping is carried out when the sun is still high, the heat of the sunlight can dry up the first sap to appear which then closes the wounds: however, in some countries, the collection of sap is done at midday, the sun's heat actually encouraging the milky sap to trickle out.

When the opium first appears, it is a cloudy, white, fairly mobile substance but on contact with air it oxidises, turning into a dark brown, viscous substance, sticky to the touch with a distinctive, delicate perfume. The opium, now a resinous gum, is carefully scraped from the pod with a short-handled blunt iron blade about 10 centimetres long. In order to prevent the blade from becoming covered in gum, the farmer wets it between plants. Poppy growers working on licensed farms, where poppies are cultivated for the pharmaceutical industry, do this by dipping the blade in water; peasant farmers, who are the vast majority of the world's poppy growers, often simply lick the blade. Needless to say, this addicts the farmers to their crop.

A pod will continue to secrete opium for some days and may be tapped up to half a dozen times. The opium yield varies according to the size of the pod and the efficiency of the farmer. The average is 80 milligrams per pod, a hectare of poppies providing between 8 and 15 kilograms of raw opium.

The farmers work their way backwards across the fields, tapping lower mature pods before the taller ones so as not to spill the opium inadvertently. This is collected in a container hanging around the farmer's waist. As they go, they mark the larger or more potent pods with coloured yarn. This directs the farmer to the pods on subsequent harvesting sessions and indicates which are eventually to be gathered in whole. These will be opened, dried in the sun and the seeds collected for the next season's planting.

In gum form, raw opium contains a high percentage of water so it is sun-dried for several days until the mass is reduced by evaporation to a sticky, dark brown substance with a strong odour and the consistency of warmed beeswax. The freshness of raw opium is judged by its pliability: when fresh, it is putty-like. It is then beaten into an homogeneous mass and moulded into cakes, balls or blocks which can be stored for months, wrapped in plastic or leaves and stacked on shelves in a shady place. As it dries, it hardens. Excessive moisture or heat during drying or early storage will cause it to deteriorate but, once dried, it is stable and will gain in value for the older it is the less water it contains and the more concentrated it becomes by weight. In some cases, harvested pods are gathered and pulped in warm water which is then sieved and simmered over a fire, resulting in a poor quality opium which is not traded but may be retained by the farmer for personal use.

Raw opium, which is slightly granular, contains more than just the coagulated latex. In the scraping of the pod, pieces of the outer wall may be removed and up to 7 per cent by weight of raw opium may consist of extraneous plant matter. What is more, it can be deliberately adulterated by the farmer with sand, tree sap or ash, although a trained opium buyer can spot these tricks and few farmers dare resort to such chicanery.

Before the opium can be smoked or further processed, it has to be cooked. As traders usually prefer it somewhat improved from its rough state, cooking also prepares it for market.

The cooking is done by adding the raw opium to boiling water. It dissolves, any impurities such as pod fragments floating to the surface with heavier adulterates sinking to the bottom. The solution is passed through cheesecloth or a fine sieve to remove impurities then brought to the boil again and reduced. It is now a clean, brown, mobile fluid known as liquid opium. Very slowly, it is left to simmer until all that remains is a thick, brown paste known as prepared, cooked or smoking opium. This is pressed into moulds or trays and dried once more in the sun until it takes on the consistency of dense modelling clay which will harden as it matures. Much purer than raw opium, the cooked opium is now ready for the addict, the trader or the drug baron's laboratories.

The remainder of the plant is not discarded. Once ripe, the seeds contain no dangerous substances whatsoever and are edible. Black, blue and grey seeds are frequently used as a decoration for cakes and bread whilst brown seeds are used in Turkey to make *halva* and to give the typical crunchiness to such traditional Turkish pastries as *silgin boereghi* and *hashash coereghi*. In India, yellow seeds are milled and added to sauces as flavouring or thickening agents.

Ripe poppy seeds yield about 50 per cent of a fixed oil made up of the glycerides of linolic, oleic, palmitic and stearic acids. Poppy seed oil has a straw-yellow colour, is odourless and tastes vaguely of almonds. It may be employed in cooking and as a salad dressing and it has been used as an adulterate of olive oil. Other uses are in the manufacture of perfumes and, because of its drying properties, as a base for expensive artists' oil paints.

In the nineteenth century, Turkish growers wasted little of the plant. Seeds were pressed to give both vegetable and lamp oil, the residual seed cake, stems and leaves being used as cattle fodder. This was historically an important factor in dairy produce, for cows fed on the detritus of poppies were said to provide the milk which made the finest yoghurt. Mixed with flour, the residuals also made a coarse bread. Seed was also sold to merchants in Smyrna who traded it on to Marseilles, where it was used in soap factories, whilst poppy heads were infused to make a traditional sedative drink.

Today, in most areas where the plant is commercially and legally grown, the opium producing stage is bypassed and the dried capsules, known as poppy straw, are milled and processed for the extraction of their alkaloids. Very large quantities of poppy straw have to be processed, but morphine, codeine and thebaine are recoverable. The seeds, which have almost as much value, are used in the food industry.

Although poppy straw morphine was extracted first in 1823 by a French chemist called Tilloy working in Dijon, it was not until 1928 that a factory was built when Janos Kabay, an Hungarian, developed a commercially feasible extraction process. During the Second World War, poppy straw processing began under German control as a source of opium during the Allied blockade. Since then, refinements to extraction techniques and agricultural development have greatly increased yields, so that today more than 50 per cent of the world's legal annual morphine demand of about 230 tonnes is derived from this source which, in some countries such as Australia, is a highly mechanised agricultural procedure.

The traditional growing, harvesting and preparation of opium however is and always has been essentially a peasant-farming activity, although there have been variations according to time and place. In Bengal, for example, it was customary to incise the pod with a sharpened mussel shell whilst elsewhere the extruded juice was placed upon a lower leaf of the plant to dry, a practice which lingers in parts of Afghanistan. However, from the late eighteenth century and with the expansion in world trade promoted by Europeans, opium growing and production became in places a highly organised, efficient and lucrative industry.

In India in the nineteenth century, opium growing was far from being a peasant-run operation. Admittedly, smallholders produced the opium but it was sold through a structured market and was big business, employing tens of thousands of growers and workers, many of whom became habituated to the drug.

As a commercial commodity, opium was an extensive branch

of Indian agriculture. Grown mostly on the Ganges plain between Patna and Benares (now known as Varanasi), it was a major revenue source for the Indian economy. Its importance is reflected in the substantial records compiled about the business which afford a fascinating glimpse of how the industry began in modern times.

Sown early in November, the crop was harvested from early February the following year. The tapping tool (known as a *nushtur*) was of similar design to that used today, whilst the collecting blade was an iron scoop (a *sittooha*) and the collecting vessel an earthenware pot called a *kurrace*. This was emptied into a shallow tilted brass dish (a *thallee*) which allowed the water content (*pusseewah*) to drain away. The raw opium was allowed to dry for several weeks, being turned and stirred daily, before being stored in clay pots in godowns, or warehouses. Once weighed, tested and valued, it was thrown into vast vats, kneaded and subsequently pressed into spheres the size of small cannon balls.

This process was an important part of opium manufacture. The factory hands sat in rows in the godown, each man in front of a *tagar*, a tin vessel holding enough opium to make three to five balls. A basin containing water, a supply of poppy flower petals, a cup of *lewah* (inferior opium) and a brass cup in which the ball was shaped made up the rest of a worker's equipment.

Taking the cup, the worker placed a petal in the base and smeared it with *lewah*. Another petal was added overlapping the first until the receptacle was lined by opium-soaked petals. An opium ball was rolled and placed in the cup so the dome protruding from the top was the same size as that contained by the vessel. This was then covered in poppy petals and *lewah*, the petals at the rim carefully interwoven to make a seal. When completed, the ball was about 15 centimetres in diameter and covered in a shell of petals. It weighed about 1.5 kilograms.

Once the ball was formed, it was placed on lattice-work racks in a drying room, a warehouse with open ends to allow the wind to pass through. Checked and turned daily by small boys, who ensured no insects were damaging the opium, it was kept until sufficiently dry then packed into mango-wood chests with two fitted trays, each chest containing forty balls in individual compartments, twenty to a tray. The chests were sealed with pitch, sewn into gunny or hides and sent for trading or to market. In Ghazipur, the centre of India's modern legal opium production system, some opium-making equipment a century old is still in use in techniques which have not significantly changed for 200 years.

The size of the opium industry can be judged from contemporary accounts. The area under poppy cultivation in 1870 was 560,608 acres. In the financial year of 1871—72, the number of chests sold was 49,695 at a trade price of £139 each. The net profit per chest was £90. The total opium revenue came to £7,657,213. At 1996 currency rates, this equates to approximately £612 million or $950 million.

The product and the style of marketing varied from place to place. While Indian opium was sold in forty-ball chests in the nineteenth century, Turkish opium from Smyrna – upon which was based a speculative commodities market – was packed in grey calico bags in oblong wicker baskets, the strength and quality of the goods being measured in carats on a 1 to 24 unit scale like gold: under 20 carats, the standard was considered poor and the opium discarded. The opium was blackish-brown, waxy to the touch, wrapped in poppy leaves and sold in irregular, flattened oval cakes weighing between 250 grams and a kilogram. The surface of each was sprinkled with the winged seeds of a species of sorrel to prevent them from sticking together. When shipped, it was transported in hermetically sealed, zinc-lined wooden cases, each sufficiently large to take an entire basket.

An alternative Turkish opium from Constantinople was a redder brown and sold in small lens-shaped cakes covered with poppy leaves whilst Persian opium from Yezd and Isfahan, where the Persian trade was centred, was usually dark brown and came in the form of sticks wrapped in grease-proof paper and tied about with cotton twine, or cones weighing 200–400 grams. Egyptian opium was formed into round, flattened cakes like ice hockey pucks, was reddish in colour and quite hard.

Aficionados, dealers, merchants and users were experts at assessing quality and strength in each and every variety and cargo. Opium was judged with all the finesse of a tea or coffee blender, the pertinent factors being its colour, weight, density, water content and granularity. Many traders could identify and judge the quality of individual samples just as experienced wine tasters can tell the vintage of a bottle of claret and from which vineyard it comes.

When and how man first discovered the potency of opium is hard to ascertain: he has been familiar with it since prehistoric times. The nineteenth century botanist, George Watts, suggested man came upon the poppy's secret by stages of gradual awareness. Watts conjectured that humans aesthetically appreciated the poppy for its flower before they came to use it as a vegetable: certainly, it was eaten in salads in India as recently as the 1890s, although this may have been for its medicinal qualities. The juice was then found to make a refreshing drink when diluted with water and, eventually, the neat juice would be discovered to have narcotic effects inducing feelings of contentment and capable of numbing pain.

However that first discovery might have been made, today it is known that opiates can be swallowed, smoked, injected, sniffed, inhaled or absorbed through mucous membranes. How it is taken affects the intensity and speed with which it has an effect upon the brain and the whole body.

Historically, there have been only two basic ways to indulge in opium: one was to eat it, the other to smoke it.

Opium eating refers, in effect, to the general swallowing of it for as well as eating it in solid form it is also possible to drink raw opium dissolved in a variety of liquids. Opium in solution might well have been the first common method of taking it as, before the technique of cutting the pods to allow the sap to ooze out, the whole poppy head was crushed and mixed with wine or honey and water. Such a solution served more than one purpose for raw opium has a bitter taste and eating it neat would not have been easy: indeed, raw opium can induce severe vomiting.

Despite this, it was taken orally in India for over 1500 years, the dictum going that efficacy improved with unpalatability. In 1687, it was recorded the Turks ate opium for pleasure but disguised the bitterness with nutmeg, cardamom, cinnamon or mace and served it with saffron or ambergris. Even then, it was essentially a medicine and regarded as an aphrodisiac. In Europe, opium was mixed with wine or wine and sugar or honey.

Smoking opium was chiefly confined to China, the East Indies, the eastern seaboard of Indo-China (particularly Vietnam) and Taiwan (formerly Formosa). It had to be concentrated before it could be used. A method of preparing opium for smoking was published in the *British Pharmacopoeia* in the early nineteenth century:

Take of opium in thin slices, 1lb; distilled water 6 pints. Macerate the opium in 2 pints of water for 24 hours, and express the liquor.

> Reduce the residue of the opium to a uniform pulp, macerate it again in 2 pints of water for 24 hours, and express. Repeat the operation a third time. Mix the liquors, strain through flannel, and evaporate by a water-bath until the extract has acquired a suitable consistency for forming pills.

Once the extract was produced, the opium mass had been reduced by about 50 per cent, the concentration more or less doubled. Known in China as *chan du*, the pills were round, pea-sized, dark-coloured and stiffly malleable.

A traditional opium pipe was quite unlike that used by tobacco smokers. There were variations but basically it consisted of a broad tube (often made of a length of bamboo about 5 centimetres in diameter and perhaps 50 centimetres long) with a smaller, usually metal, tube protruding about two-thirds of the way down, ending in a tiny cup or bowl up to 2 centimetres across. In typical Chinese pipes, the bowl was a hollow chamber with a tiny hole in the roof.

The would-be smoker reclined on his side and held the pipe in one hand. With the other he took a thin metal spike or needle about 15 centimetres long, impaling the pill of opium on the end. This task of preparing the pill was traditionally carried out in opium dens by small boys who were, on occasion, also catamites. If the pill was too moist, it was dried over the flame of a small, specifically designed spirit lamp which produced a fierce hot spot above a toughened glass cowl. With the desired consistency achieved, the opium was spread around the base of the bowl or placed over the hole of the hollow bowl by inserting the spike into the hole and pulling it free, the index and second fingers of the pipe hand holding it in place. The bowl was then inverted over the spirit lamp until the opium pill melted and began to vaporise. At this moment, the smoker took a very deep breath and sucked air rich with opium fumes through the main tube. Some early Chinese pipes were similar to hookahs, the fumes drawn through water or scented liquid before inhalation.

The action was ideally done in one large inhalation for the opium was quick to vaporise: a pipe took between fifteen and thirty seconds to run its course. The pipe characteristically whist-led while the opium was drawn in. As the smoker inhaled, he sometimes manipulated the opium with a needle-like probe to keep an air-hole open and to force the opium into the chamber of the bowl. Unvaporised opium, or vapour which had not been inhaled, solidified on the interior of the pipes: needless to say, old pipes had a value because they were coated with a residue of raw opium which could be recycled. Known as 'dross', it was a mixture of charcoal, empyreumatic oil and opium and was sold as pills to the poor or mixed with tobacco, tea or some other material smoked by them.

The inhaled fumes were retained as long as the smoker could hold his breath, exhalation made only through the nostrils to gain the best advantage of the fumes: what the lungs did not absorb, the nose might take in. A first-time user was usually nauseated by his pipe but this effect passed after two or three further pipes, diminishing with each. Experienced smokers would take three or four pipes in quick succession, a pipe consisting of one pill.

His smoking over, the smoker fell into a deep but not refreshing sleep which could last from fifteen minutes (with one pipe) to several hours. Upon waking, there were no after-effects, such as a hangover. The smoker was subdued and calm, in a state of extreme lassitude.

The habit of reclining to smoke opium had its origins in China but was not essential: it was, however, convenient for the smoker would quickly fall asleep after his pipe, the effects of which were quite rapid. As Jean Cocteau, the French writer and opium addict, observed: 'Of all drugs "the drug" is the most delicate. The lungs instantaneously assimilate its smoke. The effect of a pipe is immediate.' He called opium 'the ultimate siesta'.

The method of smoking opium has not changed and, in the few places were it is still smoked today, such as the Shan states of north-east Burma (now called the Union of Myanmar), China, Laos and Thailand, the technique and paraphernalia survive. Opium smoking is in fact legal in some countries, notably in the Middle East, where it is sold as sticks about the size of a hot dog sausage.

One does not have to be an addict, or an eater or smoker, to come under the effect of opium: passive consumption is possible. Walking through a field of incised pods can induce mild effects and poppy farmers can tell when the time to harvest is nigh because they wake in the morning with severe headaches and even nausea. Harvesters may absorb opium through their skin and excise officers and traders who come into frequent contact with it can also be affected.

Opium is still consumed by the traditional means of eating and smoking in Third World countries, especially in those where it is produced, but in more technologically advanced nations opium is not widely used today. Its derivative, heroin, is the main opiate of addiction and there are several ways in which that drug can be taken. Unlike opium, heroin is rarely swallowed because this is an ineffectual method of consumption but it is frequently smoked, either mixed with tobacco in a hand-rolled reefer or 'joint', or inserted into a cigarette filter tip.

Smoking is, however, a relatively inefficient way of taking heroin and requires a high purity to be effective. The best non-injectable way to use heroin is to sniff it in powder form through the nostrils – a method known as 'snorting' – which allows absorption into the bloodstream through the nasal mucous membranes.

The quickest, most effective way to take heroin is to inject it. This requires certain equipment: a cooker (usually a large spoon), a source of flame and a hypodermic syringe. The addict mixes heroin in the spoon with water, or glucose and water, in order to dissolve it. Lemon juice, citric acid or vitamin C may be added to aid dissolving. This cocktail is heated until it boils, drawn into the syringe through a piece of cotton wool or a cigarette filter to remove solid impurities and injected whilst still warm. An addict calls his equipment his 'works' or 'kit'.

Subcutaneous injection is known by addicts as 'skin-popping', whilst intravenous injection – injecting straight into the vein – is called 'mainlining'. The mainliner also requires a tourniquet of some sort to distend veins. When the tourniquet is released, the effects of the heroin are almost instantaneous. Most heroin is taken by injection: however, since the arrival of AIDS and the risk of cross-infection through shared needles, the habit of smoking and snorting heroin has been on the gradual increase.

Whatever the means of consumption, whatever methods of taking the drug have become tenable or fashionable, the fact remains that, well before man had developed into a civilised, social being, he had discovered the precarious magic of poppy sap.

2

The Discovery of Dreams

Opium has been used by man since prehistoric times and was arguably the first drug to be discovered. Being naturally occurring, it almost certainly predates the discovery of alcohol which requires a knowledge of fermentation.

The preserved remains of cultivated poppy seeds and pods have been discovered in the sites of fourth millennium BC Neolithic pile-dwelling villages in Switzerland. Botanical examination has shown these not to be *Papaver setigerum*, but *P. somniferum* or possibly a deliberate hybrid. As these ancient farmers also grew linseed, it is likely both crops were utilised for their oil although no suitable contemporary tools for oil extraction have been found and it is, therefore, just as likely the poppy was grown for its narcotic effect, either as a painkiller or for use in religious ceremonies – or for both.

It has long been suggested that the knowledge of opium spread from Egypt through Asia Minor to the rest of the Old World but the Swiss discoveries cast this theory into doubt. What is as likely is that the secret of opium originated in the eastern reaches of Europe – in the Balkans or around the Black Sea – and spread south and west from there.

Around 3400 BC, the opium poppy was being cultivated in the Tigris–Euphrates river systems of lower Mesopotamia. The Sumerians, the world's first civilisation and agriculturists, used the ideograms *hul* and *gil* for the poppy, this translating as the 'joy plant'. Their invention of writing spread gradually to other societies and it is from them the Egyptians probably learnt the skill: it follows they may also have learnt of opium. It may be reasoned, therefore, that the Sumerians not only gave humankind literacy but also one of its greatest problems.

By the end of the second millennium BC, knowledge of opium was widespread throughout Europe, the Middle East and North Africa. Poppy juice is mentioned in seventh-century BC Assyrian medical tablets contained in the royal library of the Babylonian King Asurbanipal, although these are thought to be copies of earlier texts. Doctors of the time considered opium a cure for almost every ailment, sometimes mixing it with liquorice or balsam: of 115 vegetable concoctions mentioned, 42 concern opium which was collected early in the morning by women and children who scraped the congealed sap off wounds in the poppies with a small iron scoop.

Yet the earliest find of opium itself comes from Egypt where a sample was discovered in the tomb of Cha, dating to the fifteenth century BC. At around the same time, the Egyptian city of Thebes was so famous for its poppy fields that Egyptian opium was known as Thebic opium. The alkaloid, thebaine, obtains it name from the city. In the *Therapeutic Papyrus of Thebes*, dated 1552 BC, and in other sources such as the *Veterinary and Gynaecological Papyri* from Kahun, dated between 2160 and 1788 BC, opium is prominently listed with other natural remedies and drugs: in the former – sometimes known as the *Papyrus of Ebers* after its discoverer, Georg Moritz Ebers – opium is included in 700 remedies, one chapter specifically prescribing it as a paregoric to calm fractious children. The prescription demanded opium be mixed with fly droppings, pulped, sieved and taken for four days.

For the Greek civilisation, opium was a commonplace. In the third century BC, Theophrastus referred to the sap of the pod as *opion* whilst he called poppy juice *meconion*, obtained by crushing the entire plant. This is an interesting fact for it suggests he had a specific knowledge that the sap contained a substance and that he may have been acquainted with separating it out although, at the time, the general method of taking opium was to crush the pod in wine or a honey and water solution. The method of incising the pod to gather the sap, developed by the Assyrians and used to this day, was lost until the technique was re-invented or rediscovered about AD 40 by Scribonius Largus, physician to the Emperor Claudius.

In AD 77, Dioscorides wrote that opium was best obtained by the careful grazing of the pod, although he was just as familiar with other applications of the poppy. He recorded:

> Poppies possess as it were a cooling power, therefore the leaves and head when boiled in water bring sleep. The decoction is also drunk to remedy insomnia. Finely powdered and added to groats, the heads make an effective poultice for swellings and erysipelas. They must be crushed when still green, shaped into tablets then dried for storage. If the heads themselves are boiled in water until the liquid is reduced to half then boiled with honey until a syrup forms, they may make a sweetmeat with an anodyne action.

Both Dioscorides and Theophrastus, whilst noting opium induced sleep and numbed pain, did not consider its effects upon the brain which were generally disregarded although the philosopher Diagoras of Melos was cognisant of the drug's snare. Living in the third century BC, he declared it was better to suffer pain than to become dependent upon opium, a view shared earlier in the fifth century BC by Erasistratus who advocated the complete eschewal of opium.

Apart from its medicinal use, opium also served the Greeks in a spiritual or occult capacity. It was most likely employed by initiates to the cult of Demeter for there is a legend which decrees that, in her search of her daughter Persephone, the goddess came to Sicyon, at one time called Mecone (the city of poppies), in the fields of which she picked the flowers and cut open their unripe pods. Tasting the gum which exuded from them, Demeter forgot her sorrows. Statues and portraits of the goddess frequently show her grasping a poppy instead of a sheaf of corn whilst the flower decorates her altars. There is a further suggestion: in her rites conducted at Eleusis, opium was taken to aid in the forgetting of the sadness of the death of the year, the short drug-induced sleep being a symbol for the passage of winter before the rejuvenation of spring. The medical priests of Aesculapeius administered opium to those who visited Epidaurus to seek a cure for illness. The sick slept in the sanctuary of the temple, the priests procuring healing dreams for them.

As long as opium was in the hands of priests it was regarded as a metaphysical substance. This supernatural attitude, however, was dismissed by Hippocrates (460–357 BC). Considered the father of medicine, he disassociated himself from the magical attributes of opium which he mentioned was useful as a cathartic, hypnotic, narcotic and styptic. A reasoned and logical thinker, Hippocrates concluded diseases were naturally caused and were, therefore, cured by natural remedies. Opium was, for him, one of the latter, which he believed required study and understanding rather than being imbued with miraculous powers. He suggested drinking hypnotic meconion (white poppy juice) mixed with nettle seeds to cure leucorrhea and 'uterine suffocation'. Like Diagoras, Hippocrates was of the opinion it should be used sparingly and under control, a stipulation which exists to this day in the Hippocratic oath which states, 'I will give no deadly medicine to anyone if asked, nor suggest any such counsel.'

It was not long before opium began to appear in literature. In the *Odyssey*, Homer writes of 'nepenthe', the drug of forgetfulness, which was an opium preparation. When Telemachus visited Menelaus in Sparta, the memory of Ulysses and the other warriors lost in the Trojan War so saddened the gathering a banquet was commanded for which Helen prepared a special cordial:

Helen, daughter of Zeus, poured a drug, nepenthe, into the wine they were drinking which made them forget all evil. Those who drank of the mixture did not shed a tear all day long, even if their mother or father had died, even if a brother or beloved son was killed before their own eyes by the weapons of the enemy. And the daughter of Zeus possessed this wondrous substance which she had been given by Polydamma, the wife of Thos of Egypt, the fertile land which produced so many balms, some beneficial and some deadly.

Homer's noting opium came from Egypt is hardly surprising: not only had this source been known of for centuries but Egyptian doctors were renowned. Even Moses shared their secret as was recorded in the Bible, Acts 7, verse 22: 'And Moses was learned in all the wisdom of the Egyptians, and was mighty in words and in deeds.'

For a long while, scholars assumed nepenthe was hashish but this is incorrect. What is plainly described is the effect of opium which, especially once established as a habit, promotes indifference towards everything except the ego and a calm euphoria in which anger and sorrow are suppressed. Hashish, on the other hand, usually produces a delirious excitement.

Homer's description was not a matter of poetic licence. He was writing about an everyday experience undergone by those addicted and it is almost certain the poet had taken opium, even if he was not habituated. Furthermore, a solution of opium in alcohol was used by the Greeks as a tranquilliser, to banish fear, anguish and hateful memories: it might also have been used to promote Dutch courage in warriors going into battle. The tradition of opium as an antidote to sorrow lingers to the modern day: in some places in the Middle East, iced poppy tea is traditionally served to mourners at funerals.

When the Greek civilisation was usurped by the Empire of Rome, more than works of art and treasure were plundered and brought to Italy. So, too, came learning, including the knowledge of opium, spread by military men returning from foreign campaigns (including those in Egypt and the Middle East), priests, physicians, intellectuals and Greek slaves many of whom were educated and employed in Rome as tutors and administrators.

Galen, in the first and second centuries AD, was the last of the great Greek physicians. Although he considered it to be influenced by the occult, he did not claim direct magical properties for opium but he did afford it the omniscient properties of a glorious panacea, claiming it resisted poison and venomous bites and cured, amongst other things, headaches, vertigo, deafness, epilepsy, apoplexy, poor sight, bronchitis, asthma, coughs, the spitting of blood, colic, jaundice, hardness of the spleen, kidney stones, urinary complaints, fever, dropsy, leprosy, menstrual problems, melancholy and all other pestilences. It was he who popularised the use of one of the famous early opium concoctions, *mithridate*, the invention of which is accorded to Mithridates the Great. Galen advocated it to all his patients amongst whom were numbered Marcus Aurelius and the Emperors Commodus and Severus. Yet, for all his apparent quackery, Galen was a serious scientist. He studied and published his findings on the toxic effects of opium and understood the concept of tolerance – that is, the ability of the body to withstand larger and larger successive doses, requiring increasing doses to gain the same effect as time goes by.

Opium

Like Homer, Virgil mentioned opium in his works: in both the *Aeneid* and the *Georgics* it is mentioned as a soporific. His lines *spargens humida melle soperiferumque paparva* (giving dewy honey and soporific poppy) and *Lethaeo perfusa papavera somno* (poppies soaked with the sleep of Lethe) indicate very clearly the accepted capabilities of the drug. Pliny the Elder wrote that poppy seed (he was incorrect) was a useful hypnotic, whilst the poppy latex was effective in treating headaches and arthritis and in healing wounds.

For the Romans, the poppy was a powerful symbol of sleep and death. Somnus, the god of sleep, is frequently portrayed as a small boy or sprite carrying a bunch of poppies and an opium horn, the vessel in which the juice was collected by farmers, whilst another popular image is that of a figure bending over a woman and pouring poppy juice on to her closed eyes. The poppy also formed part of the mysteries of Ceres, the Roman goddess of fertility, who resorted to the drug to relieve pain: a famous statue shows her holding a torch and poppy pods. Indeed, the poppy was so well known a symbol that, in later years of the empire, it was to be found on Roman coinage.

The Romans viewed opium not only as a painkiller and religious drug but as a convenient poison. For the suicide, it was a pleasant means of enticing death. Hannibal was said to have kept a dose in a small chamber in his ring, finally ending his life with it in Libyssa in 183 BC. Yet its main attraction was for the murderer.

Being easily obtained, easily disguised in food or dissolved in wine and bringing a seemingly innocent death as if in sleep, opium poisoning was an ideal assassin's aid. According to the historian Cornelius Nepos, the son of Dionysius (the tyrant of Syracuse) arranged with the court doctors in 367 BC for his father to overdose on opium. In AD 55 Agrippina, the Emperor Claudius's last wife, put it into the wine of her fourteen-year-old stepson, Britannicus, so her own son, Nero, might inherit the throne.

As a medicine, opium was taken in a number of concoctions but for leisure use – as what would now be termed a 'recreational drug' – it was eaten often mixed with honey to suppress its bitterness.

The eating of opium increased as the knowledge of its beneficial properties became more widely known. In the second century AD, it was stated that Lysis could take 4 drachms of poppy juice without being incommoded. To be so tolerant of the drug suggests he was a well-established addict: such a quantity would have killed a first-time imbiber.

Curiously, neither the Greeks nor the Romans spread the use of opium throughout the whole of their domains and they did not regard opium as an international trading commodity.

However, the Arabs did. They had used opium as a painkiller since the time of the Egyptians and it was the Arabs who developed and organised the production of, and trade in, opium which has existed ever since.

By the ninth century, Arab scholars and medical men were publishing texts on *af-yum* (or *ufian* or *asiun*), as opium was known, and its preparations. The knowledge was spread by Arab traders and doctors such as the eminent Rhazes who lived in Baghdad but travelled throughout Africa, the Middle East and Moorish Spain.

The study of opium at the time reached its zenith in the person of the outstanding Muhammadan physician, Abu Ali al Husein Abdallah ibn Sina, known outside Islam as Avicenna, who lived much of his life in Persia, in a palace in Isfahan which was noted for its poppy growing. A poet and intellectual as well as a doctor, he was, by all accounts, something of a libertine who maintained a large number of concubines and drank wine in contradiction of the Koran: the prohibition of alcohol by the Prophet's teachings did not extend to drugs such as opium and hashish, thereby encouraging their use in lieu of wine. Avicenna took opium and was almost certainly addicted. His poetry sings the praises of the poppy and wine cup. It is said he died, aged fifty-eight, of an overdose of opium mixed with wine.

Despite his libidinous life-style, Avicenna was a much respected doctor and his *Canon of Medicine* was a standard text for five centuries. He particularly noted the value of opium in the treatment of dysentery, diarrhoea and eye diseases.

Within a century of the death of Muhammad in AD 632, the Arab empire expanded rapidly. Doctors and learned men, who had studied the writings of their Greek antecedents, travelled with merchants in the footsteps of the armies, propounding the teachings of Islam and spreading their sciences of mathematics and medicine. They raided, traded and travelled west to Spain, down the coasts of east and west Africa and east through Persia into India: they even reached as far as China, although they did not establish a colony or presence there as they did almost everywhere else. Wherever they went the knowledge of, and trade in, opium went too. It was a perfect merchandise: valuable, concentrated and compact, it did not deteriorate easily. It reached Europe by sea and India either by caravan or dhow, whilst east of India it travelled exclusively by dhow, the Arab sailors being skilled navigators.

For the best part, opium was used only as a medicine. In Arabic Spain and around the Mediterranean, it was an accepted painkiller and specific cure for stomach ailments, but in India it was regarded with almost Galen-like enthusiasm and considered a cure-all as well as a form of recreation. Needless to say, once the efficacy of opium was established in a land conquered either by arms or trade, poppies were soon under local cultivation.

Meanwhile, in southern Europe, the use of opium declined as the Roman Empire collapsed and was absent for much of the Dark Ages, only to reappear with the return of the Crusaders who regained the knowledge from the Arabs whom they fought.

For the Christian knights, opium, often confused with other drugs, took on the mantle of myth. The returning warriors told fantastical stories of the raptures and powers of magical herbs and potions, recounting such tales as the Old Man of the Mountains in Persia who fortified his zealous troops with hashish to whip them into a fervour of fighting spirit, the stamina of the Tartar couriers and their horses who banished exhaustion with opium and Turkish soldiers who steeled themselves with it before the battle.

With the gradual fading of Arab influence, the trade in opium was taken up by the next great trading people – the Venetians. Venice was the centre of European trade and, once again, with goods came knowledge. Opium was imported from the Middle East with spices but it was not a major item of merchandise although, when Columbus sailed to discover the New World, it was one of the commodities he was briefed to bring back. His instructions were not unique: Cabot, Magellan and Vasco da Gama were all requested to find opium in addition to other commodities. Thanks to da Gama, the Portuguese displaced the Venetians and, having navigated a route round southern Africa, included opium in their cargoes, purchasing it on the Indian subcontinent where poppies were now widely grown, the Mogul emperors encouraging this cultivation for its significant revenue.

Although it was occasionally taken for recreational purposes, opium was regarded primarily as a medicine in Europe where, by the sixteenth century, its use was established. It is not hard to imagine what kind of an impact it must have had upon the emerging medical sciences. Here was a naturally occurring substance which, with a modicum of preparation, could eradicate pain. The potential benefits were enormous, considerable medical reputations being based upon this 'new' wonder drug.

One such celebrity was Philippus Aureolus Theophrastus Bombastus von Hohenheim (c. 1490–1541), who called himself Paracelsus. He studied and taught medicine at the University of Basle and was tutored in alchemy by the Bishop of Würzburg, alchemy and medicine being akin to each other at the time. An idea of his approach to medicine may be gathered from his writings:

> In my time, there were no doctors who could cure a toothache, never mind severe diseases . . . I sought widely the certain and experienced knowledge of the art [of medicine]. I did not seek it from only learned doctors: I also enquired of shearers, barbers, wise men and women, exorcisers, alchemists, monks, the noblemen and the humble people . . . They all tried to teach me what they did not know. For all their wealth and pomp, they are vainglorious chatterers and there is no more in them than in a worm-riddled coffin. So I looked for a different approach.

Paracelsus's different approach was somewhat radical. He tossed Avicenna's *Canon of Medicine* on to a midsummer night's celebratory bonfire, denounced other doctors as quacks and cut a dashing figure. He travelled everywhere with a copious supply of ointments, potions and elixirs, precious stones (said to have magical properties), surgical instruments and astrological as well as astronomical charts. He wore a double-handed sword he had obtained from the East and slept with it: it is rumoured the pommel was hollow and contained the Elixir of Life. He prepared all his own medicines and was, when not attacking his professional peers, a lively character according to a contemporary, Oporinus:

> In curing [intestinal] ulcers he did miracles where others had given up. He never forbade his patients food or drink. On the contrary, he frequently stayed all night in their company, drinking and eating with them. He said he cured them when their stomachs were full. He had pills which he called laudanum which looked like pieces of mouse shit but used them only in cases of extreme illness.

He boasted he could, with these pills, wake up the dead and certainly he proved this to be true for patients who appeared dead suddenly arose.

According to the legend which has sprung up around him, Paracelsus called opium 'the stone of immortality'. He wrote, 'I possess a secret remedy which I call laudanum and which is superior to all other heroic remedies.' He used the word *arcanum* to describe his secret and certainly there was hinted to be a strong degree of the arcane about his opium prescription. It was regarded as being endowed with magical powers which no one questioned scientifically. By chance, the actual ingredients are known: the recipe was 25 per cent opium mixed with henbane, crushed pearls and coral, *mummy* (a tar-like Arabic drug), bezoar stone (a concretion from a cow's intestine), amber, musk, certain oils, the 'bone from the heart of a stag' and, finally, 'unicorn'. Presumably, this last was either powdered rhinoceros horn, the ground-down bones or 'horn' of a narwhal or crushed sea-shells. The mix of superstition and alchemy with medical knowledge is obvious.

Unfortunately, despite the Renaissance and rediscovery of the classical world, few seem to have heeded the warning words of Diagoras of Melos and Erasistratus, not to mention Hippocrates. Like Avicenna and many others before him, Paracelsus was himself habituated: his sword pommel probably contained his personal stash.

The widespread use of opium produced a comparatively large population of addicts from the Middle Ages onwards although most were from the upper classes who could afford medical treatment: it is recorded that some addicts took as much as 40 grams a day, but this would have been mixed with wine or as a tincture of opium, not neat. On the other hand, the peasantry were kept blissfully ignorant of opium's enslavement by way of their poverty.

Paracelsus's success and reputation did much to advance opium usage. His disciples were many and covered much of Europe. In 1600, Platerus of Basle widely promoted the use of opium whilst Sylvius de la Boe, the famous Dutch physician, stated he was unable to practise medicine without it. A Belgian doctor called von Helmont prescribed so much opium he was nicknamed 'Dr Opiatus'. He was also addicted.

Although not exactly dissenters, there were a few cautioning voices at least outlining the potential dangers of opium. In 1546, the French naturalist Pierre Belon visited Asia Minor and Egypt, drawing attention to the abuse of opium amongst Turks. He wrote:

> There is not a Turk who would not purchase opium with his last coin; he carries the drug on him in war and in peace. They eat opium because they think they will thus become more courageous and have less fear of the dangers of war. At the time of war, such large quantities are purchased it is difficult to find any left.

On one occasion, he observed an opium-eater take 2 grams in a single dose. When Belon subsequently presented him with another 4 grams, he ate them without any sign of adverse reaction. Such a level of tolerance is easily believable when compared to contemporary statistics: in the late 1500s, it was known some Egyptians took 12 grams of opium per day, or 4.38 kilograms per annum. The scale of the opium trade was also recorded by Belon. Travelling along a caravan route, the naturalist reported seeing fifty camels loaded exclusively with opium *en route* for Europe.

He was not alone is recognising the drawbacks of opium. At about the same time, Prospero Alpino noted how it made Egyptians lose their energy and their functions, numbed them and made them so fickle their word in business could not be trusted. A Portuguese doctor, Acosta, wrote upon returning from a voyage to the Far East in 1655: 'Though opium is condemned by reason, it is used so extensively that it is the most general and familiar remedy of degraded débauchés.'

Acosta also recorded the condemnation of Arabic, Persian, Turkish, Indian, Malay, Chinese and Malabar doctors, who all decried the drug for its risk of habituation.

Gradually, the more subtle medical possibilities of opium were being realised. Garcias ab Horto, the Portuguese botanist, visiting the Portuguese colony of Goa on the west coast of India, noted opium suppressed what he termed disagreeable physical and mental impressions, adding that those under the influence 'spoke wisely about all sorts of things. Such is the power of habit.'

In England, as across much of north-western Europe, opium had been medicinally employed mainly for its narcotic properties. John Arderne, in the mid fourteenth century, used salves and potions containing opium (such medicines sometimes known as *dwale*) to procure sleep and also applied it externally as a crude anaesthetic during surgery. 'He schal,' Arderne records, 'slepe so that he schal fele no kuttyng.' In *Bulwarke of Defence against all Sickness Soarenesse and Woundes*, published in 1579, Bullein recommended opium obtained from the white poppy which 'hath all the vertues' and from the black poppy 'which is cold and is used in sleeping medicines: but it causeth deepe deadly sleapes.'

Arderne was not the first to realise the anaesthetic potential of opium. In the thirteenth century, two medical monks by the name of Hugo of Lucca and Theoderic of Cervia experimented with opium to combat pain during surgery. They invented what was termed a *spongia somnifera*. As the name implies, this was a sponge soaked with opium and other substances which was held over the patient's nose, much as a chloroform mask was six centuries later. The sponge could be remoistened throughout the operation, but the evaporation could not be controlled and the effects were very much a hit-and-miss process. If the dose was large enough to kill the pain, it might also have killed the patient and possibly affected the surgeon. As opium has a depressing effect on the heart muscles and respiration, the use of the sponge could promote heart failure. In time, the monks realised it was better to use opium after surgery to reduce pain, rather than as a simplistic anaesthetic.

Opium was the essential ingredient of the four great mainstays of the medieval apothecary and doctor: *mithridatum, theriaca, philonium* and *diascordium*. They were common palliatives and general antidotes to a vast range of medical conditions, but opium was also used specifically in a form called 'laudanum', the name deriving from the Latin verb *laudare*, meaning to praise.

The name was first coined by Paracelsus when referring to his mouse dropping-like pills, but it was the English physician, Thomas Sydenham, regarded as the founder of clinical medicine, who reapplied it in the 1660s to a tincture of opium mixed with alcohol by which it was thenceforth known.

Laudanum was a common opium preparation, the bitter taste disguised. Little different from Helen's nepenthe, it was usually strong red wine or port in which a dosage of opium had been dissolved. The combination of the two ingredients made a powerful and potentially very dangerous mixture. It was the main form in which opium was taken until well into the nineteenth century.

Sydenham's zeal for laudanum was considerable and his praise ever forthcoming:

> . . . here I cannot but break out in praise of the great God, the giver of all good things, who hath granted to the human race, as a comfort in their afflictions, no medicine of the value of opium, either in regard to the number of diseases it can control, or its efficiency in extirpating them . . . Medicine would be a cripple without it; and whosoever understands it well, will do more with it alone than he could well hope to do from any single medicine.

He was of the opinion that without opium the art of healing would cease to exist – or certainly would not advance – for, with its aid, a doctor was able to perform near miraculous cures and conduct surgery. Sydenham's eulogy for opium was so expansive it earned him the sobriquet of 'Opiophilos'.

Each doctor tended to have his own recipe. Sydenham's laudanum was far more scientifically based, doing away with the mumbo-jumbo of Paracelsus's mixture. It contained 2 ounces of opium, 1 ounce of saffron, and a drachm of cinnamon and of cloves, all dissolved in a pint of Canary wine. Other mixtures of the same period were not so logical and free of superstition or quackery. One, *Laudanum Josephi Michaelis*, published in *The Commonplace Book of an Apothecary of Great Dunmow*, included pearls, coral and amber; another, ominously named 'Lancaster (or Quaker's or Kendal) Black Drop' and originally cooked up by a Capuchin monk called Rousseau, contained opium, fermented crab-apple juice, nutmeg, saffron and yeast. Of the consistency of syrup, it was claimed to be three or four times the strength of previous versions of laudanum and it must have pleased his patients for Rousseau became a successful practitioner in Paris under the patronage of Louis XIV. His concoction had a long life: it appeared in the *Hamburg Codex* of 1845 and in the *US Pharmacopoeia* of 1851.

Thomas Dover was the inventor of another opium product, Dover's Powder, which first appeared in the *London Pharmacopoeia* of 1788 and was being used up until the Second World War.

Dover was a fascinating, larger-than-life character. As a young man he had lived in Sydenham's house in the village of Wyndford Eagle in Dorset, where he contracted smallpox. Sydenham treated and cured him. After studying under Sydenham, he became a privateer and commanded a vessel called the *Duke*, with which he raided the coast of South America: on 2 February 1709, he rescued Alexander Selkirk (on whom Defoe based Robinson Crusoe) from the Juan Fernández Islands. Dover later returned to England and set up in medical practice: although lacking any formal training other than that acquired with Sydenham, he had doubtless picked up a large amount of knowledge on his travels.

Dover's Powder was described by its inventor as a 'diaphoretic' (a substance to promote sweating), for which he gave the method of preparation in his *Ancient Physician's Legacy to his Country*, a collection of writings from his forty-nine years in the medical profession. The ingredients were 1 ounce each of opium, liquorice and ipecacuanha with 4 ounces each of saltpetre and vitriolated tartar. Dover wrote the dosage was:

> from 40 to 60 or 70 grains in a glass of white wine posset on going to bed. In two or three hours at the furthest the patient will be free from pain, and though not able to put his foot to the ground, 'tis very much if he cannot walk next day.

He declared quite bluntly that the powder was strong, adding that 'some apothecaries have desired their patients to make their wills before they venture upon so large a dose.'

Not only physicians and travellers were well acquainted with opium. So, too, were writers. In *The Canterbury Tales*, writing in *The Prologue* of the pilgrim who was a doctor, Chaucer lists, amongst others, Aesculapeius, Hippocrates, Dioscorides, Galen, Avicenna and a number of Arabic doctors (such as Rhazes, Hali, Serapion and the Moor, Averroes) who were noted for their opium use. His catalogue is not restricted to Arabs and classical figures: Chaucer also mentions John of Gaddesden, a medical authority educated at Merton College, Oxford, who died in 1361, during Chaucer's lifetime. In *The Pardoner's Tale*, the third rioter plans the death of his comrades by poisoning their bottles of wine with, Chaucer adds, a substance described by Avicenna as sure to bring on a pretty ghastly end whilst the grieving Lady in *The Book of the Duchess* bemoans that even Galen and Hippocrates could not heal her woe or ease her pain.

It goes without saying opium did not escape William Shakespeare's

attention. His most famous reference comes in a soliloquy by Iago
in *Othello*:

> Not poppy, nor mandragore,
> Nor all the drowsy syrups of the world,
> Shall ever medicine thee to that sweet sleep
> Which thou ow'dst yesterday.

The imagery is not all that poetic. Shakespeare would have known
the term 'drowsy syrup' for, in fact, it was accepted medical
terminology for opium.

Sir Thomas Browne, who was a seventeenth-century doctor as
well as a writer, used opium as an image in his work: 'The iniquity
of oblivion blindly scattereth her poppy, there is no antidote
against the opium of time' and 'I need no other laudanum than
this [his faith in prayer] to make me sleep.' Robert Burton, the
noted scholar and priest who died in 1640, wrote in his famous
work, *Anatomy of Melancholy*, of the problem of those who were
insomniacs 'by reason of their continual cares, fears, sorrows,
dry brains [which] is a symptom that much crucifies melancholy
men.' His remedy was *laudanum Paracelsi*, swallowed with violets,
roses, lettuce, mandrake, henbane, nutmegs or willows: the last
was an interesting addition for it was known that willow also
cured headaches, containing as it does a natural form of aspirin.
Alternative cures for melancholia which Burton proposed included
smelling a ball of opium (as he said the Turks did), anointing the
forehead upon retiring with an opium–rosewater mixture and
applying leeches behind the ears then rubbing opium into their
puncture marks.

Whilst most scholars and writers would have been acquainted
with opium, few would have been addicted. By taking it in small,
infrequent quantities, they would have avoided the trap. Yet there
was one who was famously habituated: he was Thomas Shadwell,
the leading Whig supporter, Restoration dramatist and poet.

His habit was widely known throughout society and he became
the butt of jokes as a result of it. Shadwell, who had a long-standing
political and literary quarrel with John Dryden, was the subject of
the latter's mock-heroic poem *MacFlecknoe*, the Prince of Dullness,
who 'never deviates into sense' and who was given a wreath of
poppies. In his *Absalom and Achitophel*, Dryden directly refers to

Shadwell's habit. Yet, whilst his addiction was ridiculed for the sake of literary enmity, Dryden did not condemn it and a mock epitaph on Shadwell's death more or less treated his habituation as an acceptable failing. It went:

> Tom writ, his readers still slept o'er his book,
> For Tom took opium, and they opiates took.

Ironically, Shadwell had the last laugh. After the revolution of 1688, he superseded Dryden as both Poet Laureate and Historiographer Royal. Clearly, his addiction was not regarded as an obstacle to his rising in both royal favour and literary stature. His death was ironic, too: despite his funeral orator stating, to his certain knowledge, that Shadwell had not taken his dose of opium and went to his maker with a clear mind, it seems more than likely he died of an overdose.

In later years, opium was to claim more famous slaves or acolytes. Clive of India was addicted to it, having taken it as a painkiller for a bowel complaint: he killed himself at the age of forty-nine with an overdose. Robert Hall, the Baptist divine, was addicted, as was Thomas Wedgwood, the father of photography. The Duke of Wellington reported that George IV took laudanum to counteract his alcoholic hangovers. In America, Benjamin Franklin, the politician and one of the authors of the Declaration of Independence, was almost certainly addicted to opium in his declining years, as was John Randolph of Roanoke, Virginia, the arrogant and eccentric politician who fought the emancipation of slaves even though he gave his own their liberty in his will.

Inevitably, with such an extensive application of opium for a huge range of illnesses, addiction was common, yet it was hardly ever addressed and was generally accepted as the price one paid for the relief of pain. One reference to the hazard of addiction may be found in Purchas's volume, *Purchas His Pilgrimage*, published in 1613:

> . . . they [travellers in Africa and Asia] suppose I know not what conjunction and efficacie both of Mars and Venus are therein; but being once used, must daily be continued on paine of death.

Dr John Jones's *Mysteries of Opium Reveal'd* published in 1700 – probably the earliest book specifically dealing with opium – mentioned the risk of addiction as well as the pleasures the drug offered. It did not specifically warn against opium, merely accepting addiction as a possible outcome of opium taking.

Jones, who as well as publishing, practising medicine and studying opium, invented a clock improbably driven by bellows, wrote that opium produced 'a dull, mopish and heavy Disposition', caused a loss of memory and generally affected the whole body. He outlined both the physical and mental contra-indications of excessive usage or high dosage, also noting the effects of withdrawal. Almost certainly an addict himself, if Jones had not undergone withdrawal he had most certainly witnessed others going through its rigours, for he reported a sudden cessation of opium taking brought on 'great, and even intolerable Distresses, Anxieties and Depressions of Spirits, which in a few days commonly end in a most miserable Death, attended with strange Agonies.'

Yet, despite such a warning, he also emphasised the pleasurable sides of opium use which he appears to have regarded as not only being a vehicle for pleasant fantasies, the dulling of pain and release from anxiety, but also for 'Promptitude, Serenity, Alacrity and Expediteness in Dispatching and Managing Business . . . Assurance, Ovations of the Spirits, Courage, Contempt of Danger, and Magnanimity . . . Euphory, or easie undergoing of all Labour, Journeys . . . Satisfaction, Acquiescence, Contentation, Equanimity' and a good deal more. As a summary, he wrote 'if [after taking opium] the person keeps himself in action, discourse of business, it seems . . . like a most delicious and extraordinary refreshment of the spirits upon very good news, or any other great cause of joy . . . It has been compared (not without good cause) to a permanent gentle degree of that pleasure which modesty forbids the name of . . .' The pleasure Jones's modesty forbade him to name might well be described as sex: addicts frequently comment on how orgasmic the sensation of opiates can seem. As for the illnesses Jones claimed opium would cure, his list covers almost every ailment from travel sickness to amputations, gout to bubonic plague and, most marvellous and ironic of all, he declared it was a cure for hypochondria.

Perhaps the most vulpine aspect of Jones's book was his claim that his was the truthful account of the ways and pitfalls of opium. Like any addict, he claimed miracles for the drug, insisting his book was written without prejudice or 'any sly or sordid Evasion, or considerable Omission (which has been the perfidious Course of Authors in this case).' In truth, he merely told what he saw through the addict's eyes. His book was also criticised by a contemporary academic, with some justification, as being 'extraordinary and perfectly unintelligible'.

Jones summarised his thoughts by concluding, 'opium does not operate by causing a grievous sensation and there being no other way left by which it may operate it must operate by causing a pleasant sensation . . . What can then cure pain and all its effects better than pleasure?'

With the development of scientific curiosity, doctors and students began to wonder what it was about opium that made it work as it did yet opium lost little of its mystery. It was still referred to as 'the Hand of God' or 'the sacred anchor of life'.

Even Robert Boyle, author of *The Skeptical Chymist* and after whom the fundamental natural law is named, believed in opium's occult secret. He was convinced it affected the 'animal spirits' and the nervous system. Dr John Freitag claimed its narcotic abilities were due to its extreme coldness, a concept dating back to the Middle Ages and the belief in humours. Monsieur Pomet, Chief Druggist to Louis XIV, explained opium's capabilities in a similar vein:

> Opium procures rest by its viscous and sulphureous particles, which being convey'd to the channels of the brain, by the volatile parts, agglutinates and fixes the animal spirits, in such a manner that it stops for some time their circulation, from the swiftness of their former motion; so that during that obstruction, or tye upon the spirits, sleep ensues; for the senses are as it were fettered or locked up by the viscous or agglutinating property of opium.

One of opium's most avid students, Pomet referred to it as a 'narcotick, hypnotick and anodyne'. It was good, amongst other things, for composing 'the Hurry of the Spirits', promoting insensibility, useful in diseases of the breasts and lungs, prevented the spitting of blood, cured coughs and colds, vomiting and looseness of the bowels, as well as being handy in the treatment of 'cholick, pleurisis and hysterick cases'. His study of opium went so far as to chronicle its sources and types. He wrote:

First, the pure from Cairo or Thebes. Secondly, the black and hard from Aden. Thirdly, the yellow and softer sort from Cambaia and Decam in the East Indies. Yet we generally at this time reckon but two sorts, being first the Turkish or Theban, which is weighty, of good consistency, thick and more solid than the Indian; of a lively fresh reddish colour, almost likes fresh aloes, of a strong poppy scent, of an acrid bitter taste, that will burn and flame; soft, easy to cut, and be dissolved in either water, wine or spirit of wine, and is pretty clean from dirt, excrements and filth. Secondly: the Indian opium, which is softer, yellower, lighter, not of so good a body, and much fouler, being in every respect inferior to the former.

Attitudes towards opium persisted broadly unchanged through the eighteenth century although occult considerations were abandoned as scientific study increased. Medical writers began to assess opium, investigate and even criticise it. In his *Family Herbal*, the eighteenth-century physician Dr John Hill recommended caution and expressed his doubt about its alleged ability to cure a mad dog's bite. George Young, in his *Treatise on Opium* published in the 1750s, and Dr Samuel Crumpe, in his *Inquiry into the Nature and Properties of Opium* in 1793, indicated the main features of addiction and touched upon the problems of withdrawal, but neither showed any sense of moral condemnation for either medicinal or recreational use. Crumpe went so far as to admit he had taken opium frequently and experienced its euphoria: there was no suggestion he took it to treat an ailment.

Even the great Dr Samuel Johnson took opium on occasion, if only for medicinal purposes. Father of the English language, compiler of the first English dictionary, sage, seer and compendium of knowledge – or so his biographer, James Boswell, would have it – he was never addicted but took it to cure headaches and stomach trouble. Johnson, it seems, was wise to the dangers and wily enough to avoid them. In *Boswell's Life of Johnson*, the biographer recorded:

On Sunday, March 23 [1783], I breakfasted with Dr Johnson, who seemed much relieved, having taken opium the night before. He however protested against it, as a remedy that should be given with the utmost reluctance, and only in extreme necessity. I mentioned how commonly it was used in Turkey, and that therefore it could not be so pernicious as he apprehended. He grew warm and said,

'Turks take opium, and Christians take opium; but Russell, in his
Account of Aleppo, tells us, that it is as disgraceful in Turkey to take
too much opium, as it is with us to get drunk. Sir, it is amazing how
things are exaggerated.'

Most people considered opium taking for pleasure a peculiarly
Eastern custom, a quaint pastime or an eccentric vice. When he
appeared in literature, as in Dr Russell's *History of Aleppo*, the
opium user was an object of curiosity rather than of censure or
alarm.

This eccentric vice paved the way for another, less common use
for opium. For most of the late eighteenth and early nineteenth
century it was, for a select few, not just a miraculous catholicon
but the key to a cupboard containing untold marvels.

3

Pleasure-domes in Xanadu

Opium alters the recognition and perception of certain sensations. Dr John Jones wrote of how it wonderfully distorted candle flames, how the sound of a pin dropped into a brass bowl was magnified and changed, how church bells sounded as if heard along a 'hollow valley'. At the end of the eighteenth and into the nineteenth centuries, this warping of sensation, in addition to the dreams and visual images opium promoted, was to have a profound effect upon the arts, in particular literature.

The period is called the Romantic Revival, its writers known as the Romantics. The name was loosely applied to a body of European authors roughly between 1775 and 1835 who rejected the prevalent rules of classicism and neo-classicism. At the core of Romantic literature was a resurgence of the imagination, flights of fancy allied to narrative rather than description. Romanticism contained a new awareness of nature and the natural world, emphasised the need for spontaneity in thought and action, attaching considerable importance to natural genius exhibited through imagination. It also embodied a more liberated and subjective expression of passion, pathos and personal feelings. Opium, and the liberty of thought it produced, was instrumental in the development of the Romantic ideal.

In Europe, the movement included such writers as Goethe, Schlegel, Hölderlin, Chateaubriand, Madame de Staël and Pushkin, whilst in Britain it embraced Coleridge, Wordsworth, Scott, Percy

Bysshe Shelley, John Keats, Lord Byron and Thomas De Quincey, the core of the period extending between 1798, when the poets Samuel Taylor Coleridge and William Wordsworth published *Lyrical Ballads*, and 1832, when Sir Walter Scott died.

The awareness of opium and its effects suddenly became a topic of discussion with the 1821 publication in Britain of De Quincey's autobiographical *Confessions of an English Opium-eater*. It was the first time opium addiction, or as De Quincey put it, 'the marvellous agency of opium, whether for pleasure or for pain', was laid bare in a book in which its author stated opium, rather than himself, was the true hero of the piece.

When De Quincey, who was born in Manchester in 1785, discovered opium is debatable. Some accounts suggest he first took it medicinally at the age of seventeen, others claiming he encountered it whilst a student at Worcester College, Oxford: he wrote it was in 1804 when he was twenty, purchased at the recommendation of a fellow law student from a chemist in London's Oxford Street to cure toothache and neuralgia. Whenever it was, De Quincey never forgot his first taste:

> . . . in an hour, O heavens! What a revulsion! What a resurrection, from the lowest depths, of the inner spirit! What an apocalypse of the world within me. That my pains had vanished was now a trifle in my eyes; this negative effect was swallowed up . . . in the abyss of divine enjoyment thus suddenly revealed. Here was a panacea . . . for all human woes; here was the secret of happiness . . .

Opium offered De Quincey new routes of evasion from his confused state of mind about his future and his misery over the loss of his companion, a prostitute with whom he lived in penury in London whilst studying law, who left him when he returned to his family. Opium became his new destination in life. He stressed it did not create anything new but embellished what already existed, heightening awareness of latent thoughts and imagination: as he put it, a man who spent his life talking about oxen would dream of oxen under its influence.

Early in his opium-eating days, De Quincey would take a draught of laudanum then set off to walk about London or to attend the opera. Knowing the drug heightened mental sensitivity to outside stimuli, he used its euphoria to expand his consciousness, to stretch the pleasure of being in the ordinary world with an ability to reach beyond the prosaic and mundane. Listening to opera became an exquisite pastime: even the sound of young ladies in the audience speaking Italian took on the qualities of the music which, heard through opium, stirred up memories, not as direct recall but 'as if present and incarnated in the music'. Even the calls of market traders and banter of customers sounded like a weird music, the opium also eradicating the concept of time and altering perceptions of space. De Quincey often walked great distances, oblivious as to how long he was out.

It was of this time that De Quincey wrote his famous eulogy to opium:

> O just, subtle, and all-conquering opium! that, to the hearts of rich and poor alike, for the wounds that will never heal, and for the pangs of grief that 'tempt the spirit to rebel', bringest an assuaging balm – eloquent opium! . . . thou buildest upon the bosom of darkness, out of the fantastic imagery of the brain, cities and temples . . . beyond the splendours of Babylon and Hekatompylos; and, 'from the anarchy of dreaming sleep', callest into sunny light the faces of long-buried beauties, and the blessed household countenances, cleansed from the 'dishonours of the grave'. Thou only givest these gifts to man: and thou hast the keys of Paradise . . .

Although the lassitude of opium frequently removes the desire to record what wonders are experienced – and De Quincey himself reported how he wanted to write down what his intellect had undergone but found himself riddled with a 'powerless and infantile feebleness' – the dreams can be so exquisite and amazing as to outstrip the powers of literacy. In time, these visions spill over from the state of narcosis into everyday thought.

This ability to visualise outside opium-induced sleep was summed up by De Quincey in four important observations. The first was 'that, as the creative state of the mind increased, a sympathy seemed to arise between the waking and the dreaming states of the brain in one point – that whatsoever I happened to call up and trace by a voluntary act upon the darkness was apt to transfer itself to my dreams.' In other words, the imagination could, in part, decide what the opium had as its raw dream material. Second came the awareness that 'my dreams were accompanied by deep-seated anxiety and funereal melancholy, such as are wholly incommunicable in words.' These emotions were surely a part of De Quincey's own psychological make-up, although a sense of inexpressible melancholy is common to many addicts' experience: it may well be an expression of the calmness opium promotes. His third observation was that 'the sense of space, and in the end the sense of time, were both powerfully affected.' This distortion provided a strange and omniscient visual imagery in addicts, often filled with fantastical buildings and structures, land- and seascapes and mountain vastnesses. Finally, 'the minutest incidents of childhood, or forgotten scenes of later years, were often revived. I could not be said to recollect them . . . but placed as they were before me, in dreams like intuitions, and clothed in all the evanescent circumstances and accompanying feelings, I recognised them instantly.' The ability to recollect experiences is the stuff of the writer's art.

In these four points, it is surprising De Quincey does not mention the manner in which opium contorts or alters colours. In ordinary dreams, colours (if they appear at all) are unenhanced and realistic. In an opium dream, reds darken to maroons and blood crimsons, blues blacken to the colour of an early night sky, whilst yellows become solid and more luminescent. What is more, colours take on an almost tangible texture so the hue becomes only a part of their impact: one does not just see them, one also feels them.

Undoubtedly, opium was a Pandora's box of literary tools to the imaginative and erudite mind. It provided unique visual images, afforded a kind of mental time travel, gave a new way of observing the mundane and acted as an *aide-mémoire*.

When De Quincey became habituated, he called opium his 'Divine Poppy-juice, as indispensable as breathing': it was his release from physical pain and mental anguish, but it gave him more. Through the freemasonry of addiction characteristic amongst addicts, he gained a sense of kinship with others with whom he shared the common belief that opium set them above normal mortals, for it gave such magnificent visions. In other words, it took him into another, miraculous universe where the incredible was accessible.

As addiction increased, his dreams changed. The visual images remained, yet they metamorphosed. Visions of Babylonian architecture gave way to torments. Emotions such as joy were replaced with guilt. De Quincey became haunted by a sense of unfathomable dread, imprisonment or of being pursued by an ill-defined, terrible hunter.

De Quincey recorded, for the first time and in spectacular detail, just such an agonising dream, the likes of which are familiar in advanced opium addiction. He had met socially a Malay trader and, although their meeting was brief, it impacted itself upon his mind, for the Malay became an incubus in De Quincey's imagination:

> The Malay has been a fearful enemy for months. Every night, through his means, I have been transported into Asiatic scenery . . . in China or Hindustan . . . I was stared at, hooted at, grinned at, chattered at, by monkeys, by paroquets, by cockatoos. I ran into pagodas, and was fixed for centuries at the summit, or in secret rooms; I was the idol; I was the priest; I was worshipped; I was sacrificed . . . Thousands of years I lived and was buried in stone coffins, with mummies and sphinxes, in narrow chambers at the heart of eternal pyramids. I was kissed, with cancerous kisses by crocodiles, and I was laid, confounded with unutterable abortions, among reeds and Nilotic mud . . . Over every form, and threat, and punishment, and dim sightless incarceration, brooded a killing sense of eternity and infinity . . . The cursed crocodile became for me the object of more horror than all the rest . . . I was compelled to live with him; and (as was always the case in my dreams) for centuries. Sometimes I escaped, and found myself in Chinese houses. All the feet of the tables, sofas, etc., soon became instinct with life; the abominable head of the crocodile, and his leering eyes, looked out at me, multiplied into ten thousand repetitions . . .

In addition to dealing with the pleasures and pains of opium-eating, De Quincey intended to write a third part to his book to counteract his critics who rightly claimed the first edition was loaded in favour of the pleasurable side of drug taking. Ironically, he was too wracked by the pain of trying to break his addiction to write it. He succeeded in reducing his daily consumption by 85 per cent but he could not completely eradicate the habit. Opium was, he stated, the only means he had of being truly happy.

De Quincey's controlled addiction does not seem to have made his life unduly miserable for he was contentedly married, kept his addiction manageable and, although he frequently locked himself away for weeks on end with his laudanum and books, he was always a keen and erudite conversationalist. Yet, had he completed his writing, he might have produced a valuable cautionary text: instead, he brought the subject into the open.

De Quincey was not unique. There was a substantial number of creative artists – most but not all of them writers – who were also addicted and who, through their addiction, changed the direction of Western literature.

One of these was George Crabbe. At the age of thirteen, he was apprenticed to a surgeon-apothecary and, three years later, to a surgeon: such training familiarised him with opium. In 1775, he returned to his birthplace of Aldeburgh in Suffolk to work as a warehouseman before setting up in medical practice. At the same time, he began to publish poetry and, in 1781, took holy orders. For the rest of his life he lived as a priest and writer.

His addiction began around 1795 when he started to take opium to cure migraine attacks. At about the same time, his third son tragically died and his wife began to develop into a manic-depressive. Whether or not the migraine was brought on by the stress or, as his doctor suggested, by an intestinal illness (perhaps a duodenal ulcer similarly prompted), or whether in fact Crabbe took opium as a release from his private anguish, is immaterial. The fact remains he became quickly habituated and continued to be so until he died, although he managed to keep his habit secret from his parishioners. His son, who was also his biographer, wrote that his father took a constant but only slightly increasing dose to which he attributed his long and generally healthy life: Crabbe died in 1832, aged seventy-seven.

Crabbe's earlier poetry had been skilful but unexciting. It was after his addiction was established that he wrote his best, most searching work. Much of Crabbe's later writing shows an influence of opium: one poem in particular, perhaps his most famous and enduring, is rich in drug imagery. It is one of a long sequence of poems collectively entitled *The Borough*, written between 1804 and 1810: it is called 'Peter Grimes'.

The story, set in the dismal estuarine creeks of the Suffolk coast which Crabbe knew so well, is the harrowing tale of a cruel fisherman who murders his father, then abuses and negligently kills two apprentice boys. Grimes gets away with the crimes but he is made a social outcast, forbidden by the magistrates to employ another apprentice. He is forced to live a solitary life in a bleak landscape of swamps, mud-banks and ditches where he grows insular and, stung by guilt, mad. Spectres of his father and the apprentices wait for him in the marshes and inlets, standing mute as he rails at them and tries to justify his sins. At last, on his deathbed, Grimes recounts the agonies he has had to endure from the ghosts.

> And when they saw me fainting and oppress'd,
> He, with his hand, the old man, scoop'd the flood,
> And there came flame about him mix'd with blood;
> He bade me stoop and look upon the place,
> Then flung the red-hot liquor in my face;
> Burning it blazed, and then I roar'd for pain,
> I thought the demons would have turn'd my brain.
> Still there they stood, and forced me to behold
> A place of horrors – they cannot be told –
> Where the flood open'd, there I heard the shriek
> Of tortured guilt – no earthly tongue can speak:
> 'All days alike! for ever!' did they say,
> 'And unremitting torments every day.'

The haunted, guilt-ridden imagery is opium-inspired, likewise the descriptions of the never-ending mud-flats where time passed with the sluggishness of an opium dream, the tides ebbing and flowing with an excruciating slowness. Grimes's death might even be that of an opium addict:

> And still he tried to speak, and look's in dread
> Of frighten'd females gathering round his bed;
> Then dropp'd exhausted and appear'd at rest,
> Till the strong foe the vital powers possess'd;
> Then with an inward, broken voice he cried,
> 'Again they come,' and mutter'd as he died.

The poem is not that of a newly acquired addiction: it is the stuff of the well-habituated user, long past the stage of the splendours of Babylon and Hekatompylos.

Another of Crabbe's contemporaries whose life and work were in debt to opium was Samuel Taylor Coleridge.

Born in Devonshire in 1772, Coleridge was introduced to opium at an early age. He was probably given laudanum at eight when he suffered from a severe fever or later, as a schoolboy at Christ's Hospital, when he contracted jaundice and rheumatic fever. What is certain is his being prescribed laudanum for rheumatism when an undergraduate at Cambridge in 1791. He was by then well acquainted with it, for he wrote to his brother in November 1791: 'Opium never used to have any disagreeable effects on me.' He took it again as a tranquilliser in March 1796, in November and December of the same year to treat neuralgia, the following year for dysentery, and in 1798 to kill toothache. It was at this time that he wrote again to his brother, saying: 'Laudanum gave me repose, not sleep; but you, I believe, know how divine that repose is, what a spot of enchantment, a green spot of fountains and flowers and trees in the very heart of a waste of sands.'

It was not until the winter of 1800, when Coleridge started taking laudanum and brandy to conquer acute back pain and swellings in his joints, that he became unequivocally addicted. By early 1802, he was taking over 100 drops of laudanum a day, a dosage he reduced by the following winter to 12–20 per day to combat nightmares and severe diarrhoea which, unbeknownst to him, were caused by his withdrawal. In April 1804, aware he was addicted, Coleridge took a voyage to Malta to break his habit. He failed.

Like most addicts, Coleridge moved in drug-taking circles, one of the characters he was familiar with being Dr Thomas Beddoes, who was at the centre of a group of drug experimentalists. Beddoes, who lived in Bristol, was a physician for whom drugs were not only a professional interest but a hedonistic one. His 'study' of drugs was not restricted to opiates: he was, in modern terminology, into the whole scene. In his Pneumatic Institution, a clinic he ran for pulmonary diseases, Beddoes toyed with opiates, cannabis and a wide range of other substances. It was here Sir Humphrey Davy first discovered nitrous oxide, or 'laughing gas', which he and others – Coleridge included – found amusing.

An example of Beddoes's intense drug involvement is revealed in a letter he wrote to his friend, Thomas Wedgwood: 'We will have a fair trial of Bang [a misspelling for *bhang*, or cannabis] – Do bring down some of the Hyocyamine Pills – and I will give a fair trial of opium, Hensbane, and Nepenthe. By the bye, I always considered Homer's account of the Nepenthe as a Banging lie.'

Coleridge, unlike many, made little effort to hide his addiction:

he admitted to it openly. His friends William Wordsworth, Robert Southey and William Cottle were aware of his entrapment, the cause of his frequently sallow complexion, dull eyes and shaking hands. De Quincey recorded Coleridge at a lecture:

> His appearance was generally that of a person struggling with pain and overmastering illness. His lips were baked with feverish heat, and often black in colour; and in spite of the water which he was continually drinking through the whole course of his lecture, he often seemed to labour under an almost paralytic inability to raise the upper jaw from the lower. In such a state it is clear that nothing could save the lecture itself from reflecting his own feebleness and exhaustion, except the advantage of having been precomposed in some happier mood.

As lecturing was an important part of Coleridge's livelihood, and as his addiction frequently meant cancellation of a lecture at the very last minute, with audiences waiting at the door, the effect on his income can be guessed and he lived much of his life at least partly supported by friends.

At times, Coleridge was deeply ashamed of his habituation, vehemently deploring it although he did not feel guilty and often dismissed it by blaming it on his weak health. He even claimed opium was essential to his earning a living, yet he was desperate to be rid of it, as De Quincey observed:

> Grave, indeed, he continued to be, and at times absorbed in gloom; nor did I ever see him in a state of perfectly natural cheerfulness. But as he strove in vain, for many years, to wean himself from his captivity to opium, a healthy state of spirits could not be much expected. Perhaps, indeed [he went on, recognising the effects of habituation upon both Coleridge's physical and mental well-being], where the liver and other organs had, for so large a period in life, been subject to a continual morbid stimulation, it may be impossible for the system ever to recover a natural action. Torpor, I suppose, must result from continued artificial excitement . . .

In 1812 and again in 1814, Coleridge sought medical help but to no effect. He even went so far as to employ a man whose job was to stand between him and the door of any chemist he might approach, forcibly ejecting him from it.

Eventually his health deteriorated so far that, in April 1816, he went to a Dr Gillman in Highgate, north London. Gillman controlled and reduced Coleridge's dependency but he was unable to eradicate it for Coleridge surreptitiously obtained supplies to give himself a temporary boost. By the time he went under Gillman's regime, he was consuming at least 2 pints of laudanum a week, occasionally 2 pints a day, the equivalent of 20,000 drops. The pharmacist who provided his 'illicit' supply claimed to sell him a 12-ounce bottle every fifth day, giving a dose of 1000 drops a day in addition to Gillman's reduced intake: 1000 drops would kill 5 first-time users.

Whatever Coleridge thought of his addiction, which he admitted affected his moral nature, he was correct in his claim that in part he earned his living from it for, whilst it may have ruined his lecturing career, there can be no doubt it was an integral part of his literary creativity which, added to his extraordinary imagination, his considerable intellect and his catholic taste in reading, produced some of the most remarkable poetry in the English language.

The Rime of the Ancient Mariner and *Kubla Khan* are the two most famous of Coleridge's many opium-influenced poems, although a fierce debate about the role of opium in the writing of the former has raged for decades. *The Ancient Mariner* was completed early in 1798, before Coleridge became addicted but certainly after his use of opium as a medicine for dysentery: the work is steeped in opium. A sensitivity to sounds, an awareness of the intricacies of colour and light, the visual images, the passage of elongated time, the sense of desolation and vast seascape and the presence of a spectral woman, all smack of opium, not to mention the central theme of an evil deed, persecution by a ghostly apparition and a catalogue of horrors. The mariner's crew were from a 'charnel-dungeon', the ocean covered with 'slimy things' which 'crawled with legs upon the slimy sea', the surface 'like a witch's oils, Burnt green, and blue, and white'. The spectre is described:

> Her lips were red, her looks were free,
> Her locks were yellow as gold:
> Her skin was as white as leprosy,
> The Night-Mare Life-in-Death was she,
> Who thicks man's blood with cold.

In *Kubla Khan*, the opening lines of which are so frequently quoted (and misquoted), the evidence of opium is also clear:

> In Xanadu did Kubla Khan
> A stately pleasure-dome decree:
> Where Alph, the sacred river, ran
> Through caverns measureless to man
>   Down to a sunless sea.
> So twice five miles of fertile ground
> With walls and towers were girdled round:
> And there were gardens bright with sinuous rills
> Where blossomed many an incense-bearing tree;
> And here were forests ancient as the hills,
>   Enfolding sunny spots of greenery.

The imagery of archaic architecture, vast caverns and dark seas precedes other examples in the poem, of voices and music heard in the distance, the tactile sense of the sunny pleasure-dome containing caves of ice and the wailing woman waiting for her demon-lover under a waning moon.

Both poems are drawn from the writing of others. *The Ancient Mariner* has its vague foundation in George Shelvocke's account of rounding Cape Horn, whilst *Kubla Khan* has its roots in Purchas's *His Pilgrimage*, with which the poet was familiar and, through it, conscious of opium and addiction. Such a talent and intellect as Coleridge possessed would almost assuredly have produced extraordinarily fine poetry without the aid of opium because, for Coleridge, opium was not the creative force behind his art, but a mere provider of material: in early 1801, he wrote to a friend that he looked back on his long and painful bout of rheumatism 'as a storehouse of wild Dreams for Poems'. In other words, as De Quincey realised, opium was the tool by which Coleridge rearranged and reassessed experiences and stimuli received either through narcotic dreams or from outside sources such as books and lucid, everyday non-drug-influenced conversation.

Yet, for all his writing obtained from the storehouse of opium, Coleridge was concerned about his addiction. Just before he died, he wrote, 'After my death, I earnestly entreat that a full and unqualified narrative of my wretchedness, and of its guilty cause, may be made public, that at least some little good may be effected by the direful example.'

There were other poet-addicts, too. Elizabeth Barrett Browning was addicted at an early age. Although there is no substantial evidence, it seems likely John Keats took laudanum before the winter of 1819—20: he admitted dosing on mercury in the form of calomel to counteract a sore throat contracted in late 1818 whilst nursing his tubercular brother and it is highly plausible, with his fear of tuberculosis, he also took laudanum. Furthermore, in March 1819, Keats was hit in the face by a cricket ball and his writings of the next day suggest he took laudanum to kill the considerable pain.

Keats's poetry suggests a more than passing familiarity with opium. In 'To Sleep', a sonnet from April 1819, he wrote:

> 'ere thy poppy throws
> Around my bed its lulling charities

'Ode on Indolence', 'Ode to Melancholy' and 'Ode to a Nightingale' all carry references to opium or the poppy whilst 'The Eve of St Agnes', written between 18 January and 2 February 1819, is rich with opium-prompted imagery which is hardly surprising for, at the time, Keats was taking medication for his sore throat and was suffering from toothache: laudanum was the common painkiller for any dental problem.

Not only poets were inspired or affected by opium. So, too, were prose-writers, the most famous being Wilkie Collins. When he was nine, Collins overheard Coleridge admitting his struggle against opium to his mother. The poet was in tears but Mrs Collins was a realist and replied, 'Mr Coleridge, do not cry; if the opium really does you any good, and you must have it, why do you not go and get it?' This exchange made a lasting impression on young Wilkie's mind. At twenty-three, he noticed how his father – the artist William Collins, who was dying of heart disease – found release from acute pain in doses of Battley's Drops, a proprietary-brand laudanum. With such experiences, it is no wonder Wilkie Collins turned to laudanum to ease a rheumatic illness which caused temporary, partial blindness and brought terrible pains to his legs. He took opium for the rest of his life.

Quite open about his habituation, Collins drank a wineglass of laudanum nightly as a sleeping draught and carried a hip-flask at all times, in addition to keeping a decanter full in his home. To ease neuralgia in later life, he also received morphine. Collins was, in fact, more than open about his habit: he was downright boastful. At a meeting with his friend, Hall Caine, he produced a glass of laudanum and, telling Hall Caine he would let him into the secrets of his prison-house, swallowed it in one. On being asked, Collins admitted he had taken such amounts for twenty years to stimulate his brain and to steady his nerves. Hall Caine questioned the ability of opium to stimulate Collins's mind and enquired if it had the same effect on others, to which Collins replied it did – Bulwer Lytton was addicted, he said, and it stimulated him, too. Yet, when Hall Caine asked if he should take laudanum for nervous exhaustion, Collins paused and quietly advised against it.

The best known of Collins's novels, *The Moonstone*, was written almost entirely under the influence of opium. Unable to write himself, Collins dictated the novel to a staunch-hearted secretary: her two predecessors had resigned their jobs, unable to face working with Collins as he writhed and groaned in pain. The plot, which is complex and tightly written, turns upon opium: the moonstone, a magnificent diamond, was taken by the hero of the tale while he was sleep-walking after having been unknowingly fed opium. When he read the book through, Collins could not recall the ending as being his work. It was not his only plot featuring opium: his earlier stories *No Name* (1862) and *Armadale* (1866) also involved laudanum.

Sir Walter Scott took laudanum whilst writing *The Bride of Lammermoor*, his doctor prescribing 6 grains of laudanum a day for a painful stomach complaint. Scott disliked opium for it depressed him and, to overcome its effects, he took long morning horse-rides to rid himself of what he called 'the accursed vapours'. When the novel was finished, and Scott read the manuscript, he stated he could remember not one incident, character or conversation from the story. As Scott's method of working was to 'lie in bed in the mornings simmering over things for an hour or so before I get up – and there's the time when I am dressing to overhaul my half-sleeping, half-waking project de chapitre – and when I get the paper before me, it commonly runs off pretty easily', it is no wonder *The Bride of Lammermoor* was so alien to its author: he would be waking and writing after a night of opium depression, a state superbly described in the heroine of the novel, Lucy Ashton, whose neurosis and anxiety lead to insanity.

That neither Wilkie Collins nor Sir Walter Scott recognised their own work does not suggest opium gave them something which had not originally existed within them in the first place. Collins had researched gemmology, India and somnambulism before embarking upon his novel and the historical background and geographical settings of Scott's tale were familiar to him. Just as De Quincey had pointed out, if one talked of oxen, opium represented them: here were sustained examples of knowledge being recycled by opium.

Other writers were indebted and, in some instances, enslaved to opium. As Wilkie Collins reported, Bulwer Lytton took opium as a tranquilliser and stimulant, most probably introduced to it as a painkiller for the excruciating earaches he experienced throughout his life: his elder brother, who lived in Constantinople, might have prompted his first dose, for he suffered from migraines and was an addict who described the effects of taking opium as being like having one's soul rubbed down with silk. Bramwell Brontë, the brother of the Brontë sisters, was an addict, whilst Byron and Shelley were occasional users. James Thomson experimented with it but he was to die from alcoholism whilst, towards the end of the nineteenth century, the poet Francis Thompson was heavily addicted. Baudelaire, born in 1821, was a heavy hashish user for many years but he turned late in life to opium, his poetry paying homage to it. There are reasons to consider others as candidates for opium usage: Hector Berlioz, Gérard de Nerval and, in later years, Arthur Rimbaud and Maurice Rollinat were also either addicted or influenced by it.

It is fair to say most writers came across opium in the first place as an anodyne and only subsequently fell under its sway, the dreams and nightmares weaving themselves into their work often to become an essential and unavoidable part of it. Yet there were those who regarded opium as a boon to their writing, who had been afforded the opportunity of giving it up but chose to keep on with it. For them, opium was a path to the unattainable, a doorway into the cosmos. None realised, or chose to heed, De Quincey's remarks that opium only displayed what was already in the mind.

For many addicted writers, opium did little to affect their characters adversely. They lived artistically successful lives, often becoming wealthy from their writings. There were those, like the guilt-ridden Coleridge, for whom addiction was a burden but they were of sufficiently strong will not to let the depression and despair of addiction oppress them.

On the other hand, there were those who were poor or burdened with the worries of everyday survival, and perhaps weak of character, who were changed by opium. They could become moody, sullen, mercurial of spirits and even suicidal, were often tormented, with their work showing this torment seething in them: a good example is Edgar Allen Poe, the American writer whose character was undermined by both opium and alcohol.

For over a century, a controversy has raged about whether or not Poe was an opium addict for at least a part of his life. Certainly, he was an opium user if not actually addicted and his work shows the unmistakable signs of opium: four of his fictional heroes are addicts. Poe tried to commit suicide by overdosing and his sister recorded often seeing him in a sad state from opium. Orphaned at the age of three and adopted by his Scots godfather who lived in Richmond, Virginia, Poe was partly educated in London, later attending the University of Virginia which he had to leave, broken by gambling debts. In 1831, he was dishonourably discharged from West Point Military Academy for deliberate neglect of his duties. Turning to journalism, he became a heavy drinker with an unstable temperament which both addictions eroded to such an extent he could not cope with his financial worries, his inner despair, the demands of his creativity and his wife's fatal consumption. He quarrelled with landlords and contemporaries – his most notorious feud was with Henry Longfellow – and died tragically as a result of wounds received in a drunken brawl in Baltimore in 1849 with, it is thought, electioneering hooligans: some claim he was drugged by his attackers but it is just as likely he was either drunk or had taken opium.

Whether through literature, personal experience or observing the everyday world around them, there was hardy a person alive in Europe or the immigrant populations of North America at the time who was not well acquainted with opium. De Quincey and his social peers may have used it for pleasure as well as a release from pain – and marvelled at its heightened dreams – but there were many hundreds of thousands of common folk for whom opium was the only way out of the drudgery of a harsh life.

4

Poverty, Potions and Poppy-heads

Throughout the nineteenth century, opium was as widely used in Britain, Western Europe and America as aspirin or paracetamol are today – if not more so – and it was the main ingredient of a vast range of medicines, patent medicines and quack 'remedies'.

The extensive use of opium was staggering. As Berridge and Edwards outlined in *Opium and the People*, consumption in Britain increased between 1831 and 1859 at an average rate of 2.4 per cent per annum. Imports rose from around 91,000 pounds (41,300 kilograms) in 1830 to 280,000 pounds (127,000 kilograms) in 1860, re-exported opium rising from 41,000 pounds (18,600 kilograms) to 151,000 pounds (68,500 kilograms), more than half selling to America.

Despite opium production in India, which was largely under British control, most of the importation came from Turkey, which was deemed to manufacture a higher-quality product. Indian opium had a low morphine content – at 4–6 per cent – which made it unsuitable for British pharmaceutical use: Turkish opium had a 10–13 per cent morphine content and could easily be exported through Smyrna, which had long been an important trading centre, used particularly by the British who had established commercial links with Turkey since the founding of the Levant Company in 1581.

The Ottoman Empire was a large market for British cotton goods, which were traded for corn, silk, raisins, wool, sponges and opium: between 1827 and 1869, 80 to 90 per cent of all imported opium was Turkish. The trading level never dropped below 70 per cent even with the advent on the market of Persian opium which was imported direct from Persia or via Constantinople where it was repackaged to look like the Turkish variety.

The Turkish near-monopoly on opium was not without detractors. In 1829, a Dr Webster stated quite bluntly that, if possible, opium should be grown in and obtained from a British colony, removing the reliance upon what he termed 'the rascally Turks'. Such a wish was, however, beyond the bounds of fulfilment. The trade was too well established to be overturned by jingoistic considerations.

At first, the trading lines followed the old silk and spice routes by way of the Low Countries, France, Germany, Gibraltar and Malta and, of course, Italy, where Venice was in the last stages of decline as a trading power. In time, alternative routes developed. Marseilles became a major shipment centre, a position it held until the 1970s. Rotterdam and Amsterdam also developed into maritime drugs centres, which they remain to this day. Yet, by 1850, most opium was shipped direct from Turkey aboard British vessels, doing away with transhipment and foreign tariff charges.

In Britain, Liverpool, Dover and Bristol were all opium ports, yet the main centre for trading in Europe was London where a cartel of importers controlled the business. Initially, these merchants were those whose firms were descended from the Levant Company: when the company finally closed in 1825, the cartel disintegrated, leaving opium susceptible to free trade. Wholesale importers moved in, purchasing opium both by private deal and at auction. As in any commodity market, there were also spot buyers who speculated when they saw prices favourably low but who were not dedicated opium traders.

The centre of opium business was around Mincing Lane in London, where 90 per cent of the trade was conducted. It had been an important market-place since the sixteenth century but, by the mid-1700s, it was associated primarily with opium and, to a lesser extent, other drugs. Opium transactions were sealed in Garraway's Coffee House, near the Royal Exchange, by a system known as 'buying by the candle'. A small candle was lit at the start of an auction and bids accepted until the wick burnt away, at which point the highest bid for the consignment 'under the candle' was accepted. Auctions took place fortnightly, began at 10.30 in the morning and were attended by about 100 buyers and brokers who bid throughout the day.

On occasion, deals were arranged between the London drug wholesale houses, such as the Apothecaries' Company or Allen and Hanburys, and individual brokers of whom there were about thirty operating in London. The method of business was thus: every Saturday, a list was published in the counting house of the Apothecaries' Company providing notice of forthcoming requirements. Brokers submitted samples the following Tuesday. The company's Buying Committee tested the samples and ordered accordingly. In these circumstances, cargoes in bond were sold prior to customs clearance.

Trading in opium required specific commercial expertise and the rewards could be high, although so too could be the risks. Mincing Lane brokers and dealers seldom worked under a 50 per cent profit margin, which could rise to 100 per cent, but it could just as readily fall. As with any agricultural commodity, prices fluctuated widely according to growing and harvest conditions and the quality of the produce. A second element reducing profit margins was the publication of a monthly current prices list allowing end-buyers, such as chemists, to shop around for the best deal. Other factors stabilising prices were the removal of import duties, the increasing efficiency of business with the advent of postage and railway parcel services and the gradual supplanting of the general import merchant by the dedicated opium dealer. A final influence upon international pricing was the encouragement by producer-governments which advocated switching peasant farming from less commercial and more risky cash crops to opium, thus improving their people's income and lives, simultaneously increasing local tax revenue.

Prices varied widely. Opium was liable to an import duty of 9 shillings per pound until 1828, then 4s per pound to 1836, when it was cut to 1s per pound, the level at which the duty remained until a free-trade agreement removed it in 1860. The reduction and abolition of tax, linked to increasing import quantities, brought the wholesale price consistently down for much of the nineteenth century.

In 1818, with duty at 9s, Turkish opium wholesaled for about £1 per pound ex-tax, 30s per pound tax paid: in 1851, the wholesale price was 21s per pound, tax paid. Substandard or poorer quality opium, such as Egyptian, was priced in 1858 at 6s 8d per pound, ex-tax. Needless to say, poor harvests or the loss of a cargo (as in 1865, when the SS *Crimean* ran aground off Smyrna with a cargo of several tonnes of opium) caused price fluctuations but, in general, the cost of opium did not rise more than 25 per cent in a century to 1900.

Despite the modest pricing of opium, there were those who sought ways to produce it without suffering import taxes or dealing with Webster's 'rascally Turks'. Between 1740 and 1830, attempts were made to grow poppies and harvest opium in Britain.

The opium poppy was an established wild plant in some parts of Britain and Ireland well before the eighteenth century. Whether it was naturally indigenous or had been introduced is uncertain but it was to be found, most notably in the Fens (the low-lying marshlands of Lincolnshire, Norfolk and Cambridgeshire) where it was used to make poppy-head tea and a variety of folk remedies.

The methods of cultivation were first described by a Mr Arnot in 1742:

> What I have found most successful is to trench a spot of new rich ground, where Poppies had not grown the preceding year; for if they are continued several years on the same Ground they degenerate. A chusing the ripest and whitest Seed of the great single-flowered Turkey Poppy, I sow it in the month of March very thin and superficially in Drills at two Foot Distance each, to allow Place for Weeding, etc. As soon as the young Plants spring up, I take most of them away, leaving only the strongest most thriving Plants at about a Foot distant from each other.

The first person in Britain to produce opium was Dr Alston, Professor of Botany and Materia Medica at the University of Edinburgh. He achieved this is the 1730s, using the white poppy because of its large pods, although it was not until 1742 that he published the fact.

From 1763, the Society of Arts began actively to promote the study of medicinal plants, starting with the cultivation of rhubarb and offering a gold medal for new discoveries. Soon the society's interest turned towards the poppy and opium, prompted by a winner of a 50-guinea prize, John Ball, who produced home-grown opium. Encouraged by Ball's success and spurred on by a new prize of 50 guineas plus a gold medal for the production of 20 pounds of raw opium, Thomas Jones set 5 acres of ground near Enfield, north of London, in 1794. Despite problems with weeds and inclement weather, he succeeded in 1800 in producing 21 pounds of raw opium and took the prize.

The prize for the development of the medicinal plant went to Dr Howison, an ex-Inspector of Opium from Bengal. In 1813, he stated that a double red garden poppy was suitable for opium production in Scotland, but it was his experiments with the white poppy near London which convinced him commercial opium growing in Britain was feasible. The problems he faced were the fragility of the plant, which could not withstand strong winds, and the care needed in harvesting the pods. Nevertheless, he received the gold medal.

The next major breakthrough came in 1820. John Young, an Edinburgh surgeon and winner of another gold medal, set out to prove opium could be harvested in a cold, damp climate. He succeeded in cultivating poppies which not only gave opium but also oil at a profit of £50–80 per acre. His yield per acre was 56 pounds of opium, several hundred pounds of oil and oil cakes, in addition to a harvest of early potatoes planted between the poppy rows, affording the young plants a protection against the elements. In all, the venture showed a profit of £110 7s 6d.

Not surprisingly, the most successful opium growers were those in the south of England, where the weather was milder. In 1823, Dr John Cowley and a Mr Staines, both of Winslow in Buckinghamshire, received a 30-guinea award from the Society of Arts for '143 pounds of opium, of excellent quality, collected by them from about eleven Acres of Land, planted with the *Papaver somniferum*.'

It was not long before reports came in of other poppy-growing ventures. Poppies were under limited cultivation in most of the southern counties of Britain. In some places, their legacy remains for opium poppies may now be found growing wild on the fringes of Sedgemoor in Somerset and in the countryside around Bridport in Dorset. Most of the growers found a ready local market for their produce for chemists were keen to buy opium at prices well below the market value, without the middleman and duty costs, although how good this opium was is hard to tell because no tests were done to verify the morphine content.

In general, the home-grown opium farmers were part-timers and none saw the poppy as a viable, long-term commercial crop. Indeed, the only successful commercial poppy product was not opium but poppy-heads.

This crop was grown in Mitcham, Surrey and was well-established as early as 1830: the London drug market for poppy-heads obtained the bulk of its supplies from this source. The pods yielded an extract known as 'English opium' with a 4 per cent morphine content. A bag of 3000 poppy capsules sold wholesale for about £4 10s 0d.

Poppy growing was never going to be successful on a large scale. The required hours of sunlight were too fickle to guarantee a high opium content, the ground could be too readily waterlogged by summer rains and the growing season, except in the far south of England, was too short.

One rural area of England, however, became synonymous with opium taking, to such an extent it was referred to as 'the opium district' and 'the kingdom of the poppy'. The per capita consumption there was higher than anywhere else in the country. It was the Fens.

The reason for the high consumption of opium is unclear. Possibly, the people in this remote area had grown used to opium over the centuries, having used the wild poppy. On the other hand, local conditions might have prompted its popularity. Before the swamps were fully drained in the mid-1800s, malaria was prevalent and fever common amongst the scattered communities. Although quinine had been discovered and introduced to Europe in the 1640s, it was expensive, at ten times the cost of opium: obviously, the people resorted to the cheaper drug or relied upon herbal brews, including poppies, to reduce malarial fever. The damp climate with bleak winters promoted rheumatism and neuralgia and opium was used to relieve weather-induced illnesses as well as muscular pain brought on by heavy agricultural labouring.

Opium poppies were grown in Fenland gardens to provide herbal cures but most opium was obtained from chemists. Those in the cathedral city of Ely, in the centre of the Fens, sold more opium than any other drug. It was bought as a pill or a thin stick at 1 penny a time, and it was so common a customer had no need to even request it: a penny coin placed on a counter meant only one thing.

In his novel, *Alton Locke*, published in 1850, the Victorian reformer and novelist, Charles Kingsley, wrote about a Fenman explaining the taking of opium to a stranger:

> 'Oh! ho! ho! – you goo into the druggist's shop o' market day, into Cambridge, and you'll see the little boxes, doozens and doozens, a'ready on the counter, and never a venman's wife goo by, but what calls in for her pennord o'elevation, to last her out the week. Oh! ho! ho! Well it keeps women-folk quiet it do; and it's mortal good agin the ago pains.' 'But what is it?' 'Opium, bor'alive, opium!'

A penny's-worth of 'elevation' was not taken merely as a medicine but, as the name implies, to lift its user out of the mire of Fenland mud and the drudgery of agricultural life. In 1863 Dr Henry Julian Hunter, a doctor in the Fens who studied the opium problem, reported: 'a man may be seen occasionally asleep in a field leaning on his hoe. He starts when approached and works vigorously for a while. A man who is setting about a hard job takes his pill as a preliminary, and many never take their beer without dropping a piece of opium into it.' Once opium was widely accepted as a medicine, it soon gained popularity as an intoxicant.

Such was the level of local addiction and the popularity of opium as a drink as well as a medicine, sales were always heavy on a Saturday night. At least one Fenland brewer, in Ely, added opium to his ale at source. The local practitioner, Dr Hawkins, reported seeing a King's Lynn farmer enter a chemist's shop, order 1½ ounces of laudanum and drink it down there and then. What was more, the man returned twice that day for a similar draught then purchased half a pint to take home for the evening.

The quantity of opium sold in the market towns of the Fens was astonishing. Whittlesea, with a population of 3700, had five chemists dealing primarily in opium whilst a chemist from Spalding testified he sold more laudanum in his four years in the town, to fifty regular customers, than he had in twenty years in another town. A Holbeach chemist took £700–800 a year for laudanum from the working classes of a single parish. Hunter reckoned each chemist sold 200 pounds of opium a year. In 1867, a King's Lynn chemist declared to Dr Hawkins that he sold 170 pounds of solid opium, 6 gallons of laudanum and 6 of calming cordial for infants in 12 months: from these statistics it was estimated that 50 per cent of Britain's imported opium was used in the Fens.

In Whittlesea, the local doctor estimated the average consumption for an addict was between 4 and 8 ounces a week and that many were restricted in their habit only by their income. Although opium was comparatively cheap as an occasional medicine, it was a financial burden on the habituated. In 1878, it was published that 'a poor family will spend eight pence to one shilling per day for opium alone', this equating to 8–11 per cent of an average labourer's wage.

In later years, despite the advent of drug legislation, Fenland opium use continued. Although adult usage declined, opium pills were still given to children whilst animals were dosed with veterinary laudanum as late as the 1920s: a government report noted the high number of applications for veterinary opiates which were doubtless being taken by humans. Officialdom turned a blind eye to this, accepting the practice as a 'local custom'.

The vast quantities of opium consumed in Britain were not used only by the likes of De Quincey or agricultural labourers. Every British person took opium at some time in their lives and many took it frequently.

Opium was, by 1800, long established in medicine. It was employed as a painkiller, a sedative and as a specific against fever and especially diarrhoea. This latter may seem insignificant today but, two centuries ago, diarrhoea was a killer and opium its best cure. Doctors serving with British companies or the military in the East knew of its success rate in the treating of dysentery and cholera, both of which dehydrated the body through diarrhoea. With the British cholera epidemics of 1831—2, 1848—9 and 1853—4, opium was heavily promoted and, mixed with calomel, saved thousands of lives.

The drug acquired the finest of testimonials. It worked. It was not a placebo, as were so many medicines, and it did away with the need for cupping, bleeding and the application of leeches upon which doctors had relied for centuries. By comparison with these crude treatments, opium was also gentle. It produced no inconvenience to the patient, save perhaps mild constipation with prolonged use, and it could be applied as a self-medication. Indeed, it was arguably the first genuine over-the-counter, commercially produced medicine for, until opium was widely available, most self-applied cures were home-brewed concoctions which were passed on either through oral tradition or such publications as *Culpeper's Complete Herbal*.

Another promotional point for opium was the common person's reluctance to visit the doctor. A consultation was expensive and could cost as much as 30 per cent of a skilled worker's weekly income. In place of the doctor, many visited the chemist who, as a dispenser of drugs, offered cheap advice as part of the sales pitch. It was commonplace for chemists to suggest a treatment, often of their own formulation, which was sold by the penny's-worth.

The sale of opium in the eighteenth and nineteenth centuries was akin to the modern-day selling of proprietary medicines in Third World countries. Whereas a modern New Yorker or Londoner goes out and buys a pack of medication, in many poorer countries the packs are split and the contents sold individually with a verbal reading of the dosage. Patients purchase only what they can afford and need.

Laudanum was immensely popular yet other mixtures were just as favoured and became so widespread as to be included in the pharmacopœia. One opium-based liquid was camphorated tincture of opium known as 'paregoric', the name deriving from the Greek for 'consoling' or 'calming': another was Battley's Sedative Solution, officially called *liquor opii sedativus*, containing calcium hydrate, opium, sherry, alcohol and distilled water.

An indication of the chemist's position in the treatment of everyday ailments can be gained from one London East End chemist who, in 1868, reported a Saturday morning income, in just three and a half hours, consisting of 209 penny customers, 12 one-shilling customers and over three shillings in patent-medicine sales. Most of this trade would have been in opium-containing preparations.

In 1857, the Sale of Poisons Bill addressed the issue of the sale of opiates with the intention of controlling it but it was debated whether such control was beyond enforcement due to such widespread use. Professor Brade of the Royal Institution commented, . . . 'there are a number of persons who are in the habit of keeping laudanum by them: they take 10 or 20 drops . . . when their bowels get out of order, or when they are apprehensive of cholera', whilst a Bristol magistrate pointed out a chemist could not be expected to keep opium under lock and key because he dispensed it at a rate of at least 100 times a day.

In time, not only chemists sold opium – so too did grocers and co-operative stores, rural general stores, booksellers and travelling peddlers. At a retail price of 1 penny for a third of an ounce, it was a bargain.

Another form of self-medication was the patent medicines. These were liable to a 12 per cent stamp-duty tax on the retail price but this did not diminish their popularity which soared throughout the nineteenth century, prompted by lavish claims in the new art of advertising. Chemists were quick to ride the patent-medicine bandwagon, offering their own similar brews at a lower price, undercutting the cost of tax and advertising. Many were harmless, coloured, sugar syrups but, needless to say, a good many contained more toxic substances such as strychnine, prussic acid, aconite and opium.

Dover's Powder was famous as a patent medicine but the most famous – which survives to the present day, although it no longer contains the drug in anything like the quantity it did – was Dr J. Collis Browne's Chlorodyne. It was invented as a cholera remedy by an Indian army doctor who sold the formula to a pharmaceutical manufacturer. It was marketed as a cure for a wide range of common ailments but it is best known today as a cure for diarrhoea. The original contained 2 grains of morphine (as hydrochlorate of morphia) per fluid ounce added to chloroform and tincture of cannabis: the modern version, now called J. Collis Browne's Mixture, consists of 1 milligram of morphine anhydrous in every 5 millilitre dose with peppermint oil in a base of ethanol and caramel which gives it an authentic opium-brown colouring. Needless to say, chlorodyne produced addicts and it was not unknown as a vehicle for suicide, murder and accidental lethal overdose. Despite its risks, chlorodyne and similar medicines were a godsend. In Britain alone, they saved countless adults and children from death by dysentery and cholera, diseases which were inevitable in the crowded, unsanitary cities where food was contaminated and sewers at best rudimentary.

Yet opium did more than save lives: it provided an escape from the miseries and vicissitudes of working-class life. Men reverted to it to calm their fears of insecurity and poverty, to kill memories of long hours at the loom, the coal face or the plough. Women took it to numb the grinding poverty in which they lived and worked, struggling to raise a family and feed a husband.

People were introduced to opium quite literally as soon as they left their mother's breast, and possibly before.

Although there were a large number of baby-calming liquids on the market – including home-made recipes such as poppy-head tea – the most famous of all was Godfrey's Cordial, a soothing syrup for babies which reduced colic and consisted of tincture of opium in a thick sugar syrup to disguise the bitter taste. Sales were astronomical. In 1808, a Nottingham chemist reported selling 600 pints a year whilst, in Coventry in 1862, it was estimated 12,000 doses were given a week. In Long Sutton, Lincolnshire, a chemist claimed to sell 25½ gallons a year to a population of 6000 – and he was not the town's sole chemist.

The 'comfort', as Godfrey's Cordial was colloquially known, had its competitors, the main ones being Mrs Winslow's Soothing Syrup – a popular sedative for babies throughout Europe and America which contained up to 1 grain of morphine per fluid ounce – Street's Infants' Quietness and Atkinson's Infants' Preservative.

Victorian baby preparations were sold to all classes, although they were primarily bought by the poor. Not only mothers purchased them for their fractious offspring. Baby-minders bought them in large quantities.

Wages amongst lower-class workers were low and both parents frequently worked at menial or physically demanding jobs for long periods. Babies, an inevitable product of poverty, were a hindrance. Infanticide was not uncommon but most infants, their mothers employed as domestic servants, in factories or in agricultural gangs, ended up in the hands of child-minders who charged about 3s a week (20 per cent of an average wage) to look after a child. The minders were most often in control of up to a dozen babies and were not only notoriously lax but they might also have had a second home job as well – say as a laundry-woman. To keep their charges quiet, they fed them soothing syrups: in this way, many children in poor areas were not only habituated to opium but spent much of their time in a semi-comatose state. What compounded the problem was that, when the mother returned from an exhausting day, she too dosed the child so she could get an uninterrupted night's rest.

There was another convenient side-effect. Opium suppresses appetite so young children were less likely to be hungry and a strain on the already tight domestic budget. Inevitably, these children were frequently undernourished and in continual poor health, with a characteristic yellowish pallor to their skin. By the age of three or four many were, as one observer wrote, 'shrank up into little old men or wizened like a little monkey'. When they grew older, few of these children were able to benefit from even the modicum of education available to them and they ended up providing the next generation of the working class, illiterate and condemned to a cycle of poverty and opium use.

The accidental lethal poisoning of children was not infrequent: opium was also used by despairing mothers to kill their own children, especially bastards. Certainly, it was used to murder infants in the infamous Victorian baby-farms and work-houses.

A poisoning inquest in Liverpool in 1876 sums up the situation and the ambivalence of most people's attitudes towards infant mortality and murder. It outlined the case of a mother, who took at least an ounce of opium a week, whose two-day-old infant died from opium poisoning. The doctor attending the death put it down to opium taken through the breast in the mother's milk. A more plausible explanation is the mother killed the infant in despair at having the responsibility of a child. The jury accepted the doctor's explanation and the husband was cautioned to control his wife's opium consumption. Such a verdict was common. Few doctors would have been willing to certify a cause of death which would implicate another member of his profession or undermine the use of opium. The attitude of many juries, comprised of common folk who knew full well what was going on, was that the death of a child, whilst to be pitied, was a mercy in disguise, an escape from the oppression of poverty or working-class life.

For adults, opium provided more than a quiet child. It was used widely by London dockland prostitutes who drugged their clients with it so they might rob them: they also took it to counteract the misery of their profession, as a relief from muscular pains after a long night's work and to counteract the symptoms of venereal disease. It is not inconceivable to think De Quincey was introduced to opium by his prostitute companion who would surely have been familiar with it. On occasion, opium was used as an intoxicant but this was not common. In the north of England particularly, drunkards took laudanum or opium pills as an occasional alternative to alcohol but in general, gin and ale were the usual tipple, being cheaper. Where laudanum drunks existed, the start of what has become a major undermining of late twentieth-century society occurred – drugs-related crimes began to appear on the records of magistrates' courts, concerning addicts stealing to support their habits.

It must be added that not all opium users, even frequent or chronic ones, were detrimentally habituated. Many cases were documented of people in their eighties and even nineties who were regular, even heavy users, but who remained in good health, apart from a tendency to become constipated and with the characteristic creamy-yellow complexion.

Despite all the signs of opium's potential for evil, addiction still aroused little public interest. For the average Victorian, opium taking was as much a part of society as the drinking of alcohol or the smoking of tobacco. Indeed, opium was more widely available in 1870 than tobacco was in 1970: and, like tobacco in the present day, it was primarily purchased by the poor and lower classes, contemporary studies showing the deeper the poverty, the greater the desire to buy opium.

In the first half of the nineteenth century, opium was seldom regarded by either the public or the medical profession as a problem although, very occasionally, concern was shown. When, in 1828, the Earl of Mar died, an investigation found he had been eating opium for thirty years, once telling his housekeeper he consumed 49 grains of solid opium and an ounce of laudanum a day. On hearing this, his insurers refused to honour his life insurance, contending his habit affected his life expectancy. A few years later, a Professor Christison of Edinburgh concluded to a Scottish court that opium-eating shortened life.

The premise that opiates were harmless began to be eroded from the 1830s, the availability of drugs worrying those members of the newly evolving public health movement as well as doctors in what was becoming a well-defined medical profession with new standards and ethics. Opium became a medical matter and, as a result of a number of inquiries, was regarded by the 1860s as a social and medical problem to be considered with other poisons, addiction becoming regarded as chronic poisoning. Mortality statistics started to register opium as a cause of death. In 1860, a third of all fatal poisonings were due to opiates and casual overdosing was so common that domestic health publications gave instructions for dealing with poisoning.

The main reason for so many accidental overdosings was the unreliable strength of opium mixtures, the non-standardisation of doses and the uneven levels of adulteration: laudanum from one druggist could be very much stronger than that from another. In addition, habitual users frequently misjudged the limits of their tolerance. Opiates also accounted for the majority of suicides throughout the nineteenth century and, although no statistics exist for criminal poisonings, laudanum was sufficiently prevalent in murders as to warrant being mentioned in the Offences Against the Person Act of 1861.

Mortality statistics gathered by the Registrar General's office caused the medical profession to press for the restriction of opiate availability on public health grounds. The statistics were also good propaganda for the growing public health movement, with infant mortality as the campaigners' central pivot. The Ladies' Sanitary Association published penny tracts with such dramatic titles as *The Massacre of Innocents* which condemned the use of soothing syrups by the poor. There was more than a hint of class consciousness in these tracts: the middle-class ladies who distributed them had little knowledge of the plight of the poor and conveniently overlooked the fact many middle-class children were also soothed with opiates.

The matter of doping infants regularly appeared in the medical press and it was debated in Parliament. Yet articles and parliamentary discussions, although they touched upon adult addiction, again only dealt with the working classes. Middle- and upper-class opium usage was either ignored or tolerated. Only the temperance movement addressed the problem across the classes, and then only in passing, allying the problem to alcoholism which was considered more prevalent in the workers.

It was generally believed that the way to combat the problem was to reduce the availability of opium and, in 1868, the first steps were made to control opiates. The 1868 Poisons and Pharmacy Act brought together the interests of legislators, doctors and pharmacists after several previous attempts at legislation had failed. The act, which listed opium and its preparations amongst a total of fifteen poisons, restricted who could sell opium and how they might do it: however, it carried no serious penalties for contravention and the concept that a law could illegalise a substance and prohibit its use or possession was far off into the future. Nevertheless, as the supply of opiates became increasingly limited, they started to acquire the enchantment of forbidden fruit with which dangerous ensorcellment they have been associated ever since.

Although registered doctors could dispense opiates under the act, chemists were appointed the only purveyors of poisons and therefore of opium, the details of every sale being recorded in a poisons register. All containers had to be clearly labelled 'poison', the skull-and-crossbones symbol coming into use. In effect, the restrictions were not at all stringent and hard to enforce but there was a small decline in the mortality statistics, with a distinct dip in infant mortality which dropped to a third of the pre-act total by 1880. Yet by 1900, the overall opium death rate remained at the same level as prior to 1868.

One hole in the act was that patent medicines containing opium were not covered. Inevitably, their sales soared as the act started to bite and a new campaign against these began amongst doctors in the 1880s, criticism of the opium trade which was being carried on with China adding to the climate of opinion in favour of further opium regulation. The main force of the attack was against chlorodyne – Dr J. Collis Browne's Chlorodyne alone earned its makers £31,000 in 1891. The next year, legislation brought patent opiate medicines under the umbrella of the 1868 act: sales from Dr J. Collis Browne's Chlorodyne fell slightly to £25,000 by 1899.

The new legislation was quickly turned to advantage by the patent medicine industry which continued to market its brands but without an opiate content. Surveys by the British Medical Association in 1909 and 1912 discovered that most remedies were free of opium, the makers keenly advertising the fact. *Liquifruita Medica* gives a good example, its advertising claiming it was 'free of poison, laudanum, copper solution, cocaine, morphia, opium, chloral, calomel, paregoric, narcotics or preservatives'. Quite what good it might do was not questioned: many former opiate medicines were now little more than syrups laced with foul-tasting herbs. The common dictum was the worse it tasted, the more good it must do.

By the end of the nineteenth century, opium was firmly in the domain of the doctor rather than the kitchen cupboard and, with new specific drugs being developed, it was no longer needed as a cure-all. Opiates became controlled substances, improvements in the medical profession reduced the degree of self-medication and opiates were prescribed for a more limited range of illnesses than before.

Yet, by now, opium's throne was under threat. Where opium itself had ruled in the past, its crown was being passed to its stronger, more powerful and seemingly more miraculous constituent parts.

5

Heroic Substances

Early in the eighteenth century, pharmacists and physicians began to hunt for the core substances of opium which produced its miraculous properties. There was an awareness – arrived at as much by guesswork as by scientific analysis – of there being what was called the 'basic principle' of opium, otherwise referred to as its 'essence': Rousseau's 'Black Drop', having three times the potency of any other opium mixture, was considered to have a super-abundance of this elusive compound, yet what it was was unknown and, as doctors were always requesting even stronger potions, there was created a growing demand for the knowledge. It was believed that, if this substance could be isolated, the potency of opium could be vastly increased by getting rid of the ineffective material in its make-up. It goes without saying the financial rewards of discovery were an added incentive.

Of course, what the hunters did not realise was they were drawing inexorably closer to the discovery of the alkaloids of opium, the organic chemical compounds at its very heart.

Several men worked independently to investigate the poppy and its products, one of the earliest being an American, John Leigh of Virginia, who published his *Experimental inquiry into the properties of opium* in 1786. Seventeen years later, a French pharmacist called Derosne succeeded in separating out a salt from opium which, in experiments on animals, proved to be more powerful than raw opium. He promptly announced he had discovered opium's essence, publishing his findings in the *Annales de Chimie* in February 1804, and immodestly naming the salt '*Sel narcotique de Derosne*'. Not surprisingly, it quickly gained popularity as a medicine.

What Derosne had discovered was one of opium's constituent parts, a substance today known as noscapine (formerly called narcotine), although his was not a pure sample.

In December 1804 another French chemist, Armand Seguin, presented a paper, entitled '*Sur l'opium*', to the Institut de France, in which he outlined a technique for obtaining another substance from opium. His discovery was not published for a decade, by which time he was in disgrace for embezzling drug supplies from the French army, and his work was dismissed. Seguin did not know it but he was on the trail of one of the most far-reaching medical discoveries of all time.

The first real breakthrough is generally credited to a 21-year-old German pharmacist's assistant from Paderborn in Westphalia, Friedrich Wilhelm Adam Sertürner. Born in Neuhaus in June 1783, he received no scientific education or training but he was apprenticed to a pharmacist for five years. Although his laboratory equipment was inadequate and rudimentary, his patience and precise scientific observation were not and, curious about opium, he spent much of his spare time investigating it. Working initially in Paderborn and later at Einbeck in Hanover, he was to alter the future of medicine. His painstaking experimentation has saved millions of lives: it might also be argued to have instigated the scourge of modern society.

In 1806, Sertürner published the results of fifty-seven of his experiments in the *Journal der Pharmacie*, twenty of which dealt with meconic acid which he termed poppy acid. He discovered pure poppy acid had a different effect on blue plant pigment than raw opium in solution did, deducing this was caused by something in the acid. He then studied the precipitates of chlorates in an infusion of opium and arrived at the conclusion that he had found a new, independent, chemical substance. What he had isolated for the first time was a pure medicinal compound which he proved to be basic as opposed to acidic. This was a revelation for up until then all organic compounds were thought to be acids. The new compound was to be known as an alkaloid – that is, an organic compound with alkaline properties.

Sertürner experimented with his alkaloid on animals. Opium

with the alkaloid removed showed no effect but the substance itself had ten times the power of processed opium. He knew he had arrived at the secret of opium which he referred to as its *'principium somniferum'*, or sleep-making principle. He named his discovery 'morphium' after Morpheus, the Greek god of dreams or sleep although, since then, it has variously been known as morphia, morphinum and morphin. We know it today as morphine.

For years after his initial work, Sertürner experimented on himself, looking to perfect his morphium, passing through its various states of euphoria, depression and nausea, learning of its therapeutic effects as well as its dangers of which he prophetically wrote, 'I consider it my duty to attract attention to the terrible effects of this new substance in order that calamity may be averted.'

At first, his work was ignored: his lack of qualifications condemned him to obscurity although he knew in his heart that what he had achieved was ground-breaking. 'I flatter myself,' he wrote in 1816, 'that Chemists and Physicians will find that my observations have explained to a considerable extent the constitution of opium, and that I have enriched chemistry with a new acid (meconic) and with a new alkaline base (morphium), a remarkable substance which shows much analogy with ammonia.' However, in 1817 the French chemist, Joseph Louis Gay-Lussac, drew attention to it although it was fourteen years before the Institut de France awarded Sertürner a 2000-franc prize and a citation for having 'opened the way to important medical discoveries by his isolation of morphine and his exposition of its character'. His achievement also sparked considerable research into the hunt for alkaloids of other organic substances: in 1817, strychnine was discovered, in 1820 caffeine, with nicotine following in 1828.

Once Sertürner's work was widely known, others built upon it. Two French chemists, Joseph Cavento and Pierre Joseph Pelletier, evolved a process for producing morphine and, in 1818, a French doctor, François Magendie, published a paper entitled *Formulary for the Preparation and Mode of Employing Several New Remedies*, the subject of which was the medical application of the alkaloid. Magendie described the case of a young girl with an aortic aneurysm who had sought in vain for a cure for insomnia produced by the pain from physicians and 'gossips, charlatans, pharmacists, magnetizers' and 'herbalists'. Claiming she could not take opium,

Magendie prescribed her two types of pills, one strong and the other weak, containing the acetate and sulphate of morphine. These calmed her symptoms and he went on to prove their efficacy with other patients.

Although morphine did not catch the attention of addicts in the first decade after its discovery, it was otherwise misused for, being of considerable strength, it was taken by a large number of suicides. So many people used it to end their lives (or as an implement of murder) that it was included with gunpowder and other man-made tools of destruction in Balzac's *Comédie du Diable*, published in 1830: the Devil himself claimed it was a primary cause for the sudden population increase in Hell.

By the early 1820s, morphine was commercially available in Western Europe: in Britain and America, its popularity as an anodyne rapidly increased after the translation of Magendie's paper. It was cheap to produce and, more importantly, was sold with a standardised measure of strength. For the first time, doctors could prescribe accurate doses. Being far more potent than opium, only ¼ grain of morphine had the same effect as 1– 1½ grains of opium. By 1840, morphine was widely accepted and used for almost as many medical conditions as opium, and the application of pure alkaloids rather than simple opium preparations was becoming commonplace.

Other opium alkaloids had been found: Robiquet identified codeine, its name originating from the Greek for poppy-head, in 1832: Pelletier found narceine in the same year: thebaine was discovered by Thiboumery, working with Pelletier, in 1835: papaverine was separated out by Merck in 1848.

Despite the arrival of morphine, opium was still popular. Dr Jonathan Pereira's standard British text on therapeutics, published in 1854, still described opium as the most important, valuable remedy available to doctors and recommended it because its effects were 'immediate, direct, and obvious; and its operation is not attended with pain or discomfort.'

It is little wonder opium was so highly regarded for the main aim of doctors was not to cure illness but to combat pain. Other painkillers existed but these could have side-effects whilst opium did not, at least in the short term. Throughout the first half of the nineteenth century, some doctors argued about the dangers of opium although, generally speaking, they side-stepped the issue of addiction through prolonged administration. The situation was still confused when, early in the 1850s, a new means was invented of introducing a measured dose of purified drug into the body. It was a turning-point in not only medical but sociological history.

For some time, doctors had been hunting for a way of administering drugs without ingesting them. Ever since William Harvey proved, in the early seventeenth century, that blood circulates through the body to all tissue, doctors had pondered how to get it to transport drugs.

A number of methods were attempted. Monsieur Pomet used a clyster (enema), writing that 'given in clysters opium operates quicker than when taken by mouth.' Suppositories made of morphine and coated with wax and animal fat were also invented. Inhalation was tried but was too time-consuming and made the patient nauseous. Epidermatic methods using skin patches and the direct smearing of opium ointment on to raw flayed flesh were also used, but they caused blistering. Clearly, something else was needed.

The subcutaneous introduction of drugs was not new. In 1656, Sir Christopher Wren injected opium into dogs using a hollow quill attached to a bulb. He even experimented on humans but little interest was taken in the process. It was not until the 1830s that the process was reconsidered when a Dr Lafargue, of St Emilion, wrote of his method of admitting morphine into the bloodstream. It was crude: a lancet was dipped into morphine solution, pushed horizontally under the skin and left there for some seconds. He later refined the process by suggesting tiny pills of morphine could be inserted under the skin with a blunt needle. Very gradually, the principle of the needle came together with the concept of the syringe, which was already known, having been invented by Hero of Alexandria, the mechanical genius of the classical world.

Who actually invented the medical hypodermic syringe is uncertain for a number of doctors began independently injecting drugs around the same time, using a glass syringe and tube with a sharpened point. Some argue a French doctor, Charles-Gabriel Pravaz, was the instigator in 1851, although Dr Isaac Taylor, practising in America, was introducing drugs into an incision by means of a blunt-nozzled syringe as early as 1839. In 1845, a Dublin practitioner, Dr Francis Rynd, injected drugs with a gravity-fed bottle attached to a hollow needle. It was, however, Dr Alexander

Wood of Edinburgh, using a syringe he had ordered from an instrument maker called Ferguson in London, who perfected the hypodermic syringe in 1853. Important modifications on Wood's design were made by Dr Charles Hunter of St George's Hospital, London. He became the first advocate of what he termed the 'ipodermic' method and widely preached its use in Britain. It caught on. Within two years, it was widely used in Europe and, by 1856, Dr Fordyce Barker was giving the first hypodermic injections in America.

Wood's technique was to inject his patient's arm, gaining a rapid effect, an advantage being the avoidance of the unpleasant gastric side-effects of oral administration. However, he and many others made an incorrect assumption: they thought injection, as opposed to ingestion, would not lead to an appetite for the drug – the noun 'appetite', meaning a craving or addiction, comes from the belief that one got hungry for the drug just as one did for food, alcohol or anything else which was eaten. Remove the act of swallowing, they reasoned, and hunger would be assuaged. With this belief, Wood injected morphine widely. A good many of Wood's patients became morphine addicts. Ironically, his wife was to die of an overdose of injected morphine, the first-ever recorded drug death by hypodermic needle.

Morphine injections were used to treat everything from inflammation of the eyes, menstrual pains and rheumatism to *delirium tremens*. The rapid effect of injected morphine and the invention of early anaesthetics, such as chloroform, also meant surgery was more readily carried out and post-operative pain easily controlled.

The widespread use of the new syringe, allied to the belief injected morphine was not addictive, lead to what became known as 'morphinism'. Many misguided doctors provided morphine and syringes for those patients rich enough to purchase them and taught them how to self-inject. Typically, morphine addicts were from the middle and upper classes: morphine, precision-made syringes and needles cost money, so most addicts were middle-aged professionals and business people. The poor, who could seldom afford a doctor's fees, rarely saw morphine. Entire families became addicted because of the ready supply, the lack of legal controls on prescriptions and the fact a prescription, having been paid for, was the rightful property of the patient who could re-use it ad infinitum.

Encouraged by medical conviction that morphine was benign, its use became a casual pastime amongst the well-to-do of Europe and the USA: even when the dangers became apparent, many ignored them, took their daily injections and went about their everyday lives not realising the truth until they were habituated. As with opium, no social stigma was attached to morphinism which it was assumed the addict had acquired through medical treatment.

Another factor causing morphinism was that larger doses were being taken than had been the case with laudanum or opium pills. One ounce of laudanum contained approximately 1 grain of morphine, so even laudanum addicts taking 2 ounces a day were dosing on far less morphine than an injecting addict. Although some kept their daily intake to 6 grains, many took over 10, with some taking up to 40 grains a day, the equivalent of 40 ounces of laudanum. When one considers a very high laudanum dose such as Coleridge's, of 38 ounces (2 pints) a week, one can see how terrible morphinism was compared to opium addiction.

Morphine's anodyne properties, however, appeared a godsend in the many wars which raged in the nineteenth century. For the first time, soldiers' wounds could be treated under anaesthetic and the subsequent pain relieved. As the fighting increased, so did the demand for opium and morphine.

In the American Civil War, poppies were cultivated across both Union and Confederate territories, with Virginia, Tennessee, South Carolina and Georgia being the main growing states. The opium was used to cure the dysentery endemic in both armies, with morphine being refined as a painkiller. A large number of wounded Civil War veterans became morphine addicts as a result: opiate addiction was so common it was known as the 'army disease' or 'Soldier's Disease'.

Opium was administrated orally to a massive extent in both armies, troops routinely dosed on a daily basis against malaria and diarrhoea. To say administration was casual is an understatement. Union Surgeon Major Nathan Mayer did not even dismount from his horse to dispense opium. He poured out what he termed 'exact doses' into his hand and let the recipients lick it from his glove. Morphine injections were also given as syringes became more commonplace. Over ten million opium pills and two million ounces of opiates in powder form and tinctures (mostly morphine) were issued in the army of the Union. One may reasonably assume a similar dosage amongst Confederate troops.

The war had another detrimental effect. More than 63,000 soldiers returned home with lingering gastric upsets for which they continued to take opium: and they brought with them a knowledge of morphine. In his book *The Opium Habit*, published in 1868, Horace Day wrote:

> The events of the last few years [the Civil War] have unquestionably added greatly to [addict] numbers. Maimed and shattered survivors from a hundred battlefields, diseased and disabled soldiers released from hostile prisons, anguished and hopeless wives and mothers, made so by the slaughter of those who were dearest to them, have found, many of them, temporary relief from their suffering in opium.

The American soldier was not unique. British troops in the Crimean War injected morphine to escape the terrible conditions in their camps and, in the Franco-Prussian War, both French and Prussian soldiers drowned their sorrows in not only alcohol but also in morphine.

It was not long before case studies were being published about the collapse of morphine addicts' health, far worse than anything engendered by opium. The symptoms were soon recognised: a haggard appearance and emaciation, loss of sexual ability or desire and, as with opium, constipation. Attempts to break habituation led to what were described as severe flu-like symptoms.

Warnings about the power of hypodermically injected morphine started to be published. A British physician, Dr T. Clifford Allbutt, reported in 1870 a lack of caution against morphine by injection, observing there were too many doctors for whom 'the syringe and phial are as constant companions as was the lancet to their fathers.' He went on to comment:

> Injected morphia seemed so different to swallowed morphia, no one had any experience of ill effects from it, and we all had the daily experience of it as a means of peace and comfort, while pain on the other hand was certainly the forerunner of wretchedness and exhaustion. Gradually, however, the conviction began to force itself upon my notice, that injections of morphia, though free from the ordinary evils of opium-eating, might, nevertheless, create the

same artificial want and gain credit for assuaging a restlessness and depression of which it was itself the cause . . . If this be so, we are incurring a grave risk in bidding people to inject whenever they need it, and in telling them that the morphia can have no ill effects upon them so long as it brings with it tranquillity and wellbeing.

The leisure use of morphine was well established by the time Allbutt published his paper. It was so widespread, writers of popular penny novels were using it as an image for dissolution. Allbutt commented on this, remarking: 'Now that the hypodermic use of morphia is brought into sensational novels as a melodramatic device it may indeed be said to have reached the height of fashion. We may thank our stars if one of us be not seen ere long, syringe in hand, between Aspasia and Clodius in the windows of the Burlington Arcade.' That was not all: morphinism soon became a metaphor as well as a novelist's dramatic tool. In 1886, Lord Randolph Churchill compared Gladstone's rhetoric on Home Rule to 'the taking of morphia! The sensations are transcendent; but the recovery is bitter beyond experience.' In actual fact, Churchill's attack was close to the bone for Gladstone took laudanum in his coffee, apparently to increase his rhetorical powers when addressing Parliament.

The first major contribution to the study of morphine was written by a German Jewish doctor, Edward Levinstein. His *Die Morphiumsucht* – published in English in 1878 as *The Morbid Craving for Morphia* – was divided into chapters on the symptomatology, etiology, prognosis and prophylaxis of morphine. It was not just a warning about the effects of morphine: it described a brand-new disease and suggested somatic origins for it. Whilst known to the medical fraternity, Levinstein's book had scant initial impact.

In 1882, *The Lancet* recorded that hypodermic injection was becoming general practice. The rapid increase in published case studies suggested an epidemic of addiction was imminent but the position was not quite so simple. Morphine use was popular and widespread but no more so than other opiates: indeed, compared to the prevalence of opium addiction in the working classes with which most doctors had little connection and which was beyond medical control, it was of far less concern. The truth was the medical profession singled out the injecting of morphine, which took on the aspects of an urgent problem, as becoming a cause for anxiety because they knew about it and it could be addressed.

Dr Norman Kerr established the Society for Promoting Legislation for the Control and Cure of Habitual Drunkards in 1876: nine years later it was renamed the Society for the Study of Inebriety. Its primary aim was to reduce alcoholism – especially when it was caused by gin – which was rampant in the working classes but it included in its brief 'narcotising agents'. Kerr believed opium addiction was less dangerous than alcoholism – although harder to cure – and he acknowledged the syringe was the most effective way of becoming inebriated. Within the medical fraternity, the society promoted the concept that inebriety from drink or drugs was a disease and the responsibility of medical men. Many doctors disagreed, regarding morphine or opium addiction (referred to as 'narcomania') as just a percentile of general inebriety. Drug addiction was actually called 'drug inebriety'.

Despite warnings about the unrestrained use of the syringe, so effective was the morphine injection, so quick was it to kill pain and so prevalent was the medical attitude towards treating symptoms rather than causes, the practice continued to grow and most standard textbooks made no reference to the risks. Not until around 1900 was drug addiction even referred to and it was not until 1910 that the dangers were fully comprehended, drug addiction becoming a separate medical issue. During the first decade of the twentieth century, the term 'addiction' was rarely used: in addition to drug inebriety, narcomania, morphinomania, morphinism, the morphine habit or opium-eating were the *bon mots*.

By 1914 and the outbreak of war, addiction was recognised and named. What was more, there were now means to reduce it for other drugs had been invented which killed pain with far less risk. Acetylsalicylic acid, trade-named aspirin, appeared on the market in 1899 and, being cheap to produce, quickly took the place of laudanum or morphine in the treatment of lesser aches and pains. Several years later diethyl-malonyl-urea, an hypnotic drug trade-named veronal, came into wide use: although a dangerous substance, it was safer than opiates, especially when used as a sedative.

However, no sooner was a knowledge of opium and morphine well disseminated than a newer, even more dangerously addictive drug appeared, deriving from but not a naturally occurring alkaloid of opium.

The year 1874 was in retrospect a black day for both medicine and society. At St Mary's Hospital, Paddington, in London, a pharmacist called C.R. Alder Wright was searching for a powerful, non-addictive alternative to morphine. He boiled morphine with acetic anhydride and created a substance which, believing morphine to be a double molecule, he named tetra-ethyl morphine. F.M. Pierce at Owens College experimented with this new substance, inducing sleepiness in dogs, dilating their pupils, causing them to salivate and vomit. In 1887, several papers were published identifying the now-named diacetylmorphine – the chemical formula for which was known to be $C_{17}H_{17}NO(C_2H_3O_2)_2$ – as a narcotic more potent than ethylated or methylated morphine: its single molecular structure was proven in 1890.

Little work was done on diacetylmorphine until 1898, when a German chemist, Heinrich Dreser, working at the Bayer Laboratories at Elberfeld – where aspirin was also developed – produced a quantity of diacetylmorphine. After brief clinical tests, it proved to be an awe-inspiringly powerful painkiller. Bayer mass- marketed it under a brand-name Dreser had come up with based upon the German word *heroisch*, meaning mighty or heroic. It was called heroin.

Whether made in a pharmaceutical facility or a clandestine laboratory, heroin manufacture is comparatively easy. Morphine is first extracted from raw opium by dissolving it in hot water and adding lime, which causes the precipitation of organic waste material, leaving the morphine in suspension as a white band near the surface. This is drawn off, reheated and has concentrated ammonia added to it. The morphine solidifies and sinks, to be collected by filtration. This is now morphine base. Ready for turning into heroin, it weighs about 10 per cent of the original quantity of raw opium: from 10 kilograms of raw opium comes 1 kilogram of morphine base which, with additional ingredients gained during processing, in turn yields slightly more than 1 kilogram of heroin.

Heroin manufacture involves several processes. First, equal quantities of morphine and acetic anhydride are heated in a glass or enamel-lined container for six hours at 85°C. The morphine and the acid combine to form impure diacetylmorphine. Second, water and chloroform are added to the solution to precipitate impurities. The solution is drained and sodium carbonate added to make the heroin solidify and sink. Third, the heroin is filtered out of the sodium carbonate solution with activated charcoal and purified with alcohol. This solution is gently heated to evaporate the alcohol and leave heroin, which may be purified further or converted to heroin hydrochloride, a water-soluble heroin salt.

Heroin, which was distributed in small boxes with a lion and a globe printed on the label, was hailed as the new wonder drug, although more as a specific than morphine which had been applied to a wide range of ailments. Its effects were much faster for heroin rapidly turns into morphine on entering the bloodstream, so the effect is that of morphine except heroin is more soluble in fats and can therefore get into the central nervous system more quickly. Although it had analgesic potential and was five to eight times as powerful as morphine, it was promoted primarily as a non-addictive treatment for respiratory illnesses and the suppression of coughs. It was stated to be non-addictive on the contention that, although it was derived from morphine, the molecular structure had been altered by the manufacturing process, thus losing the addictive agent. It could be produced cheaply and relatively simply with a high degree of purity and quality control. Only small amounts were required per dose and it could be given by hypodermic injection although it was usually administered orally as pastilles – heroin cough lozenges were popular – or tablets, or as an elixir in glycerine solution. Within two years, it was widely used across Europe and the USA.

History repeated itself. No sooner was heroin freely available than extravagant claims were made for it. It was even mooted as a cure for morphine addiction. Warnings soon began to appear, too: reports of tolerance and addiction were published in 1900, to be followed by others advising against heroin treatment for morphine addiction. The Council of Pharmacy and Chemistry of the American Medical Association included heroin in their annual publication, *New and Non-Official Remedies* published in 1906, but added the proviso, 'The habit is readily formed and leads to the most deplorable results.'

By 1910, the medical profession was fully alert to the danger of heroin and its medical use began to decline. However, factors came into play which led to the pan-global epidemic of heroin addiction which has increasingly plagued modern society.

First was heroin's effects. Its potential as a substitute for morphine, as well as being a more stimulating narcotic 'leisure' drug, became common knowledge. Second, it was introduced to society at a time when drug controls, especially in the USA, were just coming into force, thus restricting its availability: in the USA, it was used as an illicit pleasure drug by young criminals in the underworld of larger cities. Being cheaper than morphine, heroin was an ideal illegal commodity: as a white powder, it was also easily 'cut' or adulterated. In its pure form it was highly concentrated and therefore compact and easily concealed by traffickers. Inevitably, illicit heroin use grew rapidly and became the primary trade drug of the criminal underworld. Indeed, it was the criminal fraternity who originated the international heroin problem and not the medical profession who did not make addiction as widespread as they had done with opium and morphine.

Over the space of the nineteenth century, opium had evolved from being a comparatively crude natural drug to providing not only the most effective painkiller yet known but also the most terrible and arguably most addictive drug. This, in turn, was to become an agent for one of the most insidious underminings of human society ever devised.

6

God's Own Medicine

Writing at the end of the nineteenth century, Sir William Osler called opium 'God's Own Medicine' because it was a naturally occurring substance which could perform miracles and be used straight from the poppy, its active ingredients, like those of most plant-derived medicines, being its alkaloids which may be classed in two main groups. One, the pyridine–phenanthrene group, contains morphine and codeine, whilst the other, the isoquinoline group, includes papaverine and noscapine.

As well as the main alkaloid constituents of morphine, noscapine, papaverine, codeine and thebaine, trace alkaloids include narceine, meconidine, codamine, laudanine, laudanosine, lanthopine, protopine, cryptopine, rhoeadine, oxynarcotine, pseudo-morphine, gnoscopine, xanthaline, tritopine and hydrocotarnine. In all, they account for only 20 per cent of opium by weight. The morphine content of opium is not standard and can range between 4 and 21 per cent according to country of origin with noscapine being the next most plentiful at 4–8 per cent.

Today, only a very small quantity of opium is used medicinally, for example as an analgesic for patients suffering from cancer of the stomach, its main medicinal use being obtained from its alkaloids and derivatives. Morphine kills pain and euphorically relaxes the patient, although the majority of morphine is nowadays converted into codeine because the natural supply of that alkaloid is minute. Codeine is a less powerful analgesic and not as likely to cause addiction. Its usage includes the treatment of minor aches, pains and coughs. For years, it was available over druggists' counters as an alternative to aspirin, but is now strictly controlled although it is still available. Noscapine is used to counteract coughing and papaverine has dramatic effects on increasing blood flow. Thebaine is a dangerous poison, causing severe convulsions, but its importance is that it can be converted into codeine and chemically altered to form other drugs. Heroin is a strong pain suppressive but it is not widely used in medicine outside Britain.

Opiate is the generic term given to the group of drugs derived from natural opium or an alkaloid of it whilst semi-synthetic opiates are those produced by starting with a natural alkaloid then chemically modifying it: heroin may be classed as a semi-synthetic. Although synthesised, there are parts of the semi-synthetics' chemical construction which mirror or echo that of their base alkaloid. Synthetic opiates – sometimes confusingly referred to as opioids – are drugs which act in the same way as natural opiates and semi-synthetics but they are entirely man-made: their chemical structure bears little or no relation to opium alkaloids. These include pethidine, often used to relieve pain in childbirth, dextropropoxyphene and methadone.

Morphine, codeine and thebaine can all be used as the basis for a variety of semi-synthetic opiates which have become increasingly important in recent decades. Some are incredibly powerful. In the 1960s, a team working on thebaine under the prominent natural products chemist, Professor Bentley, in the Edinburgh laboratories of Macfarlan Smith & Co., made a literally unconscious discovery when someone accidentally stirred cups of mid-morning tea with a contaminated glass rod: within minutes several of the scientists were lying flat out on the floor. The company physician, Dr Simpson, was called. He monitored the comatose scientists, noting their heart rates, breathing patterns and behaviour before they revived. The drug they had unwittingly drunk was later developed into etorphine. Approximately 10,000 times as powerful as morphine, it is also known as M99 or Immobilon, and is used in dart guns to capture elephants and rhinos. Less than 2 millilitres will knock a full-grown white rhino senseless: a mere scratch from a contaminated needle can kill a man. Fortunately, there is an antidote called M50/50 or Revivon.

The problem with opiates in general is that they are addictive and, although the risk of dependence varies greatly from one to another, a frequent user will become habituated.

Addiction is the compulsive taking of drugs which have such a hold over the addict he or she cannot stop using them without suffering severe symptoms and even death. Opiates are not unique. Cocaine, alcohol, caffeine and nicotine are also addictive, but they are nothing like as powerful as opiates in their hold over their victims. Nowadays, the term addiction is replaced by that of physical dependence, which is a more accurate definition, for addicts are frequently physically dependent upon their drug: this is certainly the case with opiates.

The idea of dependence was defined in 1964 by the World Health Organisation as 'a state, psychic and sometimes also physical, resulting from the interaction between a living organism and a drug, characterised by behavioural and other responses that always include a compulsion to take the drug on a continuous or periodic basis in order to experience its psychic effects and sometimes to avoid the discomfort of its absence.' It is today considered an illness.

Opiate dependence is not a habit, nor is it a simple drive for some emotional craving. It is as fundamental to an addict's existence as food and water, a physio-chemical fact: an addict's body is chemically reliant upon its drug for opiates actually alter the body's chemistry so it cannot function properly without being periodically primed. A hunger for the drug forms when the quantity in the bloodstream falls below a certain level, the addict becoming anxious and irritable. Fail to feed the body and it deteriorates and may die from drug starvation.

This chemical relationship is easily proven. Not only humans can be addicted: so can other mammals. In Laos, where opium is commonly smoked, domestic pets such as cats and dogs become addicts by passively smoking their master's pipes. Tame macaques in India may also become passive addicts and, in the past, became addicted by licking out cold opium pipes. Today, drug-sniffing dogs employed by customs authorities are sometimes trained on synthetic opium-smelling substances because they are liable to addiction. Addicts give birth to on average smaller babies which, after the umbilical cord is severed, may exhibit symptoms of opium withdrawal having been literally cut off from a supply they have known since conception.

For the non-addict, one of the greatest mysteries is why someone takes to drug use knowing the terrible dangers. Philip K. Dick, the American science-fiction author, spoke for many people when he wrote in 1977: 'Drug misuse is not a disease, it is a decision, like the decision to step out in front of a moving car. You would call that not a disease but an error of judgement.' Clearly peer pressure, poverty and other social factors are likely to play their part in this decision-making process but the fact remains – why 'hard', very addictive drugs, such as opiates, instead of alcohol or 'soft' drugs such as marijuana? It may be that some, especially the very young, are unaware of what they are taking: this might account for the present-day world-wide trend towards younger and younger addicts. A young British addict who first took heroin at thirteen, not realising it was addictive, recently stated, 'I was feeling left out. My mates were having a better laugh, so I tried it.' A recent British survey has found Ecstasy users smoking 'skag' to ease the fading effects of an Ecstasy dose, in ignorance of what it is: skag is a street name for heroin.

Perhaps some users are hoping to find an alternative existence as summed up by Aldous Huxley in 1949:

> If we could sniff or swallow something that would, for five or six hours each day, abolish our solitude as individuals, atone us with our fellows in a glowing exaltation of affection and make life in all its aspects seem not only worth living, but divinely beautiful and significant, and if this heavenly, world-transfiguring drug were of such a kind that we could wake up next morning with a clear head and an undamaged constitution – then, it seems to me, all our problems (and not merely the one small problem of discovering a novel pleasure) would be wholly solved and earth would become paradise.

One assumption, which holds good for heroin and morphine, is the 'kick' or 'rush', the orgasmic sensuality of an injection which is particularly prevalent with heroin. For some heroin addicts, the effect is a warming of the stomach and an erotic tingling in the crotch: for others, this is heightened to a considerable erotic thrill. Perhaps the reason is summed up best by the comedian Lenny Bruce, who stated of his fatal addiction, 'I'll die young, but it's like kissing God.' The erotic pleasure can, however, be offset by a characteristic vomiting which the first shots of heroin or morphine produce.

For many addicts, heroin is favoured because, whilst allowing them to maintain full consciousness, they can withdraw into a secure, cocoon-like state of physical and emotional painlessness. Heroin is seen as an escape to tranquillity, a liberation from anxiety and stress: for the poor, it is a way out of the drudgery of life, just as laudanum was for their forebears two centuries ago.

For a long while it was believed – as an offshoot from the eugenics debate – that only certain types of people might turn to drugs and become addicted. Orientals, it was suggested, were more resistant to opium than Occidentals, the assumption based on the supposition poisons were less dangerous to an indigenous population living where the substances were naturally occurring. This, of course, was bunkum for the poppy is not native to Asia. Victorian moralists and social observers claimed the lower classes showed a greater predilection for, and were worse affected by, opium than the middle and upper classes. This too was claptrap.

Everyone, regardless of social, economic or racial background or type of physique, is a potential addict although today some doctors opine that certain people are genetically predisposed towards addiction. Opinions, such as those of the nineteenth-century American doctor, R. Batholow, are discounted: his ideal candidate for addiction was 'a delicate female, having light blue eyes and flaxen hair, [who] possesses, according to my observations the maximum susceptibility.' His opinion was not unique. Many of his contemporaries thought women particularly at risk: with hindsight, this conclusion may have been caused by the fact that morphine was so widely used to treat menstrual problems, diseases of a 'nervous character' from which women were believed to suffer and was also administered as an analgesic in pregnancy and labour. Furthermore, prostitutes used opiates not only to sustain them in their long and arduous work but also as a crude form of contraception because continued dosage disrupted ovulation.

It was also suggested that addiction was related to psychological disorders or types. As recently as the 1920s, Dr Lawrence Kolb of the United States Public Health Service expressed the belief that 'normal' people gained no pleasure from morphine except the release of pain and that pleasure was only felt by mentally unstable people. The addict, he claimed, was of psychopathic tendency. His theory is dismissed now but it is accepted that specific mental attributes may lead to drug use: these include a restless curiosity about unknown experiences and a desire to share visions with others. This may account for the quasi-religious attitudes of some addicts who see themselves in the initial phases of addiction as joining with others in a cosmic experience. For many, addiction is an entry to a special fellowship with its own mores, rules and even language. Morphine addicts in the USA spoke in an esoteric jargon – the act of injection was erroneously known as 'Chinese needlework' whilst to smoke heroin or opium was to have the 'lamp habit'.

Addicts today have their own argot – to 'shoot up' is to inject intravenously, to 'chase the dragon' is to smoke opium or heroin whilst heroin itself has a wide variety of slang names such as 'horse', 'H', 'Big Harry', 'elephant', 'stuff', 'candy', 'smack' and (ironically) 'shit'. To be addicted is to have 'a monkey on your back' or to be 'strung out' whilst a dealer is a 'pusher', 'candyman' or 'connection'. Heroin is sold by the 'deal' (a single dose in a tiny paper packet), the 'deck' (a small bagful), the 'piece' (approximately 1 ounce), the 'half-lo' (15 bags'-worth) and the 'key' (short for kilogram). The act of adulteration or diluting is known as 'cutting' because the measures of powder are traditionally mixed and separated with a sharp edge like a razor blade. Heavily cut heroin is known as 'six and four'. To be asked if one 'wants a boy' does not imply a homosexual relationship: 'boy' is a metaphor for heroin and the reply is 'no way' if one is 'anywhere' – that is, in possession. One expression, seldom associated with opium today but derived from drug-taking, is 'hip'. Meaning to be one of the in-crowd, it comes from nineteenth-century American addict slang when a 'hip' was an experienced drug taker: its root lay in the fact addicts gained sore hips from reclining on their sides on hard, opium den bed-boards. Despite such an extensive vocabulary of opiate slang, heroin users do not today have their own specific culture, as is sometimes implied by the media, unlike, for example, Ecstasy which has an accompanying culture of rave parties and its own style of neo-pop music.

So what is taking opium like? The first effect is relaxation although a few may experience a transitory, sudden rush of excitement like the erotic heroin kick. Cares, concerns and inhibitions are dispelled, to be followed by a calmness, although there may be some nausea in the early stages. The calmness grows to a serene self-assurance then a listless complacency. Nothing worries nor concerns opium takers: they often feel light, as if floating, and many describe themselves as levitating whilst under the influence. Early in addiction, mental power may be enhanced or increased and addicts believe they are having radical and unique ideas and thoughts.

As many addicted writers and artists vouchsafe, opium may stimulate visions in those with considerable imagination but, of itself, opium is not a fantasy-promoting substance. In latter stages of addiction, all opiates actually suppress imaginative creation, just as they can suppress the ability to be creative in other art forms. As Billie Holliday, the famous blues singer, said in 1956: 'If you think dope is for kicks and for thrills, you're out of your mind . . . If you think you need stuff to play music or sing, you're crazy. It can fix you so you can't play nothing or sing nothing.'

The exciting stage of drug experience does not last long: it may be sustained for a matter of months but it is more likely to begin to disappear after a few weeks, depending upon the addict's metabolism. With raw opium it may survive for quite a while although Eric Detzer, in his autobiography *Monkey on my Back*, put modern opium-eating into context:

> There's nothing classy or poetic about opium. It has the same effect as morphine or heroin. You get relaxed and energetic at the same time. Problems become unimportant. You feel sleepy, but if you go to bed you lie awake. You itch all over. You get constipated. You get hungry, particularly for sweets. You get patient and understanding. You get nice . . . An opium high can be described in one word: comfortable. It's weird that people get to where they'll give up their souls for stuff that just makes them comfortable.

With heroin, the kick reduces as tolerance rises, addicts taking larger and larger amounts, which would be fatally poisonous to unaccustomed individuals, just to feel normal. The 'high' – the plateau of experience to which all heroin addicts aspire, where reality is suborned – disappears and excitement rapidly deteriorates as dependency increases. The sought-after euphoria becomes more difficult to achieve and is then lost: by this stage dependency is firmly established and if it is not sustained, the addict slips into a state of first restless distress then excruciating physical pain. This is known as withdrawal sickness or abstinence syndrome – or, in the slang of the modern addict, 'cold turkey' or 'bogue'.

While most addicts, having lost the euphoria, build up their doses in order to try to regain it, others, desperate to feel the rush or peace again, start taking drug cocktails, such as 'speedballs' (heroin and cocaine) or ''Frisco speedballs' (heroin, cocaine and the hallucinogen, LSD) or other similarly dangerous concoctions of heroin with 'uppers' (amphetamines), 'downers' (barbiturates), 'jacket' (Nembutal) or 'crystal' (Methedrine). Inevitably, many die from an 'OD' – an overdose.

Popular belief labels all addicts as desperate characters but they are not. A minority maintain their habit at a steady dose rate, just keeping themselves above the threshold of withdrawal. They may live conventional lives, even hold down responsible jobs without detection by even close friends and family. George Crabbe was an example of such a 'secret' addict. Another was William Wilberforce: a noted evangelist, statesman, philanthropist and reformer, he succeeded against considerable vested interests in abolishing the slave trade and yet he was himself in thrall to opium, the one slavery he could do nothing to end.

Opiates in themselves are relatively safe drugs and even today addicts in receipt of opiates on prescription, and who maintain a stable, hygienic life-style, can be virtually indistinguishable from non-drug users and suffer no serious damage. A present-day consultant psychiatrist running a British drug-dependency unit has stated he knows of an 85-year-old woman from the Scottish Hebrides who has been injecting heroin for sixty years.

For those who do not control their addiction, physical deterioration is inevitable. The first symptoms of physical decline are inflammation of the mouth and throat, gastric illnesses and circulatory disorders which can weaken limbs so far as to paralyse them. At the same time, addicts become demoralised, insensitive to their surroundings and self-centred. They feel, often with justification, outcast and yet value their drug-imposed insularity. Quite often, because of their constant physical lassitude and moral turpitude, they do not bother to take any interest in personal hygiene: against such a condition, it is no wonder it is so difficult to press home the need not to share needles which leads to the transmission of the AIDS virus.

As addiction deepens, the addict grows even more mentally and physically lethargic, lacking concentration and becoming forgetful. The body debilitates and becomes emaciated as appetite for food is lost: the voice grows hoarse, constipation develops with amenorrhoea and sterility in women or impotence in men. Medical complications include hepatitis and liver damage, blood poisoning, venereal diseases, skin infections and fungal diseases, swelling and collapsing of veins too frequently used for injections, respiratory diseases, tuberculosis, psychosomatic disorders, advanced tooth decay and nervous tremors. The memory is impaired to such an extent even everyday practicalities are overlooked and the addict withdraws into an inner world. Hearing and sight, however, become acute: tiny noises are amplified and bright lights are painful. Waking hours may be filled with hallucinations with sleep bedevilled by nightmares.

This developing pattern of addiction, essentially the same for opium as for morphine or heroin, has long been known. The April 1837 edition of the quarterly journal *The Chinese Repository*, published in Canton and Macau, contained an article on a series of paintings by a Chinese artist called Sun Qua which illustrated the downfall of an opium smoker from health and wealth to pain and poverty. The subject was the son of a wealthy businessman who inherited his father's business, the pictures described as follows:

1. This picture represents the young man at home, richly attired, in perfect health and vigour of youth. An elegant foreign clock stands on a marble table behind. On his right is a chest of treasure, gold and silver; and on the left, close by his side, is his personal servant, and, at a little distance, a man whom he keeps constantly in his employ, preparing the drug for use from the crude article, purchased and brought to the house.

2. In this he is reclining on a superb sofa with a pipe in his mouth, surrounded by courtesans, two of whom are young in the character of musicians. His money now goes without any regard to its amount.

3. After no very long period of indulgence, his appetite for the drug is insatiable, and his countenance sallow and haggard. Emaciated, shoulders high, teeth naked, face black, dozing from morning to night, he becomes utterly inactive. In this state he sits moping, on a very ordinary couch, with his pipe and other apparatus for smoking lying by his side. At this

moment, his wives – or a wife and a concubine – come in; the first finding the chest emptied of its treasures, stands frowning with astonishment, while the second gazes with wonder at what she sees spread upon the couch.

4. His lands and his houses are now all gone; his couch exchanged for some rough boards and a ragged mattress; his shoes are off his feet, and his face half awry, as he sits bending forwards, breathing with great difficulty. His wife and child stand before him, poverty stricken, suffering with hunger; the one in anger, having dashed on the floor all his apparatus for smoking, while the little son, unconscious of any harm, is clapping his hands and laughing at their sport! But he heeds not either the one or the other.

5. His poverty and distress are now extreme, though his appetite grows stronger than ever; he is as a dead man. In this plight, he scrapes together a few coppers cash, and hurries away to one of the smoking-houses, to buy a little of the scrapings from the pipe of another smoker, to allay his insatiable cravings.

6. Here his character is fixed; a sot. Seated on a bamboo chair, he is continually swallowing the fæces of the drug, so foul, that tea is required to wash them down his throat. His wife and child are seated near him, with skeins of silk stretched on bamboo reels, from which they are winding it off into balls; thus earning a mere pittance for his and their own support, and dragging out from day to day a miserable existence.

Just as the way drugs are taken affects the speed and intensity with which they have an effect, the means of taking them also affects the rate with which addiction develops and may affect the ease of withdrawal. Addiction from opium smoking takes the longest, followed by opium-eating. Orally administered morphine or heroin results in quicker addiction but the greatest impact comes by intradermal, intramuscular or intravenous injection. Organic factors, such as an individual's metabolism, also play an important role in the addiction syndrome.

Morphine and heroin addiction develop much more quickly than that of opium because they are far more concentrated. It therefore follows that police narcotics officers do not – as they frequently seem to do in films such as *Lethal Weapon* and *Beverly Hills Cop* – stick their finger into a suspected drugs haul and lick it to see what they have: such behaviour is a sure-fire way to attain an addiction.

A morphine addict is not usually hooked by the first injection.

It may take several weeks of daily doses, or it may take months, before signs of chronic morphine habituation occur: but with continued use addiction is a certainty. Chronic addicts rarely survive to old age and may succumb to a relatively mild disease, or they become so weak as to die from simple infirmity. Death may come within weeks or they may linger on for years: there is no set pattern.

Of all the opium-based drugs, heroin is the most addictive and addiction can start with the very first dose. Curiously, heroin itself appears to have little adverse physical effect upon the body, much of the addict's considerable health problems deriving from his or her life-style and the fact that today many simultaneously use cocaine to counteract heroin's numbing effect.

Opium and its derivatives have posed problems for decades. Even now, although doctors and scientists understand the chemical make-up of opiates, they still have little idea how the various parts operate and there is still no guaranteed antidote.

Without an assured remedy, doctors have over the years devised scores of ways to try to fight addiction. Addicts were purged to eradicate toxins, given other opiates or opiate-like drugs as a substitute or an antagonist for certain withdrawal symptoms, and all methods tried to reduce the pain of withdrawal. Some doctors believed withdrawal was psychological or psychosomatic. Others believed it was life-threatening, yet others did not. Until well into the twentieth century, most doctors regarded addiction as they did disease: treating the symptoms but not the cause. The only common denominator was that no addiction could be reversed without the dedicated co-operation of the addicts themselves, but few fought their habit by themselves.

Thomas De Quincey was one who did. His addiction was abhorrent and he tackled it himself, yet never managed a complete cure. Of his attempt, he wrote: 'I triumphed. But infer not, reader, from this word . . . triumphed, a condition of joy and exultation. Think of me as one, even after four months had passed, still agitated, writhing, throbbing, palpitation, shattered . . .'

When morphine was discovered it was promoted as a cure for opium addiction: then, when heroin arrived it was claimed to cure morphinism. Professor Louis Lewin, in his book *Phantastica*, tells of a Chinese opium smoker who offered a reward to anyone who could rid him of his craving. One man succeeded who, with his success behind him, promptly went to Hong Kong and set up a thriving clinical business: his 'cure' was morphine injections.

Such quackery was noted by Dr D.W. Osgood of the Foochow (now Fuzhou) Medical Missionary Hospital in 1878, who observed:

> There are several varieties of pills and powders extensively advertised among the Chinese as unfailing specifics for opium smoking. Many, if not all, of these contain opium or morphia and the patient finds he is as much a slave to his medicine as he previously was to his pipe.

Osgood's own treatment was somewhat different:

> total discontinuation of opium in any form from the time of entering the asylum . . . Chloral hydrate and Potassium Bromide for the first three or four days as required. A pill consisting of belladonna, gentian, valerian, quinine and ginger is given morning and evening.

With such a regime, he was convinced he could achieve a 99 per cent success rate if the patient had 'the required grace and grit'. By contrast, Lewin firmly believed there was no substance which could cure or even alleviate opiate addiction which did not itself contain opium or a derivative.

As the patent medicine industry of the nineteenth century expanded, a parallel industry set up within it offering self-administered treatments for addiction, many of them containing the original addictive substance. Entrepreneurs, quick to see the market, cooked up various concoctions such as the 'Normyl cure for Alcohol and Drug Addictions' which contained alcohol and strychnine. 'The Teetolia Treatment' consisted of alcohol and quinine and the 'St. George Association for the Cure of the Morphia Habit' cure contained morphine and salicylic acid. All these remedies were fraudulent, offering hope without foundation and they were frequently overpriced. Some were bizarre: the leaves of the Malayan 'anti-opium plant' offered a quick cure but the only active ingredient in it was tannin.

Until the 1920s, it was believed withdrawal and convalescence were sufficient to break an addiction, the treatment maintaining the physical health of the addict, on occasion addressing the physical side-effects, such as pulling decayed teeth, and bolstering his courage with psychological help. Healthy activities were encouraged such as plenty of fresh air, exercise, sports, personal hygiene and Turkish baths to sweat toxins out of the pores. Confinement was also frequently recommended. Levinstein counselled locking addicts in a cell for up to a fortnight under medical supervision. During the first four or five days, he suggested the attendant nurses be female because male staff were more susceptible to patient bribery. The cell was to be sparsely furnished, but the addict was allowed alcohol, especially champagne, port wine and brandy. Ice compresses were applied for the inevitable headaches whilst general pain was treated with bicarbonate of soda, chloral hydrate and frequent warm baths during which stimulants, such as beef tea with port wine or champagne, were given. For some reason, champagne figured in other addiction treatments: in their account of treatment for withdrawal Allbutt and his co-worker, W.E. Dixon, noted:

> Whatever the value of auxiliary drugs, the importance of nourishment is much greater . . . When the nausea or vomiting are troublesome, cold-meat jellies, iced coffee with or without cream, iced champagne, and the like, must be tried by the mouth, and supplemented by nutritive enemas. As the stomach becomes more capable of work, turtle and other strong soups, and like generous restorative foods, must be pressed on the patient; and gentle massage used to promote absorption and blood formation.

Judging from such a menu, most cures were aimed at the wealthy. The cost of treatment was high and most doctors ignored the poor whilst those who were concerned with addiction amongst the working class mainly turned their attention to restricting supply.

In Europe, wealthy addicts mostly attended private doctors but in the USA sanatoria were founded to address the problems. Not that the patients were any better off there for many of these establishments were as fraudulent as the patent cures: they were the nineteenth-century equivalent of some modern slimming farms and in certain instances made fortunes for their proprietors who vied with each other with extravagant claims.

The emperor of the cure-masters and fraudsters was Charles B.

Towns. In 1901, he arrived in New York which had a substantial addict population. Travelling from his native Georgia, he was on the look-out for business opportunities, having been a life-insurance salesman, reputedly the most successful south of the Mason-Dixon Line. After failing in a stock-brokerage firm, he saw an opportunity in addiction treatments and invented his cure, details of which he kept secret. He somehow managed to dupe Theodore Roosevelt's physician into recommending him to Assistant Secretary of State Robert Bacon who arranged for Towns to visit China, promoting his concoction with the War Department which was seeking a cure for Soldier's Disease, and with the American delegation to the Shanghai Opium Commission in 1909, when Towns claimed he had cured 4000 opium addicts in the city. Towns became internationally renowned and was fêted by politicians, who were under pressure to do something about addiction and who lauded him for his altruism, for it was reported Towns took little financial reward from his work.

Towns's formula, finally published in 1909, was made up of one part the fluid extract of prickly ash bark, one part the fluid extract of hyoscyamus and two parts 15 per cent tincture of belladonna. This was to be administered with a complete evacuation of the bowels (usually by enema), doses of the addictive substance, castor oil and strychnine. After three days, the addict was said to pass a green mucous stool which signified the end of his discomfort and addiction. Towns's enemies and competitors referred to his formula as the 'Three Ds' – diarrhoea, delirium and damnation. By 1920, he and his cure were seen to be what they were – fakes: Towns was by then a wealthy man.

Gradually, the painful reality was realised: there was no hard-and-fast easy cure. Every conceivable scientific and quack avenue seemed to have been explored, but the rate of relapse was huge. All the cures did was temporarily divorce addicts from their drug.

In 1926, the Departmental Committee on Morphine and Heroin Addiction of the British Ministry of Health (better known as the Rolleston Committee), judged that gradual withdrawal was better than rapid but added that this was only phase one in a long treatment which could only be effective if the patient was educated in his or her problem as well as assisted with the symptoms. The patient's mental outlook and attitude were integral to the process and it was not deemed successful until the addict remained free of drug usage for between eighteen months and three years.

Over the years other less fraudulently inspired curative techniques derived from America. One of these was called CDT – Carbon Dioxide Therapy. Addict patients were made unconscious with nitrous oxide then forced to breathe a mixture of 30 per cent carbon dioxide and 70 per cent oxygen for between 20 and 40 inhalations. A coma was induced. As recently as 1972, one of the main proponents of the therapy, Dr Albert A. LaVerne, lectured on its efficacy but trials were abandoned in the same year after the death of a patient and a drop in research funding. Another therapy involved the use of lysergic acid diethylamide, or LSD. Suggested in 1952 as a cure after being used with alcoholics, it was tested on volunteer addict inmates in several prisons in Maryland. Treatment consisted of five weeks' intensive psychotherapy culminating in a very heavy LSD dosage of 300 to 500 micrograms. About a third had not resorted to heroin six months after release from jail, although whether this was due to the psychotherapy or the LSD trip it is impossible to say: a number of the convicts said the LSD helped them gain an insight into their problem. Development of the therapy was halted by a lack of research facilities.

Complex substances, such as cyclazocine or naloxone, which were classed as chemical antagonists, were tried to counter relapses into addiction by blocking the effects of heroin. They failed, the former having significant side-effects and the latter requiring huge dosages. In the early 1970s, at the Addiction Research Center at Lexington, Kentucky, a substance known as N-methylcyclopropylnorxymorphone was tested without success.

The sad truth is, to this day, no effective remedy for opiate addiction has been found and no other drugs have been so extensively researched with so little positive result: for most addicts, what keeps them habituated is a justifiable fear of withdrawal, to avoid which they are prepared to go to great lengths to ensure a continued supply.

One of the best and most graphic descriptions of the terrors of withdrawal was included by Dr Robert S. de Ropp in his study *Drugs and the Mind*, published in 1958:

> About twelve hours after the last dose of morphine or heroin the addict begins to grow uneasy. A sense of weakness overcomes him, he yawns, shivers, and sweats all at the same time while a watery discharge pours from the eyes and inside the nose which he compares to 'hot water running up into the mouth.' For a few hours he falls into an abnormal tossing, restless sleep known among addicts as the yen sleep. On awakening, eighteen to twenty-four hours after his last dose of the drug, the addict begins to enter the lower depths of his personal hell. The yawning may be so violent as to dislocate the jaw, watery mucus pours from the nose and copious tears from the eyes. The pupils are widely dilated, the hair on the skin stands up and the skin itself is cold and shows that typical goose flesh which in the parlance of the addict is called 'cold turkey,' a name also applied to the treatment of addiction by means of abrupt withdrawal.
>
> Now to add further to the addict's miseries his bowels begin to act with fantastic violence; great waves of contraction pass over the walls of the stomach, causing explosive vomiting, the vomit being frequently stained with blood. So extreme are the contractions of the intestines that the surface of the abdomen appears corrugated and knotted as if a tangle of snakes were fighting beneath the skin. The abdominal pain is severe and rapidly increases. Constant purging takes place and as many as sixty large watery stools may be passed in a day.
>
> Thirty-six hours after his last dose of the drug the addict presents a truly dreadful spectacle. In a desperate effort to gain comfort from the chills that rack his body he covers himself with every blanket he can find. His whole body is shaken by twitchings and his feet kick involuntarily, the origin of the addict's term, 'kicking the habit.'
>
> Throughout this period of the withdrawal the unfortunate addict obtains neither sleep not rest. His painful muscular cramps keep him ceaselessly tossing on his bed. Now he rises and walks about. Now he lies down on the floor. Unless he is an exceptionally stoical individual (few addicts are, for stoics do not normally indulge in opiates) he fills the air with cries of misery. The quantity of watery secretion from eyes and nose is enormous, the amount of fluid expelled from stomach and intestines unbelievable. Profuse sweating alone is enough to keep both bedding and mattress soaked. Filthy, unshaven, dishevelled, befouled with his own vomit and fæces, the addict at this stage presents an almost

subhuman appearance. As he neither eats nor drinks he rapidly becomes emaciated and may lose as much as ten pounds in twenty-four hours. His weakness may become so great that he literally cannot raise his head. No wonder many physicians fear for the very lives of their patients at this stage and give them an injection of the drug which almost at once removes the dreadful symptoms . . . If no additional drug is given the symptoms begin to subside of themselves by the sixth or seventh day, but the patient is left desperately weak, nervous, restless, and often suffers from stubborn colitis.

The rigours of cold turkey are no longer a necessary or inevitable part of overcoming addiction. Nowadays, tranquillisers and synthetic-opiate analgesics are used, the best known being methadone.

Methadone hydrochloride, a white crystalline powder which behaves like morphine or heroin, was discovered by German scientists during the Second World War. They were eager to invent a synthetic opiate to replace morphine which was in short supply due to the Allied blockade. Developed in the Mallinckrodt Laboratories, it was originally called dolophine hydrochloride. There is some argument as to how this name was arrived at: one suggests dolophine was named after Adolph Hitler whilst another states it was later invented by an American chemical company and derived from the Latin *dolor*, meaning pain. Knowledge of the drug remained dormant until around 1970 when two New York doctors, Marie Nyswander and Vincent Dole, started treating hard-line addicts with 150-milligram injections.

A powerful analgesic, methadone cancels out the euphoria of heroin and eases withdrawal, its effects lasting up to thirty-five hours as opposed to heroin's eight-hour span: it also prevents other substances, such as heroin, from working. At first, an injected dose equivalent to the addict's usual heroin dose is given but this is slowly reduced until injections are replaced by an orally administered methadone mixture or physeptone pills, then a weaker linctus. The aim is that, after stabilising on methadone, addicts will then gradually reduce their dose until they are finally able to do without it.

As methadone is also addictive, an addict may have to be weaned from it after the heroin craving is dead. In essence, methadone detoxification is not so much a curing of heroin addiction as a replacing of it by another addictive substance which is more readily overcome: but addicts on methadone say although it brings some order into their lives, they remain addicted to a drug and are trapped. They add that, in some ways, withdrawing from methadone is worse than from heroin because the withdrawal period is longer and similar symptoms may occur. In many cases, addicts spend years on methadone.

A potentially less harmful cure is acupuncture. Dr H.L. Wen, an eminent neurosurgeon working in Hong Kong in the 1970s, operated upon chronic addicts by destroying a section of their brain's frontal lobes under local anaesthetic. Worried about aspects of the anaesthesia, he decided to try acupuncture as an anaesthetic during his lobectomy. To his surprise, no sooner had he started placing and manipulating the acupuncture needles than his patient claimed his withdrawal symptoms ceased. Not convinced, Wen carried out a series of trials, since which a large number of addicts have been treated, a significant number successfully. At about the same time, a Hong Kong clinic claimed success with electro-stimulation, passing a 5-volt current through addicts' ear lobes. The drawback with both systems is that, to be effective, they have to be undergone over a long period, making them impractical and giving the addict opportunities to rehabituate.

Another approach to addiction lies in herbal or traditional medicine. In Malaysia, traditional Muslim doctors called *bomoh* treat addiction with herbal teas and the recitation of Koranic texts, regardless of the addict's religious leanings. Most *bomoh* quarantine their patients to avoid contact with drugs and to enhance their concentration on the teachings of Allah whilst others employ the use of *pembenci* (hatred charms) in a process of sympathetic magic which psychologically aids the patient. In neighbouring Thailand, addicts could attend Buddhist *wats* (temples) for herbal treatment, prayer and moral support which lasted for up to ten days. Such regimes were harsh but effective, involving herbal teas, potions which caused vomiting, herbal purgation baths and the strict vigilance of monks, or purifiers. As with Western techniques, the underlying idea was denial allied with moral assistance. Mass detoxification took place with all the addicts making a religious vow together: frequently, cured addicts stayed to help others. Sadly, this traditional approach has declined somewhat in the last twenty years as Thailand has 'modernised' and the population has become increasingly urban, relying more upon Western methods.

Other alternatives are also coming on to the market. Buprenorphine, a synthetic opiate, is proving a possible agent. In the USA a new substance, levomethadyl acetate, is being studied with clinical trials in both North America and Europe but it is not yet passed for general usage.

There is one other method of curing addiction which has nothing to do with substitute drugs, drug therapies, acupuncture needles or extract of prickly ash bark: it is not even part of a doctor's techniques.

In 1966, an English music teacher in her early twenties arrived in Hong Kong with just HK$100 and a desire to be a Christian missionary, although in what field she had no idea. Her name was Jackie Pullinger.

Armed with her love of young people and children, and the love of Christ, she established a youth club in one of the most feared and lawless barrios in the world, Kowloon Walled City. By a quirk of the 1898 Convention of Peking a tiny area of Hong Kong, about the size of a New York City block, which had once been a small walled village, became a disputed territory theoretically owned by China, ruled by the British but governed in fact by Chinese criminal fraternities whose members used it as a safe haven. By the 1960s it was a dense wedge of buildings bisected by narrow dark alleys into which the sun seldom penetrated, noxious cellars, warrens of apartments, staircases, tunnels and one-room factories making anything from fish-balls and boiled sweets to plastic sex toys.

Without a concerted police presence and aided by police corruption, Kowloon Walled City was by the late 1950s one of the world's primary heroin manufacturing centres. The presence of so much heroin not only made Hong Kong of primary importance to international drug traffickers, it produced an horrendous number of domestic heroin addicts. So prevalent was the drug in the Walled City the main thoroughfare through it, a fetid alley wider than most, was colloquially known as *Pak Fan Gai*, or White Rice Street: *pak fan* was also local slang for heroin which could be purchased openly there by the kilogram. It was in this exceptionally dangerous milieu the petite Jackie Pullinger was to find her calling. This was to cure heroin addicts. But methadone or substitute drugs had no place in Jackie Pullinger's armoury which consisted solely of the love of God and prayer.

Addicts came to a series of evangelical prayer meetings over a period of weeks. Each meeting began with a prayer and then a sermon by Jackie, followed by the singing of evangelical hymns to a guitar. All the proceedings were carried out in Cantonese which Jackie speaks like a local. Very gradually, the atmosphere grew tense, with everyone coming under a spell. Within ten minutes, the entire gathering was chanting and praying in tongues. The addicts stood up. Jackie and her acolytes, who numbered not only foreign helpers but also former addicts, encircled them singly, laying on their hands. The addicts then passed into a semi-trance, swaying and muttering, sometimes falling, to be caught, at other times keeping upright by the presence but not the contact of outstretched palms.

After fifteen minutes or so, the tension relaxed and the addicts were helped to seats. They appeared completely exhausted, some exhibiting early withdrawal symptoms. No criticism was made of the addicts' problem. It was put in the context of being an evil which only goodness might overcome.

Having undergone a number of prayer meetings, addicts were then taken to a rest centre where they were put to bed and continually attended by someone who played for or with them. In this respect, the process was similar to that of the Malaysian *bomoh* and the Buddhist regimes in the Thai *wats*: psychological support was vital. What was missing were the bowls of noxious teas.

In a relatively short space of time, the addiction was eradicated without pain. Furthermore, comparatively few addicts re-addicted: prayer gave them the psychological strength to maintain their liberty.

Jackie Pullinger has run her mission for thirty years, although latterly not in Kowloon Walled City which has been demolished in collaboration with the Chinese government: in that time, she has saved well over 500 addicts and has extended her mission to Macau and the Philippines.

In the face of such success even the most dedicated atheist has to admit to the possibility of there being a god for, if miracles do exist, then Jackie Pullinger is surely a conduit for them: to use the addict's parlance, she scores where the marvels of medicine have not. It is almost as if God, feeling guilty at having made his own medicine, is offering his own relief from it and it is perhaps not just divine inspiration but also divine irony he should exercise his love in China, for China has been at the core of the opium story for centuries.

7

The Fantasy Traders

Opium, which has been virtually synonymous with China for hundreds of years, is often thought to have been introduced by Arabs in the seventh century AD but this is debatable. There exist earlier references to opium in China so the Chinese were clearly acquainted with it before the Arabs arrived yet the fact remains the Arabs did bring it in substantial quantities, the Chinese adapting the Arabic name of *af-yum* to *a-fu-yong*. Arab dhows reached as far as Chinese waters in the sixth century and, by 900, there were substantial Arab communities in most Chinese ports. In later centuries, after Arab influence had faded in China, they took their cargoes to Malacca to trade with Chinese merchants there, bartering silks and silver in exchange for, as Duarte Barbosa recorded in 1516, 'drugs of cambray, afiam, which we call opium, wormwood and saffron'.

The likelihood is opium was either brought home by Chinese seafarers who were sailing as far as Africa in the first century BC, or introduced by Buddhist priests from Tibet around the first century AD who used it solely as an anodyne, the knowledge having reached Tibet with traders from Persia and India: or, just as likely, it arrived from India via Burma, where Chinese merchants were trading in jade and gemstones as early as the third century BC, or from Bactria (central Asia) whence the famous Chinese explorer, Chang Chien, travelled in 139 BC, meeting the remnants of the Greek civilisation of Alexander the Great there.

It was not long before the culturally and geographically isolated Chinese began to cultivate their own crops of opium poppy, which is not indigenous to China, in the western province of Yunnan.

Thus, by the time the Arab trade in opium was established, China was already originating a home-grown product in addition to importing quantities overland from India, an important point when considering the accusation it was eighteenth-century European traders who started the opium trade: whilst they certainly were to corrupt China with what was called 'foreign mud', they did not initiate the traffic.

Early Chinese literature contains a number of references to opium. The Chinese surgeon Hua To, living in the period of the Three Kingdoms (AD 220–264), used opium preparations in addition to cannabis, giving these to his patients prior to major surgery. In AD 973, the reigning emperor ordered the compilation of a medical book, or herbarium, the *K'ai pao pên tsäo*, in which opium was named as *ying-tsu-su* (*su* being the word for a pod) and recommended as a cure for dysentery. Four fleets set sail for the South Seas in 987, instructed to procure opium amongst other cargoes. At about the same time, opium was fulsomely praised in a poem by Su Tung-P'a. He was clearly familiar with it as more than a medicine, speaking of it as a potion which produced dreams and cured diarrhoea. In the twelfth century, a medical writer recorded how poppy pods were made into a paste then formed into fish-shaped cakes to be sold not only for medical use but for consumption as an expensive delicacy whilst a century later, another writer stated the fish cake paste was used also 'for diarrhoea and dysentery accompanied by local inflammation; though its effects are quick, great care must be used in taking the medicine for it kills like a knife.' The skill of scoring pods was first mentioned in China in 1488 by Wang Hi, the Governor of Kansu province. In the sixteenth century, in his *The Introduction to Medicine*, Li Ting gave an account of how *a-fu-yong* should be prepared.

The Arab–Chinese trade was comparatively small, only really supporting any shortfall in local production. Opium use was not widespread and was restricted to an upper-class élite who could afford it: most of the population, being semi-literate or illiterate, had not heard of it. Nevertheless, there was one particular section of society outside the élite familiar with opium: concubines of rich men were frequently dosed with it to keep them sexually compliant and subdued to prevent them absconding. The exclusivity of opium, which was eaten, meant very few people were addicted. However, this was to change when a particularly unique new vice, originating in the New World, was introduced to China by European sailors. It was smoking.

After the colonisation of North America, tobacco smoking spread rapidly around the world. Portuguese and Dutch sailors introduced the new fad to India, Indo-China, China and Japan. The Spanish imported tobacco from the Philippines into China around 1620, establishing the smoking habit. Had they restricted it to tobacco, matters might not have developed but, in the mid-seventeenth century, in trading posts in Java owned by the Dutch trading firm Vereenigde Oost-Indische Compagnie, sailors began smoking tobacco mixed with a pinch of opium and arsenic to give it a kick, originally believing that smoking an opium-tobacco mixture prevented malaria. The Dutch had been exporting opium from India since 1659, trading it for pepper and using it to suborn Indonesian tribal leaders. It was less than a decade before this tobacco-based smoking cocktail reached the coastal ports of China, carried via Formosa by the Dutch. In China, tobacco smoking had become so popular the Emperor Tsung Cheng prohibited it. The edict was not in force for long but by the time it was rescinded the damage was done. The prohibition had resulted in the Chinese, bereft of tobacco, smoking opium instead.

Thus was born one of the most evil cultural exchanges in history – opium from the Middle East met the native American Indian pipe.

The great social chronicler and reformer, Joseph Rowntree, summed the situation up in 1905 when he wrote:

> . . . it is quite clear that opium had long been known in China as a medicine, and that the poppy had been used there, as it is in India, as a vegetable. It is probable that there grew up in some districts a demand for the drug for vicious purposes also. But it is practically certain, from the absence of all mention of any opium habit by the Jesuit missionaries, by travellers, and in the Chinese records, that there was no general consumption of opium before the introduction of opium smoking.

Although opium smoked by itself had been known in Java in the seventeenth century, the first report of opium smoking was written in the middle of the eighteenth century when a Chinese Imperial official, Huang Yu-pu, was sent from Peking to study conditions on the island of Formosa. He reported:

> Opium for smoking is prepared by mixing hemp and the grass cloth plant with opium, then cutting them up small. The mixture is boiled with water, and the preparation mixed with tobacco. A bamboo tube is also provided, the end of which is filled with coir fibres. Many persons collect the opium to smoke it mixed with tobacco alone. Those who make it their sole business to prepare opium in this way are known as opium tavern-keepers. Those who smoke once or twice form a habit which cannot be broken. The aborigines smoke it as an aid to vice. The limbs grow thin and appear to be wasting away; the internal organs collapse. The smoker, unless he be killed, will not cease smoking.

As well as being smoked neat, opium also continued to be smoked with tobacco. In 1816, Dr Abel Clarke wrote:

> No opium is exposed in the shops probably because it is a contraband article, but it is used with tobacco in all parts of the Empire. The Chinese, indeed, consider the smoking of opium as one of the greatest luxuries; and if they are temperate in drinking, they are often excessive in the use of this drug. They have more than one method of smoking it: sometimes they envelop a piece of solid gum in tobacco and smoke it from a pipe with a very small bowl, and sometimes they steep fine tobacco in a strong solution of it, and use it in the same way.

The vice of opium smoking, so often associated with the Chinese, was not therefore a native practice. It was indubitably introduced by Westerners.

The Arabs had arrived in China by sailing the coasts of India and Indo-China: the first European allegedly to reach China, in the thirteenth century, was Marco Polo who travelled on the caravan routes north of Tibet. However, by the fifteenth century, these land routes had become unsafe and Europeans traders, who had come to supplant the Arabs, sought a sea passage to China which was considered not only treasure-filled but rich in unparalleled trading possibilities.

Of these new mercantile nations, the Portuguese were the first to arrive. After an abortive attempt to gain a foothold in 1514, in what is now Hong Kong, they were given permission to establish a single but exclusive trading base on the western shore of the Pearl River estuary in 1557. It was named Macau.

The first non-Arabic opium to be imported into China came from the Portuguese settlement of Goa, on the west coast of India, at the beginning of the seventeenth century. Known as Malwa opium and originating from the independent Maratha states of central and western India, it was not long before the trade was being competed for by the Dutch and, subsequently, the British, the control of opium passing from one seafaring nation to another. The Dutch took over from the Portuguese, bringing raw opium from India to Java, then re-exporting it to China. When, in the eighteenth century, the British superseded the Dutch, a new phase in the history of opium was opened.

Late in the seventeenth century, the Emperor K'ang Hsi grew fascinated by Jesuit missionaries who arrived at his court. Although mistrustful of his Western vassals, as he considered them – the Chinese believed all the world, known and unknown, was their empire – he decided there might be some way to make a profit from them so, in 1685, he opened the port of Canton (today known as Guangzhou) to traders. Playing safe, he issued strict regulations designed to keep them subservient. From 1720, the foreigners lived and worked in factories to the south-west of the city, outside its walls, in an area which became known as the Canton Colony. They were not factories in the modern sense (that is, places of manufacture) but trading centres staffed by a factor, or manager. Fifteen years later trading vessels, at first obliged to register their arrival in Macau, were allowed to bypass it and sail directly for Canton. From that day on, Portuguese influence began to decline.

For a century and a half, trade with China was governed by the Eight Regulations, the most important of which was that no warships or arms might enter the Pearl River (at the mouth of which stood Canton) and that merchant ships might not approach nearer the city than Whampoa, an unpleasant island with no naturally defined harbour about 10 nautical miles downriver. Malaria was endemic there and fresh water hard to obtain, the only supply being brought out to ships at anchor by sampan. All social and mercantile contact could only be effected through the Co-Hong (frequently abbreviated to just Hong), a cartel of eight to twelve Chinese merchants with exclusive trading rights with the Barbarians, as foreigners were known. Other regulations were primarily designed to humiliate and segregate foreigners.

The Co-Hong merchants obtained their trading right exclusivity from the *hoppo*, a mandarin who, in the way of the Chinese imperial civil service, was unsalaried but earned magnificent sums from the charges he made for the Co-Hong operating licences, by demanding *kum-shaw* (basically gifts which were veiled bribes), setting up spurious social trust funds and exacting fines on the Co-Hong merchants for transgressions made by the foreigners for whom they were responsible. The cost of a licence was around £50,000, excluding the obligatory bribery. The *hoppo*, in turn, had to pay back-handers to his seniors, the local viceroy and governor. The Co-Hong merchants were also on to a good thing. They maintained substantial households and lived in extreme luxury. Howqua, whose real name was Wu Bing-jian and who was one of the chief merchants in the 1830s, was worth in excess of £5 million on his death.

Despite the strictures of the Eight Regulations, trade greatly increased throughout the eighteenth century. Indeed, once the trading structure was organised to the approval of the Chinese authorities, trade flourished. Exports from China included tea, sugar, silk, mother-of-pearl, paper, camphor, cassia, copper and alum, gold and silver, silk piece-goods, lacquerware, rhubarb, various oils, bamboo and porcelain. In return, the Barbarians imported cotton and woollen piece-goods, raw cotton, iron, tin and lead, carnelian and diamonds, pepper, betel-nuts, pearls, watches and clocks, coral and amber beads, birds' nests and sharks' fins (for soup) and foodstuffs such as fish and rice. And opium.

The opium trade would not have established itself had the Chinese been more open to European merchants. With a high demand for Western manufactured goods, traders would have been satisfied and not felt obliged to commence a traffic in opium to boost their profit margins: but this was not to be. The emperors were afraid to lower their defences or to mitigate their jingoistic stance. There was a fear in imperial circles that foreign culture, ideology, religion and mores would infect the Celestial Kingdom. In part, the emperors were right: foreign influence would have had a huge cultural impact upon areas where it was allowed, but they were naïve in assuming they could keep out expansionist traders by merely restricting trade and holding it at arm's length on a noxious mud-flat thousands of miles from the capital. In other words, they underestimated the Barbarians' tenacity, determination and greed.

From the start, opium was the only import the Chinese really wanted. Indian opium was far superior in quality to the home-grown product and better for smoking. Yet more was to come for, in the latter half of the eighteenth century, the British-owned and -controlled East India Company – founded in 1600 and granted a monopoly of trade with countries 'beyond the Cape of Good Hope or the Magellan Straits' – was to start to import opium.

The East India Company – frequently nicknamed the John Company after the jovial image of the jolly Englishman John Bull – was not new to China. It had been rashly permitted by the Portuguese to establish a Macau office in 1664, from which it began trading in a small way from 1678. However, once it established mastery of trade with China, it tried to keep a firm grip on it – no British ship could officially trade with China except under an East India Company licence – until 1833 when the company charter lapsed: it did not finally wind up until 1857, when it was dissolved following the Indian Mutiny.

Inevitably, as the availability of opium rose so did the demand for it. The Chinese authorities were quick to recognise its potential harm. An edict of 1729, issued by the Emperor Yung Cheng, prohibited the smoking of opium and its domestic sale except under licence as a medicine. The severity of the penalties for opium usage imply it was a serious problem. Owners of illegal supplies were sentenced to up to 100 strokes of a bamboo cane, with an added punishment of some days or even weeks in a cangue, a heavy yoke-like wooden collar which acted as an unanchored pillory. A fixed, cage-like version was also used: few survived it. Opium dealers and den- or shopkeepers selling the drug were strangled whilst their employees were given 100 strokes of bamboo, three months imprisonment, then exile to a distance of 1000 miles. Carriers, knowing neighbours or officials who engaged in opium trafficking were similarly punished. Local customs officials were penalised for carelessness. Imperial anger was mainly directed against those who profited financially at the expense of those to whom they sold opium. The final clause of the edict expressly exempted the smoker from punishment.

Confusingly, the edict did not mention a restriction on imports and importers. It was bungled, making illegal a substance which it was lawful to import. What was more, until 1796, opium imports were liable to an excise duty which illuminates the hypocrisy of the emperors who, whilst condemning their countrymen who dealt in opium, nevertheless earned from it for their exchequer.

The edict had little impact upon European traders who took scant notice. They simply reorganised their opium business and traded more stealthily. In the year of the edict, 200 chests of opium were imported, mainly for consumption in and around Canton, Macau and the Pearl River estuary. Little imported opium reached the interior of China. By 1767, however, imports had increased to 1000 chests per annum and 4000 by 1790, most of it landing at Lark's Bay near Macau, safe from both Portuguese and Chinese interference.

In 1796, all existing edicts were renewed and their penalties increased: then, in 1799, the Emperor Kia King issued a proclamation specifically prohibiting the importation of opium, its use in China and domestic poppy cultivation.

Before this, opium was regarded like any other commodity but from 1799 it became contraband. Invariably, as soon as it was illegal, organised smuggling commenced, the illicit trade conducted not by pirates but by surreptitious arrangement between importers and local Chinese officials: corruption, not nocturnal cutters and sloops, brought opium in to Canton and elsewhere along the coast. Attracted by substantial profits, other traders defied the East India Company licensing regulations and set themselves up in the opium and general trade markets. By 1800 there were twenty private firms of various nationalities operating in Canton.

Whereas the East India Company now had to compete with other merchants in China, in India it had come to hold a virtual monopoly over opium. The cultivation and domestic trade of opium in India had traditionally been a monopoly of the Great Mogul and local princes, but this had been gradually exacted from them by the East India Company after rivalry with the Dutch had been settled to their advantage. During the reign of Charles II, the company was given the right 'to acquire territory, coin money, form alliances, make war and control civil and criminal jurisdiction.' In other words, it was more or less a state unto itself and, as the Mogul Empire began to break up in the eighteenth century, the company metamorphosed into a powerful political, as well as commercial, entity.

With the defeat of Siraj-ud-Dawlah at Plassey in 1757 by Robert Clive, the power of the Mogul Empire was shattered and Bengal came under the influence of the British. A few skirmishes occurred after this: in 1763, the British population of Patna was massacred but the uprising was quelled and the Nawab, the local puppet ruler, was dethroned. Clive was recalled from England to take control. As punishment, the Nawab lost all his possessions amongst which was the monopoly on opium production.

On his return, Clive's main task was to halt the corruption which had built up tension, culminating in the Patna massacre. He did this by setting the administration on a sure footing and paying decent salaries to its employees. To raise the revenue for this he taxed salt, tobacco and betel and levied a land tax. The East India Company in turn had to raise profits to fund Clive's reforms: opium was the ideal source.

In its early days, the company's opium trade had, for the best part, been conducted privately by its employees. Wages were so low they had been virtually dependent for their livelihoods on business conducted on the side. However, a decade after the Patna massacre, the Governor-General of the East India Company, Warren Hastings, took control of the opium monopoly, which he rightly saw as a very profitable source of revenue, although his first venture into opium was a failure. In 1781, he sent 3450 chests of opium to China in two ships one of which, an armed sloop called *Betsy*, was captured *en route* by a French privateer. Arriving off Macau, the captain of the surviving ship, the *Nonsuch*, received only derisory offers for his cargo and ended up selling it in Malacca at a considerable loss.

In India, the company attitude towards opium was restrictive. They controlled retailing by licence and under new rules introduced in 1793, all poppy growers had to sell their produce to the company. With a guaranteed market for output, opium cultivation soared. So, too, did the use of opium in India which rapidly habituated large numbers of native labour to such an extent it decreased their efficiency. In response to this, Warren Hastings unequivocally condemned its use, but he was faced with a dilemma. He was proscribing a major source of revenue. To overcome any potential fiscal loss, and to ease his conscience, he stated: 'Opium is not a necessity of life but a pernicious article of luxury, which ought not to be permitted except for purposes of foreign commerce only, and which the wisdom of the Government should carefully restrain from internal consumption.'

In the light of such bare-faced hypocrisy, a decision was made to restrict domestic Indian consumption but to develop an export trade. The company, therefore, resolved to expand considerably the sale of opium to China, for not only was opium a superb trading commodity, in that it did not deteriorate, but demand increased as addicts were created.

Had they only known, the Chinese might have had an opportunity to stop the East India Company's opium trading at this early stage. In 1793, Lord Macartney went on the first British diplomatic mission to Peking to meet the emperor. Macartney carried a letter from George III to the emperor, along with extensive gifts chosen to represent the best Britain had to offer China. In his brief, Macartney was free to make concessions, one paragraph going so far as to concede the East India Company would, if necessary, prohibit the export of opium to China. Yet the matter was not discussed, the mission being a failure because Macartney refused to kow-tow and the Chinese dismissed his gifts as rubbish.

The growth of the opium trade with China also hinged on another addiction, albeit a far less pernicious one. It was tea.

The British had taken to drinking tea and Chinese tea, considered the best, was consumed in enormous quantities: with silk, it was China's primary export. The Chinese, however, whilst keen to export tea, really wanted nothing in return except silver bullion. As the Emperor Ch'ien Lung expressed it: 'The Celestial Empire possesses all things in prolific abundance and lacks no product within its borders. There is therefore no need to import manufactures of outside barbarians in exchange for our products.'

This placed Britain and the East India Company at a serious trading disadvantage. They had to pay for tea cargoes in cash which had to come from its Indian accounts, with the result a balance of payments deficit soon accrued, much to the alarm of Parliament in London. The company had to reassess its operations or lose its charter. It took little effort to realise the commodities which could turn the situation around. Both were produced in India, where the company held such sway. They were cotton and, especially, opium. With a characteristic efficiency, the company promoted this trade with such success that, by 1804, the balance of trade was reversed and the outflow of silver halted.

The East India Company had the business methodically organised. Opium production was controlled in and around Patna, followed by the possession of the Malwa crop which brought about the end of Portuguese influence. Goa became a backwater, the East India Company attaining the opium monopoly over essentially the entire subcontinent. Some opium was also exported to China from Turkey, primarily by American merchants. The first American involvement in the trade was to be in 1811 when a Philadelphia brig, the *Sylph*, commanded by Captain Dobell, arrived in Macau with opium from Smyrna. Six years later, American traders purchased $500,000 in Turkish opium, which they also shipped to Macau, but their Middle Eastern product was inferior and unsuited to smoking: the East India Company virtually owned a world monopoly on good-quality product.

However, after the prohibitive imperial edict of 1799, in order to avoid detection, the opium-carrying ships were frequently disguised, flew flags of convenience, were armed and carried a detachment of soldiers. Opium being contraband meant no duty was levied on it, but it could no longer be landed at the factories from Whampoa. An opium depot existed on two ships permanently stationed just outside Macau harbour whilst, later, a large receiving vessel (also known as a warehouse ship) was anchored on the outskirts of Whampoa where it remained, gradually releasing its cargo, which was replenished annually, onto the market.

It was easy to smuggle opium ashore from the receiving vessels. The importer obtained payment on the spot, the opium being immediately taken ashore in armed boats with crews of fifty to seventy men, the Chinese buyer making the necessary arrangements with officials, bribing them to turn a blind eye to his business. The bribes were ironically known in the trader's vernacular as 'tea money' (also called 'squeeze'), still a common euphemism for a kickback in Hong Kong. Traders, almost but not all of them British, also paid tea money as a matter of course.

Pejorative reports about opium smuggling reached the East India Company directors in London who condemned it as 'being beneath the Company to be engaged in such a clandestine trade.' They added 'whatever opium might be in demand by the Chinese, the quantity would readily find its way thither without the Company being exposed to the disgrace of being engaged in an illicit commerce.' Nevertheless, they continued opium production and although they now prohibited their own vessels from carrying it, they encouraged other British captains, sailing under company licence, to take opium cargoes.

Under this policy of business by proxy, the opium trade grew. Merchants and sea captains were not reluctant to agree to the company's terms. Known as 'country firms', 'country merchants' or 'country wallahs' (a name given to those who traded between India and other places in the East), they were private companies or individuals who acted as middlemen to handle trade with China, willing to assume the risk of transporting and selling opium. This transference of trading responsibility had two benefits. Indian revenue from opium continued and the East India Company continued to make a profit but it could claim ignorance of what was done with its product.

The system worked thus: the East India Company produced opium under monopoly and sold the chests at auction in Calcutta. Private buyers shipped the chests to China in country firm vessels. In Whampoa or Macau, agency houses received and sold them, with the Chinese purchasers smuggling the opium into China. They paid for it in silver bullion or coin which the agencies paid into the company's Chinese office in return for bills of exchange payable at banks in India or London.

Profits varied greatly. Opium was a highly speculative trade where great fortunes were possible but so also were substantial losses. Jardine Matheson became by far the largest agency, coming into being when William Jardine and James Matheson, both leading country merchants, joined forces in 1828: their partnership, which for the first years dealt primarily in opium, was formally registered as Jardine Matheson & Co. in 1832. In Jardine's opinion, the opium trade was the 'safest and most gentleman-like speculation I am aware of.' The company exists to this day as one of the foremost trading multinationals in South-east Asia. It is the original 'noble' house although, bearing in mind its foundations, *ignoble* might be a more apposite epithet.

Both Jardine and Matheson made massive fortunes out of opium. Jardine, whom the Chinese called 'Iron-headed Old Rat' because he had once refused to run from a beating at the gates of Canton when trying to present a petition, returned to Britain, had a seat in Parliament provided for him but died of a lingering and agonising illness in 1843, substantiating for some the superstition that those who dealt in opium would come to a sticky end. A contemporary view of Jardine's political opportunism exists in Disraeli's novel, *Sybil*:

'You had a formidable opponent, Lord Marney told me,' said Sir Vavasour, 'who was he?'
   'Oh, a dreadful man! A scotchman, richer than Croesus, one Mr Druggy, fresh from Canton, with a million in opium in each pocket, denouncing corruption and bellowing free-trade.'

James Matheson lived much longer, dying aged ninety-one in 1887 after building himself a castle, also becoming an MP and endowing the professorship of Chinese at the University of London. His nephew, Donald, who became his partner in Jardine Matheson, clearly did not agree with Jardine's gentlemanly premise. He was a serious man whose conscience was pricked by the opium trade. Eventually, he became so sickened by the business he resigned from the company in 1848: later, as an old man, he was appointed a chairman of the Society for the Suppression of the Opium Trade in Britain.

   After the edict of 1799, the illicit opium trade continued for another seventy-eight years with the full knowledge and tacit approval of the British government of which, because it was governed by a charter, the East India Company was never fully independent. The charter was frequently revamped with various parliamentary committees periodically inspecting the company's activities, profitability and viability: its social or moral standing was never questioned.

   In 1830, with the expansion of the trade, permission was granted from London to extend the poppy cultivation in India, 'with a view to a large increase in the supply of opium.' This raised output by the middle of the decade to over 30,000 chests per annum. An indication of the government's knowledge of the opium trade can be seen from a report of 1832 which stated: 'The monopoly of opium in Bengal supplies the Government with a revenue amounting in sterling money to £981,293 per annum ... it does not appear advisable to abandon so important a source of revenue.' And important it certainly was for that year's opium crop formed a sixth of the gross national product of British India.

To become such a vital cash crop, vast tracts of productive land, formerly used for a wide variety of agriculture, were turned over to poppies. And, although most Indian opium originated from Bengal, there were other locations engaged in production.

There were three kinds of prepared Indian opium. That from Bengal, also called 'Company's opium', had an outer covering which was black and was therefore known as 'black earth' whilst opium from Bombay was called 'white skin' and that from Madras 'red skin'.

'Black earth' was produced in the vast East India Company factories in Patna and near Benares, as previously outlined, and sent down the Ganges River for 300 miles to Calcutta. Fleets of river craft carried the chests from late November until March, the first public auction taking place on the Monday morning before Christmas.

At an auction, there could be 4000, 5000 or even 6000 chests for sale to the highest bidders, with the terms set at a small down payment with the remainder due in an agreed number of months. A second auction was conducted in February, with a third in April; if the harvest was plentiful, there was a fourth in May or even a fifth in June or early July.

The opium was purchased by firms, such as the British-owned Jardine Matheson and Dent & Co., or American companies, such as Russell & Co. of Boston and Perkins & Company. Indians and Parsees, like Heerjeebhoy and Dadabhoy Rustomjee, also traded in opium, as well as lone British entrepreneurs. Some firms did not bid directly but through agents or purchased supplies from those who had themselves bid, paying a slight premium for the convenience.

Onward shipping was carried out by vessels which had sailed from Britain with manufactured goods or raw materials, such as minerals or bales of wool. When these were unloaded, a new cargo was taken on of India cotton, saltpetre and opium. The first port of call *en route* to China was Penang, where fresh water and fruit were loaded and some opium was traded to Malay natives as well as to expatriate Chinese who sold their opium into the deep south-west of China and the area today covered by Vietnam.

Whampoa was approached by sailing up the Pearl River estuary and into the river mouth, known by its Portuguese name of *Bocca Tigris* (the Tiger's Mouth), passing either Macau on the western shore or Lintin Island, more or less in the centre. At intervals along the shore imperial forts kept watch on maritime activity.

Before 1830, opium was carried in general cargo vessels, sturdy broad-beamed craft some over a century old. They could only sail with the wind so voyaged east from India during the summer south-east monsoon, returning in winter with the north-east monsoon which blew from October to March. With the exception of the receiving ships which held a stock of opium, trade in the drug was seasonal, just as was that of tea and silk, for the famous East Indiamen were similarly unable to sail against the prevailing wind. These old ships were so well built – often of as much as a thousand tonnes of well-seasoned timber – some of them were still afloat in 1897: one, sold for salvage in the middle of the century, realised over £7500 for her timbers, the equivalent of more than £3 million today.

A seasonal trade was disadvantageous to merchants for it meant that their vessels spent a disproportionate amount of time idle whilst the price of opium was liable to fluctuation. What was needed was a new type of ship which could sail against the wind.

The result was the designing and building of sleek ships with narrow hulls, flush decks, and the capability to beat to windward. This new breed of vessel was the clipper. The classification, based on the mariner's colloquialism 'to go at a good clip', meaning to sail quickly, referred both to small vessels which sailed against the monsoon as well as the later craft, such as the famous *Cutty Sark*, ten times the size, which beat every wind in the tea trade. The opium clippers were to become famous, beautiful ships – state-of-the-art vessels in their day. The subject of many paintings, they carried three slanting masts and a wide spread of canvas. Most of the British, American and Parsee opium-trading companies owned at least one of them.

It is believed the first opium clipper was a craft named *Red Rover*. With a displacement of 254 tons, she was built on the Hooghly River in 1829 and named after the pirate hero of James Fenimore Cooper's latest novel. She was modelled on the *Prince de Neufchatel*, which had captured nine British merchantmen during the British–American War of 1812. Her builder, Captain William Clifton, guaranteed he could provide a vessel which would do the India/China round trip thrice annually and who, before the launch, staked his reputation by announcing she would beat the monsoon on her first voyage. She did, completing the round trip from Calcutta to Macau in eighty-six days. Later, she established a record of eighteen days for the voyage from Calcutta to Lintin Island, a remarkable maritime achievement. *Red Rover* spawned an entire generation of vessels and was eventually bought by Jardine Matheson in the late 1830s as an addition to their fleet of over a dozen clippers.

Another much copied ship was the *Sylph*, not to be confused with Dobell's American craft mentioned earlier. She was a 251 ton barque, even faster than the *Red Rover*, designed by Sir Robert Seppings, Surveyor to the Royal Navy. The opium merchants also used ex-naval warships, their fire-power an effective deterrent to Chinese pirates and customs vessels: most clippers carried a complement of five guns either side, with a 68-pounder, known as a 'long-tom', amidships. James Matheson purchased HMS *Curlew*, an eighteen-gun brig, in 1823, which served as an opium runner for many years under the name *Jamesina*.

During the first twenty years of prohibition, little serious attention was paid to the 1799 edict or any of the restrictions which followed it but, in 1820, new severe penalties were laid against opium importation. Any Chinese found in possession was executed. The penalties made the captains of the receiving ships lying off Whampoa restive. A decision was made to move the receiving ships to Lintin Island, today known as Neilingding Dao. Meaning 'Solitary Nail' because of its single 1000 foot peak, Lintin is positioned 80 miles south of Canton (today called Guangzhou) and 20 miles north-east of Macau. Although a mere 3 miles long with no natural harbour or convenient landing, it became the entrepôt port for the opium trade. Its geographical position in the estuary made it convenient for importers and buyers alike and it was not unusual to have fifteen clippers lying offshore.

As Lintin became established, three older and slower vessels – the *Merope* (owned by Matheson), the *Samarang* (owned by Dent) and the *General Quiroga* (owned by a Spanish consortium based in Manila) – were permanently moored off the island, to be joined in time by others. One, the *Lintin*, owned by an American soldier of fortune called Forbes, made him so much money in three years from 1830 that he retired, requesting to be buried in a coffin made from her mainmast. By then, up to twenty-five receiving ships rode at anchor off the island.

These hulks had their masts removed and their decks covered with either a bamboo roof or canvas awnings tailored from the sails. Their guns were not removed and they became floating fortified opium warehouses commanded by British officers, but crewed by Lascars, with Chinese craftsmen. The Lascars (known as 'Black Barbarians' by the Chinese) were single but many of the Chinese maintained families ashore on Lintin whilst the vessels even carried the families of their British officers and became small, self-contained communities. Life for the officers could be quite pleasurable. They scaled the peak to shoot ducks and paddy-birds although they always went in parties to avoid being robbed, or 'bambooed'. A few houses onshore offered a respite from ship-board existence and the ladies often exercised on the beach. There were even picnic outings and social dinner parties.

Chinese merchants purchased opium from the receiving ships either cash on delivery or acceptance, or paid for in advance to agents in Canton. The opium was taken out of its chest, which remained on board, and packed into bags of woven-grass matting which were loaded on to armed, two-masted Chinese river craft with fifty oars, known as 'centipedes', 'fast crabs' or 'scrambling dragons'. When loaded, they made for shore, evading imperial patrols. Once safely up one of the many estuarine creeks, agents took collection and distributed the opium.

A contretemps between an imperial official and Chinese opium smugglers was witnessed in about 1836 by a young British doctor, C. Toogood Downing. After hiding itself up a creek, a mandarin's boat laid an ambush for a centipede, which at first got away. Then, as Downing recorded, the chase began:

> The screams and yells of the smugglers were mixed with the ricketty sound of their vessel and the orders and cries of the mandarins behind them. Every now and then the long ornamental gun [on the mandarin boat] was turned upon its swivel, and a loud report reverberated across the country as it was discharged against the chase but with little effect: the shot was generally seen dancing along the water wide of the mark . . .

Unbeknownst to the smugglers, another mandarin boat was hiding up another creek and suddenly hove into view, trapping the centipede.

> The mandarins rushed to the attack without hesitation, and laid about them in right good earnest, with their swords and pikes, frequently cutting and wounding in a dreadful manner; but the poor smugglers appeared to act on the defensive . . . Many of the defeated jumped overboard, and as they struggled in the waters to gain the shore, formed excellent marks for the spears and javelins of the conquerors. The great mass of them, however, were seized . . . The long pigtail served instead of the coat collar . . . when twisted two or three times round the hand . . .

That the smugglers put up only a defensive resistance is not surprising: any smuggler taken alive was sent to hard labour for life but if a mandarin or member of his crew was killed, the whole smuggling gang would have forfeited their lives.

As a general rule, such official craft kept clear of Lintin Island, although war junks frequently moored offshore, firing their guns to salute passing mandarin vessels, to tell the hour or keep evil spirits at bay. Otherwise, they made no attempt to intervene in the opium trade. They were not just afraid of a diplomatic incident but also of the superior fire-power of the opium clippers and fortified receiving vessels.

Occasionally, a show of imperial compliance was made. When a clipper sailed, a fleet of war junks would close on it. The clipper captain would maintain a speed which allowed the war junks to keep in touch so they might fire on the clipper, deliberately aiming wide or short. From time to time, Chinese smugglers were executed but the customs patrols were corrupt to such an extent even their commander, Rear-Admiral Han Shao-ch'iung, was in for his kickback. In 1832, patrols were abolished as next to useless.

No real effort was made to counteract smuggling, mainly because so many officials benefited from it: whilst opium was the main contraband, smugglers also ran any merchandise upon which a heavy duty was levied. Everyone from the viceroy to the lowest mandarin gained from the trade, the Emperor's exchequer the only real loser.

The opium trade grew as the years progressed, expanding from an annual production of 4494 chests in 1811–21 to 9708 chests in 1821–28, 18,835 chests in 1828–35 and over 30,000 chests in 1835–39. These amounts were for importation from India alone and excluded opium brought by sea and overland from Turkey, as well as that deriving from domestic cultivation. Until about 1830, there were extensive poppy fields throughout southern China, especially in Chekiang province, but the suppression of farmers in 1831 successfully restricted cultivation to isolated districts and regions where, by the late 1830s, a substantial amount of opium was once more being grown. Being inferior to Indian imports, it was usually used to blend with the latter rather than to be smoked on its own.

Opium profits were enormous and a large number of foreign nationals were engaged in the trade with or without official support from home. Other than the British, the Americans were particularly active, accounting for about 10 per cent of the trade: although prohibited by their government in 1858, many ignored the ruling. Often, the Americans tried to conceal their involvement in opium but it was just as vital a part of the American tea trade as it was the British tea trade and many prominent American families grew rich from it. At some stage British, American, Greek, Dutch, Swedish, French, Spanish, Danish, and Latin Americans operated Canton factories. Throughout the 1830s, the opium trade was worth up to £3 million per annum, the British accounting for over 80 per cent of the turnover. In 1837, the British mercantile contingent in Canton exceeded 150.

All the foreigners still had to reside in the Canton Colony, which amounted to a foreign enclave. They lived in thirteen factories, rather grand buildings rented from the Hong merchants, which were curious architectural hybrids with European and Oriental features. Each contained apartments or houses for expatriate staff, commercial offices for one or more firms and stores built around courtyards vaguely in the manner of a Chinese *yamen* or administrative centre. To the east was a noxious creek which served as a *nullah*, or open sewer. Close by, between the factories and the Pearl River frontage, was a square, later segregated into two small parks, the American and British Gardens. The riverbank was thronged with fishing and commercial sampans moored in lines and small cutters used by the merchants to reach Whampoa. Across the river, which was not bridged, lay the settlement of Honam, a temple and a fort. Residency was not year-long: to avoid the humidity and heat of the summer and, no doubt, the stink of the creek, merchants decamped from May to September to Macau where their families lived: foreign women were forbidden to occupy the factories.

Each factory had a local agent, known as a *compradore*, the name taken from the Portuguese: in Cantonese, he was known as the *mai pan*. They were middlemen employed by the merchants (known in Cantonese as *tai pans*) to manage all contact with Chinese traders and money dealers. They were essential because foreigners were prohibited direct contact with Chinese businessmen. Needless to say, *compradores* were in a prime position to indulge in corruption and often sold opium themselves. In time, some became incredibly wealthy, companies they founded thriving to this day as multinational corporations based in Hong Kong.

In 1828, the Viceroy of Canton had issued a proclamation denouncing the smoking of opium and ordering the rigorous enforcement of the law. The results were that opium continued to be smoked and smuggled but the trade spread out along the China coast where receiving ships were anchored at places like Namoa. Here, the usual corruption assured trade away from the prying eyes of viceregal spies.

Sending vessels along the coast was risky. The waters were uncharted and, in places, local officials were zealous in their application of the law: but, worse, every vessel ran the chance of piracy. A clipper was worth capturing for any pirate knew it was sure to be laden with opium and silver bullion or coin, the currency of the opium trade. For a clipper captain, it was never easy telling which Chinese craft were innocent and which manned by pirates: frequently, as was the case on the China coast, junks were both, the fishermen ready to turn to piracy if the opportunity arose. In general, of course, a clipper was safe because of her manoeuvrability and speed but if the wind dropped she was in real danger for many junks could be rowed.

Apart from these obvious hazards, opium runners were faced with having to do business without the convenience of a bilingual *compradore*. Some enterprising local Chinese officials learnt pidgin English whilst some traders employed multilingual expatriates to act on their behalf: as any Chinese found teaching his mother tongue to a foreigner was sentenced to death, competent linguists were rare and valuable. Jardine Matheson relied upon a Prussian missionary, Dr Karl Gutzlaff, whom Jardine had taken on a trading trip in 1832 1600 miles up the China coast.

A one-time corset-maker and the widower of an English heiress he had married in Malacca in 1829, Gutzlaff had a home in Macau where his second English wife ran a school for blind children. From here, he travelled widely, dispensing medicines and handing out tracts: his medical prowess was described as 'of the most moderate character.' During his journeys, he acquired a command of Chinese etiquette and a number of dialects: this was very important not just in communicating but also in knowing when, who and how much to bribe. An account of Gutzlaff's contribution to the opium trade was drawn from Jardine Matheson archives by the Far Eastern scholar, Maurice Collis:

> At Chinchow Bay six mandarin junks anchored close by after sunset in such a way as to suggest that the officials on board intended to prevent dealers from coming to buy. Captain McKay, who was in command of the *John Biggar*, asked Gutzlaff to row over and tell them to go away. In a letter to the firm McKay describes what happened: 'Doctor Gutzlaff, dressed in his best, which on such occasions is his custom, paid them a visit accompanied by two boats made to appear somewhat imposing. He demanded their instant departure and threatened them with destruction if they ever again anchored in our neighbourhood. They went away immediately, saying they had anchored there in the dark by mistake, and we have seen nothing more of them.' It was disclosed afterwards that the officials, though really willing enough, had not dared connive at the smuggling because the *John Biggar* was lying out in the roadstead in full view of the town. A mandarin had always to reckon on the danger of rivals or enemies reporting him if he openly flouted the law. Such a report might not mean punishment, but certainly entailed a heavy bribe to escape it.

Gutzlaff paved the way for a Jardine Matheson-led syndicate to acquire the opium trading rights to Chinchow by buying off the local mandarins with $20,000 per annum tea money.

In exchange for Gutzlaff's assistance, Jardine Matheson donated to his missionary work which included printing prayer books and selling patent medicines, some of which contained opium. It seems Gutzlaff had no conscience about opium: it was part and parcel of spreading the Word of God. Other missionaries were also connected to the traders. Robert Morrison, the first Protestant missionary to China, had became official translator to the East India Company in 1809: his Chinese dictionary was printed by the company.

There were other priests who took a different view. As early as 1838, an English clergyman denounced the fact that millions of Chinese were being brutalised by the drug. They were not alone: the East India Company was still brutalising large numbers of Indians despite attempts to control opium in Bengal. In 1840, a Mr Sym, manager for the Company opium agency at Gorakhpor, wrote: 'The health and morals of the people suffer from the production of opium. Wherever opium is grown it is eaten, and the more it is grown, the more it is eaten.'

James Matheson responded to critics who argued against opium on moral grounds by stating: 'We have every respect for persons entertaining strict religious principles, but we fear that very godly people are not suited for the drug trade.' This does not say much for his opinion of Herr Gutzlaff.

As the opium trade was conducted in part to facilitate the tea trade, the East India Company was always searching for ways in which it might grow its own tea and, in the early 1820s, the search discovered wild tea growing in Assam, in north-eastern India. A side-business sprang up, shipping indented labourers on clippers returning to India to work on plantations there. These poor wretches were promised a fixed wage, but rarely collected it. A quarter died in transit, the rest succumbing to diseases to which they had no immunity. A third of the work force died every six months.

It was little wonder that, by the mid-1830s, humane observers were letting it be known what the tea and opium trades were doing to native Chinese. This understandably enraged the Emperor.

It was not the only bone of contention between the mostly British foreigners and the Chinese. The former resented sailors being tried in Chinese courts for unruly conduct ashore. The Chinese authorities resented the opium trade and the arrogance of foreign traders whom they saw lacking in humility and gratitude and who smuggled poisons into the empire. These differences were irreconcilable.

In the India Act of 1833, the East India Company's trading monopoly rights in China were annulled. Within a year the British government realised something had to be done to safeguard opium, without which the economy of India would be in dire straits, though the trade was still not admitted to nor even mentioned.

When the East India Company withdrew from Canton in 1834, it left a vacuum in the expatriate community, for senior company officers had provided leadership and a focus for the foreigners. The merchants required a regulatory authority so the British government appointed three Superintendents of Trade in China to oversee British business, with Lord William Napier, a career sailor, selected as Chief Superintendent.

Napier arrived with ill-defined instructions as to how to deal with opium. From the moment he disembarked in Canton, he set off on the wrong foot by presenting his credentials direct to the viceroy rather than going through the Chinese merchants. The viceroy refused Napier's credentials, telling the Co-Hong merchants to get rid of him. At the affront, trade was halted and the factories besieged. Napier sent a signal to two Royal Naval frigates at anchor not far from Lintin Island to sail for Canton but after an exchange of fire with the Bogue forts, which defended the river mouth, a blockade of fire boats kept them out of the city approaches. Napier, who had fallen seriously ill, was obliged to ask permission to retreat to Macau. After this was granted, he went to the Portuguese enclave, complained about the ringing of the church bells (which the Portuguese considerately silenced) then died.

The other Superintendents of Trade, realising Chinese opposition towards foreign merchants and opium was increasing, sent memoranda to London warning that the Chinese edicts on opium should be heeded if a confrontation was to be avoided. One of the Superintendents, Sir George Robinson, resided on Lintin Island specifically to observe opium smuggling. His blunt reports were uncompromising:

> Whenever H.M. Government direct us to prevent British vessels from engaging in the traffic, we can enforce any order to that effect, but a more certain method would be to prohibit the growth of the poppy, and manufacture of opium in British India.

However, Parliament and the British Foreign Secretary, Lord Palmerston, still refusing to acknowledge openly the opium trade, disapproved of Robinson's forthrightness and dismissed him. His successor was to change the course of British history in China. He was Captain Charles Elliot, RN, formerly captain of a hospital ship, Protector of Slaves in British Guiana and Captain Attendant to Lord Napier, being in the cutter *Louisa* at the attack on the Bogue forts, prominently seated in the stern under a sun umbrella, observing the fighting and impervious to the crash of gunfire all around him.

Elliot was, from the beginning, in an impossible situation. The Chinese held him responsible for the opium trade and its results but his instructions from London were to control only lawful trade with China – which opium was not. He was bound to protect and represent the interests of the British merchants but the Chinese interpreted this as safeguarding opium smugglers. Aware of the delicate situation and the position it put him in, Elliot knew matters could only worsen and he attempted to force the British government to act on the opium trade. They did not and, by 1838, Chinese forbearance was all but spent.

The merchants themselves exacerbated the situation. They were growing tired of regulation and wanted to open Chinese eyes to the realities of international trade. A consensus of opinion was that a threat of war might do the trick. Partly to annoy the Chinese and partly to flex their muscles, some traders bypassed Lintin Island and shipped direct to Canton. This flouting of the rules was inflammatory, to say the least. The Viceroy of Canton, Teng Ting-chen, and the Governor of Canton stood to lose a substantial sum in tea money and direct investment: the former owned a fleet of opium-transporting junks, but they had to act to support the regulations for they had too many enemies ready to report any dilatory behaviour to the Emperor.

The action the Viceroy took was short and to the point: he ordered nine leading British opium dealers to leave China. They did not. He made no attempt to force them out but still he had to show his enemies he meant business. In December 1838, a boatload of coolies was arrested as they brought opium ashore from a British ship off Whampoa. The Governor admonished the British, adding he would be benevolent and avoid an investigation. The coolies were the scapegoats, being publicly executed by strangulation.

Another public execution in the American and British Gardens shortly afterwards caused further conflict. As the foreigners were forbidden entry to the city or the rural hinterland, the gardens were the only open space where merchants, their staff and sailors from visiting ships could take the air.

A mandarin entered the gardens accompanied by his retinue and a prisoner in chains. Attendants commenced erecting a wooden cross. William C. Hunter, an American partner in the firm of Russell & Co., who was the only available foreigner fluent in Cantonese, approached the mandarin to protest that the merchants' park was being used as a place of execution. The mandarin replied it was still Chinese soil and the prisoner was an opium dealer. Clearly, the execution was intended as a veiled threat to the foreigners. A large crowd assembled. The execution was well under way when a band of drunk British seamen arrived and, demanding fair play, felled the cross, smashed the mandarin's table and palanquin and tried to free the prisoner. The mandarin and his entourage retreated with the prisoner who was executed elsewhere.

Anti-foreign hostility was aroused by the routing of the mandarin. The mob swelled to 10,000. Factory doors were stormed and windows smashed. Hunter and another American merchant called Nye ran along the roof of the American factory and reached Howqua's office. As the most senior of the cartel merchants, Howqua contacted the chief magistrate and Chinese soldiers restored order. Yet the damage was done. The foreigners had exceeded the mark and tension gradually grew.

On 26 February 1839, to save face after this debacle, another alleged opium dealer was strangled in front of the American factory at a time of day when most foreigners were out taking exercise or sailing on the river. The execution was over in a few minutes, with little fuss, the body whisked away immediately afterwards: but the Chinese point was made.

In the months after the riot, Elliot received no guidance from London. He was left to rely upon his own assessment of the situation and do the best he could with it. He attempted to mediate and smooth things over but it was only a lull before the storm.

Imperial civil servants in Peking were increasingly concerned about opium and the ineffectuality of the edicts. In 1836, opium had been at the centre of heated discussion from which appeared the concept of legalising importation and taxing opium. Others argued that legalisation would spread the habit. The general consensus was that opium smoking had to be curbed because it was undermining the morality and health of the nation: worse, the exchequer was losing huge quantities of silver which were being exported, the currency being based on silver. The drain on the silver reserve was massive. In 1793, it contained 70 million taels of silver (approximately 2.6 million kilograms, one tael equalling about 37.5 grams), but by 1820 this was reduced to about 10 million taels. The Chinese also regarded opium as an agent of foreign aggression, debasing Confucian ethics and encouraging selfish idleness.

It was estimated 1 per cent of the population was addicted, usually men between the ages of twenty and fifty-five. This sounds minuscule, but amounted to four million people: C. Toogood Downing reckoned the amount of opium imported in 1836 would cater for more than twelve million addicts. In the coastal Kwangtung and Fukien provinces, where smuggling occurred and contact with foreigners was possible, 90 per cent of the adult population was habituated. Foreign travellers and missionaries recorded opium shops and divans to be as frequent as gin shops in London. Opium use was widespread amongst Imperial civil servants who, by dint of their jobs, had sufficient leisure time to indulge in it: they were corrupted by it too, often engaged actively in its smuggling and retailing.

The Chinese government was caught in a cleft stick. They could not eradicate smuggling for they had no operational navy and a huge coastline. Their officials were rotten to the core. British interests in India relied heavily upon opium revenues. International trade regarded it as a staple commodity. Too many people had too many vested interests. Even the emperors were hamstrung: when Emperor Tao Kwong was asked to legalise opium, he said: 'It is true, I cannot prevent the introduction of the flowing poison; gain-seeking and corrupt men will for profit and sensuality, defeat my wishes; but nothing will induce me to derive a revenue from the vice and misery of my people.' He had a personal as well as a moral interest in banning opium: three of his sons were addicts and were killed by the drug. He died, it is said, of a broken heart.

It looked like, even as late as 1838, the Chinese would not act and opium would maintain its status quo. The merchants in Canton believed nothing would happen and the edicts and laws were, in James Matheson's own words, 'so much waste paper.'

Yet times were changing. Early in 1839, the Emperor appointed a special commissioner, Lin Tsê-hsü, commanding him to eradicate the opium trade.

Lin was born in Foochow in 1785. A very intelligent and learned man, he graduated from the University of Peking in 1811. He was a career civil servant with a good record of service: he was also almost unique in that he was a resolute and competent administrator, a just and fair applicator of the law and – most amazingly, bearing in mind his peers – incorruptible. What was more, he had successfully closed down the opium trade elsewhere in China, particularly in his own province of Hunan.

Convincing the Emperor he could clean things up, Lin made an explosive proposal. All smugglers, foreign or Chinese, were to be treated the same under Chinese law. The Emperor agreed and sent Lin to Canton as high commissioner, with plenipotentiary powers and supreme command of Chinese forces in the city. He was specifically briefed to 'investigate port affairs', a euphemism for looking into foreign trading and the opium business in particular: it is rumoured the Viceroy fainted and remained unconscious for an hour on receiving the news.

A realist, Lin knew he was not only taking on foreign merchants but also his own countrymen: viceregal authorities would be obstructive, the Chinese navy's loyalty doubtful and the Hong traders uncooperative.

The Chinese found it inconceivable that the opium trade was conducted with the knowledge of the British monarch and in 1830, before relations had begun to break down, the then Governor-General of Kwangtung and Kwangsi provinces had advised that the best way to stop importation was to appeal to the leaders of the foreign merchants' nations. Lin, who wrote that the British 'are ruled at present by a young girl. But I am told that it is she who issues commands, and on the whole it seems that it would be best to start by sending instructions to her,' was to send a long and closely argued letter against the opium trade to Queen Victoria.

William C. Hunter, who was asked to translate the letter back into Chinese from English to make sure it conveyed the sense of the original draft, states in his memoir *The 'Fan Kwae' at Canton*, published in 1882: 'The document was a most extraordinary one. Prominent is the bombastic style, the outcome of ages of dominion, ignorance of Western official forms through an absence of diplomatic intercourse.'

The letter was delivered to Captain Warner, master of the *Thomas Coutts*: however, what happened to it is unknown. The *Thomas Coutts* reached London, but the letter never reached Queen Victoria. A charitable explanation is that Warner transferred it to a mail-packet using the Suez overland route on which mail robbery was rife. Another opinion has Lord Palmerston holding it back.

Palmerston was of the opinion the opium trade was a Chinese problem and they should counteract it by controlling consumption: besides, he also argued that to stop it would bankrupt India. On the other hand, Lin contended the sale of opium was inhumane and offended conscience. Had his attitude been aired in Britain, he would have had a number of supporters amongst the humanitarian movement and those who would have seen, in the long run, that Britain's reputation would suffer.

With more powers than the Viceroy and the Governor, Lin arrived in Canton in March 1839. He demanded the arrest of the most infamous opium offenders and ordered all opium commerce to halt forthwith, simultaneously demanding all existing stocks be surrendered within three days with every merchant – foreign and Chinese – signing a bond to guarantee a cessation in opium importation. Foreign merchants were reminded they were permitted to stay only as a courtesy. The Hong merchants were criticised for their close relationship with the foreigners, the threat made to execute a few to teach the rest a lesson, based upon their proven collusion.

At first, the foreigner traders and especially the British assumed this outburst was like all the others, a storm which would pass. They also considered themselves outside the reach of Chinese civil law and therefore safe from arrest or prosecution. They were wrong.

Lin then prohibited the foreigners from leaving for Macau. Chinese troops were mustered and armed junks patrolled the river. The merchants rejoined by saying they required more time to gather up the opium stocks.

Fully aware of their part in the opium business, Lin again threatened the Hong merchants who approached the foreign traders: 1037 chests were collected and handed over in the hope this might placate Lin. It did not. The next day, a Saturday, Howqua and his grandson, Mowqua, the most important Hong merchants, were paraded in chains. John Dent, one of the sons of William

Dent, the founder of Dent & Co., the second largest trading firm, was instructed to visit Lin, who said if Dent was not in his office by 10 o'clock on Monday morning, 25 March, he would be taken there under guard.

On the Sunday, Elliot arrived. Staying in Macau, he had received news of developments and acted swiftly. All British vessels were gathered to the north-west of the island of Hong Kong and put under the charge of the only Royal Navy warship in the region, the eighteen-gun sloop HMS *Larne*.

Lin permitted Elliot entry to the factories then strengthened his blockade, withdrew all Chinese servants and employees and cut off food supplies. The foreigners – with Elliot – were besieged. No one would starve: the factories were well stocked and, besides, the Hong merchants risked sneaking food in at night. However Elliot, acting without consultation with London, decided the British merchants had to comply with Lin's demands and, in May, they handed over their entire stock of 20,283 chests of opium, Elliot undertaking as the Crown's representative that they would be indemnified against loss. He had no power over the merchants of other nationalities but suggested they followed suit.

Much to Elliot's surprise, the merchants complied. Privately, they were more than pleased for they had imported so much back stock of opium they were having a hard time selling it. The price had dropped to an all-time low by February 1838, a chest of Patna opium bottoming at $450. Now they had a buyer in the government. The value of the stock was in excess of £2 million.

Lin was also surprised and pleased. Elliot had not sought to strike a bargain but simply acted. The Hong merchants were appalled: they knew the matter could have been settled with the surrender of less than half the whole stock. Matheson recorded their comments to his partner Jardine in Britain: 'What for he pay so large? No wantee so much. Six, seven thousand so would be enough.'

It is sometimes stated the Chinese confiscated the opium. This is untrue. It was volunteered by Elliot but he had acted alone, in the name of the British government but without their agreement, which would have been difficult to obtain. Letters took months to reach London and he had to act as a matter of urgency. There was no time for the niceties of domestic British political consideration.

Elliot was not unlike Lin. He was a conscientious, courageous and, above all, honest and sincere man of principle. A career sailor, he was personally against the opium trade which he regarded as evil and a disgraceful stain on British character. In a report to London he described it as 'discreditable to the character of the Christian nations under whose flag it is carried on.'

Lin's success posed a problem: how to dispose of so much opium? He could not send it to Peking for it would have been stolen *en route* and he could not burn it because the residue left over could still be pilfered and smoked. Instead, he decided to dissolve it. At Chen k'ou, near the present-day town of Tai Peng, 20 miles south-east of Canton, a huge bamboo stockade was erected in which stone- and wood-lined trenches 150 feet long, 75 feet wide and 7 feet deep were dug and filled with water. The 500 coolies employed for the task were made to work in the barest minimum of clothing and were strip-searched at the end of each work shift.

The opium was floated in the trenches to which salt and lime were added. Coolies stirred the brew with poles. When the opium was rotted, it was allowed to flow down gullies into the river. Lin wrote to his emperor:

> The inhabitants of the coastal region are coming in throngs to witness the destruction of the opium. They are, of course, only allowed to look on from outside the fence and are not permitted access to the actual place of destruction, for fear of pilfering. The foreigners passing by in boats on their way up to Canton and down to Macao all get a distant view of the proceedings, but do not dare show any disrespect, and indeed I should judge from their attitudes that they have the decency to feel heartily ashamed.

However, two foreigners were permitted to witness the destruction. Both Americans, one was C.W. King of Olyphant & Co., which had never dealt in opium, the other Elijah Bridgman, the first American missionary in China. Whilst attending the stockade, they observed a coolie being beheaded on the spot for being found in possession of a small amount of opium. Afterwards, King was called to an audience with Lin who asked him who was the most straightforward of the foreign merchants to which question King, a devout Quaker, was unsure, much to Lin's amusement. King then warned Lin the British were going to bring steam-powered gunboats to China, which clearly worried him: Lin was aware of British technological supremacy.

Lin was pleased with his opium-destroying success. He removed the blockade of the factories, let trade in legitimate goods recommence and allowed merchants to join their families at Macau: but in doing so, he made a grave miscalculation. He had the foreign merchants over a barrel and could have bargained for an end to opium smuggling. Yet he did not.

Whilst they handed over their opium, the merchants refused point-blank to sign any bond. Elliot, conscious this meant matters were only partly resolved, advised them all to withdraw to Macau. Indeed, he ordered the British merchants to go. Everyone left, save two dozen Americans who continued everyone else's business on a commission basis.

Lin had also made another serious error. He did not reckon with either the power of the market-place or that of addiction for, by removing an entire year's opium supply, he pushed up the speculative price on the next year's harvest to previously unknown heights. Additionally, addicts were desperate for supplies and the price of opium soared.

Despite his missed opportunities, it seems Lin became obsessed with the idea that he had to build on his success and gain further control over the foreigners. In June 1839, he thought he saw his chance.

A number of British sailors rowed ashore to the village of Chien Sha Tsin (now Tsim Sha Tsui) on the Kowloon peninsula opposite Hong Kong. They visited a Chinese inn, became drunk, demolished a small temple, then killed a Chinese peasant, Lin Wei-hsi, in a brawl.

Lin demanded a British sailor, Thomas Tidder, be charged with murder under Chinese law, in a Chinese court. Elliot, who compensated the dead man's family according to tradition, tried and punished the brawlers himself but could not prove who had actually committed the murder. Lin was not to be put off: he wanted a British life for a Chinese one. This was what the Manchu Penal Code laid down. Elliot refused to comply. Lin interpreted this refusal as defiance against the Emperor and issued a proclamation to the 'savages of the further seas', ordering them to repent their sins by submitting to the Celestial Empire or suffer the consequence. In August, he ceased all trade, besieged the Canton factories again and went with a military force towards Macau where all the British merchants were staying with their families.

As a safeguard, Elliot ordered the British residents on board the merchant ships lying off Hong Kong. Lin forbade local villagers to provision the vessels and ordered any foreigner found ashore to be shot on sight. To such a provocation, war seemed inevitable.

In the first week of September 1839, the predominantly British merchant fleet, anchored in what is today Hong Kong's western harbour, was blockaded by war junks. Elliot sent an emissary ashore: his emissary was Gutzlaff, who had written the letters he was carrying. One demanded the mandarins lift their threat, the other asked local villages not to poison the wells from which the British ships drew their water. The mandarins refused. At 2 p.m., Elliot sent an ultimatum which was ignored. Just before 3 p.m., the British opened fire on a junk. The skirmish, known as the Battle of Kowloon, was the first action in what *The Times* was to call, on 25 April 1840, the Opium War.

The British ships did not succeed in lifting the blockade but, on 3 November, two British frigates opened fire upon a fleet of war junks in the Battle of Chuenpi. The junks were routed, European supremacy was established and the war got going in earnest.

Throughout the war, Gutzlaff continued to play an important role. Exceedingly familiar with many Chinese – his Chinese name was Kuo Shih-li – he was a major spy for the Europeans. With the help of a Chinese pimp, Yu Te-ch'ang, he enlisted over forty spies who obtained Chinese maps and reported on troop movements: eventually arrested, Yu shopped all of them. Through another spy, Chen Ping-chun, Gutzlaff acquired vital naval intelligence: Chen was also caught and executed. After the war, Gutzlaff served as Chinese Secretary to the Hong Kong authorities then, in 1849, returned to Europe where he lectured extravagantly on his success at converting the heathen masses through a band of acolytes. Another missionary, smelling a rat, investigated him. It was discovered the acolytes were not Christians: a large number were opium smokers and several had criminal records. Most of them had never left Hong Kong. Gutzlaff, distraught at the disclosures, died in August 1851 of dropsy.

In retrospect, one of the most important facets of the war occurred in January 1841 when Elliot sent five warships to attack the Bogue forts. The forts were captured and Elliot signed the

Convention of Chuenpi, a treaty of his own devising which he hoped might end hostilities. Conscious the British needed a land base from which to regroup, Elliot demanded he be granted possession of the island of Hong Kong. His demand was met but again he had acted without permission from London. When Palmerston received news of the latest British possession, he was annoyed Elliot had not pressed for more far-reaching concessions.

With hindsight, the war was little more than a series of skirmishes, British occupation of various towns and insignificant naval clashes. The Chinese methods of warfare were outdated and they were usually defeated. The British suffered comparatively few losses from gunfire: most of the casualties in the 10,000-strong force which arrived from Ceylon in April 1840 died of malaria and, ironically, dysentery which could have been cured with opium.

The fighting was spasmodic. Neither the legitimate nor opium trades were halted by the war although they were inconvenienced. Several truces came into force but were broken. Through the early months of 1840, letters passed between Lin and Elliot containing proposals about shipping, trade and opium, with Lin still keen to settle the murder of Lin Wei-hsi.

The war, over which neither London nor Peking had any direct control, sputtered on until August 1842 when, with Shanghai taken, the Royal Navy sailed up the Yangtze River (closely followed by vessels carrying opium) and reached Nanking. There, aboard HMS *Cornwallis*, the Treaty of Nanking was signed. Known with some justification by the Chinese as the 'Unequal Treaty', it ended the war.

The treaty opened up China as never before. Canton, Amoy, Foochow, Ningpo and Shanghai were termed 'Treaty Ports' and became centres for foreign trade. An indemnity of 21 million silver dollars was imposed to cover, among other things, the opium destroyed by Lin and Hong Kong was ceded in perpetuity to Britain. The Hong merchants in Canton lost their monopoly, fixed tariffs being set for all imports from Britain. Opium was hardly mentioned in any of the negotiations, nor in the peace terms: the only reference to it was oblique – 'it is to be hoped [that the] system of smuggling which has heretofore been carried on between English and Chinese merchants (in many cases with open connivance of Chinese custom-houses officials) will entirely cease.' By this omission, the treaty allowed for the continuance of the opium trade.

The primary reason why opium was not touched upon in the Treaty of Nanking was because, by mentioning it, the British government would have had to plan a future policy for the trade and they preferred China to do this instead by legalising it. Both Sir Henry Pottinger, by now the Chief Superintendent of Trade and his successor, Sir John Davis, tried to force the Chinese hand but failed. Smuggling continued.

Opium imports rose sharply. Criticism of the trade increased in the British Parliament. The future seventh Earl of Shaftesbury spoke for many when he stated in 1843, 'I am fully convinced that for this country to encourage this nefarious traffic is bad, perhaps worse than encouraging the slave trade.' Yet nothing altered. Colonial policy was untouched and the Indian economy was preserved.

It was considered with hindsight that the war had been inevitable. Opium was merely one of the pretexts. The British considered the issues were more fundamental and involved forcing China to open up to world trade, although Sir George Staunton, an authority on Sino-British relations, declared in Parliament, 'I never denied the fact, that if there had been no opium smuggling, there would have been no war.' From the Chinese viewpoint, however, opium was the principal cause.

For many in London, the Chinese opinion was valid. Dr Thomas Arnold condemned it as 'so wicked as to be a national sin of the greatest possible magnitude' whilst Gladstone denounced it with the words, 'a war more unjust in its origin, a war more calculated to cover this country with permanent disgrace, I do not know and I have not read of.'

Two political casualties of the war were Elliot and Lin who, in their own ways, were joined in a fight against opium. Lin was dismissed in late 1840: Elliot lasted until Pottinger was appointed in his place in August 1841.

They both made mistakes. Elliot demanded less from the Chinese than his government had instructed, whilst acting on his own initiative, and Lin failed, through no fault of his own, because the mission he had been sent upon was impossible. They were both naïve, too honourable for the dirty business into which they became embroiled, and they had such forces massed against them – the military power of the British, the corruption of the Chinese government and the devious immorality of the opium dealers.

Lin finally left Canton on 3 May 1841, exiled to Turkestan.

Throughout the war, his Emperor blamed him and the Chinese military leaders for the failure to drive the barbarians out. It was not their fault: they were fighting superior, experienced soldiers and politicians. Yet Lin was humbled. He had caused the Emperor to lose face. As for Charles Elliot, he was appointed British chargé d'affaires to the newly constituted Republic of Texas, a British diplomatic posting equivalent at the time to Turkestan. Despite Queen Victoria's opinion of him as a man 'who completely disobeyed his instructions and tried to get the lowest terms he could', Elliot went on to become governor of Bermuda, Trinidad and St Helena and, when he died in 1875, he was an admiral with a knighthood. Yet to this day, no mention is made of his part in founding Hong Kong: the British *Dictionary of National Biography* ignores the fact completely.

International relations between Britain and China remained unstable. The Opium War might have been over but it settled nothing.

With the increased amenities offered by the five treaty ports and the new colony of Hong Kong smuggling continued, expanding dramatically. The losers were China, which did not rid itself of either opium or foreigners and Britain whose international standing was reduced by the iniquities of the war.

In short, opium was not only the cause of the first Anglo-Chinese conflict but also the winner.

8

The Government of Opium

Without opium, Hong Kong would not have evolved. Not only was it originally obtained as a result of a skirmish over opium but its initial fortunes were linked irrevocably to the trade. Within a year of being established, it had become the main opium trading centre on the China coast. The receiving ships of Lintin Island were superseded by well-built storehouses in Hong Kong.

Not only the British moved to the embryonic colony. So too did other nationalities, especially Americans and non-Europeans such as Parsees. By the mid-1840s, about 100 foreign businesses were competing with each other along the Chinese seaboard. The British free-trade policy and colonial political climate were ideal, providing a stability the merchants had not had in Canton and were unable to find not only in China but also in Siam, Japan, Formosa, Vietnam and the Philippines. Needless to say, under British rule of law, a lack of Imperial Chinese regulations – not to mention an absence of corrupt officials – enabled not only general traders to thrive: so did opium merchants who were free to get on with their work. Opium dealing was the colony's main business alongside tea and the smuggling of salt which was an imperial monopoly.

Around the opium trade was built a substantial Hong Kong shipping business. Vessels were made in the colony as well as serviced and provisioned and crewed by Chinese sailors. Local businessmen founded banks which acted as bill-brokerage firms and insurance agents. Ships' chandlers arrived. A local currency was established, based upon South American silver dollars, especially the Mexican dollar. Within five years, the northern coast of Hong Kong island was lined with impressive European trading houses whilst the mountain behind was being encroached upon by private homes, a burgeoning native quarter, military barracks and the trappings of colonial administration. The slow development of the treaty ports and their non-colonial status aided in the colony's rapid growth.

As a result of the Treaty of Nanking, China was increasingly opened up to foreign cultural and economic incursions. Close to the treaty ports, Western fashions started to creep in. The Chinese merchant élite began to mix with foreigners, especially at the racecourse: the Chinese being inveterate gamblers, horse-racing was quick to catch on wherever Europeans set up race clubs. Yet, despite such social minglings, the Chinese were generally cautious of doing business with foreigners, and the British in particular. They were also far less inclined to import from Britain as the traders had hoped. Only those merchants whose commerce was based upon opium prospered, trading in which continued into the twentieth century.

Indeed, opium controlled not only its millions of addicts but it also orchestrated British expansion into China, other nations quickly following the vanguard. The British government relied upon the opium traders for political and economic intelligence whilst the traders added their own interpretations of what they gleaned and saw, and even suggested policy. When the government required, the merchants provided ships, experienced coastal pilots, cartographical data and effected introductions. In short, the traders who operated a business for which their government still refused any responsibility were *de facto* spies and surreptitious diplomats.

The official British attitude towards the opium trade was to ignore it. In a dispatch to London in January 1843, Sir Henry Pottinger, the first Governor of Hong Kong, whilst simultaneously Superintendent of Trade, expressed the situation bluntly:

> HM Government have not the power to put a stop to this trade . . . but they may perhaps impede it to some degree by preventing the Island of Hong Kong or its neighbouring waters from being used as the point from whence British smugglers shall depart on their illegal adventures.

Yet this was wishful thinking. The British government had banked on China legalising the trade after the Treaty of Nanking so it could be controlled through taxation, yet during treaty negotiations the Chinese had affirmed the emperor's prohibition was to remain. And, of course, the British had to keep on with opium dealing because India's economy was reliant upon it.

Knowing this, the British merchants ignored an attempt by Pottinger to control them. Matheson, one of the doyens of the merchant community, was forthright in his response: 'The plenipotentiary has published a most fiery proclamation against smuggling but I believe it is like the Chinese edicts, meaning nothing and only intended . . . for the gratification of the Saints in England.'

A suggestion was made to ban opium clippers from Hong Kong harbour, the finest – indeed, only – all-weather, non-silting natural harbour on the coast of China from Vietnam to Shanghai. The Foreign Office declared excluding opium vessels would merely shift the trade elsewhere: Pottinger subsequently reasserted the opinion that the Chinese were responsible for withdrawing their own people from trading in opium, ultimately concluding it was 'neither desirable nor necessary to exclude our opium trading ships from Hong Kong harbour.'

Aware now the trade was to be neither hindered nor legalised, the traders set up camp. Jardine Matheson anchored a receiving vessel, the *Bomanjee Hormusjee*, in the harbour, from which opium was sold straight to Chinese craft. With other traders, they erected substantial godowns on shore. It was only months before Hong Kong became a more stable version of Lintin Island. By 1844, the situation prompted the new governor, Sir John Davis, to report 'almost every person possessed of capital who is not connected with government is employed in the opium trade.'

It was boom time. Profits from opium soared as the Chinese authorities virtually gave up trying to stem the flood of imports. In 1845, eighty vessels based in Hong Kong were running opium, nineteen of them owned by Jardine Matheson which also maintained fourteen receiving ships along the coast of China. One, moored at Woosung, close to Shanghai, sold opium up the Yangtze River, thus spreading the drug into the heartland of China.

By 1849, an average of 40,000 chests of opium were stored in Hong Kong and 75 per cent of India's opium was traded through the colony, to the tune of £6 million a year: against this, other trade consisted of £11.5 million of British-made goods and £1.5 million of other goods, mostly manufactured in India.

Clipper crews were the highest paid merchant seamen in the world, smartly uniformed and as disciplined as the Royal Navy. The speed of clippers, such as the Jardine Matheson ships *Mazeppa* and *Lanrick*, was such that the colonial authorities and the government used them as official mail carriers. This was not the only service provided by the opium traders: they also furnished banking facilities to British consuls, the receiving ships being safe deposit vessels such as at Ningpo where all the consulate's money came from a receiving ship owned by Dent, anchored 12 miles downriver from the town.

Opium was also retailed to local Chinese in Hong Kong. Within weeks of the Union Jack being raised on the island, the *Canton Register* predicted 'Hong Kong will be the resort and rendezvous of all the Chinese smugglers. Opium houses and gambling houses will soon spread; to those haunts will flock all the discontented and bad spirits of the empire.'

The assessment was correct for crime and vice soared. Brothels provided for the needs of sailors, military personnel and the hordes of lonely Chinese men who migrated to Hong Kong from the hinterland of Kwangtung province to seek their fortunes. Large numbers of opium dens or divans sprang up. Aware of the potential revenue, the governor set up a local monopoly by which the right to deal in opium in Hong Kong was sold annually to the highest bidder. The opium franchise was known as an opium 'farm', the noun deriving from the verb 'to farm', meaning to pass responsibility, the successful bidder for a farm monopoly agreeing to pay a certain annual amount by way of a licence, with whatever he could make on top of this being his profit. It proved impossible to enforce so the monopoly was dropped and, from 1847, a system of licensing dens was introduced with the stipulation that owners had to display their licences on the premises, could retail opium only for cash and were obliged to keep armed persons out.

Tension between Britain and China remained high, however. Humiliated by losing the conflict and still burdened by opium, the Chinese authorities deeply resented the foreign presence in their kingdom. Opium addiction was rapidly growing, the treaty ports became hives of corruption, crime burgeoned and imperial authority was increasingly undermined. This led to another problem. Piracy and banditry burgeoned.

In 1847, the receiving ships at anchor between Amoy and Foochow were all attacked, their crews massacred: then two opium vessels, the *Omega* and the *Caroline*, were boarded and the crews killed. Even the *Sylph*, Jardine Matheson's clipper, was taken in 1849. When the Chinese commander of the Bogue forts reprimanded local pirates in 1844, they kidnapped him, sliced off his ears, then ransomed him.

Some pirates sailed under British protection for a large number of the Chinese racketeers involved in opium based themselves in Hong Kong and gained British nationality. In addition, a colonial ordinance was instituted whereby a Hong Kong Chinese-owned vessel could be granted a British register, allowing it to fly the British flag and come under the same protection as a British-owned vessel. This meant a fair number of China coastal pirates sailed under the British flag.

Not only Chinese pirates preyed on shipping. In 1845, an English pirate named Henry Sinclair was sentenced in Hong Kong to transportation for life but the most infamous was an American, Eli Boggs. He operated – as did Sinclair – throughout the South China Sea. Boggs commanded a fleet of thirty war-cum-fighting junks crewed by Chinese. He attacked numerous vessels before being caught by the Royal Navy in 1857. His actual murdering of captured crews not being able to be proven, he was sentenced to Victoria prison in Hong Kong.

Of the many Chinese pirates who attacked opium clippers or general cargo vessels, the most notorious were Chui A-pou and Shap Ng-tsai. They raided the whole South China coast with substantial fleets of junks, taking any vessel they could or charging a toll on passing ships. Chui A-pou's fleet of junks, based in Bias (now Daya) Bay north-east of Hong Kong, was destroyed on the night of 1 October 1849 by HMS *Columbine* and HMS *Fury*. Within a fortnight, Shap Ng-tsai's fleet was cornered, 58 of his 64 junks being destroyed with 3150 men killed. Shap Ng-tsai escaped with 400 men and set up a pirate base on Hainan Island: he was subsequently persuaded to give up piracy and was made an Imperial naval civil servant.

The last major skirmish against pirates was the Battle of Hahlam Bay on 4 August 1855, when the USS *Powhattan* and HMS *Rattler* sank 10 junks and killed 800 pirates: this was a rare instance of the Royal Navy and the United States Navy joining forces to protect trade routes – especially those carrying opium. Thereafter, piracy was conducted by small bands who were more easily handled.

With such a volatile situation, it was certain to be only a matter of time before something happened. In October 1856, it did.

The *Arrow* was a Chinese-owned, Hong Kong-registered *lorcha*: a *lorcha* was a type of craft unique to the Far East, being a vessel with a Western-type hull but rigged with junk sails and frequently carrying Chinese-type superstructure – it may still be seen in Hong Kong waters, without the sails and powered by marine diesels. Although flying the British flag, she was attacked by armed Chinese junks, sequestered in Canton and charged with piracy. Crewed by Chinese, the *Arrow* was commanded by an Englishman. Theoretically, she should have been safe but for the fact her annually renewable certificate of registry had expired eleven days before. The captain and crew were returned unharmed to Hong Kong but their ship was impounded.

The British dismissed the expired registration as a minor administrative matter and requested the craft be restored: the Chinese authorities were adamant. After a series of failed negotiations and using the incident as an excuse to take on the Chinese who refused to revert certain parts of the Treaty of Nanking which the British required altered, a British naval force under the command of Admiral Seymour attacked the Bogue forts. In retaliation, the Canton factories were torched and the passengers on a steamboat, the *Thistle*, were massacred.

So began the second Sino-British conflict. Known as the Second Opium War or the *Arrow* War, the hostilities lasted from 1856 to 1860, the campaigns being far bloodier than in the previous opium war.

This time, however, the British were not alone. After the Battle of Fatshan Creek to the west of Canton, in June 1857, the French joined in in response to the murder of a French missionary. The Chinese militia was no match for the highly trained European forces and was beaten. During the war, in June 1858, the Treaty of Tientsin was signed. Opium was not specifically included in the treaty but it was made abundantly clear to the Chinese that, unless it was legalised, relations between the countries would remain fragile. Lord Elgin, who had been sent from London to negotiate a peace, was confidentially informed that opium was the most important matter to which he was to address himself.

Despite the Treaty of Tientsin, the war continued. Eventually, British troops marched into Peking, razing the Summer Palace and 200 other Imperial buildings to the ground. On 24 October 1860, Lord Elgin signed the Convention of Peking. Prince Kung, the equivalent of the Foreign Minister and brother of the Emperor Hsien feng, conceded to the British demands that new treaty ports be established, the Yangtze River be opened to trade and foreigners be given unhindered access to the Chinese interior. With such concessions and those of subsequent treaties, credit and transport systems developed, banks were founded or expanded, insurance and shipping companies burgeoned and blossomed. Hong Kong, as the hub of transport and commerce with China, flourished.

The most important of the Convention terms, however, was the placing of a tariff on the importation of opium which more or less legalised the trade.

The duty, identical to that placed upon ordinary goods under the Treaty of Nanking, was set at 30 taels (39.75 ounces) of silver per picul (approximately 133.5 pounds) of opium. It was much lower than the Chinese had requested: the British kept it down so as not to upset the Indian exporters and rock the Indian revenue boat. As Sir Rutherford Alcock, a British Ambassador to Peking, informed the British Parliament in 1871, 'we forced the Chinese Government to enter into a Treaty to allow their subjects to take opium.'

Ironically, the Convention allowed for missionaries as well as traders to enter China, the preaching of the gospels being legalised along with opium. Many missionaries did not approve of this and petitioned Queen Victoria to change the situation regarding the drug trade, but to no avail. Understandably, a good number of Chinese identified Western evangelism with the drug trade. Opium and morphine – which was sometimes erroneously employed by well-meaning missionary doctors to cure opium addiction – were frequently referred to as 'Jesus-Opium'. Such was the link between the Christians and opium that when Alcock left Peking in 1869, Prince Kung told him if he removed opium and missionaries from China, traders would be welcomed.

The Convention provided not only for an excise duty on opium but also led to the foreign administration of the Chinese Imperial

Maritime Customs which, under predominantly British control, developed into a highly effective organisation usually beyond the taint of corruption. Their efficiency produced a downturn in smuggling activity, although some running continued because even the low duty was considered worth avoiding. Smuggling, however, increased again after 1876 when, under the Chefoo Convention between Britain and China, the inland revenue on opium (known as *li kin*), was gathered along with the import duty. Amounting to a total of 110 taels per picul, it was considered well worth evading.

Not only immediate concessions were granted the foreigners. The Treaty of Tientsin had included a revision clause allowing a reassessment of the terms every decade and intended to give the British a chance to rewrite the rules without recourse to more gun-boat diplomacy. Yet this cut both ways and, in 1869, the Chinese Foreign Office sent an appeal to the British government. It read in part:

From Tsung-li-Yamen to Sir Alcock, July, 1869
. . . the Chinese merchant supplies your country with his goodly tea and silk, conferring thereby a benefit upon her; but the English merchant empoisons China with pestilent opium. Such conduct is unrighteous. Who can justify it? What wonder if officials and people say that England is wilfully working out China's ruin, and has no real friendly feeling for her? The wealth and generosity of England are spoken by all; she is anxious to prevent and anticipate all injury to her commercial interests. How is it, then, she can hesitate to remove an acknowledged evil? Indeed, it cannot be that England still holds to this evil business, earning the hatred of the officials and people of China, and making herself a reproach among the nations, because she would lose a little revenue were she to forfeit the cultivation of the poppy!
The writers hope that His Excellency will memorialise his Government to give orders in India and elsewhere to substitute the cultivation of cereals or cotton. Were both nations to rigorously prohibit the growth of the poppy, both the trade in and the consumption of opium might alike be put an end to. To do away with so great an evil would be a great virtue on England's part; she would strengthen friendly relations and make herself illustrious. How delightful to have so great an act transmitted to after ages!
This matter is injurious to commercial interest in no ordinary degree. If His Excellency the British Minister cannot, before it is

too late, arrange a plan for a joint prohibition, then no matter with what devotedness the writers may plead, they may be unable to cause the people to put aside ill-feeling, and so strengthen friendly relations as to place them for ever beyond fear of disturbance. Day and night, therefore, the writers give to this matter most earnest thought, and overpowering is the distress and anxiety it occasions them. Having thus presumed to unbosom themselves they would be honoured by His Excellency's reply.

This appeal was accompanied by a confidential memorandum from Sir Rutherford Alcock who pressed for it to be taken seriously. For months, the Chinese waited in anticipation of a response. None was ever forthcoming.

Alcock, who was personally dismayed by the evils of the opium trade, warned Parliament in 1871:

There is a very large and increasing cultivation of the poppy in China; the Chinese Government are seriously contemplating – if they cannot come to any terms or arrangement with the British Government . . . – the cultivation without stint in China, and producing opium at a much cheaper rate. Having done that they think they will afterwards be able to stamp out the opium produce among themselves.

Small quantities of opium from countries other than India were still arriving in China but it was the Chinese home product which started to hit at Indian profit margins. The trade in domestic opium was almost exclusively Chinese operated. Some had long been grown in China, especially in the western and south-western provinces, and by 1800 domestic production was greater than imported opium, despite the 1799 prohibition. In 1830, poppy farming had been recorded in the provinces of Chekiang, Fukien, Kwangtung and Yunnan whilst six years later, when the debate on legalisation was raging in Peking, a large imperial correspondence dealt with the domestic product. By the 1860s there was a considerable increase in poppy cultivation, much of it successfully hidden from the authorities.

There were those in China, as Alcock reported, who advocated an opium industry. This had so alarmed the Indian Board of Revenue an envoy was dispatched to China in 1868 to study the situation.

He reported Chinese opium, previously thought to be very inferior to Indian, to be now of much better quality and observed Chinese addicts mixing their native drug with only small quantities of Indian opium. This, he suggested, would lead to a taste in Chinese opium and he recommended his superiors 'send in future such increased quantities of opium to China, and at such low prices, as to prevent indigenous cultivation and competition.' Eventually, when the price of the Chinese opium dropped well below that of imports, many of the British traders were not only worried but also indignant, arrogantly believing the Chinese did not have the right to compete with them.

The majority of Chinese were concerned by the growth of their national opium industry which increased addiction and disrupted agriculture. Land which had previously been put over to food production was lost to poppies: in some districts, food shortages occurred and even starvation was reported. The problem was that more money could be earned from poppies than from wheat or rice: furthermore, the poppies were hardy and not prone to disease.

In 1870 the Censor, Yew Peh-ch'uan, warned against poppy farming, declaring opium was the greatest national danger to food production. His estimate was that 10,000 *mow* (approximately 17,000 acres) were dedicated to poppy cultivation at any one time. The situation markedly deteriorated, as was mentioned in an article in *The Times* of December 1888:

> By 1887 the relations between the Chinese and the Indian drug are found to have altogether changed ... In all parts of the Empire, except the islands of Formosa and Hainan, it is said to be produced in substantial quantities. It is estimated that a third of [Yunnanese] cultivation is devoted to poppy fields [and] this huge stock of Chinese opium is raised for the supply of scores of millions who never smoked before. Si-chuen [Szechuan province], for instance, contains 70,000,000 of inhabitants. Seven-tenths of the adult male population, it is computed, now are opium-smokers. Probably twenty-five years ago only a fraction had contracted the habit ...

The founder of the China Inland Mission and one of the first Englishmen to travel deep into the Chinese interior, Revd J. Hudson Taylor, commented in 1893: 'When I first reached China [in 1854] the opium habit was comparatively rare, but it has spread very rapidly during the last twenty years, still more rapidly during the last ten; it is frightfully prevalent now.' As he visited ten of the eighteen provinces of China, his comments are an even more terrible indictment of the opium trade.

Until 1890, Chinese poppy cultivation had been unofficial but that year the emperor revoked all the prohibition edicts and Chinese opium was legitimised. The move was not made because of a sudden official change of heart, an acceptance of opium, but as a means of quashing imports. It was a desperate act and it was to do more harm than good for it merely encouraged an even wider use of opium, making it harder than ever to eradicate in the long run.

Meanwhile Hong Kong prospered, remaining a more stable place in which to live than China: much of the nation was in turmoil with the Taiping Rebellion which raged between 1851 and 1864. Despite the risks from civil unrest in China, piracy, occasional typhoons and other natural disasters, substantial profits were made in Hong Kong. By 1892, the colony had a population of a quarter of a million, dealt with 40 per cent of China's trade and had an annual turnover exceeding £20 million.

Economic, religious and political refugees fled to the colony in ever increasing numbers, bringing their opium habit with them. By 1882 the sale of opium, which had gone back to being an annually renewed 'farm' monopoly in 1858, accounted for one-sixth of colonial revenue. The opium was provided by the farm concessionaire who sold it to divans or dens whilst, at the same time, collecting a tax from it. Smoking took place either in the divans or at home, the drug also being sold on a take-away basis.

As in China, opium crossed all the class barriers in Hong Kong Chinese society, from scholars and merchants to rickshaw pullers and coolies. The wealthy, who tended to smoke in the privacy of their homes, owned their own opium pipes which were expensive and often beautiful works of art fashioned from jade, ivory, tropical hardwoods, silver and even gold. Today, a genuine, top-quality antique pipe costs thousands of dollars for they are rare: when opium was finally banned completely, pipes were confiscated by, or surrendered to, the police and destroyed, creating *objets d'art*. Those who could not afford their own pipe and had no private place in which to indulge their habit frequented the divans or dens where they used pipes provided by operators.

The licensed opium divans, along with the beautiful Oriental whores who occupied the brothels, built an exotic reputation for Hong Kong but this apparent climate of vice was in fact still strictly controlled. To operate a divan, the proprietor had to prove to the chief police magistrate he was a fit and proper person who could furnish 'suitable accommodation for the use of customers, in order to prevent nuisances or offences to decency.' A divan was obliged by bye-laws to give on to a public thoroughfare and it had to keep to strict opening or licensing hours: the opening times were regulated as being from midday to ten o'clock on Monday to Saturday. In theory, divans were closed on Sundays out of deference to the Christian community. In fact, these restrictions were often ignored by both the authorities and the proprietors. It was impractical to restrict a man's craving to a rigid timetable.

For most of the nineteenth century, opium was smoked but, in 1893, a new phenomenon began to appear, as it had already done in the West – the injection of morphine solution with a hypodermic syringe.

In Hong Kong dens, just as was to happen later in opium shops and pharmacies in Shanghai, opium smokers or coolies buying pills for medicinal purposes were on occasion given a free morphine injection and told they could have another *ex gratia* shot with their next purchase of pills. Once hooked, of course, the injections were charged for, though they were up to a sixth cheaper than smoking.

While the hypodermic syringe was a convenient method of drug taking for European addicts, the syringe had a drawback in the East. With a native ignorance of hygiene, many syringes were rarely cleaned, needles were usually dirty and not disinfected between users and contaminated water was used to make the morphine solutions. The result was a widespread incidence of abscesses, blood poisoning and hepatitis.

The injections were not at first self-administered but given by Chinese doctors whose surgeries were little more than morphine dens. The Hong Kong government analyst, a Mr Crow, visited a doctor's surgery and wrote:

> I entered, and observed three men asleep on mats, and about twelve or fifteen standing in the verandah. Some had just had injections; the others were waiting their turn. There were numerous puncture

scars on their arms. The quantity used depended on the amount of opium the patients had been in the habit of smoking.

The holder of the opium monopoly at the time was the Hau Fook Company. The directors officially complained to the government, accusing the doctors of an unethical infringement of their monopoly. As the charge for an injection was so low – at 1 cent a shot – they were losing business. The police investigated the matter and discovered eighteen morphine surgeries but the government took no action until 1923 when it set up a dangerous drugs ordinance.

By 1880, opium imports were dropping. Chinese domestic production and sound commercial sense were the main cause, most of the merchant houses diversifying as China opened up to more general trade. Even Jardine Matheson had stopped dealing in opium in 1872. In the 1890s, the trade declined even further because of price rises in India and the improved strength of Chinese opium. Commercial commentators also reckoned, as China reduced her opium imports, she would have more income with which to import a general range of manufactured goods.

Yet there was another, uncommercial reason for giving up the lucrative trade: it was the increasingly vociferous criticism of opium back in Britain. The 'Saints', as Matheson had sarcastically called them, were blowing their trumpets and calling for justice. Humanitarian interests were merging with commercial selfishness.

Public opinion in Britain against opium had started to gain a voice in the 1870s, spurred on by the devastating effects of the trade in China and upon the native population of India which was such that, at times, the amount consumed in India exceeded the amount exported. It was proving impossible to prevent addiction in the country of manufacture where workers had started to pilfer from the godowns of Patna and Benares to feed an addiction either acquired by illicit eating or by absorption through the skin whilst handling huge quantities of the raw drug.

The move against opium was not restricted to British activists. In 1881, the government of Bombay prevented the government of India from promoting poppy cultivation in its domain on the grounds that it demoralised the work-force. They cited what had happened in the state of Gujarat where crime and corruption had soared after the introduction of poppy farming.

The opium trade had developed purely as a business founded on the basic commercial principles of supply and demand and ready profitability supported by the premise of if-we-don't-sell-it-somebody-else-will. Morality did not come into the equation and only slowly evolved over many decades. There were always a few enlightened observers or critics and, at the time of the opium wars, there were anti-opium organisations but they were short-lived and carried no influence.

For many years, the Earl of Shaftesbury was associated with anti-opium work. In 1843, as Lord Ashley, he had introduced a Parliamentary motion stating the opium trade and monopoly were 'utterly inconsistent with the honour and duties of a Christian kingdom'; fourteen years later, he raised the opium question in the House of Lords but to little avail. Others were equally condemnatory, even those who saw a good side to opium. A missionary, Revd James Johnstone, although accepting the opium trade had a beneficial side, admitted: 'I shall have to present such an array of dark facts on the other side that you shall pronounce the whole trade to be a foul blot on the fair name of England, as well as a curse to India, and a deadly wound in the heart of China.'

At last, by the 1870s, British public opinion was roused against the trade. Addressing a meeting in London in 1874, a Chinese speaker against opium, Ng-a-Choy, said:

> There cannot be, I think, two opinions about the desirability and necessity of abolishing the opium traffic, because of the pernicious effects produced by the use of opium. The whole nation of China has been demoralised by it. It is a proverb among us that of the four common vices, drunkenness, gambling, fornication and opium smoking, opium smoking is the worst.

A reform movement grew up to fight opium cultivation and trade in the British Empire but, from the start, the reformers knew they were up against the odds. This was poignantly outlined by Sir John Strachey who wrote 'Next to the land revenue, the most productive source of the public income [in India] is opium.' When it became realised, people were appalled to find 17 to 20 per cent of the gross national product of the Indian subcontinent was entirely due to the demoralisation of millions of Chinese.

In 1874, the Anglo-Oriental Society for the Suppression of the Opium Trade was founded in Britain with Shaftesbury as its president and, for a decade, it was extremely active. Its inspiration and funding derived from the Quakers. The man behind the Society was Joseph Grundy Alexander, a prominent Quaker and barrister of unimpeachable integrity. Determined and imperturbable, using a lawyer's dispassionate approach to argument, he was a formidable opponent whom even the opium traders viewed with respect. Appealing on moral and humanitarian grounds to liberal middle-class values, the Society gained a substantial following, also pressing the need for further domestic opium regulation beyond the remit of the 1868 Poisons and Pharmacy Act.

The society aimed at educating public opinion and applying parliamentary pressure to obtain political action. It extensively published anti-opium books, tracts and a magazine called *The Friend of China*, set up local offices throughout Britain, held public meetings, raised money, lobbied and petitioned the House of Commons. In 1882 alone, 489 petitions were presented to Parliament by the society.

These came to little. Every society member knew the only way to eradicate the opium trade was to fundamentally change the financial structure of India. In 1876, Lord Salisbury, then Secretary of State for India, informed an anti-opium delegation that there would be no extension of the opium trade in India but this was as far as the government was prepared to go. Pro-opium lobbyists had more political clout than the do-gooder disruptives.

Businessmen involved in the opium trade were naturally perturbed by the anti-opium movement but they had a powerful ally. The press supported them and government policy. For every 1000 words printed against opium, 5000 words in its favour were published in newspapers and periodicals.

The primary pretexts in favour of the trade were spurious and devious: opium-smoking, it was claimed, was not overtly injurious; the British government had not forced opium upon China, but merely met a demand; the Chinese authorities were insincere in professing the desire to stop opium smoking and the cultivation of opium poppies in China proved it. These facts were backed up by the if-we-don't-others-will thesis and the historical fact that Britain was merely continuing a trade begun by others. It was also frequently aired that if opium was injurious, it was no more so than alcohol was in Britain: indeed, if anything, it was less so for an opium addict was not noisy and belligerent like a drunkard. An American doctor even went so far as to say alcoholics should change to opiates, thereby causing less harm to their health and families.

Typical of pro-opium propaganda was an article from the *Pall Mall Gazette* of 1879. It asked why, if opium smoking was such an evil, no inherited ill effects were visible and went on to state that opium smoking retarded digestion which was beneficial to the Chinese who purportedly ate a virtually vegetarian diet. Opium, it was suggested, was even good for the Chinese who lived on undrained ground and worked in rice paddyfields where fever was endemic. A more outrageous claim stated the Chinese were largely immune to bronchial diseases because the antiseptic qualities of opium smoke protected their lungs.

Not only the popular press sided with opium. In the winter of 1881—2, *The Times* published two letters from Sir George Birdwood who defended the trade, differentiating between eating and smoking opium but assiduously avoiding mention of its addictive potential. He wrote:

> I hold it to be absolutely harmless. I do not place it simply in the same category with even tobacco smoking but I mean that opium smoking in itself, is as harmless as smoking willow bark or inhaling the smoke of a peat fire, or vapour of boiling water . . . I hold opium smoking, in short, to be a strictly harmless indulgence, like any other smoking, and the essence of its pleasure to be not in the opium in itself so much as in the smoking of it. If something else were put into the pipe instead of opium, that something else would gradually become just as popular as opium, although it might not incidentally prove so beneficial . . . I repeat that, of itself, opium smoking is almost as harmless an indulgence as twiddling the thumbs and other silly-looking methods for concentrating the jaded mind.

The absurdity of this ignorant bigot's diatribe, because it appeared in *The Times*, gave it some import and many pondered if, in fact, the opium issue was not misguided. Surely, it was argued, no one would so risk his reputation with such remarks if they were unfounded: what few realised was Birdwood was well connected with the Indian government and had substantial trading interests in the subcontinent.

W.H. Brereton, formerly a solicitor in Hong Kong, also equated opium smoking with tobacco smoking. In his book *The Truth About Opium*, which was far from truthful, he wrote:

> The difference between opium smoking and tobacco smoking appears to be this:- In the one case you take into your mouth the mere smoke of a valuable aromatic drug, which when passed into the stomach as a medicine has powerful curative properties . . . In the case of tobacco a foul and poisonous weed is taken, with no curative powers whatever . . . I fully believe that when medical men come to study opium and opium smoking more fully it will be the established opinion of the faculty that opium smoking is not only perfectly harmless, but that it is most beneficial.

It is ironic that Brereton was correct in his assessment of the other greatest health scourge of recent centuries – tobacco – but was unable to face the facts of opium.

Dr William J. Moore, Deputy-Surgeon-General of the Bombay Presidency, was another who held the impression the British public was being misled. More of a realist than Sir George Birdwood, he stated that the English would not agree to losing the considerable boost the exchequer received from opium revenues, especially when they would be giving up the income 'for the purpose of preventing a comparatively few Chinamen suffering from the abuse of an agent which many more Chinamen find to be a source of enjoyment, of comfort, a necessity, and even a blessing.'

The effect of such statements allayed the public conscience. India and China were far away and it was thought best to let the government handle the issue as it saw fit.

Yet there were still some far-sighted and vocal prophets, even if they were ignored. In an address to the Total Abstainers of Great Britain and Ireland in 1877, one speaker saw into the future, saying:

> One remarkable distinction between alcohol and opium is this, that whereas the abuse of alcohol dates back to the time of Noah, and is widespread almost as the human race itself, the opium vice is comparatively modern, appearing to be subsequent to and in some degree consequent upon the diffusion of Mohammedanism. We know alcohol, and I hope we know its worst. The opium plague is yet in its infancy. With the exception of China, no country has

been strongly inoculated by it. In China its prevalence dates back only two or three generations. Who then can insure us against the spread of the opium vice within our own borders?

One has to wonder what the speaker would think today, walking the streets of London or Los Angeles.

Membership of the Society for the Suppression of the Opium Trade (the Anglo-Oriental prefix was dropped) declined from 1885 but, four years later, Alexander became secretary and instigated a revitalised campaign.

New motions were laid before Parliament and failed but then, in 1891, one was carried with a majority, although an amendment 'talked it out' (the motion running out of debating time), so never reaching the statute books. Two years later, a motion was proposed that the system by which Indian opium revenue was raised was morally indefensible. The government realised they could no longer put off the reformers. Gladstone, the prime minister, who when younger had denounced the opium trade as 'this most infamous and atrocious trade', now trod a little more cautiously. He proposed a counter-resolution, which was passed, setting up a Royal Commission instructed to report on the situation: but China was omitted from the terms of reference.

It was soon apparent the commission was a stalling measure. Bar one, the commission members were all pro-opium government supporters. To ensure a bias, the members could not delve freely into conditions in India, were only allowed to visit places the government approved whilst witnesses and officials were tutored in what to say. Sir Henry Wilson, the odd man out on the Commission, and Alexander who went to India with him, found the truth elusive.

What unbiased information was gathered, from doctors and missionaries, was reduced or misrepresented with the result the Commission, apart from Wilson, reported the evil effects of opium in India to be greatly exaggerated. Comparing Indian opium taking with the 'temperate use of alcohol in England', the Commission pointed out India could not afford the loss of opium revenues. The blame for addiction in China was laid firmly on Peking. In the Commission's opinion, it was China's fault her subjects were allowed to take opium.

The Commission report was not published until 1895. In the

meantime, no more political moves could be made. When *The Times* published a summary of the Commission's report, the public believed Alexander and his Society had been whipping up a storm in a teacup. All that came of the Commission was a government declaration that opium trade controls would be introduced in the future. No date was specified. It took the Society ten years to overcome the defeat.

By 1906, the Society was on its feet again, with over 200 candidates standing in the general election, vowing to promote the end of opium if they were elected. Few won seats but the Liberal Party took the election and in May, a Liberal Member of Parliament tabled a motion based upon that of 1893, that 'the Indo-Chinese opium trade is morally indefensible, and requests His Majesty's Government to take such steps as might be necessary for bringing about its speedy close.' It was carried and the Secretary of State for India responded by declaring if China seriously wanted to restrict the consumption of this drug, the British government would not close the door.

In response, the Chinese government issued an edict abolishing poppy cultivation which, in 1908, at last resulted in an agreement with Britain.

A reform movement had also grown up in China and, in 1906, prompted by the statement made in Britain, an imperial decree was published demanding the cessation of opium smoking and the closure of all opium dens. It set a target date of 1917 by which time China would be cleansed of opium. A proviso excluded people over sixty: it was inserted because Tzu-hsi, the Dowager Empress, was herself addicted and did not wish to break her habit.

Having set a deadline for eradication, China and Britain came to an agreement by which India guaranteed to reduce opium exports to China by 10 per cent annually whilst China would decrease cultivation and imports from other countries at the same rate, thus gradually weaning the nation off opium.

The problems now shifted to India where the agreement necessitated a considerable change in agricultural policy and a redistribution of the two types of opium produced, 'provision', or export, opium and 'excise', or domestically consumed, opium. The area under poppies was reduced from 613,996 acres to 350,000 acres between 1905 and 1910. Initially the *ryots*, or peasant farmers, were reluctant to change: opium was easier to grow than other crops and produced a higher return, especially once production was cut and prices rocketed. Eventually, they were retrained to grow other cash crops and, from 1914 to 1919, they were even reluctant to return to opium production to meet the demand for painkillers brought on by the First World War. The Indian Opium Agency had to provide special inducements to satisfy demand.

In 1909, the British government forced the colonial authorities in Hong Kong to cease exporting prepared opium to China, where imports were controlled by special customs permits. In the same year, after more than two centuries of spreading opium slavery throughout Asia, the government of India ceased exportation. So, officially, ended the terrible trade by which Britain, for the best part, along with a number of lesser mercantile nations, had earned vast revenues – not to mention acquiring what was to become her most successful, lucrative and thriving colony – by poisoning a substantial proportion of the Chinese population.

The Chinese government, more concerned with opium suppression than many historians have allowed, was also moving to take the initiative. In April 1905, an opium combine was set up to administer huge areas of land set aside for poppy farming, the aim being that if the government controlled production it could manage consumption. The combine was only patchily effective. In some provinces the anti-opium drive was lax whilst in others it was strenuous and efficient.

A Mr E.S. Little, having journeyed through western China in 1910, reported 'all over the province of Szechuan opium has almost ceased to be produced, except only in a few remote districts on the frontier.' Eric Teichman, the Chinese secretary to the British Legation in Peking, supported this statement by noting poppy growing in Kansu province was virtually non-existent.

Despite localised successes and some uncompromising punishments – forty-seven people were executed for growing or smoking opium in Hunan after the Wuchang Uprising of 1911 – enforcement of the ban was difficult and tens of thousands of addicts were left untouched by the reforms. Many had salted away supplies whilst an illegal and highly lucrative trade continued, run by mercenary foreigners, corrupt officials and conveniently blind government departments. Inevitably, many senior government personnel and politicians in the new Republic of China, which was founded as a result of the Wuchang Uprising and dethroned the last emperor, were strident in their condemnation of the opium trade at the same time as they, or their families, were taking part in it and, as landowners, were frequently producing opium. Sun Yat-sen, the mastermind behind the revolution and the acknowledged father of modern, post-imperial China, raised money for his cause by taxing all the opium dens in Canton.

This double standard reached high places. While Sir John Jordan, British Ambassador to Peking in 1917, optimistically reported a massive decrease in opium production and usage, a vice-president of China purchased £4 million worth of Indian opium which he sold in his own country for an enormous return.

Against such a background, the problems continued because although attempts were made to control production and consumption, little was done to dismantle channels of distribution which were well organised and long established. Along these routes opium was still smuggled and the trade even went so far as to export opium from China, the first instance of this occurring in any significant way.

The situation did not last long. China was plunged once more into political chaos in 1916 with the death of the president, Yüan Shih-k'ai, and entered into the era of the warlords who emasculated the national government and ruled their own domains with medieval baronial savagery. The grip the authorities had been putting on opium was lost and both the production and use of opium resumed on an extensive scale.

In some areas, opium cultivation became virtually mandatory. Local warlords used it as a source of income to fund guerrilla warfare. Farmers were forced to abandon food production and cultivate poppies, with the opium harvest being commandeered. The cultivation of poppies and transportation of opium were taxed, as were opium dens, shops, pipes and the little lamps used to set the pipes going.

The dire and variable situation was recorded in 1921 by the writer, E.G. Kemp. She wrote of the locality of Hunan province around the town of Changteh which contained a regional army headquarters. The town had been captured in 1918 by Northern forces under General Feng Yu Hsiang. Feng was a Christian who made his men study the Bible, forbidding them to smoke tobacco or opium and to drink alcohol. He educated illiterate soldiers, training them in trades so they would not be destitute when demobilised. He realised it was impossible to ban the opium trade on a large scale and later used opium as a source of revenue to address poverty and disease through social welfare programmes and free education.

By the time Kemp arrived in Changteh in 1920, the town had undergone what she called 'a wonderful purification.' All the gambling premises, opium dens and whorehouses had been closed. Severe fines were levied on opium dealers, soldiers found selling opium were executed and civilians, after paying their fine, were publicly flogged then paraded around the town with a placard around their necks proclaiming their evil. The addict, however, was dealt with sympathetically. General Feng, aware of the grip of addiction, opened official refuges for smokers who were registered by being photographed on entering and leaving each refuge.

By contrast, Kemp also visited Yunnan, a very poor province which depended to a large extent on the export of opium to other parts of China for its income. Kemp wrote:

> We heard much about the poverty of the district and the increasing cultivation of opium poppy. It is tragic to see this when a few years ago the land was filled with crops needed for the daily food of the people. In some parts half the crops are opium, and it demands a great deal of labour! The land has to be twice ploughed, the second time crosswise, well manured and the seed (mixed with four times its quantity of sand) is sown three times between October and March. After the sowing the land has to be harrowed, then the young plants are hoed and weeded, generally by the women and children. I have seen the women sitting on stools to do it on account of their poor little bound feet.

An investigation in 1923—4 by a world-wide reform agency, the International Anti-Opium Association, indicated opium was being produced in a majority of Chinese provinces. In some, local governors were attempting to enforce the prohibition but they could not prevent smuggling or trading because of the anarchy ruling the land, the inaccessibility of much of China and the under-funding or non-provision of soldiers to police the law. For many governors, the army had to be retained intact: to send a patrol out on opium-seizing duties was to send it to a certain death at the hands of bandits or warlords. The result was history repeating itself: as in the 1870s, the increase in poppy farming brought about localised famine.

The anarchy of banditry across China was extensive and the brigands no strangers to opium themselves. In *Ten Weeks with Chinese Bandits*, published in 1926, Dr Harvey J. Howard, an American ophthalmologist at Peking Union Medical College, told of his capture by outlaws in northern Manchuria. He recorded how they lived a hard, probably short life: the only consolation they had was opium, which they would do anything to get. The bandits constantly discussed the price and supply of opium much, as Howard recorded, as Western soldiers talked about whisky or beer. He reported that:

> Opium smoking seemed to fill their every need. It often took the place of food, sleep and recreation with them. In fact every necessity and all other luxuries were as nothing compared to the indulgence in this one vice. When they had plenty of crude opium, their happiness appeared to be complete. When they were without it, they were demons to live with. Undoubtedly the craving for this drug had driven many of them into the bandit business.

From the 1890s, some Chinese smokers had started to follow the developing Hong Kong trend for morphine: by 1900, this form of addiction was spreading fast. To combat it, the government first taxed morphine in 1902 then banned its import and refining in 1909. The ineluctable result was to propel a previously legitimate trade underground. By 1920, a pound of morphine which wholesaled for £12 in the London pharmaceutical industry fetched £210 in Shanghai.

Morphine smuggling was conducted primarily by the Japanese who ran it into China by way of Manchuria, Formosa, Hong Kong, French Indo-China and Korea. All the morphine was manufactured in Britain and the smuggling of it did not abate, despite restrictions on sales.

The dangers morphine posed the addict, which were far greater than those of opium, were not unknown. The *Peking and Tientsin Times* published an article just before Christmas 1924 commenting on the rise of morphine use in China. The account mentioned a wholesale morphine pill-maker, named Wang Lo-shan, in the town of Ch'u Hsien, who made a daily sale of 500,000 pills within his district, a small army of peddlers covering a daily round. It was noted once a morphine habit was acquired, the addict would not revert to opium unless morphine was utterly unobtainable. The article continued:

> The man who swallows a dozen morphia pills a day has swallowed more physical destruction than the average opium smoker, and he does it without the loss of time involved in the laborious smoking process. Reports from many parts of China show an increase in the habit of opium-eating because it is easy and less expensive. The desired effect is produced by a very much smaller quantity [and] many coolies divide their daily quantum into three parts; two are eaten during the day, and the third smoked in the leisure of the evening.

Once comparative political stability returned with the coming to power of Sun Yat-sen's Kuomintang, or National Party, government in Nanking in 1924, China carried on its war against opium. By now, the prevalence of the drug throughout China was so extensive babies were reportedly born in the opium-producing areas of Yunnan with an in-built addiction and, in the city of Kweichow, the local chamber of commerce adopted opium as the official standard of exchange.

With the warlords submitting to Kuomintang authority, it looked as if matters might change for the better. The Criminal Code of 1928 prohibited the sale, possession, importation and exportation of opium and its derivatives. Under the code, drug traffickers were liable for the death penalty. A Chinese Central Commission for the Suppression of Opium was appointed in 1936 and passed a decision to abolish poppy cultivation gradually. Provision was made for the building of hospitals and hospices for opium addicts, with more than 100 being opened within a year. They were desperately needed if opium was to be stamped out for it was conservatively estimated there were 3,500,000 registered addicts in China. How many unregistered sufferers there were beggars the imagination.

Regardless of the progress made by Britain and other countries over the opium trade, China was still bedevilled by the extra-territorial rights of foreigners who resided in foreign concessions and in such enclaves as Portuguese Macau, British Hong Kong and the extensive foreign quarters in Shanghai where Chinese authority could not be brought to bear.

Of these, Macau was notorious. It had always had a raffish atmosphere but this was magnified by opium which was openly prepared in large amounts for smoking in the many opium dens where smokers indulged their habits on four- or five-tiered bunks like, it was said, racks of loaves in a bakery. So plentiful were these dens, and so easily accessed, they were regarded as worthy of sightseeing and featured on tourist itineraries.

As with the morphine trade, the Japanese were a particular obstacle to opium control and their concessions in Hankow and Tientsin were specifically opprobrious. After the Japanese took control of Manchuria in 1931, they became the main supplier of heroin down the China coast. In the 1930s, Japan earned over $300 million a year from the distribution and sale of Manchurian opium and heroin. The Japanese had a reason for being involved in narcotics smuggling into China. For centuries, the two countries had been enemies and the Japanese were only too aware how effective narcotics were as a social weapon. When, after more than a decade of antagonism, this animosity finally erupted into the Sino-Japanese War of 1937, Japan had already undermined a section of Chinese society.

Not only officials were corrupted by opium. Even Empress Wan Jung, also known as Elizabeth and wife of the tenth and last Ch'ing emperor, Hsuan Tung, known as Henry Pu Yi, was eventually heavily addicted to opium which she had first smoked at the age of nineteen, originally supplied by the Japanese in Tientsin. Her addiction was used for propaganda by the Japanese, her butler being their spy, keeping his masters fully informed. In the year from 10 July 1938, she smoked 740 ounces of what she termed ointment for the increase of longevity. At about 2 ounces a day, this was a heavy dosage, lethal to any non-habituated smoker. She might have been Empress of China but not for her were there ivory and jade pipes: she used whatever cheap instruments she could have purchased for her in the market place. Her death, when it came in June 1946, was directly attributable to opium. Imprisoned by the Communist Chinese forces, she was locked in a cell in Kirin where, prevented from receiving opium, she went into withdrawal. Her companion, Hiro Saga, a distant relative of the Japanese royal family, described her dying days. As Communist soldiers and curious peasants filed chattering and laughing past her cell door to get a glimpse of her, she screamed for opium to such an extent the other prisoners yelled for her to be put down so they might have some peace. When not screaming for opium, she begged for it from the sightseers or her guards and hallucinated that she was back in the Forbidden City, calling out for servants to run her a bath or fetch her food. Her cell was messed with her own urine, excrement and vomit into which she sank for periods of unconsciousness. The guards refused to feed her, wash her or even enter the filth of her cell. She died of malnutrition and the effects of opium withdrawal.

The Sino-Japanese War badly disrupted any drive against opium. Social administration was in upheaval and the addict hospitals were given over to wounded troops. The Japanese flooded China with opium, morphine and cocaine in a systematic attempt to create new addicts and to encourage former ones to rehabituate. Aware of the potential harm it could cause, they also widely reinstated poppy farming in areas they occupied.

Muriel Lester, writing in the *Manchester Guardian* in April 1938, wrote a lengthy personal account of the opium situation:

In the old Japanese concession [of Tientsin] is a street in which about 50 per cent of the houses are drug 'joints'. They are not allowed to sell to the Japanese, but foreigners and Chinese, men and women, are offered the stuff openly as they walk through the street.

In Peking I spent a morning visiting various drug 'joints'. There are plenty of them . . . The Japanese are no longer allowed to carry on this trade. The drug shops are all left in charge of Koreans under Japanese protection, but Chinese police arrest any Chinese trafficker whom they find. Death is the penalty . . . We were able to buy as much as we liked, but our usual purchase was only twenty cents worth . . . Small boys were on the look-out for customers and led us genially along the *hutongs* [back alleyways]. A middle-aged procurer took us to a brothel where we purchased heroin . . . A Chinese trafficker looked very frightened when we appeared. The difference between his furtive expression and the self-assurance of all the Korean dealers was marked . . .

The thing that troubled me most in Peking was the number of small clinics which the Japanese are opening. They are well lit and attractive. One of them displays the red cross . . . They advertise in the papers the various diseases which they cure. The procedure in many of them seems to be that each person on entering is given a cursory examination by an unqualified doctor or dispenser, and is then registered as suffering from some specific disease. After that

he is allowed to buy as much heroin or morphine as he likes . . .
Three hundred addicts were set free from the city treatment centre
last week and the place was closed down. There is no longer any
clinic available here for the cure of addicts. Some Japanese here are
known to pay their [Chinese] servants or business employees half
in cash, half in drugs.

A foreign Christian appealed to five Koreans newly settled in
a Chinese town and running opium dens. 'Why do you come to
China?' he inquired. 'We were sent here,' they answered. 'Why do
you ply this trade?' he asked. 'That was the part assigned to us,'
they explained.

Apart from traditional opium smoking, Chinese addicts began
to experiment with opiate cocktails, including heroin. Margaret
Goldsmith, in her 1939 volume, *The Trail of Opium*, published a list
of items which could be purchased in opium shops in Tientsin just
before the Second World War. It consisted of heroin smoked with
cigarettes, White Powder (also smoked with cigarettes), Yellow
Powder (similar to white powder, but for smokers with a more
advanced craving), Sweet Pills (also called Golden Pills, smoked
with a pipe), *k'uai shang k'uai* (translating as 'Quick up Quick'
and smoked with a pipe), paper rolls (impregnated paper rubbed
between the palms), Black Plaster (the dust of which was scraped
off and smoked with cigarettes), opium, morphine and cocaine.

From the late 1920s, through the 1930s and the upheaval of the
Sino-Japanese and the Second World Wars, despite some official
measures, in practice opium was given a more or less free rein
in China. The Kuomintang authorities, which had been headed
by Generalissimo Chiang Kai-shek since Sun Yat-sen's death in
1925, were busy trying to unify China, fight the Japanese, woo the
British and Americans and fend off the Communist forces of Mao
Zedong. Yet their preoccupation with politics and military matters
was not the only reason for opium's freedom. Chiang Kai-shek and
his administration were themselves heavily dependent upon opium
revenue. Chiang had had his early political career bankrolled by
an infamous Shanghai gangster called Tu Yueh-sheng, also known
as Big-eared Tu, who ran the Green Gang, a large, particularly
well-organised and ruthless Chinese secret criminal fraternity. Tu
owned extensive poppy-growing interests in Chekiang and Kiangsu
provinces and controlled most, if not all, of the opium trade along
the Yangtze River and in Shanghai itself, a major opium trade hub.

Throughout his time in China, before he fled to Taiwan upon losing the country to the Communists, Chiang Kai-shek had an ambiguous relationship with opium. What the Japanese did not do to China with opium, he did.

Chiang Kai-shek knew if he controlled opium, he could fund his army. In 1927, the finance ministry organised an official opium monopoly, facetiously entitled the National Anti-Opium Bureau. Things went well until the monopoly was extended to Big-eared Tu's opium-growing regions. Here Tu's opium-handling company, the Da Gong Si, held sway. Within a fortnight, the Nationalist government cancelled the monopoly and closed the anti-opium bureau.

The international outcry which accompanied this move forced Chiang Kai-shek, who was keen to develop relations with the West, to reinstate the bureau as the National Opium Suppression Committee. Chiang Kai-shek announced grandiloquently: 'The National government will not attempt to get one cent from the opium tax. It would not be worthy of your confidence if it should be found to make an opium tax one of its chief sources of revenue.'

It was a charade.

Words, like human life, were cheap for Chiang Kai-shek. The following year, 1929, his government took $17 million in what was euphemistically termed 'opium prohibition revenue'. To add insult to injury T.V. Soong, one of the wealthiest men in China and the Harvard-educated Finance Minister, purchased 700 chests of Persian opium through Big-eared Tu in 1930 to supplement a temporary shortage in home product, using Kuomintang soldiers to off-load and guard it in Shanghai. Soong took a hefty commission.

That was not all. In 1931, Chiang Kai-shek struck a deal with Big-eared Tu. Tu's Green Gang would be afforded government protection in all aspects of opium, have a veto over the appointment of government opium officials and take a large percentage of the earnings in exchange for a down-payment to the treasury of $6 million against forthcoming profits. In the long run, the deal fell through but the intentions behind it were plain. Tu controlled opium and therefore Chiang Kai-shek. To err on the side of caution though, Big-eared Tu lived in the French concession in Shanghai, safe from Chinese law.

Tu was also an opium and morphine addict and, later, he became a heroin addict. Further, he was the main heroin producer in China where it was available as pills and tablets for swallowing or pink pills for smoking. Yet his infamy extended well beyond Shanghai and Chinese politics.

Over 50 per cent of Big-eared Tu's heroin was exported to France through official channels. The police force in the French concession was administered from Vietnam, then French Indo-China. The captain of police, Étienne Fiori, was a Corsican and a representative of the Union Corse, the Corsican equivalent of the Sicilian Mafia. With French Consul-General Koechlin, he was beholden to Big-eared Tu who paid both the diplomat and the police captain hefty bribes in addition to providing them with concubines. On Tu's behalf, Fiori assisted in setting up his distribution route to France. Heroin, manufactured by Tu in Shanghai, was shipped to Paris via Hanoi, Saigon and Marseilles. Tu paid a substantial part of his profits to key civil servants and politicians in France to ensure the French government kept its inquisitive nose out of Shanghai.

This protection did not last long, despite Tu increasing his Parisian bribe level and sending as his undercover emissary Mme Wellington Koo, wife of China's representative at the Treaty of Versailles negotiations. The French government was not for turning. Fiori and Koechlin had let down and possibly double-crossed Tu. In 1933, both were poisoned at a farewell banquet before retiring to France. Koechlin died in extreme pain (along with a few other misfortunates who shared his serving dish) whilst Fiori was ill for months, his health broken.

The Farmers Bank of China, colloquially known amongst expatriate Europeans as the Opium Farmers' Bank, was inaugurated in the same year. Chiang Kai-shek was closely involved in it and used it for his private banking transactions. A conduit for heroin and opium revenue, it issued its own currency notes, Chiang increasing the print run when his funds ran low. The reserves were never audited nor the books opened for inspection.

Perhaps the greatest public irony of all was Chiang Kai-shek's fiftieth birthday present from Big-eared Tu. For several years, aware China needed to be strong to defend itself (and his way of life), Tu had spent millions of dollars purchasing American fighter aircraft to build up the air force. On an auspicious day in 1936, Tu presented Chiang Kai-shek with an aircraft bearing the name *Opium Suppression of Shanghai* on its nose. The hypocrisy and arrogance of the two men were staggering. A poetical expatriate witticism of the time went:

A way at last has now been found
To get opium suppression off the ground.

By the end of the 1930s, it was estimated 10 per cent of the Chinese nation (about 40 million people) were opium addicts, the Japanese occupation during the Sino-Japanese and Second World Wars not significantly reducing the figures: it was in Japan's interest to keep as many Chinese as possible habituated. In Shanghai, even after the privations of the latter conflict, opium was readily available to all levels of society. Opium poppy growing at the time was still so common as to be found in the suburbs of Canton. Domestic production and importation continued unabated until 1949 when, after four years of bitter civil war, the Kuomintang army was defeated by the Communists.

Within months of assuming control, in February 1950, the Communist government State Administrative Council banned poppy growing, the production, importation and sale of opium and all narcotics. Only a required quantity of licit medicinal opium was produced under rigorous control.

This ban was comparatively easily conducted for China went through massive land reforms. Landlords were displaced (or beheaded), the peasants put in control of agricultural production, communes established and cash crops replaced by food. Communist oratory, a vital aspect of mass ideological education, attacked opium and poppy growing as an imperialist plot which, in a sense, it was. Local cadres, responsible for the presentation of political theory at grass-roots level, were not only able to preach the anti-opium creed: they were also able to pinpoint local opium vendors, addicts and poppy growers.

Opium stocks were publicly burned, divans were destroyed, dealers were either killed or sent for 'political re-education' in labour camps. Poppy fields were burnt and ploughed. Pipes were publicly destroyed. Opium taking was listed officially as unhealthy, anti-social, anti-socialist and a capitalist activity. Addicts were not condemned for their vice but offered medical help and rehabilitation centres were set up. Those who were antagonistic towards treatment were sent to labour camps whilst those who re-addicted or were intransigent were paraded before the public as criminals and imprisoned.

Between 1949 and 1953, the addict population dramatically shrank. By 1960, China was virtually free of drug addiction. Anyone dealing in opium was summarily executed, often without the inconvenience and expense of a trial. In 1971, China produced exactly 100 tonnes of raw opium, precisely its medicinal requirement.

Whilst mainland China was going through civil wars, uprisings, famines, social and political renaissance, Hong Kong went about things in its own way.

The news of the reforms promoted by the 1906 Liberal government back in London had created some dismay. The opium monopoly revenue made up a substantial part of local tax income.

It was reckoned that up to a third of the Hong Kong Chinese population used opium on a fairly frequent basis, although nothing like all of them were addicted. A Chinese merchant, Ho Su-cho, summed up the state of affairs:

> Many use it occasionally, but are not addicted to the habit; they can use it or not, as they choose. Most Chinese who use opium do so for pleasure, just as other people smoke cigars or cigarettes. When a visitor calls at a place he is offered opium to smoke. Apparatus for smoking is kept in most places of business, so that when a customer comes he may be entertained by being offered a smoke of opium . . . The effect is bad in all cases. The moral effect, however, is not so degrading in the case of the rich or well-to-do as it is in the case of the poor. This is due to the fact that the rich man has the means with which to buy the opium he wishes, whereas the poor man is often compelled to resort to theft and other dishonest methods in obtaining the money with which to buy the drug . . . Formerly a shop for the smoking of opium was considered disgraceful; but now in most homes and places of business as well as in the public shops apparatus for smoking the drug is kept, in order that visitors and friends may be entertained. The use of opium has become more respectable and as a result has increased.

In May 1908, another motion was put before the British House of Commons. It suggested steps be taken 'to bring to a speedy close the system of licensing opium dens now prevailing in some of our Crown Colonies, more particularly Hong-Kong, the Straits

Settlements and Ceylon.' It was carried unanimously and the Secretary of State for the Colonies declared the opium divans of Hong Kong were to be shut.

In the colony, this pronouncement was met with angry indignation. The Governor, Sir Frederick Lugard, worried at the potential loss of tax revenue, claimed matters were under control and assured his political masters in London that opium dens were not as bad as they were made out. 'They were,' he said, 'places where the tired coolie may rest and enjoy a little opium, or where friends of the better classes may meet and discuss affairs. Such places contrast strongly with a public house, in that they are quiet and orderly. Women and children are absolutely excluded.' Nevertheless, all the dens were closed during 1909 and 1910, the operating of one becoming an offence. However, the purchase and consumption of opium was still not illegal and it continued to be supplied by the monopoly holder.

In 1914, the monopoly system was closed once again, the opium concession now being held by the government which prepared smoking opium in its own factory, retailing the product throughout the colony. The vicinity of the factory soon became a mecca for poor coolies who sniffed at the steam coming from the waste-pipes in the hope of getting a free sample.

Opium was sold through a system of licensed offices, the price being fixed by the government. However, Hong Kong's main *raison d'être* having always been to turn a dollar, the government actually paid licensees a commission to promote sales where demand fell short of projections. In the first ten months, the scheme brought in HK$3.5 million, peaking in 1918 at HK$8 million or 46.5 per cent of government revenue. Just in case reformers should get wind of this, however, the income was disguised in the accounts as 'Licences and Internal Revenue not otherwise specified.'

It was another thirty-two years before opium was made illegal in Hong Kong.

Although illegal, opium dens continued to exist openly for the maximum penalty for operating one was a fine of only HK$500. Colonial pragmatists and realists knew they could not simply do away with opium overnight. Addiction, as well as moneyed interests, precluded it. Even under the Dangerous Drugs Ordinance of 1923, opium was fairly safe. The only serious offence concerned the counterfeiting of government opium labels and wrappers, by which tax might be avoided.

The number of Hong Kong opium users was little changed from the figure estimated seventeen years before and was not expected to drop until full prohibition was introduced. The status quo remained until 1932 when the Opium Ordinance allowed the police new and increased powers of search which led to a resolve to close down all the dens. Most were shut, although a number continued to operate illegally, but as opium possession and use remained legal, provided supplies came from a licensed source, the closure of the dens had little impact on opium consumption.

By 1935, there were some seventy retail shops selling opium under licence at HK$14.50 a tael. This price was out of the reach of the ordinary coolie, whose daily wage was in the region of 50 cents, so a black market quickly developed in which opium cost about HK$3.50 a tael. The source of most of this cheap opium was China, with a small amount being either pilfered from government stocks or smuggled from Persia.

For the poor user, illegal dens were the only alternative they had to smoking up an alley: as most coolies who did not live on the streets resided in crowded boarding houses, sleeping in common beds on a rota, dens with an individual *kang* on which to lie must have seemed luxurious indeed. In fact, they were seedy, squalid places, often little more than cubicles in run-down tenements. It was officially estimated Hong Kong had about 2500 illegal divans in 1935, each catering for about 40 smokers a day. The police often raided these dens but did not necessarily close them down, the Chinese constables and some of their European superiors often using the raids as an excuse to collect protection money from proprietors.

Despite its traditional popularity, opium use was beginning to wane. The fashion was shifting to Shanghai heroin which was obtained mostly as pink pills for smoking. The escalation of heroin can be judged from Hong Kong police statistics: in 1931, 5000 pills were seized but by 1933, the haul had risen to 500,000 per annum. In 1937, the Hong Kong water (now marine) police made their first seizures of heroin. The defendants were arrested, bailed then – predictably – vanished.

Severe punishments were meted out for heroin possession, including long prison sentences. At the same time, operating an opium den was still only liable to a fine. The hard line taken against heroin was caused by two factors: first was the recognition that heroin was far more dangerous than opium, and second, it was feared heroin, being illegal and therefore untaxed, was more than likely to undermine the revenue potential of opium.

All attempts to halt smuggling and, therefore, to protect the revenue base were ineffective. Hong Kong harbour allowed unrestricted access by sea and the land border was open. Poverty and civil strife in China gave an added incentive to smuggling. Opium was run into Hong Kong mostly by ocean-going junks which traded along the China coast. Each could carry several tonnes of cargo, a small percentage of opium easily out-valuing the rest of the load. The Hong Kong coastline – of little sheltered bays and fishing hamlets full of compliant locals for whom piracy had been a pastime for centuries – provided ample cover. It also gave shelter from customs officers who frequently followed their police colleagues' example and either colluded with smugglers or charged them protection money. Officially, the colonial administration did not recognise the corruption in its ranks. It blamed the apathetic, indifferent attitude of the local Chinese for opium addiction and accused them of not wanting to assist the police.

As an entrepôt port, Hong Kong had a very important place on intercontinental steamship routes. This, in turn, made it an ideal centre for international traffic in drugs which, by the time a report on the subject was published in 1936, was well organised, well financed and wide-reaching. What was more, the colonial government had neither the manpower, expertise nor funds to fight it. On the other hand, the financial report for the year 1938/9 recorded a steady increase in government opium sales.

Addiction patterns were changing. The older addicts were mostly habituated to opium but the younger were trapped by heroin. The report of 1936 concluded Hong Kong (just the island itself, excluding the crowded peninsula of Kowloon and the 200 or so miles of the rural New Territories) contained over 40,000 opium addicts and 24,000 heroin pill addicts. Many were female, with over 90 per cent of the prostitutes addicted or frequent users. Addicts amongst the coolie population were malnourished and in poor health and, although some were admitted to hospital for treatment, most of them lived, smoked, dreamed and died on the streets. What was more, Europeans still frequently smoked opium at Chinese banquets, as guests of Chinese businessmen or while doing business with a Chinese firm. However, very few indeed were actually addicted.

The sight of opium addicts in the streets of Hong Kong was a commonplace which most Chinese ignored but which even long-term expatriate residents could seldom see without a shudder of sympathy. In the 1930s, it was possible to see into dens when passing by outside, the addicts lying on shelf-like bunks or *k'angs*. They were invariably skeletal, sorry wrecks of human beings who, under the effects of their pipe, were suddenly active, returning to their usual manual labour with a vigour which soon wore off requiring them to take another pipe to keep going.

During the Second World War, Hong Kong was occupied by the Japanese who, at first, imported opium into the colony with the intention of demoralising the Chinese: they had no need to for disease, starvation and Japanese cruelty were sufficient not only to demoralise and kill large numbers but to cause many hundreds of thousands to flee into China. As the war progressed, and Japan came under increasing pressure from Allied forces, supply lines were disrupted, with first opium imports and then stockpiles being depleted. In the occupied territory, many thousands of addicts died from withdrawal, insane or broken, but a good number survived through to non-addiction.

When the Japanese surrendered Hong Kong in September 1945, the colonial government, most members of which had been incarcerated in a prisoner-of-war camp on Hong Kong island, did not immediately take over the running of the colony. An interim administration was set up under the British Commander-in-Chief. He issued a proclamation which abolished the opium monopoly thereby preventing any possible revenue being derived from it. Quite possibly, had there been a civilian administration in place, they might have argued against or even prevented this move. The police were made responsible for the closing of all opium dens and suppressing any opium dealing whatsoever. Needless to say, an illegal trade quickly appeared and began to thrive.

Yet, for the first time since Hong Kong was ceded to the British, opium was illegal there and was, at last, banned by every facet of British government, at home and abroad. The pernicious legitimate trade was finally over.

9

Coolies and Conferences

With the Far East and especially China steeped in foreign opium for the better part of two centuries, it was perhaps inevitable, in due course, the tables would start to turn. When this revenge began there was a certain ironic justice about it for it involved, once more, an exploitation of the Chinese.

From around the middle of the nineteenth century, large numbers of Chinese – particularly men – started to emigrate. There were two main reasons for this migration. First, conditions in China were intolerable for the average peasant. Landlords were grasping, the Ch'ing emperors imposed crippling taxes which were ruthlessly collected, starvation was rife due to a combination of poor administration and natural causes and the nation was torn apart by the Taiping Rebellion. Second, there was simultaneously a massive international demand for labour. Across the world, roads and railways were under construction, mining was booming and vast areas of previously untouched continents were coming under the plough. From time to time, gold rushes added an extra incentive to migrants throughout the world.

Millions of Chinese peasant labourers – coolies – emigrated with the dream of striking it rich overseas, sending money home to support their extended families or, having made good, bringing their families to their new home.

The first immigrants headed into South-east Asia, to the tin mines and rubber plantations of the Malay peninsula. An indication of this migration can be seen in population figures: by 1910, the first reliable census, there were recorded 60,000 Chinese living in Rangoon, 120,000 in Saigon and 200,000 in Bangkok. In Singapore, they were the racial majority. Such large immigrant numbers brought about a high demand for opium: in Singapore in 1881, a third of the adult Chinese population was addicted – this was a higher addiction than in China. To try and regulate supply and use it as a source of tax revenue, every South-east Asian country and colony had a state opium monopoly in place by 1900, state-licensed opium dens being commonplace: opium taxes substantially increased government incomes and significantly encouraged economic development.

Most coolies came from the southern, coastal provinces of China, especially Fukien, Kwangtung and the area around Canton which had long been associated with the opium trade. Just as in the 1820s, when coolies were exported to the tea plantations of Assam, large numbers of men were shipped out through Hong Kong, Macau and other ports such as Amoy. They were, from the very. start, exploited by Chinese coolie shipping agents and ships' captains – over a third of whom were Americans – then abused and treated atrociously by their employers. The trade in these unfortunate souls was known colloquially as the 'Pig Trade': the 'Poison Trade' was slang for the opium business. Crowded into corrals like slaves they were, as the British Consul in Canton observed in 1852, frequently painted with letters such as P, C or S meaning Peru, California or the Sandwich Islands.

Whilst some were convicts on release or kidnap victims (we still use the contemporary expression, 'shanghaied'), over 95 per cent were indentured workers who, having had $50 paid for their sea passage on their behalf by would-be employers who regarded it as a loan against future income, were offered a wage they never saw for their loan and deductions for living expenses exceeded their earnings. Their travelling conditions were grim but because money had changed hands they were not legally slaves so no action could be taken against their shippers. Many died *en route*: one British-owned vessel, the *John Calvin*, lost 50 per cent of its passengers whilst American ships were often known to have 40 per cent mortality rates. Some attempt was made by Britain to regulate this human trade with the Chinese Passengers Act (1855) but this resulted in the trade merely shifting away from Hong Kong.

Women were sometimes part of 'Pig Trade' cargoes. Under Chinese law females could not emigrate but coolie employers overseas wanted women: the aim was to make their indentured coolies settle in their new countries, thus alleviating the need to import more. The women were mostly either kidnapped or purchased under a Chinese system, known as *mui tsai*, which allowed for the sale of young girls as servants or concubines-in-training. This aspect of the trade was invidious: in 1855, the British vessel, *Inglewood*, hove to off Amoy with a cargo of female children all under the age of eight. The crew, disgusted at what comprised their cargo, reported it to the British consul who arranged for the children to be returned home.

Once abroad, many of the Chinese lived oppressed, miserable lives with only one familiar means of release – opium smoking. Not only did opium relieve the physical pain of labouring, it suppressed sexual desire in predominantly male immigrant work environments and the mental pain of homesickness: opium has the ability to make anywhere seem familiar so, for the coolie in a strange land, his nostalgia for China could be dulled by a pipe.

Many coolies, of course, were not addicted or even frequent users: indeed, a good number only took to smoking once they arrived at their destinations. In some instances, opium was even cited as an incentive to emigrate because it was legal in many places outside China whilst employers were reluctant to stamp out opium smoking for they feared without it they might suffer a labour shortage. This was certainly true in the Malay peninsula, where workers were housed in primitive conditions, suffered terrible physical labour and were exposed to a variety of tropical diseases: opium kept the work-force going. It must be said, however, the Chinese migrants did not introduce opium to South-east Asia for it was already used by Indians and Malays along with cannabis: it was just that the Chinese greatly enlarged the propensity towards it.

The main initial thrust of international emigration outside Southeast Asia was to Australia, the USA (particularly California) and Canada and later, further afield to South America with, later still, South Africa. With the coolies came Chinese traders who serviced the expatriate communities with everything from rice and joss-sticks to prostitutes and opium. It was not long before opium smoking spread to sections of the non-Chinese population wherever they settled.

By 1870, there were 50,000 Chinese working as miners and general labourers in Australia, with predominantly male Chinese communities established in the Lower George Street area of Sydney and the Little Bourke Street precinct of Melbourne. Opium smoking and dens were common. The lack of females encouraged poor white women to move into the Chinese milieu where they worked as servants, prostitutes and even married Chinese men which set white society against the Orientals and their fallen women who were deemed to be corrupted by opium. Anti-Chinese racial attitudes were the norm and when, in 1888, a ship called the *Afghan* arrived in Port Melbourne with 250 Chinese immigrants aboard, a mass picket of the docks prevented them disembarking.

Opium imports into Australia indicate the size of the smoking habit: in 1890, 17,684 pounds were landed of which only 400 pounds were for medicinal use. Fines for smoking or operating a den were lenient. The problem was to enter the political agenda in April 1890, when it was discovered there were 700 European smokers in Victoria alone. A concerted anti-opium – which meant racially inspired anti-Chinese – movement sprang up. A passage from the story 'Mr & Mrs Sin Fat', published in 1888 by the Australian writer Edward Dyson, sums up the prevalent attitude:

> The curious European on a voyage of discovery saw in [Mr Sin Fat's] room, through the clouds of choking evil smelling, opium fumes, debilitated Chinamen, with faces like animals floating to hell in the midst of visions of heaven . . . and worst of all, European girls . . . of sixteen, decoyed in at the front door by the sheen of silk and the jingle of gold, and then left to percolate through that terrible den, to be finally cast out amongst the slime and rottenness of the lanes . . .

It was artful racist writing – both 'Sin' and 'Fat' are Chinese names, but have different connotations in English – which appealed to the indignant and self-righteous masses but did nothing to rid Australia of the Chinese. They had arrived to stay and, despite racially motivated opium legislation, imports rose far higher before the tide was turned. By 1991, just under 5 per cent of the Australian population was of Chinese ethnic origin.

Such was the dream the Chinese had of the USA it was colloquially known in China as the Golden Mountain: 30,000 Chinese left Hong Kong for San Francisco in 1852 alone. Tens of thousands flocked to the western seaboard to work predominantly as labourers on the railroads and in mines. Many headed for the gold-fields. Mostly indentured, they were racially abused, cheated of their earnings and considered of little importance. The Celestials, as they were called, were considered below even native American Indians. When the gold-mines closed or failed, when the railroads were completed, most of the Chinese were simply cast adrift. They had no money to repatriate themselves. It was then the ubiquitous Chinese laundry came into being: the Chinese, ever entrepreneurial, set up in business running chop houses, acting as cooks on ranches or cattle drives, owning laundries, bakeries and tailors' shops and, inevitably, opium dens.

Through the coolie trade opium diffused across the world. Typical of this expansion was the way opium arrived in Peru, outlined in *All About Opium* by Hartmann Henry Sultzberger and published in 1884. An Anglicised German opium merchant, Sultzberger had an acquaintance who became involved in the trade through his employer, a coolie importer bringing Chinese labour from Macau. To see if there was a means of maximising profits, the importer brought in a few cases of opium as a trial. It proved so profitable a regular trade was established in both coolies and opium.

At first, opium entering Peru was duty-free. Then the Peruvian authorities seized their chance and heavily taxed it with the prompt result 80 per cent of the country's opium was smuggled. Concerned about lost tax revenues, the levy was considerably cut and companies operated by Chinese merchants in Lima imported substantial quantities from China via San Francisco. The situation was summed up by Sultzberger, who wrote:

> To my knowledge there never was any attempt made in Peru to 'prohibit' the importation of the drug, which most likely may be accounted for by the entire absence out there of those well-meaning missionaries who think that John Chinaman cannot take care of himself . . . On the other hand we see that those most directly interested in getting all the work they can out of John Chinaman, i.e. his employers, actually 'facilitate' the sale of this so-called deadly poison to him.

In other words, opium and coolies were seen as inseparable business opportunities.

The spread of opium, allied to an awareness of its effects, led to the birth of international drug control. Until 1900, international attention had been directed at and against the opium trade between India and China but, by the time the agreement between Britain and China was reached in 1908, the situation in the remainder of the world was out of control, despite occasional treaties between individual governments. It was realised that the trade could not be policed by individual countries and that the main thrust of action lay in the prevention of distribution. This was seen to be all the more relevant with the discovery of morphine and the other derivatives which not only exacerbated the problem but, being concentrates, could be easily transported licitly or illicitly across international borders.

One of the first moves against opium on an international front was made by America. As a result of the Spanish–American War, the United States annexed the Philippine Islands in 1898, inheriting a substantial opium problem for the Chinese minority of the Philippines was heavily addicted, their supplies coming from Persia, Turkey, Indo-China and China. Just after the turn of the century, there were 190 opium dens in the Philippines catering only for the Chinese, 5 per cent of the total population of Manila being habituated.

The Spanish had allowed opium trading under a monopoly system: dealers bid for their franchise and the exchequer benefited. At an annual revenue loss of $500,000, the Americans closed down the system and banned opium dens. Despite this, addiction rates rose so a commission was appointed in 1903 to address the problem and study the Far Eastern opium trade. The report of the Philippines Opium Commission led to the prohibition of importation into the Philippines except for medicinal purposes, the legislation coming into effect in 1908. Spurred by this success, America set about establishing a global narcotics policy involving both consumer and producer countries.

In 1906, Bishop Charles Henry Brent, a member of the Commission, wrote to President Roosevelt suggesting the time was ripe to call for international action to fight opium traffic and to help China eradicate the drug. Roosevelt agreed but not just on humanitarian grounds: it gave him a chance to strengthen Sino-American relations which had suffered by a ban in 1887 on the importation of opium into the US by any subject of the Emperor of China, thus monopolising the opium trade for American dealers.

In February 1909, the first international congress was convened into opium and its alkaloids. Known as the International Opium Commission, it met in Shanghai, ironically deferring its first meeting by a month out of respect to the recently deceased (and addicted) Dowager Empress. Thirteen countries attended, most of them with territorial possessions or substantial Far Eastern commercial interests. From the start, there were problems. Turkey, the major producer after India, refused to send a delegation whilst Persia merely appointed a local merchant to represent its interests. The Commission was also toothless. It could not draft a convention and no one was bound to any definite policy. Resolutions were debated but only as recommendations which did not have to be ratified by governments.

Despite its impotence, the Shanghai meeting was seminal in finally acknowledging a world problem and, by its fifth resolution, publicly promulgating the danger of addiction. The wording stated that:

> . . . the International Opium Commission finds that the unrestricted manufacture, sale and use of morphine cause a grave danger, and that the morphine habit shows signs of spreading; the International Opium Commission therefore desires to urge strongly on all Governments that it is highly important that drastic measures should be taken by each Government in its own territories and possessions to control the manufacture, sale and distribution of this drug, and also such other derivatives of opium as may appear on scientific inquiry to be liable to similar abuse and productive of like ill effects.

Yet they were just words and it was plain, if lasting reforms were to be brought about, delegates to future conferences had to be given powers.

Hamilton Wright, an American delegate to Shanghai, persuaded the US Secretary of State of the Commission's need for political leverage and he, in turn, contacted the participating nations. Their response was lukewarm; vested interests were reluctant to impose international controls.

After considerable political procrastination, a conference was called at The Hague on 1 December 1911 with twelve nations attending: Turkey remained absent and the Austro-Hungarian delegation, present at Shanghai, chose to withdraw. Those who did attend were cautious and protective of their interests: the statement of a principle was one thing but the curtailment of a profitable multi-national industry was another. The Germans protected their vast pharmaceutical industry, the Portuguese defended their Macanese opium businesses, the Persians minded their thriving poppy cultivation, the Dutch guarded their narcotic trade in the East Indies and the British were still apprehensive for the Indian economy. Nevertheless, the conference was a watershed for delegates were empowered to formulate a convention to place before their respective governments which, after ratification, allowed international legislation to be discussed. By January 1912, the meeting resulted in an agreement providing for the control of opium production and the prohibition of its non-medical use.

It looked better in print than it was: it certainly addressed the subject of international traffic, and the signatory nations agreed to control manufacture and distribution of medicinal opium, morphine and heroin (amongst other drugs) and to confine consumption, but it did not define the term 'control' and there were many more ambiguities in the Convention than there were pledges for action. As before, the various governments were loathe to risk losing tax revenues although they conceded there was an international narcotics problem. Where the convention was of use was in providing a blueprint for future legislation as well as in chemically defining both opiates and cocaine, thus stymieing many smugglers who had used loopholes in existing national laws to get away with trafficking substances by claiming they were mere derivative or substitute compounds.

Getting governments to agree to the Convention was one thing: getting them to approve it was another. Although it was mutually accepted the Convention would not come into force until the end of December 1914, and interim meetings in 1913 and 1914 were convened to chivvy matters along, only eleven countries ratified it. Three days after the last meeting ended, Archduke Ferdinand was assassinated, the Great War intervened in the situation, control measures went by the board and drug production and use rapidly escalated to cope with military demand. Meanwhile, in the Far East, opium smoking continued unaffected.

With the cessation of hostilities, the opportunity to draw all nations together against a future war was seen as a chance to bring them together in drug control. Measures concerning opium were contained in the Treaty of Versailles and, in 1921, the League of Nations set up an Advisory Committee on the Traffic in Opium and other Dangerous Drugs which co-ordinated international drugs information and recorded instances of smuggling. This quickly showed an alarming trend: international drug smuggling was rampant and increasing fast.

In November 1924, two conferences were called a fortnight apart. Known collectively as the International Opium Conference, they were held in Geneva, the first dealing with opium in the Far East and China, the second with opium manufacture. To the former only six governments, with colonial administrations in South-east Asia, and China attended. It was a fraught meeting. The Chinese were still peeved at the presence of foreign traders on her shores providing a cover for drug smugglers whilst the other nations accused China of exporting opium. By the end of the discussion sessions it was agreed to abolish all concessionary opium dealerships with governments taking control of opium through a system of licensing and prohibiting re-exportation. Sadly, this provision only referred to opium: smugglers could continue to run morphine and other opiates with virtual impunity.

Thirty-six governments were represented at the second conference. The USSR stayed away, piously stating it had already put its house in order. The meetings soon degenerated into farce. Universal agreement was impossible. User nations felt defenceless unless the producers halted production, thus robbing smugglers and traders of supply. The producers refused to ruin the livelihoods of their farmers. India claimed it needed opium for home consumption whilst Persia declared it was impossible to find an alternative cash crop. Only China as producer – rather than user – was prepared to consider a reduction but would not act alone. When it was clear no one would face the reality that the only way to address the problem was to cut production, the Americans walked out, followed by the Chinese.

Not all was lost, though. The first international control rules on opium and its alkaloids were instigated and it was agreed to maintain a statistical database of global opium production, the needs of the pharmaceutical industries and routes of traffic and to trade with an official body called the Central Board constituted to police the regulations.

In 1929, the League of Nations sponsored another abortive conference but, two years later, at the Geneva Conference on the Limitation of the Manufacture of Narcotic Drugs, fifty-seven nations assented to a Convention which established a rigorous drug classification system, including provision for new derivatives, forbade the exportation of heroin without the consent of the importing nation and declared a positive need to drive against illegal trading.

Every producer nation was obliged to publish annual estimates for drug demand and a quota system was organised. A supervisory body was established to monitor international drug movements and, where countries refused to comply, it assessed their trade in order to find out where illicit supplies originated. The Convention, which aroused one of the most important tools in the fight against drug smuggling – public opinion – was deemed 'a bold conception without precedent in the history of international relations and international law.'

Gradually, international treaties were taking effect and governments which did not want to be condemned by the international community were being forced to restrict their opiate trade. Despite the seemingly confused situation, and the apparent ineffectuality of the many treaties, the world's opium supply actually fell steadily, from 42,000 tons in 1906 to 8,000 tons in 1934.

In 1936, the Conference for the Suppression of the Illicit Traffic in Dangerous Drugs was called to deal with criminal aspects of drug smuggling. Detection methods were discussed, along with a code of punishment for narcotics offences. It was essentially a waste of time: mere prohibition was ineffectual. Towards the end of the decade, the League of Nations Advisory Committee started looking into the limitation of production but developments were tentative.

In summary, by 1939, there existed a substantial corpus of international legislation controlling opium and its derivatives, but basically the laws were often loosely drawn up, the main obstacle to getting them passed being the reluctance of countries with vested interests: resolutions were frequently watered down to the point of ineffectuality in order to be acceptable to all parties. In many instances only the Americans, who had been the initial driving force from the turn of the century, mooted for really robust laws. Producing-nations protected their revenues – just as the British had over a century before – and their farmers for whom poppy growing was an essential livelihood. Almost every nation gained from taxing drugs coming into their country or colonial possessions whilst others made substantial profits from opium derivative manufacture which they would not restrict.

Governmental opium control in the Far East for example, as suggested by the first 1924 conference, meant a lucrative opportunity for raising tax revenue by the licensing of opium retailers and the official control of opium stocks. All the colonial powers in Asia, although overtly trying to cut down on opium smoking by reducing the number of retail outlets, earned magnificently from opium taxation. An indication of this may be gleaned from official accounts: in 1918, opium accounted for 46 per cent of the revenue of the Unfederated Malay States and in 1923 for 48 per cent of the total in the Straits Settlements. In 1920, with the 'farm' system still running, the following story appeared in the *Shanghai Gazette*:

> Macao, May 21. The bidding was very keen to-day for the opium monopoly for the three years commencing August 1st, the first offer being $2,500,000 [Mexican silver dollars] annually. Spirited competition brought the price up to $3,950,000 and the farm was adjudicated to the Lee Sing Company, Hong Kong.

Three years later, the *China Year Book*, a gazetteer for merchants, remarked:

> The revenue of the colony [of Macau] is mainly derived from gambling and opium . . . There is unquestionably strong feeling in South China regarding the possession by the Portuguese of a colony which derives the bulk of its revenue from sources which have been proclaimed illegal within the territories of the Chinese Republic.

Some observers blamed the colonial powers, and Britain in particular, for dragging their feet. One, Ellen La Motte, in *The Ethics of Opium* published in 1924, condemned colonial nations for their attitudes. She astutely remarked, 'If opium is produced for the Orient, the overflow of that output must necessarily filter back into Europe and America.' She could not have foreseen the prophecy in her words.

The complexities of applying the new laws in opium dependent countries are illustrated by the problems India faced. The government there insisted opium eating was a legitimate use akin to that of the medicinal, arguing eaten opium was non-addictive, was a legitimate stimulant in lieu of alcohol and not detrimental to public health. An Indian Government publication brought out in 1923 and entitled *The Truth about Indian Opium* stated:

> The prohibition of opium-eating in India we regard as impossible . . . Opium is in virtually universal use throughout India as the commonest and most treasured of the household remedies accessible to the people . . . The vast bulk of the Indian population, it must be remembered, are strangers to the ministrations of qualified doctors or druggists. They are dependent almost entirely on the herbal simples of the country . . . To prevent the sale of opium except under regular medical prescription would be sheer inhumanity.

It also argued opium was essential to the country because of its extensive veterinary use in cattle and because elephants also ate large doses although the reason for this is unclear for a drugged elephant can hardly be an adequate beast of labour.

The non-detrimental argument was not universally believed and statistics gathered by anti-opium groups suggested possibly up to 85 per cent of the opium sold fed addiction. As in Britain, infants were calmed with it. *Bala goli* was a common opium sweet given to children, the bitterness of the drug disguised by sugar or spice whilst wet nurses and mothers with querulent babies often smeared opium on their nipples.

Opposition to opium did not just rest with religious or social organisations. Mahatma Gandhi ran a campaign against opium in Assam in 1921 and instituted a 250,000-signature petition with Ramanamdra Chatterjee and the poet Rabindranath Tagore which was presented to the first of the 1924 international conferences. At the same time, sympathisers on the All-India Congress Committee condemned the opium policies, Gandhi remarking: 'It will be no defence to urge that the vice has existed in India from time immemorial. No-one organised the vice, as the present government has, for the purposes of revenue.'

For a while, running as a strand through the conferences, an argument simmered as to which was more harmful, opium eating or smoking. In the past many had held the opinion eating to be the less deleterious but the argument arose that it had to be more harmful than merely inhaling fumes, some of which would not reach the mouth from the pipe but drift into the air. The government of India, which produced mostly eating opium, was of the former opinion which it maintained to the 1930s. Their argument, however, was succinctly put down at the 1924 conference by one delegate standing up and declaring to a pro-eating speaker: 'Very well, I have two cigars. I propose to demoralise myself by smoking one of them, while you eat the other.'

Gradually, throughout the 1930s, the influence of the League of Nations Advisory Committee began to take effect. Poppy cultivation in India in 1935 was down by 90 per cent over the figure of a decade before, although there was a government-held opium mountain and the drug was still a substantial revenue contributor. Yet opium's days seemed numbered. Gandhi's message, linked to that of the international conferences, was informing public opinion against drug taking.

Not all nations were in favour of international controls and some deliberately flouted them, Japan in particular. Wherever there were Japanese businesses or consular offices in China, there was opium, morphine or heroin. A Chinese delegation went to Geneva to try and press their case with the Advisory Committee: they even had film footage of Japanese drug dealings but they were not allowed to screen it in the name of international co-operation.

The film showed opium refineries in the Japanese concession in Hankow, discovered after the Imperial Japanese Army was routed from the city. It was not all it seemed. Certainly, the Japanese were refining opium into morphine base and heroin, but what the film did not go into was the source of the raw opium which was provided by Tu Yueh-sheng, a share of the profits going towards Chiang Kai-shek's army which, in turn, was fighting the Japanese.

As well as continuing to encourage opium usage and addiction in those areas of China she controlled, Japan also secretly encouraged and even financed drug smuggling as a form of passive international terrorism in the run up to Pearl Harbour. Later, during the Second World War, Japanese involvement in opium was to continue: officials in the administrations of Japanese-controlled territories, such as Hong Kong, joined with local underworld figures and war profiteers, obtaining their co-operation by bribing them with opium.

In the years leading up to the Second World War, international co-operation in Geneva broke down as the League of Nations itself began to disintegrate. International smuggling increased further and legal opiate production was stepped up as countries gradually began to prepare for the inevitable conflict ahead.

The anti-narcotic organisations which had been put in place by the League of Nations were retained when the United Nations (UN) was set up after the war, the Advisory Committee being continued as the Commission on Narcotic Drugs, which formulated international agreements and controls whilst co-ordinating the drive against narcotics abuse and sale.

The first new control, the Paris Protocol of 1948, provided for new drugs to be included under international control measures. This was followed by a protocol in 1953 which sought to limit world opium output to medical or scientific use, a group of only seven producer nations being allowed to export opium: they were Bulgaria, Greece, India, Iran, Turkey, the USSR and Yugoslavia, in which poppy farmers were obliged to be licensed and strictly overseen. Other countries were permitted to produce domestically used, non-exportable opium. The acreage of poppy farming and opium production would be calculated by the UN according to estimated international pharmaceutical demand.

The protocol meant well but ran into problems: the proviso allowing domestic production was a huge loophole through which the bandwagon of illicit opium could be driven unhindered. Only fifty-three countries signed the protocol: those who were already opium producers, such as Thailand, Burma, Laos, Afghanistan and Pakistan, rejected it. Afghanistan went so far as to request permission to be a legitimate exporter, arguing opium was a vital cash crop supporting up to 90 per cent of the peasant farming population. The request was denied, the Afghan question remaining on the agenda for some years but doomed never to be resolved.

The Single Convention on Narcotic Drugs of 1961 sought to incorporate all nine of the drugs conventions tabled since 1912. To simplify matters further, the Permanent Central Opium Board and the Drug Supervisory Body were merged into the International Narcotics Control Board (INCB) which was responsible for monitoring the licit narcotics trade and policing international agreements. Amongst its first moves were the tightening of control over cannabis and poppy straw, the international prohibiting of opium and hashish smoking and eating, and coca-leaf chewing, but 'after a transitional period to permit the countries concerned to overcome the difficulties arising from the abolition of these ancient customs', by which proviso, of course, the INCB created a massive catch-all, opt-out clause.

In effect, the Single Convention was not much more than a compromise. Although eighty countries signed it, the register of official exporting nations was closed down in an attempt to address the Afghan problem, to be replaced by a stipulation that only countries which traditionally produced opium for export could carry on supplying world pharmaceutical needs. If other countries wished to join the exporters they had to gain INCB approval. This was not likely to be forthcoming. The INCB attitude was confirmed when Burma's application to export was rejected in 1964, although the American demands for even stricter regulation were also turned down.

Faced with a still increasing international drug problem, the UN began a Fund for Drug Control in 1971. Its purpose was to fight opium production on an economic front. Projects were proposed which covered addiction, the viability of crop substitution and drug enforcement in opium-producing countries. The fund target was initially $95 million but only just above $2 million were raised, most of it by the USA. Other countries sat on their hands: the richer governments said they were not funding what was basically a drive against America's massive drug problems whilst the poorer saw little reason to pay to alleviate what was in their eyes a First World dilemma. UN involvement remains extant today in the UN International Drug Control Programme.

The 1961 Single Convention was amended by the 1971 Convention on Psychotropic Substances and, later, a 1972 protocol. In 1988, another convention, the Convention Against Illicit Traffic in Narcotic Drugs and Psychotropic Substances, was introduced. The publishing of conventions and protocols was, and remains, all very well but it cannot really address the subject. In characteristic UN fashion, there has been much talk but relatively little result. Fine words have often not led to firm actions. Merely determining policies, making intentions to eradicate addiction, setting world quotas on opium production and suggesting ways of counteracting the trade do not necessarily achieve anything. To be effective, the

UN has to flex its muscle, wave the stick of trade sanctions, institute trade and aid embargoes, even endorse military intervention. Yet it does not and it cannot. To be effectual, the UN has to have a series of criteria in place as a foundation: every nation must be effective against opium within its own borders and there must be an international regard to drug laws so they are more or less equal in every jurisdiction, closing cracks through which drug traffickers may squeeze. The UN must be given enough international diplomatic strength to override national political and economic interests.

If the UN has lacked the clout to effectively address such problems as the war in the former Yugoslavia, the commitment to sort out political problems in Somalia, the means to prevent genocide in central Africa and starvation world-wide, what hope can one have that it will be of any use in the fight against opium and its derivatives?

10

Junkies and the Living Dead

For centuries, addiction was regarded as an unavoidable inconvenience of opiate consumption and rarely considered a problem: 100 years ago doctors frequently referred to users, without any alarm or censure, not as addicts but as 'habitués'. Addiction was not seen as evil but a minor social vice although there was often an underlying apprehension it might lead to worse. This misgiving very slowly grew as the notion of addiction came to be feared and the addict came to be regarded as a corrupted, perverted menace. This change of opinion, the addict metamorphosing from harmless misfortunate to loathsome criminal, came, as did the first moves for international control, from the USA.

From its earliest years, America had an opium problem. It was used as a therapeutic medicine in the colonial era and was extensively relied upon during the War of Independence by both American and British forces, to the extent there was such a shortage some doctors, like Dr Thaddeus Betts, grew their own. In fact, at various times throughout American history, poppies have been cultivated in states ranging as widely as New Hampshire, Florida and California. As the post-colonial population expanded, and immigration increased, epidemics raged through the eastern states so that, by 1840, opium taking, both as a medicine and to maintain medically inspired addiction, was widespread. As well as laudanum, a Dr Barton invented what he called 'The Brown Mixture', a concoction of opium and liquorice similar to that of the ancient Assyrians, which also became a common medicine. By 1860, opium posed a major social issue in America, as it did in Europe, the American Civil War considerably magnifying the problem. An article by Fitzhugh Ludlow in *Harper's Magazine* in 1867 stated:

> The habit is gaining fearful ground among our professional men, the operatives in our mills, our weary serving women, our fagged clerks, our former liquor drunkards, our very day laborers, who a generation ago took gin. All our classes from the highest to the lowest are yearly increasing their consumption of the drug.

Furthermore, the patent medicine industry boomed with such opium containing concoctions as 'Hooper's Anodyne, the Infant's Friend' (a baby soothing syrup), although opiate usage was not as widespread as in Britain, for the people led different life-styles and the poor were not always so trapped in industrial ghettos but often living a more pastoral existence. Nevertheless, as opium began to gather a dubious reputation, the patent medicine industry held out against legislation for the publication of ingredients on labels. Many popular brands contained high levels of opium until 1906 when the Pure Food and Drugs Act came into force, after which people saw what they were taking and morphine and opium demand plummeted. It might be remembered not only opiates were involved. Until 1903 Coca-Cola contained cocaine: it was indeed 'The Real Thing' in those days. John Pemberton, its pharmacist co-inventor, was a morphine addict.

Not only opium addiction increased. Amongst the well-off, morphinism spread with the introduction of the hypodermic syringe, many of the addicts being society ladies. Indeed, addiction was far more prevalent amongst Caucasians than coloured or native American Indian groups, no doubt because these latter lacked the financial resources to buy medicines or hire doctors. Their poverty protected them. By 1875, the southern states had a much higher addict population because of the prevalence of subtropical diseases and the after-effects of the Civil War.

A typical southern addict was female, Caucasian, reasonably well off and addicted through medicinal use. Mrs Henry Lafayette Dubose in Harper Lee's novel, *To Kill a Mockingbird*, is a fictional portrait of such a woman: widowed and living in a small Alabama town, she is a picture of discreet decay. As was the case with many well-to-do addicts, she was regarded sympathetically and ultimately died, weighing only 28 pounds, having kicked her habit: Atticus, her neighbour and lawyer, held her up to his children as an example of extreme courage, a woman battling addiction and winning against the odds.

As the dangers of opium and morphine became more widely known, the reformers more vociferous and effective and the addicts created by the Civil War and medical ignorance died off, demand in America fell but, as long as they existed, opiates were seen as relatively devoid of evil and addicts not considered an evil threat but objects for compassion. It was not until the 1920s that public perception radically altered, when addicts who had become hooked through medical use were replaced by recreational drug takers of whom the public grew afraid. These were not the ill or invalids but self-indulgent, irresponsible, lower-class members on society's periphery. By 1930, the likes of Mrs Dubose were out of date, to be replaced by less agreeable fictional characters like the hustling poker-playing addict in Nelson Algren's novel, *Man With the Golden Arm*. This change of attitude was mainly caused by legislation brought in to address the increase in recreational drug taking.

Recreational drug use in America was not new. Opium smoking had been known since the first Chinese coolies arrived, spurred on by the California gold rush of 1848—9. Over the next two decades, wave upon wave of southern Chinese labourers landed on the west coast, bringing with them the habit and the institution of the opium den. At first, it was contained within Chinese communities, where dens became more than just drug-taking shops. They evolved into iniquitous dives, offering an opium divan, gambling, prostitution, loan-sharking and Chinese food: in short, they became corrupt community centres and a further drain on the coolies' meagre earnings, creating a vicious spiral. The coolie, whose dream was to return eventually to the land of his ancestors, earned a wage but lost much of it in deductions; of what he was left (about $1 a day was average) he spent half in the dens. This retarded his chances of returning to China and, made miserable by the thought, he smoked more. The coolies were in thrall to opium and, consequently, to the *tongs*, Chinese criminal secret societies which were the forerunners of modern Triad groups.

The effects of the habit were known but largely ignored by both medical and social circles unless they impinged upon the community at large outside the embryonic Chinatowns. The general opinion was voiced in 1874 by Dr J.P. Newman, Chaplain to the United States Senate, who said:

> The Chinese come in great numbers as domestic servants, washermen, labourers, miners etc. We are doing what we can to civilize and Christianize them – for we are giving them schools of learning and temples of religion – but they have come to us debilitated, they have come enervated by the influence of opium. We need them as labourers, need them as servants, we need them as citizens; for in that great region from the Missouri to the Golden Gate there is less than one million of white inhabitants. We therefore bid them welcome, but we cannot bid them welcome as opium smokers.

In other words, they were welcome as minions but only so long as they could work: and there was no mention of helping them kick the habit.

As they frequently do to this day, the Chinese communities kept to themselves in self-imposed ghettos, often on the rough side of town where other racial groups spurned them. It was therefore inevitable the only non-Asians they met were other outcasts, those of the criminal underworld.

The first white man to smoke opium is said to have been a gambler called Clendenyn, in San Francisco in 1868. Presumably as a saloon gambler and perhaps a petty criminal, he was working the Chinese dens. The practice soon gained popularity. The exclusivity of the dens gave a sense of protection and identity to these minor outlaws, shunned by their own kind but willingly hosted by the Chinese. The dens, colloquially known as 'dives' or 'joints', became centres of criminal activity. The origin of the words is interesting: 'dive' is an abbreviation of divan and therefore directly related to opium whilst 'joint' derives from an Anglo-Irish word for a low ante-room, such as was found in brothels where prostitutes entertained their clients.

As the American West opened up eastward, the Chinese spread and established their communities, each with at least one den providing not only a smoking base and meeting place but also a network of safe houses for the non-Asian criminal fraternity. Some dens were elaborate multi-bunk houses – of the twenty-six operating in San Francisco's Chinatown in 1885, most catered for twenty-four smokers at a time and were located mainly in an area bounded by Stockton, Washington, Dupont and Pacific Streets. Others were just rooms of chop-houses or Chinese laundries, stores or lodging houses.

Opium smoking reached its summit in 1883 with the importation, mostly through San Francisco, of 208,152 pounds of smoking opium. The actual size of the addict population was unknown but the *San Francisco Evening Post* estimated in 1875 there were 120,000 opium addicts in the United States, but said the figure *excluded* the Chinese.

From the late nineteenth century, opium dens were to become more than just houses of addiction and crime. They were the birthplace of the American drug subculture, a cosmopolitan fusion of Oriental and Occidental mores, myths and values. An esoteric argot developed: 'the long draw' was an ability to inhale an entire opium pill with one breath, those who prepared opium pills and pipes were called 'chefs' and the smoking habit was known as 'yen', from the verb 'to smoke' in the Peking dialect. Many of these words later entered the general vocabulary, carried by non-criminal bohemian smokers such as actors and writers who imbibed: today, 'to have a yen' means to possess a longing for something.

Although opium smoking was nothing like as widespread as morphine injecting, it was viewed by the public with horror. This was not based upon the fear of addiction but upon racial hatred: the Chinese were regarded as the Yellow Peril and to be avoided.

This racial attitude affected not only public but official opinion. It was said, without much foundation, that respectable women were visiting the dens to engage in sexual intercourse with the dreaded Celestials, their sexual appetites having been aroused by opium. That opium was a narcotic was conveniently overlooked by the xenophobes. None the less, reports of debauchery circulated: a San Francisco doctor, Winslow Anderson, claimed he saw the 'sickening sight of young white girls from sixteen to twenty years of age lying half-undressed on the floor or couches, smoking with their lovers. Men and women, Chinese and white people, mix in Chinatown smoking houses.' Probably one of the first instances of the association of race, drugs and sex, it was surely inaccurate: any woman to be found in such a state in an opium den was likely to be a prostitute.

It was only a matter of time before action was taken. In 1875 the San Francisco municipal authority, under the pressure of offended public opinion, passed an ordinance forbidding the smoking of opium, the possession of opium or the paraphernalia needed to smoke it and the organising of a smoking house. Virginia City, with a substantial Chinese population, followed suit in 1876. Enforcement was patchy. Those dens to which whites went were closed down, on racial grounds, but smaller establishments catering primarily for Chinese were ignored.

The result of the ordinance in most places was simply to transfer non-Chinese smokers to boarding houses owned by Caucasians on the fringes of Chinese residential areas, where they continued their habit, whilst wealthy users frequently set up their own dens for well-heeled clients and friends. Supplies were obtained through Chinese opium merchants.

Despite local ordinances being passed in twenty-seven states by 1915, opium smoking steadily increased until federal legislation was enacted which made the vice so risky and expensive smokers turned to other opiate use. In this lay part of the root of the problem as it exists now: smoking, whilst harmful, was far less dangerous than injecting morphine or, in due course, injecting or smoking heroin.

Imported smoking opium or domestically produced supplies made from raw opium imports were heavily taxed, the levy of 75 cents an ounce sufficiently exorbitant as to encourage vast smuggling operations run almost exclusively by the *tongs*. In addition, large numbers of Chinese set up in business as 'cooks' running 'opium kitchens' in which, in direct contravention of the 1890 law prohibiting non-native Americans from engaging in opium manufacture, they processed raw opium into the smoking product.

By the end of the century, demand for smoking opium reached a plateau then began to fall, mainly because the Chinese population similarly began to drop due to immigration controls and voluntary repatriation in the face of racial abuse. Nevertheless, it was realised the only way to combat opium was not in individual state legislatures but federally.

Hamilton Wright, preparing for the 1909 conference in Shanghai, lobbied Congress for federal legislation. If the USA was to lead the world against opium, he argued, it had to put its own house in order, too. Yet there was more to it. With some states prohibiting opium and others not, there was a brisk inter-state smuggling traffic which had to be addressed.

Just before the Shanghai conference, the Senate passed the Smoking Opium Exclusion Act which illegalised all imports of opium save those brought in by registered pharmaceutical firms. Severe fines and terms of imprisonment were put in place and possession was sufficient cause for arrest. Suddenly, opium was regarded as a criminal substance to which was attributed the romantic thrill of the danger of illegality. It also suggested opium was an alien substance, contrary to the American way of life – a filthy Oriental habit – which set the tone for drug enforcement. As might have been expected, smuggling increased sharply, the street price of opium rose and criminal gangs started to make substantial profits.

Wealthy smokers, especially those connected to show business, high-class call-girls and rich criminals, maintained their smoking habit, protected by their riches or position from arrest or shortage. By the 1920s, most of the major American cities had opium-smoking locations: those with gangster residents, such as Miami, New York and Chicago, were particularly well catered for as was Los Angeles with its movie industry. In Errol Flynn's autobiography, *My Wicked, Wicked Ways*, he describes in detail his smoking of opium in a den, being introduced to the place by a Chinese girl called Ting Ling. Inevitably, Flynn insists opium improved his sexual capabilities, rather than suppressing them.

Opium smoking was fashionable. Smokers, colloquially known as 'pipies', considered themselves a drug élite and superior to heroin users. Newspaper stories circulated about parties held for smoking, the guests arriving in their pyjamas as if ready for bed: sex and drugs were already inseparable. For the vast majority of smokers, who were not protected by fame or fortune, there was only one alternative: they turned to morphine and heroin which were cheaper to buy, easier to hide and less conspicuous to use. In time, the smoking élite also turned to other drugs, as smoking opium became more and more rare and less was smuggled because of its bulk.

The crackdown also affected the Chinese. The Californian police mounted a concerted, 18 month drive starting in 1913, resulting in 1200 convictions and a public bonfire of opium and pipes. Many of these were not merely drug equipment but valuable antiques centuries old. Reluctant at first to give up smoking, the Chinese were also eventually forced to change to morphine and heroin, the last smokers disappearing in the New York area during the Second World War.

Hamilton Wright continued his campaigning but, for all his philanthropic intention, he was also a scaremonger playing upon xenophobic and racial unease, stressing the dangers drugs posed to white people: in 1910, he published a report, playing upon racial fear, in which he wrote negroes in the South were taking cocaine which put white women at risk, presumably from fornication. This was clearly bunkum but it set a trend, an attitude towards drugs which has survived. What was more, statistics released to the public grossly exaggerated addict numbers so the drug problem seemed far greater than it was: from 1910 to 1940, attitudes towards opiate addiction which, at times, verged on the hysterical, were profoundly influenced by erroneous and occasionally deliberately manipulated figures, though obtaining accurate statistics about addicts has always been difficult because they do not volunteer to be counted.

After agreement made at the Hague Conference of 1911 and due to Wright's work, the Harrison Narcotic Act – called after its instigator, Congressman Francis Burton Harrison – was passed in 1914. It did not actually prohibit narcotics as force doctors, chemists and other legalised dealers to register, pay a nominal tax and maintain records of drug transactions. There was, however, a loophole depending upon medical opinion and legal interpretation. If addiction was considered a disease, a doctor was obligated to cure it: if it was seen to be a vice, his prescription might maintain (or feed) addiction, thus making him commit a criminal offence. In 1919, the Supreme Court came down in favour of the latter interpretation and, over the next quarter of a century, 25,000 doctors were prosecuted for prescribing narcotics to addicts. The ruling gave rise to 'dope doctors', corrupt general practitioners who prescribed opiates for cash, the addict's alternative being the criminal underworld. This further reduced addiction amongst middle-class white women who were loathe or afraid to associate with criminals.

Illicit heroin was readily obtainable throughout metropolitan areas in America. It was cheaper than morphine and gave a bigger, quicker kick. Those who could not inject it, snorted it. Addiction being what it was, criminals charged increasing sums for supplies, driving their clients to petty crime to pay for their habit. Simultaneously, cocaine was legislated against, leading many users to move over to heroin.

Heroin had for some time been used by young men in the underworld but rarely outside it. From 1910, however, heroin usage spread like wildfire across America. By the time alcohol was prohibited in 1920, heroin was well established and, with the added repression on liquor, the stage was set for the arrival of the junkie.

The term 'junkie', so common today, is thought to have been coined in the early 1920s, although opium was referred to as 'junk' at the turn of the century. Originally, it meant a junk-man, a rag-and-bone man or totter who travelled the streets buying scrap metal, wood and cloth. Aware of the fact garbage could have a value, New York City addicts earned money by picking through the city dumps for discarded metal to sell.

Other American colloquialisms existed from time to time: an addict was variously known as a 'schmecker' (from the Yiddish *shmek*, meaning a smell or sniff), a 'hype' (from hypodermic) and a 'hophead'. The latter has a fascinating derivation. In the late nineteenth century, when the Chinese were the main suppliers of opium, the drug was known as 'hop'. This was an Anglicised, shortened version of the colloquial Cantonese name for opium, *nga pin*, pronounced *ha peen*, and meaning bird or crow shit. In white American society, this was melded with hops, as used in beer, to imply a substance of intoxication.

Most heroin addicts were addicted in their late teens or early twenties, although a substantial number were older, having transferred from opium or morphine. The vast majority were male and, until the 1940s, Caucasians outnumbered blacks. New York street gangs were especial breeding grounds for addicts. Heroin use was a part of gang initiation, an aspect of the destructive and dangerous pastimes in which gang members traditionally indulged. Indeed, New York was as now the heroin centre of America, the base for almost every heroin dealer in the nation: 90 per cent of America's heroin addicts lived within 180 miles of Manhattan. Downtown precincts were the addicts' territory, the tenements and low-cost housing blocks containing poor families in which addiction was frequently rife. Addicts roamed the streets, looking like bums. Those addicts who were not reduced to sorting junk typically held low-paid, semi- or unskilled jobs whilst the small number of female addicts were virtually all prostitutes.

For several years from 1919, addicts in cities across America were catered for by a chain of forty-four clinics which sought to gather statistics on addiction, register addicts, supply them with drugs and examine their problem. One, set up along strict disciplined lines by the New York City Health Department, was a visitor attraction like a working theme park and featured on city tours. The clinics were a failure because widespread street peddling supplied addicts without their having to submit to a clinical regime, attendance at them was not compulsory and the 1919 Supreme Court judgment in effect made them illegal because they were seen as maintaining a vice. By 1921 all but one – in Shreveport, Louisiana, which remained open until 1923 – were closed by the federal authorities.

Gradually, heroin usage spread first from New York to other eastern seaboard cities, then westwards. By 1930, heroin was to be found nation-wide. Furthermore, from about 1925, the pattern of addiction began to alter with large numbers of negro workers migrating north. To counter their misery and poverty in the cold, northern cities, they played jazz, sang the blues and used heroin.

By the 1920s, heroin was being injected. At first, it was injected subcutaneously or intramuscularly but it was not long before mainlining became the mode. There are several reasons suggested for the popularity of the hypodermic but the primary one is the lowering standard of heroin purity caused by the success of legislation on production and by the selling methods employed by Italians who took over distribution from Jewish gangs, leading to an increase in price and higher levels of adulteration. The heroin was cut with finely ground sugar, milk powder or talc to give it bulk but this reduced its effect so any method which could release a dose into the system quickly and thoroughly was eagerly followed. By 1939, street heroin was only 27.5 per cent pure.

Addict statistics may have been inflated but the problem was serious. The Italians were ruthlessly efficient. Some peddlers, eager to extend their customer base, were reported to resort to giving free initial samples which acted as loss-leaders: once an addict was hooked the demand was established. This creation of a market was not as widespread as common myth would have it although crime rates started to build where there were addict-rich communities.

Scandals in Hollywood did nothing to allay public apprehension concerning drugs: if the popular heroes of the silver screen were susceptible, then no one was safe.

Surviving as much on calumny as celluloid, Hollywood was a quidnunc's dream and several high-profile drug scandals provided good copy. Olive Thomas, one of Ziegfeld's most beautiful show-girls and a rising actress, was found poisoned in Paris in September 1920. It came as a shock when it was found she had been obtaining drugs from a US Army captain, called Spaulding, who was a heroin and cocaine dealer. Her death prompted an outcry, culminating in Cardinal Mundelein of Chicago issuing a pamphlet entitled *The Danger of Hollywood: A Warning to Young Girls*. Two years later, Wallace Reid, Paramount's main star, was committed to a sanatorium. Addicted to morphine, first taken at the instigation of a fellow actor to counteract exhaustion whilst filming *Forever* in 1920, he died in the sanatorium in January 1923, his addiction and his health broken. The next film his wife Florence made was called *Human Wreckage*: it was an exposé of the drug trade and prohibited in Britain because of its vivid scenes of drug taking.

The same actor who hooked Wallace Reid, who worked on the Sennett lot, was pusher to the stars. Known as The Count, he also addicted Mabel Normand, Barbara La Marr, Alma Rubens and Juanita Hansen. Barbara La Marr died in 1926, aged thirty, of an overdose of opiates and cocaine: the studio put it about she died of anorexia. Alma Rubens tried to break her habit but she was physically too degenerated to survive: she died in 1931, aged thirty-three. Juanita Hansen was comparatively fortunate. She kicked her heroin habit but lost her career, later founding the Juanita Hansen Foundation which crusaded for doctors to wage war against addiction.

The US government made a number of attempts to counteract the growing problem. A Committee on Drug Addiction was set up in 1921: the Narcotic Drugs Import and Export Act of 1922 increased penalties and established the Federal Narcotics Control Board. Congress effectively outlawed all domestic use and production of heroin in 1924 and, three years later, formed the Bureau of Prohibition, the commissioner being made responsible for enforcing the Harrison Act, previously the responsibility of the

Internal Revenue Service. In another three years, responsibility was passed to the Justice Department which inaugurated the Federal Bureau of Narcotics (FBN), not only to enforce the Harrison Act but to provide international liaison and co-operation and delegates to conferences.

All these changes had little effect. Heroin addiction did not substantially fall and smuggling continued as before.

Such was the problem that, by 1930, 35 per cent of all convicts in America were indicted under the Harrison Act. The Public Health Service instituted federal hospitalisation of addicts in narcotic 'farms' at Fort Worth, Texas, and Lexington, Kentucky. Many in the medical world considered addiction was the result of personality disorders akin to a form of insanity, requiring compensatory institutionalisation. Accordingly, these 'farms' were austere premises built like prisons, staffed by warder-like nurses and with régimes to match.

With hindsight, it can be argued the Harrison Act was positively harmful. It forced addicts across the legal divide, criminalising them and causing them to seek underworld drug supplies. It also consolidated the connection between the addict and the criminal which had always been there but was weak in the face of a legitimate or semi-legitimate drugs trade. In the eyes of the public, the act tarred all addicts with the same brush, be they down-and-out petty criminals or members of the establishment. It can further be argued, at the time of the Act, drug use had reached a peak and was beginning to fall naturally, affected by the problems of prescribing morphine and the development of alternative medicines. The Act exacerbated, even exaggerated, the situation by giving drugs the status of illegality, suggesting the problem to be greater than it was and providing criminals with a new commodity.

Not only the US government aimed to eradicate addiction: so did others who, in the 1920s, sought their goal through fear and near public hysteria. One of these was Richard P. Hobson, a pious, Prohibitionist zealot who, once liquor was banned, redirected his attention to dope. Described as a person of virtually unlimited moral indignation, he was not interested in preventative measures. He wanted a crusade. To this end, Hobson promoted the idea that heroin propelled addicts into the most heinous acts. Broadcasting nation-wide in 1928, he referred to addicts as criminal zombies, the Living Dead. Addiction, he declared, was like leprosy but not as remediable and far more readily contracted, addicts being carriers of this disease which, he went on, threatened the whole of mankind with violence and crime. The threat he perceived was genuine enough and Hobson's rabid zeal only further alienated addicts. It was no wonder attitudes hardened and, by the outbreak of the Second World War, where there had previously been a variety of addicts from the southern lady to the Chinese coolie, the saloon gambler to the street gang member, there was now only one – the despised, depraved and villainous junkie.

The Second World War greatly disrupted international trafficking and many thousands of addicts were forced to undergo cold turkey. The FBN found its workload shrinking for the addict population dropped from around 200,000 to 20,000 by 1945.

As the war took hold in Europe and the Far East, heroin supplies came mostly from south of the border in Mexico. It is said enterprising Chinese from San Francisco, realising poppies would probably grow well in Mexico, took seeds to farmers in the hills of Sinaloa province, inland from the cities of Culiacán and Mazatlán on the Gulf of California, who cultivated them. Mexican heroin was rough stuff, never over 50 per cent pure (and sometimes as impure as 30 per cent) and a dirty brown in colour. To make it go a long way, the dealers adulterated it by as much as 97 per cent with sugar or milk powder. Morphine was cut by 35 per cent with novocaine, baking soda, powdered boric acid and talc. Some dealers sold counterfeit heroin which had no result in the addict whatsoever and a good many, faced with virtually non-existent supplies of opiates, turned to such drugs as marijuana.

Between 1945 and 1970, the penalties for drug dealing in the USA underwent a series of sea changes. At first, capital punishments were levelled: the federal penalty for the sale of heroin by someone over eighteen to a buyer under eighteen was death at the jury's discretion. Drug dealers were sent to the electric chair or the gas chamber but this penalty and others created a strong reaction in society and the onus of responsibility for the control of drugs was passed to doctors and psychotherapists. The threat of Death Row had not had the desired effect. Addiction rates steadily rose, fuelling crime against property. With a new faith in medical and psychological treatment, penalties under federal laws were reduced to mandatory minimum gaol sentences, obligatory participation in detoxification programmes, flexible sentences and even the maintenance of addiction under medical supervision.

The demographic nature of addiction altered, too. In the immediate post-war years to 1950, there was a sharp increase in heroin abuse in the black and Latino ghettos of northern cities to which southern blacks had migrated over the previous two decades and to which Latin Americans had flocked during the war. This development so worried the FBN that, in 1951, a mandatory minimum sentence of two years was instituted for a first conviction of narcotics possession.

This minimum sentence entered the statute books just as the dread of Communism and Soviet aggression was growing to the mania of McCarthyism. It was a natural progression of Senator McCarthy's rabid zeal that narcotics be linked to the Communist conspiracy.

The FBN associated China's need for foreign currency with her determination to destroy Western society and the trafficking of heroin into the USA. Claiming most heroin in North America was of Chinese origin, the US government frequently complained in the UN. Harry Anslinger, Director of the FBN, declared in 1954 that the Chinese had a twenty-year plan to finance political activities and spread addiction in the USA. Although he continued to voice this opinion into the 1960s, he was wrong. FBN reports in the 1960s showed China was neither exporting any opium or opiates nor producing them, except for her exact pharmaceutical requirement.

By 1965, the heroin epidemic had spread into suburban middle-class neighbourhoods. The post war 'baby boomers' had come of age, the population in the 15–24 age group increasing by 50 per cent over five years. It was these white middle-class youngsters who began experimenting with heroin on the campuses and street corners of America. The culture of permissiveness, free love, pot and rock 'n' roll promoted experimentation: the catchphrase was 'be cool'. Between 1960 and 1970, the number of heroin users rose from approximately 50,000 to 500,000.

Many of the new youth sought heroes: most found them in sports personalities, political activists and pop stars but for a significant number, particularly those with a modicum of education, the hero was a writer – Jack Kerouac.

An American of French-Canadian and Mohawk-Caughnawaga

Indian extraction, Kerouac was the archetypal addict writer who described himself as a strange, solitary, crazy, Catholic mystic. A university drop-out with a good education and a sharp intellect, he was a rebellious drifter who wandered America like a hobo, rejecting, commenting upon and criticising the safe foundations of the American dream. He started his drug career with benzedrine then moved to marijuana. When he fell under the influence of another American writer, William Burroughs, he was introduced not only to the underworld characters of his stories and poetry but also to morphine and heroin. It was Burroughs who called his apartment a 'shooting gallery' – his friends could shoot up there: the phrase entered every addict's dictionary. Later, in Mexico, Kerouac experimented with mescaline, peyote, and goof-balls (barbiturates): he was also an alcoholic.

Most of Kerouac's innovative writing was done under the influence of drugs. He abandoned accepted literary techniques, turning to hallucinatory and stream-of-consciousness styles, using words as jazz musicians used musical phrases. His novel, *On the Road*, was published in 1957 and it is arguably the most influential American novel of the twentieth century. The hero is a young man, Dean Moriarty, a foot-loose traveller who became the archetypal American hero, a spiritual extension of the pioneers of old who lived free. Criticised for its hedonism, degeneracy and disregard for established social mores, young people saw it as an adventure. It started a whole new youth culture of which drugs were an accepted part: it might be said to have caused the birth of the modern drug 'culture.'

The drastic rise in addiction in the 1960s was met with a massive programme for the building of mental health centres throughout America which heralded new attitudes. The mental health establishment had a different view of addiction from the one held by the FBN: addiction was a physical or psychological disease requiring treatment and, as law enforcement had failed, it was perhaps time to try a new approach. Gradually, it was accepted that crime and drug abuse were widespread throughout society, cutting across class and ethnic boundaries and that the real criminals were the pushers, dealers and organised crime bosses, not the addicts.

Outpatient clinics offering methadone maintenance created a favourable response to the medical treatment of heroin addiction and led to the 1963 Presidential Commission on Narcotic and Drug

Abuse which supported relaxing mandatory minimum sentences and increasing funding for research into all aspects of narcotic and drug abuse. Three years later, the Bureau of Drug Abuse Control of the Food and Drug Administration was set up under the umbrella of the Department of Health, Education and Welfare. Then, in 1968, both it and the FBN were abolished and the Bureau of Narcotics and Dangerous Drugs (BNDD) established with international responsibilities and contacts. Funding was increased, agents were trained and a long-term programme of enforcement and regulation begun. New legislation, such as the Drug Abuse Prevention and Control Act of 1970 and the Controlled Substances Act, strengthened the resolve of the authorities.

In June 1971, President Nixon launched a war on drugs campaign, the USA leading a large scale offensive against opium producers and traffickers. In a long, televised speech, Nixon said, 'America has the largest number of heroin addicts of any nation in the world . . . The problem has assumed the dimension of a national emergency . . . If we cannot destroy the drug menace in America, then it will surely in time destroy us.' Drugs rose to the top of the political agenda. Famous public figures joined the crusade, including Elvis Presley who, by now, was probably America's best-known (yet – at the time – least realised) junkie.

The BNDD and US Customs received substantially larger budgets. Agent numbers increased severalfold. Political pressure was applied to other governments to adopt a more hard-headed attitude towards opium production and trafficking. Nixon augmented a Special Action Office for Drug Abuse Prevention and, a year later, the Office of Drug Abuse Law Enforcement and the Office of National Narcotics Intelligence. So many different organisations were unwieldy so, in 1973, the Drug Enforcement Administration (DEA) was created with all the functions of the various agencies rolled into one.

The DEA's mission included – and still includes – enforcing federal drugs laws, freezing and seizing drug traffickers' assets, liaising with Interpol and foreign enforcement agencies and furthering co-operation and co-ordination of international, federal, state and local law enforcement programmes. It is, furthermore, established on a world-wide footing with agents in overseas offices.

Before 1940, American narcotics agents operated only inside America. In the late 1940s, a few agents started to work overseas out of American embassies and consulates. By 1995, the DEA had over seventy-five offices in fifty countries. In those from which opium or heroin originate, DEA agents are almost paramilitary personnel who actively participate with local enforcement agencies, dressed in camouflage combat clothing and armed with the latest automatic weapons. Their role is to arrest opium traffickers and producers, seize evidence and destroy heroin laboratories. The DEA is also at the forefront of the scientific war against drugs: for example, the Heroin Signature Program is capable of identifying the geographic source of a heroin sample by the recognition of specific chemical characteristics. The organisation has an official annual budget of nearly $1000 million: it has been estimated though by some observers that, in total, counting every aspect of its work both nationally and internationally, the US war on drugs is a $13.3 billion dollar a year effort.

Initiatives created by the DEA have proved to be as effective as they have been innovative. One of these is called asset-sharing. When DEA agents succeed in seizing a drug trafficker's assets, the income is shared with those countries which assisted in the case on the condition the sum earned (which can be substantial) is spent on furthering the fight against drugs. This system of co-operation has proven very popular with almost every participating country. Only Britain has ever rejected the share offer, saying the money earned would be placed in the general exchequer and spent as the government saw fit: on that occasion, the DEA withheld what amounted to several million dollars. Another initiative, within the USA, is the Demand Reduction Program, based on the obvious fact that demand drives the drug business – if no one was buying, then no one would be selling. The user is targeted, not with custodial penalties but with social ones which strike home harder. For example, in Tennessee, a juvenile convicted of a drug offence loses his driving licence, even if the drug offence was unconnected to a motor vehicle.

For a while, in the 1970s, the DEA had some outstanding successes which resulted in the American addict population dropping from 500,000 to 200,000. But then, in 1979, there was a new heroin importation explosion. Even the DEA was swamped. Addiction soared to former peaks. New laws were passed with mandatory prison terms, including an Anti-Drug Abuse Act (1986), and the American police forces stepped up arrests and convictions of traffickers, doubling the country's prison population in the 1980s.

Today, the DEA operates what is called its Kingpin strategy. This concentrates American and international law enforcement against key personnel and organisations in the global drug underworld, deliberately seeking to destabilise their businesses and generally making it difficult for them to operate at full efficiency: in other words, they legally hassle them and keep the illegal trade on the hop.

Additionally, the USA has a National Narcotics Intelligence Consumers Committee (NNICC), set up in 1978 to collect, analyse, disseminate and evaluate drug related intelligence from both foreign and domestic sources. NNICC plays a seminal part in providing the data which informs the development of drug policy, the deployment of anti-drug resource and operational tactics.

Despite all the efforts of the DEA, the USA has a huge drugs problem, exacerbated by the number of street pushers who are themselves addicts. It is a known fact when heroin addiction reaches a certain stage, the addict finds it advantageous to become a dealer rather than feed his habit with other criminal activity. The trade therefore has to expand to self-perpetuate itself: a vicious circle is formed. Heroin addiction has declined amongst the middle class but it is rampant in inner-city areas amongst the poor, blue-collar workers and unskilled labourers. In Harlem, New York City, where over 60 per cent of households have incomes below the federal poverty line, it is hardly surprising heroin is rife for it not only alleviates the drudgery of life but.it also affords a lucrative way out of the poverty trap. Many poor youths turn to the drug trade to make a living for heroin, whilst it will not make a street dealer rich, will bring him in more than many a legitimate wage packet might.

Urban drug dealing inevitably leads to high crime rates. Gangs fight for territory. Automatic weapons are readily available. Drug related murders are commonplace. By 1989, the situation was so bad President Bush followed Nixon's example. He announced a new $7.8 billion programme, declaring war on Latin America's *Narcos*, the narcotics barons, raising the budgets of the DEA, the US Coast Guard, the Central Intelligence Agency (CIA) and other agencies and giving hundreds of millions of dollars in aid to Peru, Bolivia and Colombia. In December of that year, he ordered

US troops into Panama to capture General Manuel Noriega who was taken to Miami to face cocaine smuggling charges. This was a new and important development for it was the first time regular military units had overtly joined the battle.

It has been reckoned at least 50 per cent of all crimes committed in American cities are drug related: this figure may be considerably higher in inner-city zones, although in rural areas it is significantly lower. An article in *Newsweek* as far back as 1971 stated that New York was in a virtual state of siege. The city, the article declared, was being killed by heroin and there were other cities on the death list. The situation is little changed today. Drugs are still at the forefront of the American consciousness, as opinion polls show: most Americans consider drugs the greatest problem facing their nation.

11

DORA, Isabella and Olivia

Over the Atlantic in Britain, the rate at which the problem developed had been slower and the manner different.

A shifting Chinese community, mainly seamen on leave between vessels, had existed in Britain since the eighteenth century, centred almost entirely upon the London East End boroughs of Stepney and Poplar, close to the docklands, where it occupied just two streets, Pennyfields and Limehouse Causeway. Its numbers were insignificant. By 1861, the resident Chinese population of the entire country was 147, rising to 665 over 20 years. Several opium dens existed but they catered exclusively for Chinese.

Few non-Orientals ever went into a den. Indeed, as with modern London Chinese gambling establishments, outsiders were positively discouraged. The only foreigners to enter them were Victorian sensationalist press journalists looking for sleaze, corruption and vicarious excitement or exotic danger. What they wanted to find, they found. Dens were described quite uncensoriously as humble, wretched places but they were not regarded as sinister: they were objects of curiosity and opium smoking was considered as little more than an exotic foible of John Chinaman.

This concept is well described in an essay about a London den at Palmer's Folly, published in the *Daily News* during 1864, which reads:

A dreadful place . . . We become conscious of a peculiar smell of burning, the aroma from which is not unpleasant . . . We push at a half open front door, and at once find ourself in a small, half-lit, shabby room on the ground floor, in which a large French bedstead occupies the most conspicuous place. The smell has grown in intensity as we neared this house, and, once here, it becomes trying both to eyes and head. . . On the bed, which is devoid of sheets or counterpane, and has its pillows and bolster placed lengthwise along its sides, are three Chinamen, sprawled round a small japan tray, in the centre of which is a tumbler half full of a thick brown syrup, of the consistency of treacle, some brass thimbles, one or two bits of wire about the size known as 'blankets'; a burning taper and some pipes . . . The old Chinaman on the end of the bed nearest the window seems in a half trance, though he smokes vigorously, and in his cadaverous face, painfully-hollow cheeks, deeply-sunken eyes, open vacuous mouth, and teeth discoloured, decayed, and, it seems, loose as castanets, you read the penalties of opium smoking. This is the proprietor of the house, whose preparation of the drug is so exceptionally skilful that Chinamen come from all parts of London to patronise him. Before you hastily form a judgement as to the wreck of vitality you think you see, learn that the old man is seventy-five years old, that he lives quite alone, and is his own housemaid, scullion, and cook; that he is diligent in his business, such as it is; rises daily at 5 a.m., and is celebrated throughout his dingy neighbourhood for the energetic particularity with which he scrubs and washes pots, pans, and house, and for the scrupulous care wherewith he purchases and prepares his food . . . Beside the bed, there are chairs, a table, cooking utensils, and a clothes-line stretching from one corner of the room to the other. On this hang the coats and waistcoats, collars, and cravats of three young fellows . . . They are evidently of a respectable class of Chinamen, they are clean in their persons, and both socks and shirts are of commendable purity . . . The young fellow with the particularly jolly smile . . . shows us how a pipe is charged, lighted, and smoked. One of the blanket pins is thrust into the syrup, and then twisted round and round in the flame until all the stringiness hardens down, and a pill-like globule can be inserted in the small hole in the thick barrel of the pipe. This is lit, and finished in a series of vigorous puffs, which are apparently continued for about a minute. The half-tumbler of black-brown syrup is opium duly prepared for smoking, and is worth twenty-five shilling, while the thimbles at its side each hold a shilling's worth . . . Each man helps himself, potters about the little place and lounges on the bed with perfect freedom . . . The club-night at, say, the 'Three Jolly Pigeons', when the grocer, the baker, the parish clerk and the small farmer meet to chat over the gossip of the week, with pipe and glass, is a fair English illustration of the manners, demeanour, and general free-and-easiness of this batch of smokers.

A dreadful place it might have been yet malefic and vice-ridden it was not: the opium den was, as the writer put it, little more to the Chinese than the public house was to his English working-class contemporary.

Yet, as in America, attitudes began to change with the start of legislation, with the Pharmacy Act of 1868 and the establishment of the Society for the Suppression of the Opium Trade. Public opinion was swayed, equating opium with something evil.

This attitude was latched on to by a number of popular authors. In Charles Dickens's last novel, *The Mystery of Edwin Drood*, published in 1870, there is a powerful indictment of opium. The main character – one cannot call him the hero, for he becomes one of Dickens's most fascinatingly dislikeable characters – is John Jasper, the choirmaster of Cloisterham Cathedral and an opium addict. The novel was unfinished, but the way in which it was developing shows how Jasper's double life was catching up with him and highlights his despicable side. He courts the fiancée of his disappeared and presumed dead nephew, Edwin Drood, whom it is likely the novel would have proved Jasper had killed.

For Dickens, opium was a symbol of degeneracy, of a surrender of basic human values, a corruption of decency. A man of double standards – Dickens proclaimed a healthy Christian morality but maintained a secret mistress and a bastard child – it is not remarkable he wrote so powerfully and critically about an aspect of society of which, like infidelity, he had some insider's knowledge. In the last years of his life, when he was writing the story of Edwin Drood, he frequently took laudanum, and not just to relieve pain. On a reading tour of America in 1867, he dosed himself to calm his nerves after an emotive public reading of the death of Tiny Tim from *A Christmas Carol* and used it for some months as a cough mixture. Furthermore, Dickens researched the story by visiting the slums of London with the police where he saw an old crone smoking opium from a home-made pipe, a scene he used in the novel.

Dickens's novel introduced an intolerance of opium and opium dens but, in 1891, a new novel appeared in which an opium den was used as the setting for the dramatic, blasphemous revelation of man's inner evil. It was Oscar Wilde's famous tale, *The Picture of Dorian Gray*. Gray, the main character, lives two parallel lives. He is on one plane a witty, handsome and charming man yet he seduces young women and corrupts young men. The portrait of himself as a young man ages as time goes by whilst Gray himself does not. The mockery of the picture prompts him to murder its artist, by which act he sees himself as set apart from civilised society. In an attempt to escape the realisation of the killing, he goes to a London opium den 'where one could buy oblivion'. In the den, however, Gray meets not oblivion but two of his former despoiled companions driven to addiction by his actions. One is intent on killing Gray but he does not: he cannot believe the man standing before him is forty years old. Gray is spared, saved by the picture which does his ageing for him, but he is reminded of his past and realises there is no escape from it. The opium, from which there was also no escape, is an image of entrapment: no amount of opium can alter the truth.

A year after Wilde's story was published, Sir Arthur Conan Doyle wrote of the effects of opium addiction in one of his Sherlock Holmes tales, *The Man with the Twisted Lip*. The story starts with Dr Watson entering an opium den in the East End of London to rescue an addict friend. There he meets Holmes, in disguise, who is investigating the disappearance of a respectable businessman, Neville St Clair, whom it is believed has been kidnapped and robbed by a deformed beggar, the man of the title. The beggar is duly arrested and put in gaol. Holmes, after a night considering the case, rushes to the police cells where he washes the beggar's face to find the cripple is St Clair in disguise. St Clair is, in fact, not a businessman at all. Unknown to his wife, who sees him leave for the office every day, he is a highly successful beggar. The opium den is used by him as a base where he might change from his suit and top hat into rags, making himself up to appear physically repugnant. The opium den, therefore, becomes an image for transformation from truth into deceit, just as it was for the addict customers who escaped reality there.

Dr Watson's visit to the den was not out of character for a middle class Victorian professional man. Such was public curiosity about the naughty side of life, opium dens actually drew not only curious voyeurs but even tourists doing the sights of London.

For many, however, the dens were a sign of decadence and contact with Chinamen, as with other coloured races, was seen as socially polluting. That this commingling might involve the sensuality of opium as well was abhorrent and rumours of debauchery and racial degeneracy abounded. They were unfounded. There was little meeting of East and West in the opium dens of London: the working-class East Enders – dockers, stevedores, prostitutes, sailors and longshoremen – did not smoke opium. They kept to their own forms of opiates, along with gin and ale.

Despite the fact opium had been taken for pleasure for decades, the idea grew up that such drug taking signified deviant or eccentric behaviour. Artists, painters and writers, such as Oscar Wilde, Aubrey Beardsley and Dante Gabriel Rossetti, occasionally smoked opium: Wilde, in particular, was known not only for his absinthe drinking but also his Egyptian cigarettes containing tobacco soaked in opium tincture. Yet even at their most numerous, these bohemians were a very small group.

For the first decades of the twentieth century, opium slipped from the limelight. However, after the Great War, matters changed. Drugs returned to the social agenda as a serious social menace: that addiction at the time was falling was by the way.

Whipped up by the press, encouraged by popular 'penny dreadful' novels and films, often made in America, the public was inundated with what would now be termed hype, much of it inaccurate. Narcotics were seen to have escaped from London's East End to infect the nation, depraving the young who fell for their insidious charms. Panic ensued.

The increase in the Chinese population fuelled this panic. There were about 1300 Chinese in Britain in 1911: by 1921, there were nearly 3000. Compared to America, or even France, where there were large numbers of Sino-French exchange student workers (Zhou Enlai and Deng Xiaoping amongst them), this total was minuscule but it was sufficient to alarm the public. Journalists wrote sensationalistic articles about opium dens, white girls in slavery and Chinese criminal conspiracies bent on spreading vice to corrupt the English. When, in 1918, the actress Billie Carleton was found dead in her flat, the press had a field day: the case contained all the elements they wanted – sex, drug use and an opium den. Generally speaking, however, it was all rubbish. The only white girls to be involved with the Chinese were those who had married them, there being a considerable shortage of women in Chinese circles.

The dangers of opium, sex and crime soon became the stock-in-trade for pulp-fiction writers. One writer, called Arthur Ward, had visited Limehouse. There he saw a Chinese man who gave him a brief but incisive idea. Writing as Sax Rohmer, Ward invented the arch-villain, Dr Fu Manchu.

First appearing in 1913, Dr Fu Manchu embodied all the evil the public saw in the Chinese. He was set on the domination of the West, used opium against his enemies and was himself an addict. Ward may have been biased but he knew a good character when he saw one and not all his inventions were fictional: in one story, a fictional drug dealer called King was based upon a real-life one in London who went by the name of Brilliant Chang. A significant number of the stories were also filmed, spreading the image of the Chinese as all being potential Fu Manchus.

Other authors jumped on Ward's bandwagon. Newspapers published details of sex and drugs and 'dance dope dens' where a 'sickening crowd of young aliens' preyed on 'pretty, under-dressed' English girls. Aleister Crowley – named by the press as the wickedest man in the world for his drug taking, sexual perversions and occult reputation – wrote of heroin and cocaine addiction in his *Diary of a Drug Fiend*, released in 1922. In him, the press had just the scapegoat they needed and they laboured the point off and on for twenty-five years. Due to a chequered career which included operating an occult temple in Sicily, engaging in sexual magic with both male and female partners, allegedly eating babies as part of satanic rituals, running a troupe of dancers called 'The Ragged Rag-Time Girls' and indulging in drug taking which included smoking opium, sniffing cocaine, eating hashish and swallowing liberal doses of laudanum, veronal and anhalonium, as well as smoking and later injecting heroin, he was regarded as the archetypal drug fiend. Severely addicted, Crowley was to die impoverished in Hastings in 1947, a heroin addict to the grave.

The sense of danger was communicated to an even wider audience through the cinema. Hollywood and British-made Fu Manchu films, which were still in production in the 1960s, famously starring Christopher Lee and Tsai Chin, did much to encourage fear: real-life Tinseltown tales, such as that of Wallace Reid, did more.

These scandals gave the media the ability to shape public opinion, the man in the street being informed (or more often mis-informed) by sensation-hungry, circulation-driven editors. The Chinese, the most law-abiding ethnic minority, were hounded as drug-sodden corrupters of youth. Although few people in Britain ever came upon any drugs other than their doctor's prescription, a public outcry built to demand government action.

No legislation against Chinese smoking opium existed until 1909 when the London County Council passed a by-law prohibiting opium smoking in seamen's boarding houses, but it was another seven years before opium was regarded as a narcotic rather than a poison. The Hague Conference of 1911, however, changed things. Britain became obligated to legislate and a scandal in 1916 revolving around cocaine being supplied to Canadian troops stationed in Britain brought about a seminal piece of legislation, known as DORA 40B, the acronym drawn from Regulation 40B of the Defence of the Realm Act. It made supplying drugs to troops in wartime a serious offence and was then extended to apply to civilians, possession without a doctor's prescription becoming a crime.

Under the drug clauses in the Treaty of Versailles, Britain was obligated to legislate again and, in 1920, the Dangerous Drugs Act entered the statute books. It was basically DORA 40B altered to meet the demands of international opium legislation.

Armed with the law, the police set about a successful and sustained crackdown. Hundreds of prosecutions were made, one of the high points being the arrest and conviction of Brilliant Chang in 1924, followed by his deportation after serving a prison sentence, in 1926. Drug trafficking in Britain was virtually at an end, drug usage dropping to the level of less than a dozen convictions per annum whilst certification of exports prevented illegal international traffic in British-manufactured morphine: but there was one loophole in the Dangerous Drugs Act which permitted doctors to prescribe for addiction without necessarily trying to cure it. The phraseology in the act was legally ambiguous so, in the same year as Chang was arrested, the Ministry of Health established a committee to address the problem.

The Rolleston Committee, which published its report in 1926, was named after its chairman, Sir Henry Rolleston, President of the Royal College of Physicians. Addicts were to be considered patients not criminals and it was agreed a doctor could maintain an addiction without fear of prosecution if the patient could not otherwise survive. These decisions have shaped attitudes towards addiction in Britain ever since because, in effect, the committee had made it official policy to treat addiction as a medical rather than a law enforcement matter.

Mercifully, Rolleston did not imitate the Harrison Act and thus prevented Britain from following the USA. Most British addicts continued to obtain their supplies through doctors and avoided reliance on criminal dealers. They were also not prosecuted or sent to state institutions.

Recreational drug use in Britain through the late 1920s and 1930s was insignificant. The Chinese smoked opium in their tiny communities but it did not travel nation-wide with them. Some upper-class and artistic or theatrical people took drugs, but mostly cocaine. Heroin was rarely seen.

There were other reasons for the low addiction rates in Britain. First, alcohol was not prohibited, as it was in the USA. Second, society in British cities was more or less stable whereas in America it was in a state of considerable flux with wave after wave of immigrant arrivals, youth gangs and crime groups running the streets.

By the late 1930s, drugs were all but absent from the press and the cinema. People had other concerns with the Depression, the rise of national socialism in Germany and the inexorable approach of war. The 1930s were, in effect, a lull before the post-war drug storm.

In the literary and artistic worlds, however, interest in opium remained. In the 1930s, Aldous Huxley started to become intrigued by drugs and put them as a central theme in his seminal novel, *Brave New World*, published in 1932. Opium usage was common amongst European intellectuals before and immediately after the Second World War. Raymond Radiguet, Pablo Picasso, Guillaume Apolinnaire, Francis Poulenc, Georges Auric, Louis Laloy, Jean Cocteau and many of the Surrealists were smokers or users, if not addicts. Laloy went so far as to publish a book on the subject, *Le Livre de la Fumée*, which was an opium smoking manual. It became a best-seller and is said to have been the instigation for the rise of opium smoking in fashionable European society between the world wars.

Yet the most famous modern descriptions of opium smoking were given by Graham Greene who first smoked opium in 1951 in Vietnam and developed a passion for it as an antidote to his fits of deep depression: but he was never addicted. Most of his opium experiences were undertaken in the opium dens (or *fumeries*) of French Indo-China although, on occasion, he was invited to smoke with acquaintances. He was fascinated, as many Europeans were, by the ritual of opium smoking, the ambience of the den with its subdued lights, burning opium lamps and young girls who prepared the pipes.

The first few pipes left Greene drowsy but the next few revitalised his mind, making him alert yet pacific. It was after his first smoking experience that he underwent what smokers referred to as a 'white opium night'. He lay awake and was then suddenly plunged into a deep, narcotic sleep which seemed to last for hours but, in fact, lasted only twenty minutes. Waking again, he stayed conscious for a short while before, once more, dropping into a long sleep 'compressed' into minutes. On another occasion, Greene and a friend took a young girl from an opium den back to their hotel in Hanoi: inevitably, both men were unable to enjoy the girl sexually because their opium smoking had killed their sexual capability. Indeed, Greene was to write of what every addict already knew, that opium was a grand substitute for sex and suppressed desire.

For Greene, opium was an escape from reality, a means of suppressing depression, fear and self-loathing and an aid to his literature. He described smoking a pipe in his novel, *The Quiet American*, set in Vietnam before the start of the Vietnam War, closely basing the description on personal experience. He later also wrote about opium smoking in his autobiographical *Ways of Escape*. Needless to say, he only got out of it what he put into it, as De Quincey had suggested. Greene, obsessed at the time with sex, his mistress Catherine Walston and his abiding love–hate relationship with the Roman Catholic faith, had opium dreams mingling erotic sex with religion, exotic Eastern scenes, strange architectural shapes, the Devil himself and places with which he was familiar (such as the entrance to a gentleman's club in St James's Street, London), all thrown together with a rapid passing of time and the colour gold in the form of coins.

Opium gave *The Quiet American* a certain risqué quality. Readers were attracted to the book's romantic setting and the vice of opium smoking just as previous generations had been by the writings of Coleridge or Wilkie Collins, Elizabeth Barrett Browning or George Crabbe, Dickens, Wilde and the pulp fiction authors.

Government reports in Britain in the immediate post-war years believed drug addiction was restricted to two groups: a quarter of all registered addicts were in the medical profession, the remainder being in what was termed the alien population, covering Chinese and black immigrants in urban areas. The founding of jazz clubs in wartime London played a significant part in addiction, providing a multi-racial milieu where drugs were used and from which, after the war, they spread, a doctor writing in 1956, 'the addicts we have in this country . . . are nearly all instrumentalists in jazz bands.'

Every now and then, the press commented upon the growth of drug use but the authorities generally tended to ignore these early warnings, although the Home Office began to record heroin addicts as a separate category in 1954 and had fifty-seven listed. The number increased slowly in the 1950s but heroin was certainly not a problem.

Only around 1960 did matters change in both Britain and Western Europe, when an American-style pattern of addiction started to appear with pushers actively creating new addicts, particularly teenagers, most often males. Morphine use dropped and all but disappeared. Heroin was 'in'. Over a matter of two years, addict numbers rose from around 250 to several thousand.

A catalyst for this rapid increase was the number of heroin addicts fleeing to Europe, especially Britain, to escape a harsh penal code for drug offences introduced in Canada in 1958. By 1962, seventy Canadian addicts – a fair proportion of them having narcotic-related criminal records – had arrived, and yet they were not necessarily the cause but merely a symptom of the problem.

Teenagers were changing. They had more freedom, more spending power and more social status than ever before. A teenage culture developed on the back of pop music and from this extended a drug subculture which started in London and then spread to other cities. A market in heroin developed and the word 'junkie' entered everyday English. Although the number of addicts remained small by comparison with the USA – about 3000 existed in 1969 – it was five times the 1961 figure and did not augur well for the future.

The Ministry of Health convened the Inter-departmental Commission on Drug Addiction in 1958 under the chairmanship of Sir Russell Brain. Three years later, the resulting Brain Report decided there was no need for any real worry or change. The main problem, it reported, lay in a small number of bohemianly inclined doctors who were over-prescribing to addicts, who then passed on their surplus to others: a case was cited of one doctor who prescribed 6 kilograms of heroin in one year. Another case concerned Lady Isabella Frankau who prescribed substantial quantities of drugs – one sixth of the national total of prescribed heroin in one year – on the genuine assumption she was undermining the black market she abhorred. In fact, she was supplying it, Brain informing the Home Office, 'Your problem, gentlemen, can be summed up in two words – Lady Frankau.'

Until the escalation in addiction, the British way of handling the problem was adequate but when addiction soared it was first swamped then collapsed, unable to handle the new drug subculture and its devotees. The government feared British cities would become like American ones and a second Brain Report was commissioned and published in 1965. This took a different view, suggesting tight restrictions on doctors and their prescribing, the establishment of addiction clinics and more competent search methods by customs officers to halt smuggling: yet the report held to the policy that addiction was a medical problem. The report created the foundation for the new Dangerous Drugs Act of 1967 and the setting up of drug treatment centres, the doctors of which were the only ones permitted to prescribe to addicts.

To the present day, Britain is virtually the only country in the world where, under certain conditions, a doctor may prescribe heroin which is deemed elsewhere as so dangerous even doctors may not handle it: partly, of course, the general incorruptibility of the British medical profession allows this state of affairs. British doctors may prescribe heroin for pain relief, such as in the care of the terminally sick. Furthermore, it occasionally appears in other medical usage: a 1995 report, which created an outcry and was roundly condemned, stated that some doctors in Scotland were giving pregnant women injections of heroin to relieve the pain of childbirth, favouring it for its speed and efficacy.

The Misuse of Drugs Act (1971) integrated existing drug laws, extending them where necessary and making the system sufficiently flexible as to add new drugs to the prohibited register. In the Act, drugs were also divided into three categories, A, B or C, according to their degree of harmfulness, with opium, morphine and heroin being placed in group A, penalties being decided according to the category of drug and the type of offence. However, due to the convoluted history of past legislation, anachronisms remain in the Act. It is still an offence to attend or permit premises to be used for opium smoking and to possess opium smoking or preparation equipment: even the ownership of antique opium pipes for aesthetic reasons is technically forbidden. The smoking of opium in Britain is rare today but not entirely unknown: the interception of 15 grams of raw opium in the mail led to the discovery of a seedy opium smoking divan in Dundee in 1989.

These acts, with the Drugs Trafficking Offences Act (1986) mentioned later, remain the backbone of drug legislation and control in Britain.

Britain has no equivalent of the DEA. H.M. Customs and Excise investigate illegal importation whilst police regional crime squads investigate distribution, often targeting the criminal rather than the crime, drug distributors being an important aspect of their work which may bring them into alliance with customs officials. Each police force in Britain has a drugs squad which investigates drug dealing within their jurisdiction whilst local police deal with drug possession and abuse. Scientific analysis of finds is conducted by the government chemist who has also developed a chemical fingerprinting system similar to the DEA signature programme.

Despite the law, addiction has continued to rise with cheap heroin arriving in Britain and Western Europe as a whole. When prescribing became tightly monitored, heroin from South-east Asia began to come into Europe, smuggled in by Chinese crime syndicates: the British resident Chinese population provided cover for the traffickers. In later years, heroin from Afghanistan, Pakistan and Iran also appeared.

One of the best known of the Chinese heroin traffickers was a young Malaysian-Chinese woman. Shing May Wong came from a well-to-do bullion dealer's family and was educated at Roedean. At her trial in 1977, she claimed she had infiltrated a heroin-smuggling syndicate in order to avenge a Chinese criminal syndicate of her father's death: he had been murdered in Singapore. She sold her beauty salon and shop, left her husband, became a hostess in Singapore and, with her lover Li Mah, who was a syndicate member, arrived in Britain to set up a heroin importation ring. With a second Chinese accomplice and an Australian, May Wong brought in heroin worth £20 million over a two-year period. She was entrapped by a police sting operation and sentenced to fourteen years.

During the 1980s, heroin became the focus of both media and government attention. No longer was it seen as just a foible of bohemian jazz instrumentalists and aliens: it was capable of touching everyone's lives and it showed no boundaries in claiming its victims. Even members of the nobility and the children of government ministers became enmeshed. Olivia Channon, the Oxford undergraduate daughter of government minister Paul Channon, died in 1986 of a heroin/alcohol overdose. The Marquis of Blandford has been addicted to heroin and has led a life peppered by petty crime, including being gaoled for stealing drugs, whilst Alice Ormsby Gore, the sister of Lord Harlech and an ex-girlfriend of rock guitarist Eric Clapton, himself a one-time addict, died of a heroin overdose in 1995.

Rock musicians themselves, perhaps as an extension of the old jazz musician junkie tradition, seem very susceptible to drugs. Drummer Ginger Baker, one of the trio of the seminal super-band, Cream, first took heroin in the late 1950s after being told it improved his playing: his heroin addiction lasted twenty years. Baker has said it was difficult to kick his habit because fans who were also dealers frequently gave him drugs free – he was the ultimate endorsement of their product. As well as Baker and Eric Clapton (also a member of Cream), Boy George, Sid Vicious of the Sex Pistols and Keith Richard of the Rolling Stones, Pete Townshend of the Who and singer Marianne Faithfull have all at some stage been addicted: when Clapton and Boy George kicked their habit, much was made in the media of their success. Overseas, heroin took – and still takes – its toll on other rock musicians. Janis Joplin died of a heroin overdose in a Hollywood hotel in 1970. Lou Reed survived his addiction but wrote a famous song about it entitled, not surprisingly, 'Heroin'. Kurt Cobain committed suicide by shooting himself, but he had also heavily dosed himself with heroin to which he was addicted. Jerry Garcia, the key member of the Grateful Dead, died in the summer of 1995 in his sleep – but at the famous Serenity Knolls drug-rehabilitation clinic. He had told friends he was going on a scuba-diving trip. He, too, was addicted to heroin for many years.

Public education campaigns, school lectures, training for teachers in drug awareness and government advertising campaigns have targeted the vulnerable which is in effect every member of society. In 1985, the House of Commons Home Affairs Committee stated drugs – and heroin in particular – were the most serious peacetime threat to ever face the nation. It was a prophetic statement: addiction rose 20 per cent in 1989 and 1990. There were 34,000 registered drug addicts by the end of 1994 but the official estimate of overall addiction to opiates, including heroin, pethidine, methadone and morphine, was put at approximately five times that figure, most of the addicts young and addicted to heroin.

Social workers across Britain have recorded a recent sharp increase in users particularly in the sixteen-to-eighteen age-range, although many are younger and some are addicted for several years before being identified. This said, it is a misconception that drug use is exclusively a youth issue. There has also been a recorded increase in the 1990s of middle-aged and elderly addicts. Some have been addicted from youth but others are newly addicted through searching for a relief from loneliness or chronic pain. Registered addicts aged over fifty increased by 52 per cent in 1993: many others are unregistered.

Another increasing trend is the use of heroin by professional people who are confident they will not become addicted, usually starting with a casual experimentation. They claim heroin calms or relaxes: some believe it to be glamorous and take heroin as a social activity much as others might take alcohol. Many become 'hidden' addicts, supporting their habit with above average incomes and thus avoiding criminality. Such is the situation now that one recent study suggests high income earners are in some areas the majority of illegal drug users.

Some addicts may hold important posts. Dr Clive Froggatt, a very senior government health adviser to both Margaret Thatcher and John Major, was addicted to heroin, allegedly taking up to eight fixes a day: colleagues put his mood changes down to overwork and the stress of responsibility. Four successive government health ministers remained ignorant of his secret which was uncovered when police conducted routine checks of pharmacists' records to find he had been making out heroin prescriptions in either fictitious names or those of deceased persons. Froggatt was arrested and given a suspended prison sentence in April 1995. He stated he did not believe heroin had affected his clinical judgement but he did believe it made him much more ruthless and less compassionate as to the effects the wide-ranging and much criticised health service reforms he devised would have on patients.

The professional addicts generally keep a low profile: it is the poor addict who most frequently comes to public notice. Just as was feared in 1965, British cities are beginning to resemble American ones. Heroin is rife on the housing estates of Manchester, the streets of Bristol and the inner suburbs of London: the horrendous Handsworth riot in Birmingham in 1985 was blamed by police on drug dealers. One of the underlying causes for the rapid growth in heroin usage is believed to have been the 1983 Brinks-Mat bullion robbery from a warehouse on a trading estate near London Heathrow airport, when much of the £26 million haul was invested in the drugs trade: it was – and remains – common practice for criminal gangs to finance drug deals with money gained from armed robberies, especially of security vans. A van robbery of, say, £500,000 could return up to £3 million from heroin.

In 1994, chief superintendents of police warned Britain now has a drugs crisis as serious as that of the USA. Manchester police estimated the average heroin addict in their area spent £30,000 per annum on his habit, raising the money from burglary, theft, prostitution and street dealing. In Glasgow, heroin was, for a time, infamously sold through a network of ice-cream vans and mobile shops. Gangs from different cities have set aside their animosities to establish a national supply system. There are differences between Britain and America: the former has as yet no massive organised crime network and the British black population is not riddled with heroin as it is in America. Yet addicts are becoming younger and drugs are becoming synonymous with lawlessness. The fear of the junkie is now felt in the heartland of middle England.

12

Carpets, Condoms and Cats

For a good deal of its history, other than for medical use, opium has been an illegal commodity: even the centuries-long, Indo-Chinese opium trade was, for much of its existence, nothing more than a smuggling enterprise, albeit a vast one. There has, thus, always existed a strong bond between opium and criminality.

It is inevitable that so long as world opium production exceeds basic legitimate demand, for medicinal or research purposes, there will exist an illegal market developed for the surplus and controlled by criminal traffickers who will have a vested interest in maintaining or expanding this market at every opportunity, increasing the size of the surplus. Drug traffickers are, save in their illegality, no different from any other commodity entrepreneur operating in the best spirit of free trade and, because of the addictive nature of their wares, they will have no problem selling their product. As William Burroughs noted in the introduction to his novel, *The Naked Lunch*, published in 1959: 'Junk is the ideal product . . . the ultimate merchandise. No sales talk necessary. The client will crawl through a sewer and beg to buy.' Any risks traffickers take are countered by substantial profits: no addict can complain about the cost of his fix.

Traffickers have always drawn supplies from one of two basic sources. First, they have purchased opium from countries where poppy cultivation is legal but where a percentage of the harvest escapes the attention of the authorities, despite state or tax controls.

Quantities have depended upon governmental efficiency in the control of trading and farmers. An example of such a source was Turkey where, prior to 1972 when the government banned poppy growing, 25 per cent of the opium harvest vanished into a black market: in 1971, Pakistan legally produced 6 tons of opium, but approximately another 200 tons over-production was similarly diverted. The respective authorities could not prevent this 'hidden' trade as the farmers received higher returns from the illegal traders and were thus encouraged to grow more than was legally required.

Second, supplies have been purchased from countries where poppy cultivation is officially forbidden but enforcement lacking due to inefficiency, undermanning of police and excise agencies, corruption or a governmental inability to address the general situation. Sometimes illegal poppy crops have been either undiscovered or officially regarded as non-existent and therefore ignored.

The situation has changed little in three-quarters of a century. In the 1920s, it was reckoned for every medicinal ounce of opium sold internationally on the legitimate market, 10 ounces traded illegally on the global black market. A League of Nations publication in 1938 stated, between 1925 and 1930, at least 90 tons of morphine had been manufactured in excess of legitimate requirements and sold illegally: virtually no country was free from illicit opium, the trade increasing pro rata with the political instabilities in the Far East and Europe as the Second World War approached. At the time, most smuggled raw opium came from Iran or China with Turkey providing the clandestine factories for the manufacture of morphine.

Then, as ever, the traffickers' aim was profit at as high a margin over cost as the market (in other words, the addict) could sustain. Two vague categories of trafficking existed: the first was smuggling into countries where opiates were illegal, the second importing into countries where they were legal but controlled and subject to excise. The former were drug runners in the modern sense, the second contraband excise dodgers in the age-old tradition of the buccaneer.

Merely by evading duty, the buccaneer-type smuggler stood to turn a tidy profit. A 1909 smuggling case illustrates the possible profit level involved in even a modest operation. Stewards aboard the North German Lloyd line passenger steamer, *Kronprinzessin*

Cecilie, regularly smuggled opium and codeine into New York, where it was subject to an importation levy. With the co-operation of the ship's watchmen and a corrupt customs inspector, they passed the drugs to an American confederate who sold them to pharmaceutical firms. Customs agents caught the ring in February 1909. It was discovered the stewards had purchased codeine in Germany for 440 Deutschmarks a kilogram, about $1 per ounce. The duty evaded was $1 an ounce and the supply was sold at $5 an ounce.

High profit margins have always meant traffickers have been sufficiently well bankrolled to outwit or bribe the authorities. One example out of thousands was to be found in the early 1920s on the railway line running to the Chinese province of Shansi. A locomotive driver on a monthly salary of $40 would be paid $200 for carrying a small packet of morphine. The provincial governor promised a $3 reward for every packet seized: the traffickers paid railway inspectors $6 for every undetected packet. Every so often, the inspectors were permitted to make a worthwhile seizure to bring them credit and give their work viability. The remainder of the time, they carried out superficial checks and confiscated nothing. Almost everyone was a winner – the drivers got their smuggling fees, the inspectors got their bribes (and an occasional reward bonus) and the gubernatorial authorities thought they had the situation under control: the only loser was the addict who had to foot the bill.

Traffickers have not just relied upon something as coarse as corruption to meet their ends. Many have been familiar with the legal systems of their target countries, using these to their advantage, especially in the early years of international control when legal complexities occurred because more than one country was involved in a transaction. What was legal practice in one place was not in another. The Advisory Committee was told in 1927 of three-quarters of a ton of morphine found in the possession of known traffickers who had purchased it through the French office of a Swiss pharmaceutical company which had imported it legally into France, there being no import licence required. Such loopholes were widened further because many governments were lukewarm to the idea of controls and usually set light punishments for trafficking. Other smuggling opportunities arose in the early years through the naming and classification of drugs.

The constant invention of new drugs meant smugglers could trade in them before they were listed as controlled. The 1925 Convention controlled morphine and its salts. The smugglers promptly traded in benzoyl-morphine, a derivative but not a salt, yet from which morphine could be recovered.

Smuggling networks have often been very complex and convoluted. From 1906, when opium was made illegal in China, there grew up a substantial smuggling network of both foreign opium into China and Chinese-grown opium out of it. In 1925, Hong Kong customs seized 3.5 tons of allegedly Chinese opium, along with a hoard of documentation outlining the existence and the *modus operandi* of several powerful Chinese smuggling syndicates. The current total consumption of legal Indian opium in Hong Kong was 22.5 tons per annum. The documents showed just one syndicate was smuggling such an amount annually. They were not just dealing in Chinese product: 8.5 tons of raw Persian opium was found in a cave on an island near Hong Kong and a seizure of drugs and documents in Shanghai in 1925 proved the extensive importation of Turkish opium shipped from Constantinople via Vladivostok. At the same time, huge quantities of morphine were being smuggled into China via Manchuria by Japanese traffickers.

Macau was also a smuggling centre. Under an agreement with China in 1913, Macau was permitted to import 260 chests of opium a year for domestic consumption and 240 chests for re-export outside China. However, this was usually smuggled into China, the destination disguised by erroneous way-bills or the opium substituted: one opium consignment bound for Mexico was seized by Chinese authorities but found to consist of molasses. The opium was *en route* for Canton. Such opium was often wrapped or labelled to appear to come from China itself, a trick employed globally to place the blame for trafficking upon the Chinese. A huge haul of 14,000 assorted packages of heroin, morphine and cocaine was made in an hotel on West 40th Street, New York City, in 1922: amongst the narcotics were printing plates for Chinese opium labels.

Before the advent of the airliner, most smuggling was inevitably done by sea. Not only were ships trading internationally but a vessel offered a multitude of hiding-places. On 25 February 1929, 194 pounds of opium were found on SS *Kut Sang* in Hong Kong harbour, the drugs concealed in the hollow base of an anchor davit.

The original rivets of the base plate had been replaced by screws with heads resembling rivets. This was no more ingenious than in many other instances, such as the morphine and heroin seized by Chinese customs at Tientsin in 1921 from the Japanese vessel, SS *Awaji Maru*, concealed in blocks of sulphate of soda. Customs records across the world are littered with reported hidey-holes: morphine in canvas sacks suspended down ventilator shafts; opium buried in coal bunkers and coke holds, tucked into blanket lockers or, on SS *Montauk*, hidden in a cavity cut into the aftermast. In 1938, 850 hermetically sealed tins of opium were found by New York customs in a false bottom to a fuel-oil tank on a British ship, SS *Silveryew*. Cargoes provided good camouflage: opium or heroin has appeared, amongst many others, in cargoes of dried shrimps, soap (with opium cakes looking like the bars of soap), in duck egg shells packed alongside real eggs, in Bologna sausage skins, in barrels of cement, in loaves of bread and in tins marked pickled cabbage. False labelling often disguised the true nature of a cargo, with just a few containers holding drugs, the remainder being the genuine article. Passengers also carried drugs, with the ubiquitous false bottomed suitcase being a favourite method.

Where a ship was found to be smuggling, a common penalty was to fine the ship's owners although, on occasion, the captain might be able to convince the authorities of his, the crew and the owners' innocence. The captain of SS *Silveryew* succeeded in allaying a fine, the manager of the Silver Line stating on behalf of the owners:

> This is the work of an organised gang who try it on all ships going from the Far East to America . . . No one knows how they work or get the opium on board. It is a great mystery to me how they could have got that enormous amount of dope aboard without being seen. The only way they can be found out . . . is when one of their own gang gives them away. I think this happened in the present case.

The Second World War generally made things difficult for international smugglers, with supply regions being cut off. Illicit opiate sales dropped sharply in 1939—40 and only slowly increased during the war years. As the war continued, most smuggling was conducted on a small scale by individual merchant sailors or troops returning home.

In the United States, heroin from Mexico began to arrive, carried by peasant couriers: they were colloquially known as 'mules', a name which has stuck to drug couriers ever since. Opium, being bulky, was brought across the Rio Grande on rafts to be onward transported in baggage on trains, buses or in private cars. For what is probably the first time in the history of narcotics, it was also flown in by light aircraft.

In the Middle East, military transport was used to shift drugs around the region but so too were camels, which were made to carry opium in smooth-ended metal cylinders they were forced to swallow. A smuggling camel could be discovered by the wounds on its mouth caused by the forced feeding. It was said a camel could hold 7.5 kilograms in its belly for at least a month without discomfort. The habit lasted after the war for in 1952 Egyptian customs officers impounded a camel suspected of smuggling. In time, it became drowsy and was slaughtered. Inside its stomach were found twenty-eight rubber containers of opium of which at least one had leaked, causing the beast's stupefaction. Rubber was used to avoid discovery by a metal detector and the trick was still in use at least to the 1970s for the transport of heroin by camel over the Turko-Syrian border.

The ingenuity of opiate smugglers is renowned. A famous instance of the smugglers' artifice concerned opium from Hong Kong entering North America inside the horns of imported cattle. The beasts had their horns cut off, hollowed out and fitted with an inner screw thread. Packed with opium, the horns were then screwed back on to the animals. All went well until an astute customs agent spied one animal with its horn dangling downwards. Less exotic, hollowed out objects have been favoured for years: heels of boots and shoes, oranges and grapefruit, bars of soap, dolls and toys, plaster busts, fake antiquities, books, picture frames and even lengths of timber and grindstones. Any potential container is considered by the smuggler: bottles of medicine and toothpaste tubes in personal luggage, musical instruments (especially those with hollow sound boxes, like guitars), knobs of brass bedsteads, fountain pens, portable typewriters, shoulder pads, cameras, empty wrist-watch cases, photographic film cases marked *do not open* – the list is almost endless. Refrigerator casings, car panels and chassis members, railway carriage doors, spare tyres on commercial vehicles (and, in recent years, those actually on the road wheels), fuel tanks, barrels of tar, aircraft roof and wing cavities, bicycle frames and fire extinguishers have all been utilised.

On occasion, the smugglers resort not to hiding drugs but actually simply disguising them. Opium has been smuggled shaped like peanuts and inserted into ground-nut shells, made into candles, shaped as vehicle wheel-chocks and carved into *objets d'art*. In 1952, opium was being smuggled from Afghanistan and Pakistan into India inside walnut shells which had been emptied of their kernels, re-sealed and placed amongst ordinary walnuts, the authorities only becoming suspicious because the nuts were sent by parcel post rather than in bulk. Heroin, being an off-white or white powder, lends itself to overt smuggling. A Persian carpet importer smuggled heroin by liberally sprinkling it over suitably coloured carpets, which were then rolled up and shipped: the recipient hoovered them clean. Animal skins, to which white powder often clings as a residue of the preservative process, have also been similarly used. As an extension of the cow-horn scam, another instance concerned a Chinese woman carrying her pet cat and its recent litter of five new-born kittens who was arrested for smuggling opium. The pet cat was clean but the kittens had all been drowned, dried off, eviscerated, stuffed with opium and replaced alongside their mother. Kittens are not the only young creatures to be stuffed with heroin; there is the case of a dead human baby also being used, cradled by its erstwhile mother.

International courier services were, for a while, used by drug smugglers, but today this has largely stopped as companies refuse to accept packages from unknown customers unless these are open and able to be inspected. Ordinary postal services, however, are liable to abuse and have long been used by smugglers. The bulk of ordinary mailed parcels carried internationally makes comprehensive detection virtually impossible, despite modern technological methods to counteract arms smuggling and terrorism. Thousands of kilograms of heroin were smuggled out of Vietnam during the Vietnam War through the US Army Post Office; with half a million troops in the theatre of war, comprehensive parcel examination was impossible. Organised rings were established amongst troops who, in some instances, made vast profits from their trade. A particularly unsavoury side to this business was the smuggling of heroin inside body bags returning corpses home for burial: heroin was also smuggled back to the USA hidden in deep wounds in cadavers.

On numerous occasions, traffickers have used children with whom they have travelled, the latter sometimes carrying the contraband: in some instances, they have even used their own offspring. In 1989, in a case dubbed the 'Heroin Baby Trial', an Australian couple were sentenced to life imprisonment in Thailand after trying to smuggle 5.53 kilograms of heroin out of the country in a pillow in their year-old infant's pram. The method of using children is based upon the knowledge that law enforcement agencies are reluctant to prosecute children because of their age, the complex laws governing minors, the difficulty of proving intent on the child's part and the fact that many are ignorant of what they are doing.

Chemical trickery is also in the smugglers' evasive arsenal. The plainest method is merely mixing a powdered drug, such as heroin or morphine, with another similar-looking powder. Morphine has been smuggled in rice and flour whilst heroin has been hidden in cosmetic powder or talc. Separation is a simple matter of dissolving and evaporation. This can, of course, go wrong. A Chinese smuggler was caught in 1947 through his own stupidity. He dissolved 125 grams of opium in boiling water then soaked a length of cloth in it and left it to dry -- but forgot opium smells, especially when it is warm. He was arrested on a crowded bus and executed.

A particularly clever quasi-chemical technique was used in smuggling by sea. A lightweight sealed box containing drugs was tied to a bag of salt or sugar and dropped overboard. When the sugar or salt dissolved, the sealed box floated to the surface to be collected. A modern variation on this theme came to light in 1994. It involves a boat dropping a consignment overboard in a waterproof box, attached to weights, a buoy and a tracking device consisting of a transponder beacon and a receiver. The weights hold the consignment on the sea-bed. At a later date, which can be weeks ahead, a collection vessel arrives following the transponder and, by sending a signal to the receiver, triggers the release of the weights. The buoy carries the consignment to the surface to be picked up.

A major factor favouring smugglers is the high value of heroin in relation to its volume. A kilogram of pure heroin takes up little more room than an average book: after cutting, it can provide up to 200,000 doses. This makes the smuggling of small quantities economically feasible and allows drug syndicates to accept a degree of discovery. It is, from their point of view, better to spread their risk than to put all their eggs in one basket – and the odd arrest is to their advantage for it mollifies the authorities. Recently, heroin has been found being smuggled out of Hong Kong in postcards which have been carefully peeled into two halves, with a small amount of heroin being inserted and the card repasted.

With small quantities being viable, smugglers frequently hide heroin about their persons. Body packs are taped onto the torso or around the thighs: women enhance their busts with shaped packets inside their bras whilst men can appear as beer-gutted football supporters or well-padded fat cats. Two American women were arrested at Bangkok airport as they boarded a Seattle-bound flight in March 1992 with 3.5 kilograms of heroin strapped to their legs. 'Pregnant' women are sometimes podgy with body packs rather than a foetus: one smuggler was caught with tiny bags of heroin under his dentures, his slurred speech giving him away. Some resort to tailor-made undergarments fitted with pockets. As an extension to the powdered carpet trick, some passengers (particularly elderly ones) rub heroin into their grey hair and shampoo it out at their destination.

Heroin is also carried internally by two methods. First, the drug is placed into a sealed metal or heavy rubber container known colloquially as a 'charger', lubricated with Vaseline and pushed up the anus or vagina: such traffickers are known as 'stuffers'. An example of the type is a British woman, Sandra Gregory, who was arrested in Bangkok in 1993 as she tried to board a plane to Tokyo with 142 grams of heroin concealed in her vagina. Second, it is put into tiny flexible rubber containers and swallowed: these smugglers are called 'swallowers'. Condoms tied with dental floss or fishing line are ideal containers being easily swallowed, the smuggler easing them down smeared with syrup: on occasion, the lubricated surfaces suffice. The rubber is also highly elastic and less likely to fracture. Fingers cut from latex rubber gloves (usually of the surgical rather than kitchen variety) have been found, also tied with dental floss which is far more tensile than cotton, resists stomach acids and does not stretch when wet. At their destination, the smugglers either pull the chargers out or take a heavy dose of laxative.

All is well unless the smuggler is X-rayed. One of the earliest recorded cases of smuggling by ingestion dates to June 1945 and involved a Mrs Chowning who was taken at Laredo, Texas, *en route* from Mexico. Fluoroscopic examination revealed foreign objects in her stomach. She was dosed with laxative and excreted thirty-one packages of heroin. Since then, swallowers have increased the number of packages they ingest. The average is 70 to 80, but British customs have found 260 in one person: it may yet prove to be the world record.

If customs officials suspect a swallower, they apprehend and continuously observe them twenty-four hours a day – this is referred to as 'baby-sitting' – until the suspect defecates and passes the packages which are then collected. Frequent urine samples are also taken and, if drug urine levels start to rise, implying a package is leaking, the smuggler is instantly hospitalised and operated upon, a customs officer present at surgery to seize any removed evidence.

Things can go badly wrong for the smuggler without customs officials' involvement. Amongst other occurrences, in February 1982, 42 condoms each containing 4 grams of heroin were obtained from the stomach and lower intestine of an American *en route* by air through Hong Kong. The haul was found during the autopsy. One condom had burst, bringing the carrier a particularly nasty death. Most ingested seizures range from 0.5 to 1.7 kilograms. More recently, in 1992, a Colombian woman was picked up in Bogotá as she was about to board a Miami-bound flight. It was discovered she had 752 grams of heroin, in 16 sealed plastic bags, surgically implanted into her buttocks.

Nowadays, airlines co-operate with law enforcement agencies, for a good number of individual smugglers fly long-haul. Cabin staff on flights in-bound to America are given cash incentives by US Customs for pointing out passengers who did not eat or drink: they might be swallowers. Some airlines note passengers who refuse food, too frequently visit the lavatory, seem deliberately not to sleep and who are uneasy in their seats for no apparent reason. On certain routes, specific nationalities are carefully observed: for example, Chinese and Thai nationals are watched in-bound to London, with West Africans outward-bound from Hong Kong where they are infamous as smugglers.

Smugglers often take roundabout routes to throw customs officials off their trail. They fly from a drug producing to a drug-free territory, stay a while and then fly onwards after re-ticketing, thus disguising their original point of departure.

Some syndicates use relays of carriers to the same effect whilst flight-loading is also used whereby several carriers embark on the same flight: if one is stopped, the others may get through. A Filipino smuggling ring intercepted bringing heroin into the USA in 1970 had eight couriers on a single flight.

The most effective protection a trafficker can hold against detection is a diplomatic passport which affords total immunity from customs searches at air- and seaports. For decades it has been used, and remains, as a means of smuggling. At one time, in the 1960s, it was such a widespread method of avoiding detection that customs officers in both Europe and the USA wryly suggested the initials CD (meaning *Corps Diplomatique*) should stand for *Contrebandier Distingué*.

Examples of diplomatic traffickers are legion but several stand out because they were Ambassadors. Maurico Rosal (Guatemalan Ambassador to the Netherlands and Belgium), along with Salvador Pardo-Bolland (Mexican Ambassador to Bolivia), smuggled heroin worth at least $5 million between them, running it from Europe to the USA: Pardo-Bolland was successfully sentenced to eighteen years' imprisonment in the USA. In 1971, the Laotian Prince Sopsaianna arrived in Paris to take up the post of Laotian Ambassador to France. As a result of a tip-off, his baggage was stopped and searched, one of his suitcases being found to contain 60 kilograms of heroin. The matter was covered up but the French government refused to recognise his diplomatic credentials and he returned to Laos.

Most modern heroin transhipment is done by containerised freight aboard ships, air freight cargo, vehicles, international mail parcels, concealment on commercial airline flights and light aircraft. The largest shipments go by cargo container, such as the seizure of 494 kilograms of South-east Asian heroin by US Customs near Oakland, California, in 1991. It originated in Thailand and was shipped via Taiwan, hidden in a consignment of plastic bags. Taiwan was used as a way-post to disguise the country of origin of the container by redocumentation. Another means of shipment is in torpedo-shaped containers bolted below the water-line onto the bilge-keels of large vessels. These are impossible to detect without examination by a diving team.

Recent statistics of heroin smuggling into Britain give an indication of the world-wide situation, although Britain, being close to continental Europe, receives a disproportionately high percentage by road. The figures are 33.9 per cent brought in by vehicle, 19.9 per cent by freight or cargo, 14.9 per cent in baggage, 3.9 per cent on person, 1.6 per cent concealed internally, and 25.8 per cent in other ways, including post, sea drops, diplomatic bag services and light aircraft.

The high volume of modern international trade and passenger movements makes the searching of every likely means of smuggling impossible. An example of the task may be seen in the small area covered by Hong Kong where, in an average year, customs authorities have to contend with over 52,000 ocean-going vessels, 250,000 smaller craft, 71,000 aircraft landings, 42 million travellers, 7 million vehicles and 11 million packages of cargo. Searching or even observing such a volume of traffic is beyond human abilities.

Despite the complex subterfuge needed to smuggle, traffickers have not and will not be put off. They accept some of their shipments will be intercepted and budget accordingly in the knowledge their profit margins are so high. And there are always people willing to act as mules. These may be petty criminals looking to make a career in the trade, international prostitutes obliged to carry for their pimps, tourists who think they can get away with it, global back-packers and hippies short of money for the next leg of their journey or, as is frequently the case, simply poor people in dire financial straits, hoping to raise some capital. In their need or greed, they forget the one traffickers' maxim – mules are expendable: and they are now so plentiful they are often referred to as ants.

In the modern world of intercontinental trade and tourism, it is well nigh impossible to apprehend more than a small percentage of smugglers and dealers. Many factors other than the wiles of the traffickers gain relevance. Geographical location is an important element.

The USA has always had a huge problem, due to the length of its borders and seaboards which are impossible to police. Access is easy through the many settlements along the Mexican or Canadian borders, small ports on the West Coast or the Gulf of Mexico, so close to the Caribbean islands. The Mexican–USA border follows the Rio Grande for 1900 kilometres, most of which can be crossed. Expanses of desert allow light aircraft to fly below radar and land at disused airfields or even in the desert itself. Cargoes can be dropped undiscovered by parachute. Of the Canadian border, 5000 kilometres run through unpopulated wilderness. Add this to the millions of vehicles which cross the frontiers annually and the millions of passengers who arrive by scheduled airline, not to mention private aircraft and yachts, and the problem seems truly insurmountable.

Other countries face similar problems caused by the international nature of the drug trade. European countries are all land-linked, which helps smuggling, whilst the European Union's removal of border controls further abets traffickers. Large itinerant populations of migrant workers provide a supply of mules whilst some countries, like the Netherlands, have so relaxed the enforcement of drug laws as to make a near mockery of international enforcement measures.

The smugglers, traffickers and mules are only the 'front' of the trade. Behind them stand the drug barons and their efficient organisations, many of which are internationally based. They might almost have learnt their trading methods from the East India Company, for many of them are modelled on commercial multi-national structures with world-wide contacts, political protection and vast financial resources. Their ingenuity is seemingly inexhaustible. Since the 1960s, they have accrued such wealth they can pay top dollar to employ the best lawyers, financiers and advisers, meet any bribe level and corrupt whomsoever they chose to protect them, from police officers to commissioners, civil servants to government ministers, magistrates to cardinals.

These organisations are frequently ethnically exclusive. For decades, the traffic in the USA was conducted by Italians. In France, the traders are Corsican, in Italy they are frequently Sicilian, in Germany they are Turkish and in Asia usually Chinese or Japanese. New groups are emerging all the time. Nigerians are now players, with the latest new boys on the opiate scene being Russians, Albanians and Romanians.

The strength of such ethnic bondings is powerful. Laws of silence are paramount, ethnic honour or pride firmly rooted. The groupings have specific codes of discipline which are ruthlessly enforced whilst there is collective protection for loyal members. From the law enforcement aspect, they are usually impossible to infiltrate, although the American authorities have successfully penetrated the American Mafia with spectacular results. However, despite ethnic ties, alliances between such groups have also become commonly accepted: with the international nature of the drugs trade, such co-operation between criminals is essential.

In the early stages of international control, the problem of the international gangs was underestimated and there was insufficient legislation to combat them. International police co-operation was also muddled and makeshift. However, in 1923, the International Police Commission, or Interpol, was set up with headquarters in Paris. Today it has 136 member countries and, although it targets all international crime, it is a strong tool in the fight against drugs with its massive database accessible to the world's police forces.

Tip-offs and criminal contacts, stool-pigeons, narks and grasses were for years the drug squad officer's main weapon and these are still important but the odds favour the trafficker who, often amongst the élite of the underworld, knows the terrain whilst the police work in the dark. Both police and drug organisations tap sources for information: gang rivals, addicts hungry for a fix and vengeful dealers are always ready to snitch to the police or anti-trafficking organisations. Enforcement agents buy information and may infiltrate local rings, posing as potential clients. It is dangerous work and may lead to the agent being murdered when found out. They have a reasonably good success rate but they catch only street pushers and perhaps the middlemen suppliers. The bosses escape the net.

The invention of the computer has considerably aided drug enforcement. An early example of the use of the microchip dates to the early 1970s when Chinese heroin gangs targeted the USA. Unsure of the trustworthiness of their American contacts, two couriers usually carried out each delivery, one a representative of the American buyers, the other a Chinese to keep an eye on him. Several arrests were made by feeding computers with aircraft passenger data, highlighting repeating patterns of two people, one an Asian, flying on the same aircraft to the same destination. At about the same time, American cross-border vehicle data also started to be collected to watch for patterns of travelling frequency.

In the last decade, airline ticketing computers have become immensely sophisticated. They can track a passenger across the world, note where and when he breaks his journey or omits a segment of the route. For example, a passenger might fly from London to Calcutta, then take a boat to Thailand, pick up some heroin, go by train to Kuala Lumpur and fly on to Los Angeles via Tokyo, changing airlines along the way. The computers will record this, noting he did not fly from India to Malaysia. Quite often, possible candidates for smuggling are stopped by airport customs officers who ask not to see inside their cases but their tickets and passport. A recent Thai visa stamp but no Thai ticket stub, for example, is cause for suspicion.

Airport customs offices maintain internationally accessible, computerised reference files of convicted or arrested criminals and released or suspected smugglers amongst other undesirables. The passenger lists of every in-bound aircraft are liable to scrutiny whilst the aircraft is *en route*, the data obtained from the airline computer network, customs officers especially targeting high-risk flights, usually those from or near source countries. Organised syndicates today bribe computer operators rather than police and customs officers whilst hackers can be employed to access computers to alter or erase crucial files.

Whilst old-fashioned detective work, sharp eyes, hunches and experience remain effective weapons, the enforcement agencies have other handy tools at their disposal. Dogs, trained to sniff out drugs, are used widely at border posts, in ports and airports, given a free rein to range over off-loaded baggage and cargo: their noses are acutely tuned to scent specific drugs. Furthermore, a dog cannot only find infinitesimally small traces of drugs but differentiate between it and all the other smells it comes across. This negates smugglers' attempts to mask the scent of their drug by packing it with mothballs, onions, garlic powder, pepper, perfume or coffee. A dog may also be given the run of an aircraft cabin, sniffing the seats: if a seat proves positive, the information is radioed to the baggage hall, the passenger who occupied it identified through his boarding pass record or baggage tags and appropriate action taken.

Two classifications of dogs are generally used, the active and the passive. The former are usually eager, excitable breeds such as spaniels which are positioned in airline baggage sorting halls. They run all around and over the incoming luggage and, when they get a scent of narcotics, become excited, barking and furiously wagging their tales with glee. Passive dogs are from less volatile breeds such as Labradors and Setters. They wander the transit lounge or mingle with airline passengers at baggage carousels.

When a scent is picked up from a passenger, the dog sits down next to them, briefly glancing up at their face: this is the signal to customs officers the passenger is carrying.

A US Customs sniffer dog called Snag had, up until 1993, made 118 drug seizures worth $810 million, the most any canine has discovered: he has his place in the *Guinness Book of Records*. Two other dogs, Rocky and Barco, made so many seizures along the Texas–Mexico border in 1988, the Mexican smugglers put a $30,000 price on their heads. The dogs held the rank of honorary Sergeant Major and were reported to wear their stripes on duty. In May 1995, an Irish sniffer dog named Jake, working at Rosslare – who has found £9 million worth of drugs – was kidnapped. He was found a few days later after an appeal to the public, locked in a shed where it was presumed he had been left to die by drug traffickers.

Military spin-off technology is also now used in the war against the smuggler. Sophisticated radio communications equipment and bugging or long-range listening devices all play their part. Aircraft fitted with electronic monitoring sensors, originally ready to lock on to enemy aircraft in the Cold War, now intercept light aircraft flying at zero altitude. Satellite logging and pinpointing find the same targets whilst earth resource satellites can identify areas under poppy cultivation, allowing them to be targeted for destruction. High-speed launches and combat helicopters are also on line.

Despite all this, it is still estimated 90 per cent of all drugs dispatched arrive safely at their destination. DEA statistics estimate as much as $200 billion worth of narcotics enters the USA annually, a sum equivalent to one-third of all national imports. In the fiscal year 1992—3, the US Customs and US Coast Guard, backed up by the US Navy, spent $1.1 billion intercepting drug smugglers. It is no shame to them, in the light of the business, they utterly failed.

Colonel Arthur Woods, one-time Police Commissioner for New York and the first police expert appointed as an assessor to the League of Nations Advisory Committee, stated in 1923, '. . . in the contest with law-breakers as rich, as powerful, as well organised, and as far-reaching as these, the police must act strongly . . . In the struggle between traffickers and police, the advantages still lie with the traffickers.'

His words are just as true today.

13

Enter the Mobster

After the Harrison Act became law, the growth in trafficking in the USA became increasingly controlled by gangsters, a collective noun which appeared in the 1920s to refer to members of organised crime gangs which began to form in metropolitan areas such as New York and Chicago.

In the first years of the century, huge numbers of immigrants arrived in America, mostly from Europe. Amongst these were Italians fleeing poverty in Italy and Sicily: and amongst those from Sicily were members of the Mafia, a loose association of criminal groups which were first formed in feudal times to protect the interests of absentee landlords. Bound by *omertà*, an oath of secrecy and a strict code of conduct, they were by the late nineteenth century a network of loosely organised, autonomous bandit gangs operating in the Sicilian countryside. When they moved to America, where they became colloquially known as the Mob, they organised along the lines of the home country, controlling towns or urban areas as they had the Sicilian countryside. It was not long before the word *mafia* became, as it is in Italy, a generic term for organised crime.

Through the years of prohibition, the Sicilian gangsters accumulated considerable wealth, running speakeasy dives and dealing in illicit alcohol, and learning how to run a national syndicate network. This allowed them to expand into racketeering, gambling, protection and the infiltration of the labour unions. Their heydays were the 1950s and 1960s, although they remain even now influential in certain spheres of activity.

The prohibition of alcohol and the crack-down on drugs in the 1920s provided commodities criminals could exploit. Surprisingly, the Mafia in America seemingly initially ignored this golden opportunity because a code of honour forbade dealing in narcotics or prostitution; discussions about activity in these businesses were to be raised again over the years, such as at the famous meeting of the 'godfathers' at Apalachin, in upstate New York, in 1957. It was often felt narcotics trading was a bad idea because it gained a bad press: it was, the godfathers said, one thing to buy judges and run rackets but quite another to deal in dope.

Many Mafia-watchers feel that this anti-narcotics attitude was just something the mobsters liked to put about, developing a myth which has extended itself into popular mass consciousness – such as through *The Godfather* series of films – and that the Mafia have, in fact, been involved with narcotics right from their beginnings in the USA. Most Mafia bosses tried to stay out of sight, avoiding any direct entanglement in the business, but despite some strict directives put out by the Mafia hierarchy, narcotics dealing was certainly common throughout upper- and mid-level echelons of the organisation.

It is true that trade in drugs, especially heroin, was left at first to another ethnic gangster system organised by Jews which had dominated the underworld prior to the rise of the Mafia. These Jewish gangs, led by such infamous characters as Waxey Gordon, Meyer Lansky, Arthur 'Dutch' Schultz and Benjamin 'Bugs' (or 'Bugsy') Siegel, smuggled supplies from Europe and Asia. Their dealers purchased through criminal contacts who bought at source, quite legally, in Paris in the 1920s or Shanghai in the 1930s.

During the 1930s, the majority of US heroin originated in China where it was refined in either Shanghai or Tientsin: the remainder came from France and the Middle East. An example of the trade may be seen in the activities of a Jewish gang led by a leading New York gangster, Louis Buchalter. Heroin was purchased through a Greek syndicate which controlled illicit exports from legal Japanese laboratories in Tientsin. Six trips were made to Shanghai between October 1935 and February 1937, resulting in 649 kilograms being shipped to the USA in steamer trunks.

The Mafia liquor business flourished through the Roaring Twenties but, in 1930–31, a gang war changed the game. Out of this conflict rose new mob leaders, the most infamous being Salvatore C. Lucania, otherwise known as Charles 'Lucky' Luciano. Luciano was a rebel with little time for the traditional avoidance of narcotics, who had his Mafia opponents killed, made alliances with the Jewish gangs, especially those run by Meyer Lansky, and skilfully built the Mafia into the most powerful criminal syndicate in the USA, probably in the world. When liquor was made legal once more Luciano, requiring a new and equally lucrative commodity, turned to running prostitution rackets and dealing in heroin.

At first, the Jews ran the distribution but, as the 1930s progressed, the Mafia began to supersede them, driving them out of the New York distribution system by every method available from beatings in alleys to murder and the fire-bombing of Jewish premises. The Mafia's advance was not without set-backs for, in the late 1930s, state enforcement agencies and the Federal Bureau of Investigation (FBI) instigated a major drive against organised crime in which Luciano was arrested and convicted. At the same time, Mussolini conducted a campaign against the Mafia in Sicily, emasculating but not eradicating it.

With the Second World War making smuggling from such traditional sources as France and China virtually impossible, by 1945 the USA could have been purged of heroin. Organised crime was at it weakest throughout not just North America but globally. The mobsters, however, had an unforeseen ally which put them back in power and to an extent they would not have dreamed in 1939.

The details were kept secret for decades and only became widely known in 1972, with the publication of a book entitled *The Politics of Heroin in Southeast Asia* by Alfred W. McCoy. This remarkable and intensely researched study, now a seminal volume in the history of international narcotics trafficking, created an uproar in America which was, at that time, fighting a losing battle in Vietnam where drug addiction amongst troops was rife. McCoy showed how the American government's fear of global Communist expansion in the immediate post-war years caused the CIA to form alliances with any organisation which could be used to obstruct the Reds. Amongst these were the Mafia and their Corsican underworld counterparts. Under the CIA anti-Communist banner, international drug dealers were able to restore their war-battered business and considerably improve upon it throughout the four decades of the Cold War.

The story, as told by McCoy, is both shocking and outrageous. During the Second World War, US Naval Intelligence built up Mafia contacts which proved of vital importance in the planning and execution of the invasion of Sicily. After this, the Mafia in Palermo co-operated with the occupying American forces, establishing a local black market and quickly becoming powerful and spreading, as the US Army advanced up Italy, to the whole country which was in post-war turmoil.

In 1946, 'Lucky' Luciano was paroled on the grounds he had aided the war effort, and deported to Italy where he was soon joined by other American *mafiosi*. Through his political and international contacts, and with the aid of Corsican gangsters who controlled a number of skilled heroin chemists, Luciano established a powerful world-wide narcotics syndicate.

At first, heroin was illegally siphoned off from the Italian pharmaceutical giant, Schiaparelli, without its knowledge, but only until a trafficking system was put in place which smuggled morphine base from Turkey, through the Lebanon to Sicily where it was refined into heroin. Setting up a citrus fruit and vegetable exporting business, Luciano sent heroin to *mafiosi* in a number of major European cities, the supplies hidden in consignments of produce and, later, confectionery. From these European way stations, it was sent on to the USA. Some went direct to New York but a substantial amount was shipped via Cuba where the corrupt governments of successive presidents welcomed organised crime for its economic potential. Then, in the early 1950s, the Mafia closed its laboratories in Sicily and the refining was transferred to Corsican operators in Marseilles.

It was the start of the notorious French Connection, although France had been a heroin staging post *en route* to America since not long after the First World War. Until the International Convention of 1931, morphine and heroin manufacture was virtually unrestricted in Europe. French dealers legally bought direct from pharmaceutical firms then smuggled their purchases into the USA. After 1931, they recruited chemists from the pharmaceutical firms and organised secret laboratories in and around Paris. Morphine base or opium was smuggled overland from Turkey through Greece and Yugoslavia: the Orient Express was a frequent mode of transport, carriage attendants the couriers.

When Marseilles ousted Paris as Europe's heroin capital, opium and morphine base naturally arrived by sea where it was handled by the considerable criminal underworld operating in the city. Corsican criminals had been established in Marseilles since the 1920s. Amongst these were François Spirito and Paul Bonnaventure Carbone who, in response to the 1931 convention, did a no-harassment deal with the city's Fascist deputy mayor and became involved in the trans-Atlantic drugs trade. There was, however, another factor which elevated Marseilles to such narcotic prominence. It was the CIA.

Formed in September 1947, one of the CIA's early projects was the funding of Corsican gangsters, especially in Marseilles, to disrupt Communist-led unions which organised labour strikes in 1947 and 1950. The underlying aim was to destroy or ineffectualise the French Communist Party. From this covert operation two Corsican gangster brothers, Antoine and Barthélemy Guerini, rose to such power that, after the 1950 dock strike, they themselves controlled the Marseilles docks. The assistance this gave to the heroin industry need not be spelt out.

To maintain the anti-Communist status quo, the CIA continued to finance and supply weapons to the Corsicans which gave them a strong power base from which they cemented their relationship with the Mafia. In 1951, the first Corsican heroin laboratory started refining in Marseilles. It was good timing for the Italian Mafia were at that moment looking for a new source of heroin.

It has been said the Corsicans also received political protection from the French government in exchange for an under-the-table agreement that all the heroin would be exported. With characteristic French self-interest, the idea was to ignore the damage done to other countries, even those of war-time allies. Rumours also exist to the effect that the Service de Documentation Extérieure et du Contre-Espionage (SDECE, the French equivalent of the CIA) was also involved in organising drugs shipments to the USA: certainly, they were heavily involved in the opium trade in French Indo-China.

Although the Corsican gangs were not as tightly organised as Mafia groups, their supply lines were very efficient. Field traders bought opium in small batches direct from poppy farmers in Turkey, reselling to a broker who arranged for it to be smuggled into Syria. At Aleppo, it was transhipped on to Beirut and converted into morphine base. Lebanese banks guaranteed strict client confidentiality and the trade provided a good income for various political groups. From Beirut, the morphine was shipped to Marseilles where it was either landed at a dock or hermetically sealed and dumped at a pre-arranged place offshore, attached to a brightly coloured fishing buoy, to be collected later by 'fishermen'. Some morphine base arrived from Indo-China where the Corsicans also operated on a smaller scale.

The refining laboratories, staffed with the best heroin chemists (nicknamed 'cooks'), were very hard to discover. Some were sited in remote houses in the countryside around Marseilles, some in cellars, outhouses or garages, and some in city tenement blocks. Many were systematically moved from location to location to avoid detection through the characteristic smell of acetic acid which accompanies the chemical process. At the pinnacle of production in the mid-1960s, there were about two dozen laboratories operating around the clock, outputting high-grade heroin of a purity usually difficult to attain.

Success in busting the laboratories was patchy but a high point was reached in October 1964 when a French narcotics squad raided a house near Aubagne and caught Joseph Cesari red-handed. The arrest was the result of a two-year-long surveillance and Cesari was a major catch. A leading Corsican heroin chemist, he was capable of achieving 98 per cent purity and had been refining 40 kilograms per week for some years in a complex permanent laboratory. His capture resulted in all laboratories being more mobile to confound detection.

Around the time of Cesari's bust, Turkish traders began to make their own morphine base, sending it direct to Marseilles, at first by sea and then overland, carried by Turkish migrant workers living in West Germany. By 1972, three-quarters of the morphine in Europe originated in Turkey, with Munich as the way station and transit warehouse.

After the morphine was refined in Marseilles, the resulting heroin was sent on to New York with merchant seamen couriers. When the authorities caught on to this, the transhipments were shifted to go via Canada or Latin America. The Latin American route was devised and run by one of the Mafia's all-time most powerful godfathers, Santo Trafficante, Jr., who 'owned' Florida and the Caribbean. He established a select band of couriers and distributors, opening up routes bringing European heroin into

Miami through Latin America. At the time, travellers from France were always suspect in the eyes of the US Customs: those from Latin America were not. Trafficante's couriers were further aided by the fact the heroin often went by way of the French possessions of Martinique and Guadeloupe, where a French national was not subject to customs formalities, thence to Puerto Rico, an American possession, from which it could be sent on to Miami without passing through customs.

As long as the Guerinis controlled Marseilles, a moratorium existed on drug trafficking within France but, by the mid-1960s, their influence was in decline and they were being ousted by younger, more thrusting characters like Jean Jehan who was the inspiration behind the Hollywood movie, *The French Connection*. The newcomers considered such a ban irrelevant and contrary to good business: it was not long before France deservedly developed her own heroin problem.

For twenty years, until 1972, the Corsicans in alliance with both the Italian Mafia (which it is alleged, until the present day, have had high political protection in their home country) and the American Mafia, ran the US heroin market: they accounted for over 80 per cent of American consumption.

Once in the USA, the heroin was taken to cutting and packing centres known as 'heroin mills', such as those in Pleasant Avenue in New York's East Harlem, where it was adulterated and repackaged for bulk, retail or street sale. By the 1970s, the avenue and the area around it was a wholesale heroin market, known as the Pleasant Avenue Connection. Some of the tenements contained 'cut houses', small mills in stifling, air-tight rooms in which, under armed guard, women, naked due to the heat, cut heroin and weighed it into small plastic bags which retailed at $5 each. Outside, teenagers called 'movers', paid up to $2000 a week, loaded and unloaded pure heroin from sellers' to buyers' vehicles. The business was conducted overtly with the connivance of certain corrupt police officers from a supposedly untouchable New York Police Department squad known as the Special Investigations Unit (SIU). Its members collaborated with the Mafia to create a local heroin epidemic amongst neighbourhood blacks and Puerto Ricans, Jewish dealers acting as middlemen. The Pleasant Avenue Connection was finally closed down in 1973 when a specially constituted squad of untouchable police and federal agents side-stepped the SIU. Nearly a hundred gangsters were arrested. One of these, caught with a million dollars, was asked what he was going to do with the money: he sarcastically replied he was going to buy a newspaper.

Some sections of the American Mafia also trafficked in heroin (called *babania* in Sicilian slang) from Sicily, their trade known as the Sicilian Connection. In Sicily itself, friction in the Mafia between traditionalists and the new realists had produced a new breed of *mafiosi* who not only held America in thrall but, through their international connections and by dealing with other overseas suppliers, were to become intercontinental heroin brokers.

French addiction rates soared after the moratorium ended and the police substantially increased their Marseilles operations from 1971, encouraged by the American 'war on drugs' initiative instigated by President Nixon and aided by the US drugs agencies. Huge heroin stocks were seized. Traffickers were arrested. In 1972, six laboratories were unearthed, one being run by Cesari who had recently been released from prison. In the same year, the Turkish authorities outlawed poppy cultivation under pressure from the American government.

This was a major victory in Nixon's drug war. Poppies had been cultivated in Turkey for centuries whilst opium could be exported from the Ottoman Empire without restriction until 1923 when the state took control and a compulsory purchase scheme was introduced. By 1964, although only certain provinces were permitted a harvest quota, Turkey being one of the few countries allowed by international convention to export opium for pharmaceutical use, production was mostly unrestricted. Inevitably, peasants secretly held back a proportion of their opium to sell on the black market where prices were higher and traffickers paid cash on delivery. Considering Turkey the main opium source for heroin bound for the USA the Americans, using the threat of diminished military and economic aid, forced Turkey first to reduce, then eventually close down, its poppy farms to starve the French Connection.

Public opinion in Turkey was outspoken, the Ankara government criticised for caving in to American demands and being made to pay the penalty for the failure of drug enforcement in France and North America. A negotiated settlement was sought and Turkey received $35.7 million in compensation. It was one-tenth of what the Turks demanded and a fraction of their legitimate per annum opium trade earnings. Only two years later, the Turkish state monopoly decided to resume business and allow poppy growing once more but, in the meantime, the Americans claimed a moral victory: Nixon gained political kudos and the Franco-Turkish criminal relationship was broken. The ban was long enough to seal the fate of the French Connection and, although the Italian Mafia and the Corsicans re-entered the trade in the late 1970s, establishing isolated heroin laboratories across rural southern France and Italy, their hold on the US market was broken. The cutting of the supply of Turkish morphine base forced the American Mafia to find a new heroin source, for which they had in fact already been searching, appreciating the pressure being put on Turkey to stop production.

Geographically speaking, they did not have far to look. Poppy cultivation was common from Turkey to Tibet in an area loosely termed the Golden Crescent and consisting of the mountains of Iran, Afghanistan and Pakistan where opium had been produced since at least the sixteenth century.

In Pakistan's North-West Frontier Province there exist autonomous regions belonging to the Pathan (also known as Pushtun) tribes where the laws of the Karachi government hold no sway whatsoever. Fierce and proud, the Pathans have been a thorn in the side of governments for centuries: the British colonial rulers, unable to suppress them, had instead made a loose alliance with them, allowing them to keep their arms and autonomy in exchange for a quiet time. The tribesmen run their own affairs, pay allegiance to local chiefs and refuse to acknowledge national boundaries which they traverse at whim. They are, therefore, the region's smugglers, bringing contraband into and out of Afghanistan. Their main stock in trade was munitions but, in more recent times, they have turned to drugs.

Under British rule, the area produced little opium although poppies have been farmed in the Mahaban Mountains along the Pakistan–Afghanistan border since the nineteenth century when the British started planting the crop for the legal opium trade. It is perfect poppy country with suitable soil, steep and well-drained hillsides, long hours of sunshine and the right amount of rainfall. There being no other forms of income apart from agriculture, it follows that the opium poppy provides an ideal cash crop. In the 1970s, opium was sent to Afghanistan and thence distributed internationally, although the amounts were comparatively small: today, there are extensive poppy growing areas on either side of the Pakistan–Afghanistan border.

The Afghan government passed a law in 1958 prohibiting opium but no penalties were levied so it was ignored. By the early 1970s the Afghanis, with no heroin problem of their own, still saw no need for action: furthermore, the country was very poor and politically unstable. There were, officials said, other more pressing priorities. In fact, even had they decided to act, the Afghan administration would have been powerless. It lacked law enforcement resources, the poppy-growing areas were geographically remote and inaccessible, the peasants had no other livelihood, the tribesmen were liable to armed rebellion if they were interfered with and corruption was endemic. On top of this, opium was a foreign currency earner. The capital, Kabul, was on the 'hippy trail' of the late 1960s and 1970s and hippy transients were prepared not only to imbibe but to act as couriers for the opium dealers and heroin refineries which were being set up, funded by well-placed and -funded Afghanis including government ministers.

Afghanistani and Pakistani opium and heroin, the latter in fairly small amounts, were run across the border to Iran. It was a frontier beyond policing, being 500 miles long and very rugged, criss-crossed with mule tracks and rough roads. From Iran, some of the drugs went west to Turkey or south to the Persian Gulf, especially Dubai, whence they were shipped on to Europe and the rest of the world. Most of the opium, however, went no further than Iran which had a huge addict population caused by the years when the country was a major opium producing nation.

In the nineteenth and early twentieth centuries, opium had been a major Iranian export commodity, accounting for 15 per cent of its foreign income. Medicine was backward and opium so commonly used it was known as *teriac* (cure-all) rather than *afyon*, the Persian for opium. When official smoking shops were introduced in 1931, ostensibly as a form of treatment clinic, the already widespread addiction rocketed. By 1949, it was estimated 11 per cent of the adult population were habituated with 90 per cent of the population smoking opium in some regions. Villages of 600 inhabitants might have up to 16 smoking shops whilst Tehran contained 500 opium dens: the country had an estimated two million addicts who consumed two tons of opium per day in the mid-1950s. The ruling families, including those closely allied to the Shah, owned vast acreages of poppies and earned substantial incomes from them. Weak laws and corruption made sure they were protected.

In 1950, Iran began to reduce opium production until, in 1955, poppy cultivation was halted and addicts given six months to cure themselves, after which poppy growing and opium smoking, selling or possessing meant imprisonment. It was reported the Shah took this move because of the poor quality of military recruits due to addiction and under international pressure.

After the 1955 ban, addict numbers reduced but many turned to the black market for supplies. Production increased in Turkey, Afghanistan and Pakistan. The traffickers demanded payment in gold bullion. Such was the size of the trade, the national reserves began to dwindle. Then heroin grew in popularity, particularly amongst the urban young, because it was less obvious when used. Illicit refineries were established in Tehran, linked to suppliers in Afghanistan and Pakistan.

By 1968, 70 per cent of the Iranian prison population were inside on narcotics offences and the government did a *volte face*. Blaming neighbouring countries for their plight and the failure of the outright ban, which was accepted to be ineffectual, they announced a provisional resumption of poppy cultivation and opium production.

The international community was incensed: it was said the decision was the greatest setback to global drug control since 1945. Yet Iran was adamant and cited the social and economic effects the blanket ban had had on the country. A law was ratified in June 1969 authorising opium production to satisfy domestic demand, poppy cultivation being condoned only in rigidly controlled areas. No sooner was the law passed than poppy fields sprang up everywhere.

Under the provision of the law, opium could only be legally used by addicts over sixty years old and by those who were unable on medical grounds to undergo detoxification. Most addicts overcame the restriction by failing to register and by buying their opium illegally. Although the law carried the death penalty for trafficking, corruption and the widespread use of opium made it impractical.

Until about 1972, the drug output of the Golden Crescent stayed largely contained within the confines of Afghanistan, Pakistan and Iran. As long as the Iranian ban lasted, there was good money to be made from a sizeable addict population there. With the ban lifted and Iran growing her own opium again, some of the Golden Crescent product was released for the international market but it was several more years before it was to become a significant source.

With the collapse of the French Connection, therefore, the Mafia and other criminals were unable at that time to obtain large scale supplies of narcotics from the Golden Crescent and they set their sights further afield on South-east Asia. The region was already producing up to 70 per cent of the world's illicit opium and Chinese chemists in laboratories in Hong Kong were refining heroin of comparable purity to that of Cesari. This, the gangsters decided, was the area in which to expand so contacts were built up between them and both Corsican syndicates operating in Indo-China and Chinese criminal fraternities existing in Hong Kong, Malaysia, Thailand and Taiwan.

The next development in the opium story, and one of the most shameful, was just around the corner.

14

Soldiers and Secrets

In 1969, the US Bureau of Narcotics reckoned only 5 per cent of the heroin on American streets originated in South-east Asia. This was more than likely a gross underestimate. However, in three years, the guestimate had gone up to 30 per cent and was rising. The source of the heroin was the Golden Triangle.

The Golden Triangle, a name made popular by journalists in the 1970s, is an area of at least 225,000 square kilometres, roughly three-sided and straddling the frontiers of Laos, Thailand and Burma, just south of the Chinese border. It is a mountainous, isolated region of sharp ridges, wide plateaux and tall peaks, the uplands formed of limestone and ideal opium poppy country, especially for the Yunnanese variety of the opium poppy which prefers a temperate climate: at altitudes above 1000 metres, conditions are perfect.

Other factors make the Golden Triangle a top quality opium producing region. Opium has been a trade commodity here for at least two centuries. Like the Mahaban Mountains on the Pakistan–Afghanistan border, the area is remote and inaccessible, beyond the laws of the respective governments and politically chaotic: that the Thai, Laotian and Burmese governments are also riddled with corruption more than helps. The collusion of many politicians, officials and military leaders is virtually certain. If not, a tolerance of the trade may be relied upon.

The population consists of independent hill tribes for whom opium is a traditional part of everyday life. They are not indigenous to the region but migrated here from the southern Chinese coastal provinces in the latter half of the nineteenth century, bringing their opium habit with them. The main tribes are the Hmong (also known as the Meo, a derogatory name given them by the Chinese and used by European colonials) and the Yao who migrated to escape Chinese persecution: lesser tribes include the Lisu, Kachin and Lahu who settled on the Burma–Thailand border. Some of the tribes occupy hilltop villages, others leading semi-nomadic existences and cultivating opium in slash-and-burn jungle clearings. Opium poppy farming is the main livelihood of these tribes and, suitable land being at a premium, has caused considerable deforestation. In some areas, 90 per cent of cultivated land is devoted to poppies.

Itinerant traders, often of Chinese origin, move through the villages, purchasing opium and selling trade goods, the opium subsequently sold to warlords and drug merchants. The main purchasers are, or have been, army units of the Kuomintang (KMT), the Nationalist Chinese losing side led by Chiang Kai-shek in the war against Mao Zedong in 1949, various ethnic rebel armies in particular bands from the northern Shan states of north-eastern Burma who have been trying since 1960 to secede from Burma, and Yunnanese-descended opium warlords who are, in essence, autarchic warlords with private armies to guard their trade routes and opium caravans. Nowadays, they command forces of several thousand well-trained and armed soldiers, often with their own uniforms.

Just who rules in the Golden Triangle or any segment of it – or has done over the last three or four decades – is beyond firm definition. It is impossible to be succinct about the situation. Opium being the only main source of finance, the region has been, and remains, in a state of flux with different forces fighting to control the opium harvest, the opium highlands and to retain or gain military supremacy with different parties forming and breaking and reforming allegiances in a continual search for wealth and power.

Being land-locked and remote, the region has no direct outlet to international drug markets so private armies are essential to escort the opium through the mountains and jungles to remote heroin factories in Burma, Thailand and Laos. There have been two primary routes along which the opium and heroin reached the outside world. One, by air from isolated airstrips in northern

Laos to Saigon, was closed after the fall of Saigon in 1975: the other main route exists to this day and goes overland through Burma and Thailand to Bangkok, now the world's chief heroin distribution centre.

Opium has always been important to South-east Asia. In the nineteenth and early twentieth centuries, government monopolies supplying a predominantly Chinese opium smoking population imported it by sea from India and by mule caravan from Yunnan, taxing the trade and thereby creating a black market, especially in Yunnanese opium. En route, the traders from Yunnan bought and sold the tiny domestic harvest raised by the hill tribes, promoting trade and creating a link between them and demand in the lowlands: some tribes inevitably began growing opium as a cash crop for the illegal market but their contribution was minuscule.

Prior to the 1940s, French and British colonial government campaigns to halt poppy cultivation kept local production low and government revenue high for imports were taxed and addicts charged inflated prices. However, as the 1950s progressed and colonial power waned, outside influences came to the fore and greatly affected the regional narcotics trade. The moving force behind this was the fight against Communism.

In order to check the spread of Communism in Asia, tribal headmen and warlords struck deals with the French intelligence services and, more especially, with the CIA. By associating themselves with local leaders, CIA operatives were also building links with the opium business for the two went unequivocally hand in hand. Furthermore, to keep the warlords in power, the CIA allowed them to maintain their opium dealing and even provided them with open access to American munitions and air transport to further their opium or heroin distribution. In short, the CIA became inextricably entangled with the Golden Triangle opium trade, handling opiate consignments, flying drug runs and tolerantly turning a blind eye to the affairs of their criminal allies.

For those who served in the Vietnam War, or covered it as journalists, CIA involvement in the narcotics trade was suspected, if not publicly acknowledged: it was McCoy's *The Politics of Heroin in Southeast Asia* which blew the whistle. The CIA went to great lengths to ban his book, claiming it was a threat to national security whilst it was really an embarrassing exposé of America's obsession with and mismanagement of the Communist threat, and the ineffectuality of Cold War strategies.

The background to CIA involvement is important to the understanding of how the present-day international heroin situation arose.

As soon as the Japanese were defeated and left South-east Asia in 1945, opium imports started again, supplies coming from Iran and Yunnan. The number of addicts quickly rose but it was not long before their supplies were heavily curtailed. The Communist victory in China in 1949, and the subsequent banning of poppy growing and closure of the Chinese border, halted the Yunnan trade whilst the signing of the UN protocol in 1953, in which opium producing nations agreed not to sell on to the international market, further cut imports. The only answer seemed to lie in domestic production and this set off widespread poppy cultivation in the Golden Triangle.

Anxious to dam the flood-tide of Communism arising from China's change of political structure, in 1950 the CIA set in motion a number of covert operations along the Chinese border in the Golden Triangle area and purchased a local airline, Civil Air Transport (CAT). This had belonged to General Claire Chennault, the leader of the famous 'Flying Tigers' during the Second World War and had flown military cargoes over 'The Hump', the mountains of Indo-China, into Kunming and Chungking in support of the Allies and Chiang Kai-shek's army. CAT was later renamed Air America, although there were those who nicknamed it Air Arlington (after the Arlington, Virginia, headquarters of the CIA) and, more pertinently, Air Opium.

As they had done in the war, the aircraft continued to support the Nationalist Chinese cause by supplying and arming remnants of the KMT which had fled China to settle along the border in the Shan states. Within months of buying CAT, the CIA was parachuting in arms and ammunition with military advisers who trained the KMT survivors, along with some hill tribesmen, into a 12,000-strong guerrilla army with which it optimistically invaded southern China in 1951–2.

These invasions unavoidably failing, the force then extended itself along the Burma–China border against anticipated Communist Chinese incursion. Then, in late 1952, it began to expand into the Shan states, soon becoming the only effective government in the remote region. This was fortuitous for the Shan states were the prime Burmese opium producing area: it was only a matter of time before the KMT started to trade in opium, financing themselves from the same source as they had been funded under Chiang Kai-shek in China. Members of the KMT have confirmed the instructions to deal in opium were personally made by Chiang Kai-shek with his son and eventual successor as president of Taiwan, General Chiang Ching-kuo, again ratifying it on the Generalissimo's death in 1975.

Equipped with the latest American arms and expertise, the KMT were able to dominate the local population. With characteristic Chinese entrepreneurialism, they levied general taxes to finance and increase their hold on the opium traffic, centralised the opium market and charged an annual opium duty to every poppy farmer. They also consolidated their infiltration of the hill tribes by marrying into them. With their hopes dashed of winning back China, they metamorphosed into a highly proficient opium militia. By 1962, they had transformed the Golden Triangle into the world's single largest poppy growing area with opium production increasing drastically. UN statistics assessed Burmese annual output as rising from 40 tons in 1945 to 400 in 1962, Thai annual output from 7 to 100 tons and Laotian from 30 to between 100 and 150 tons per annum.

From time to time, conflict flared up between Burmese forces and KMT troops. The latter considered the former a threat to their opium business whilst the Burmese were worried the KMT were inciting separatist tendencies in the historically volatile Shan states. In 1953, Burma protested to the UN and a number of KMT soldiers were flown out to Taiwan but nothing changed: the KMT were keen to retain control because of opium.

This control was consolidated further because of the Burmese political scene. As a federation of states, tribes and races with no common language, religion or political centre, Burma was (and still is) hard to govern. The Shan states especially have always been difficult to govern from outside. Even the experienced British colonial authorities were essentially impotent, the tribes owing allegiance to feudal *sawbwas*, tribal chiefs who controlled every aspect of local life but especially commerce. Faced with such localised power bases, the British gave the *sawbwas* responsibility for internal Shan state affairs: by so doing, they set the seal on the future of the opium trade. It was placed beyond external law and became a major source of revenue for the *sawbwas* who levied their own tax upon it. In 1948, when Burma gained independence, these local rulers were cajoled into accepting a place in the new Union of Burma by being promised autonomy by secession in ten years. This assurance was reneged upon in 1958 when the prime minister, U-Nu, repealed the promise, thereby setting the scene for the growth of nationalist movements.

The diversity of Burmese society has also had the country in turmoil for decades. The minority Kachins, Shans, Karens, Lahu, Wa, Mons and others have long been waging a guerrilla war against the central government. Furthermore the Burmans, who barely make up 50 per cent of the population, only hold 40 per cent of the area of the country, none of it opium growing land. Even if they wished to control opium, they could not: and the income from it furthers the separatist ambitions of the minorities.

Most opium in Burma is grown along the Chinese border in Shan- and Kachin-controlled regions, with hardly a vehicular road cutting through impenetrable, mountainous jungle. The population has no other source of income other than opium which, since 1959, the various Shan separatists parties have used to obtain arms to fight the Burmese government and sometimes each other. The leading groups, amongst many others, have included the Kachin Independent Army (KIA), the Kachin Liberation Army (KLA), the Lahu National Liberation Army (LNLA), the Mon National State Army (MNSA), the United Wa State Army (UWSA), the Karen National Union (KNU), the Shan State Army (SSA), the Shan National Army (SNA), the Shan National United Front (SNUF) and the Shan United Army (SUA). To say the situation has been chaotic and anarchic is a gross understatement. The rebels have fought each other, forged treaties, broken them and reforged others on a frequent basis whilst still attacking the Burmese forces.

In many respects, opium has been the underlying cause of Burmese upheaval but the official government too has never lost sight of its economic value. When, in 1964, it sought to become a world exporter in pharmaceutical provision, a UN mission concluded it could not endorse the proposal to allow controlled opium production. It was clear the Burmese were not in command of the country.

By the end of the 1960s, the mission's conclusion was further proven. The opium highlands were occupied by over 100 separate, capricious, armed groups. The fabric of society had collapsed with only the opium trade flourishing. To try and gain some control over – others would suggest gain a foothold in – the opium trade, the government had set up local militia groups, the Ka Kwei Yei (KKY), in 1963, to organise some aspects of the trade whilst at the same time fighting the rebels and undermining their financial base. All that happened was the situation was further confused. KKY troops saw the financial advantages of opium and several warlords were created from their ranks. In effect, all the government could do was allow the trade to continue because, even if they could not control or tax it, it was at least a huge national foreign currency earner.

Originating as an internal matter, by the 1970s outside interests in the form of the KMT, the CIA and the government of Thailand were all concerned with the instability in the Shan states. The KMT were satisfied to be sending their opium collectors throughout the Shan states, unhindered by the Burmese, who were kept busy with the separatists, and the CIA was similarly content. The confusion provided cover for American intelligence gathering along and over the Chinese border. As Thailand was Burma's traditional enemy, the Thais provided arms for the rebel bands, ensuring a buffer zone between the countries.

Prior to the KMT's move into Burma, some opium had been sent out through Thailand but the trade was insignificant. However, as the power of the KMT increased so too did the trade, with opium being transported by mule or light aircraft to Chiang Mai then freighted on to Bangkok with the connivance of Thai police, on occasion on CAT or Air America flights.

Like Burma, Thailand regarded opium as a major, if illicit, export commodity. It had been an important part of the economy for over a century. As Siam, the country legalised opium in 1851, the Chinese population of Bangkok being keen customers: the King of Siam and later rulers became immensely rich on the revenues. When Thailand was occupied by the Japanese in the Second World War, the national army hid out in the Shan states where it was quick to establish contact with the local warlords and the KMT Nationalist Chinese army in Yunnan. When the war ended, the Thai government had in place not only a protective shield against Burma but all the contacts it needed in the opium trade which became a major source of military funding. For four decades, the

Thai authorities assisted the opium traders of the Golden Triangle, took an informal tax on opium crossing into Thailand and used the proceeds to finance political aims and many a private income: it must be remembered corruption was, and to some extent still is, endemic throughout Indo-China.

From the 1940s, the Thais increased their own poppy production and, with KMT-owned Burmese opium entering the country as well, it was not long before the capital, Bangkok, became an important opium distribution centre.

The military rulers of Thailand, who came to power in a coup in 1947, survived on opium. It financed their take-over and bankrolled their armed forces, successive military administrations increasing their hold on the Thai economy including the trade in, and smuggling of, opium. General Phao, head of the CIA-equipped and -trained national police force, took personal control of the opium trade and, in exchange for CIA support, furthered KMT political aims, protecting their supply lines and opium business interests and establishing what is considered the Burma to Bangkok opium corridor. He consequently became one of the most powerful men in the country. By 1955, Phao's police force was the largest, best organised trafficking syndicate in Thailand, pivotal to every aspect of the business. By now, Bangkok was the main centre for international opium trafficking in South-east Asia, with Thailand the world's primary distribution hub. Phao's power was not to last. Press exposure of police corruption in 1955 undermined his position and, after a coup two years later, he fled the country, a very rich man indeed.

At first, the new Thai government seemed no better: it entered into the opium trade to swell the exchequer. Then, in 1959, opium use was forbidden with opium production and sale outlawed. This was all very well but, like the Burmese, the Thais had little control over the remote Golden Triangle and poppy farming continued.

The ban caused a new development. Heroin began to appear. The Thai addict population rose from 71,000 opium smokers in 1959 to around 400,000 heroin addicts in 1976. Due to indigenous corruption, little effort was made to halt the trade or the transport of opiates through Thailand by the syndicates of Chinese who had come to operate it. Military commanders and government officials continued to cream off their cut and accepted protection money from the Chinese traffickers based in Bangkok. Despite the law, it was business as usual.

The situation altered in 1961. Fed up with the KMT in the Shan states, the Burmese joined with the Communist Chinese People's Liberation Army (PLA) and drove the KMT into Laos and Thailand where the Thais, having successfully concealed their opium entanglements, classified the soldiers as civilian refugees. At the same time, the Taiwanese Nationalist Chinese government reduced the financial support it had given the KMT since 1949 which forced it to become even more reliant upon the opium business to survive.

From northern Thailand, the KMT carried on sending buying missions into the Shan states, where their middlemen – Yunnanese traders – bought opium in exchange for everyday consumer goods. The opium was collected at a number of central rendezvous points then transported by armed mule trains into Thailand. The KMT trade increased and their hold grew not only on opium production in Burma but in northern Thailand where they took over from local officials who had left the opium trade after the 1959 ban.

The mule trains were enormous with over 100 mules – on occasion as many as *600* – carrying up to 20 tons of raw opium protected by 300 heavily armed troops trained in jungle warfare. So efficient were the troops that Shan state rebel and private merchants' mules sometimes travelled with them, paying for the service. Those who did not seek protection were charged a KMT levied import duty to enter Thailand.

Despite such power, the KMT did not have it all their own way. There was a potential usurper in their midst. His name was Chan Chi-fu, sometimes given as Chan Shee Fu. He is best known today as Khun Sa: *khun* is a Shan word meaning 'lord' whilst *Sa* is the name of his stepfather, a Shan prince. In the usual way of Oriental names, it has an alternative interpretation for *Sa* may also mean wealthy: therefore Khun Sa can also mean Lord of Prosperity.

At that time, Khun Sa was the only well organised, highly proficient warlord smuggler in the Shan states. Half Chinese and half Shan, he is descended from a Chinese Yunnanese merchant family although he has claimed descent from a noble Shan family. He was born in the Shan states in 1933 and joined the KMT at the age of eighteen when he was military trained and tutored in the finer points of the opium trade. At the age of thirty, he began trading in opium on his own, supported by his own unit of KKY members. Very carefully, he consolidated his power base, gained territory and earned the respect of local hill tribes. Aware of the difficulties of transporting bulky opium, he astutely set up a simple refinery turning out morphine bricks. Within three years, he commanded a private army of 2000 and was the most important opium warlord in the Shan states.

His rapid rise caused a KMT backlash. In 1967, there was fought a local opium war between Khun Sa's forces and the KMT in loose alliance with the Royal Laotian Army. A Khun Sa controlled caravan set off from the Shan states for Ban Houei Sai in northern Laos carrying 16 tons of raw opium. KMT soldiers went to head off the caravan, concerned that Khun Sa was challenging their long-standing domination of the opium trade with Burma. As the fighting warmed up, the Laotian General Ouane Rattikone arrived with a government force, attacked both the KMT and Khun Sa's men, defeated them both and seized the opium.

This was not, however, all it seemed for Ouane Rattikone had ordered the opium from Khun Sa in the first place: he was to become one of the most important heroin manufacturers in the Golden Triangle, operating laboratories around Ban Houei Sai to process Burmese opium.

Khun Sa was beaten, his force considerably reduced and his power removed. Two years later, he was captured by the Burmese Army whilst visiting Taunggyi, a town on the western extremity of the Shan states. He was held in solitary confinement for five years, but his supporters maintained command of several opium districts. It was not the end of his career.

Regardless of the 1967 war, the KMT further tightened its hold on opium. When Hmong tribesmen revolted between 1967 and 1971, the Thai government employed the KMT to eradicate guerrilla bases. Claiming the Hmong to be Communist, the Thais also enlisted the support of the CIA. By 1972, the KMT purchased opium from virtually the whole of the Shan states and dealt in 90 per cent of the region's produce. They also established heroin factories at several places in the Golden Triangle.

The only area in the region not to produce opium in any substantial quantity at the time was French Indo-China, now Vietnam, yet the colonial and post-colonial governments were still deeply involved in the trade. Like other colonial administrations, the French ran an opium monopoly which they organised very effectively and which engendered substantial revenue. In 1939, opium accounted for 15 per cent of taxes collected, catering to over 100,000 addicts, but the costs of addiction were high. The labouring classes, mostly Chinese and Vietnamese Chinese, upon whom the predominantly agriculturally based economy relied, spent much of their earnings on opium. Families starved to death, disease was widespread and the drug undermined workers' abilities. The French-trained native civil service élite were most of them addicts and corrupt. When anti-colonial, nationalist sentiments began to be voiced, the opium monopoly was cited as the worst aspect of French domination and one of the linch-pins of Ho Chi Minh's anti-colonial propaganda.

It was the French who enticed the Hmong hill tribes of northern Laos to change their cash crop to opium during the Second World War, obtaining their co-operation by promising political support. Production rose by 800 per cent from 7.5 tons in 1940 to 60.6 tons in 1944 and the Hmong tribes, arguing over opium rights and revenues, split into factions which caused a quarter of a century of civil war. In neighbouring Tonkin, the French politically sided with Tai feudal leaders who purchased Hmong opium but double-crossed them when it came time to pay, causing the Hmong to take sides with the Viet Minh against the French. The Viet Minh and, therefore, ultimately the Viet Cong, had their struggle partly aided by the opium trade they detested.

The French stopped the opium monopoly in 1946 but, upon losing the revenue from it, unofficially sanctioned French intelligence organisations to take over the trafficking of opiates to fund covert operations in the First Indo-China War of 1946–54.

With typical Gallic guile, corrupt French intelligence officers in collaboration with Corsican gangsters operated the Indo-Chinese based international drugs trade. The money they earned was vital. The war was underfunded from Paris, where public opinion was against it, so French military and intelligence officers took a new tack. In Operation X, they dealt in opium to pay and arm local groups in order to keep the Viet Minh at bay. The French, therefore, increased the illicit traffic in opium, taking a cut of the profits to pay what were, in effect, mercenaries: individual French officials and military personnel also creamed off percentages for themselves and became rich on the proceeds. This practice did not stop until the French quit Indo-China.

The raw opium in which they dealt was purchased from the Hmong then flown by French military transport to Saigon where it was prepared and distributed to dens and dealers by the Binh Xuyen. This was a Vietnamese criminal syndicate which controlled organised crime in the south of the country and to whose nefarious activities the French turned a blind eye in exchange for their co-operation and occasional help against the Viet Minh. The Binh Xuyen leader, Le Van 'Bay' Vien, became the richest man in Saigon by 1954 for he not only ran the domestic opium market but he sold any surplus on to Chinese and Corsican syndicates.

With French colonial power receding and Vietnam partitioned, the Americans, who were increasing their influence in the new South Vietnam to counter Communist expansion, supported a new prime minister, Ngo Dinh Diem, who was fiercely opposed to the Communist Viet Minh. Diem destroyed the Binh Xuyen which he perceived as a political threat. With the departure of Le Van Vien and his cohorts, and the closure of Operation X, opium smuggling in bulk from Laos ceased with selling left to petty criminals.

The vacuum was quickly filled by the Corsican syndicates who had had representatives in Saigon and Vientiane, the capital of Laos, since the French Expeditionary Corps had arrived in the late 1940s, sent out to fight in the war. Connected to comrades in Marseilles, they had been running gold, gemstones, currency and narcotics between the French port and Saigon throughout hostilities.

They instigated a number of small charter air freight companies, collectively referred to as Air Opium (not to be confused with Air America). Some pilots were French criminals and some ex-Resistance fighters from the Second World War, including the famous double agent, Henri Déricourt. Under the leadership of Bonaventure 'Rock' Francisci, a Corsican gangster who operated Air Laos Commerciale, they flew morphine base from the Golden Triangle to Saigon then freighted it onward by sea to Europe.

Whilst the Corsicans were setting up a South-east Asian branch of the French Connection, the government of Ngo Dinh Diem was running short of funds. He legalised opium dens in 1958 and, as other South Vietnamese governments were to do, used the revenue to pay for the fight against the Viet Cong. Diem relied for opium supplies upon Vietnamese intelligence agents in Laos and Corsican gangsters whom he personally knew, shipments arriving in Corsican aircraft or, in time, Vietnamese air force transports bringing loads in from Vientiane.

In common with its neighbours, Laos also had severe monetary problems after gaining its independence from colonial rule. To address the budgetary shortfall, the government tacitly accepted arms, gold and opium smuggling whilst realising opium was their only viable export and promoting its traffic. However, it was not until the Americans withdrew their support for the government in 1962, in the face of a Cold War confrontation with Russia over their Laotian policies, that right-wing government members seriously started to enter the drug trade.

The man in charge was General Ouane Rattikone, chairman of the quasi-official Laotian Opium Administration and subsequently Commander-in-Chief of the Laotian Army from 1965 to 1971. He controlled a highly successful international drugs ring with agents in Bangkok, Saigon and Hong Kong. A skilful businessman and entrepreneur, he regarded opiates like any other commercial commodity and even brand marked his goods. He owned the infamous 999 morphine trademark, his base morphine pressed into blocks with 999 stamped into them and printed on the wrapping: the figure was taken from the 99.9 fine gold standard, although most South-east Asian morphine at the time was around 50 per cent pure.

By monopolising the opium trade, Ouane Rattikone put the Corsicans and their airlines out of business and took to flying drugs in Laotian government aircraft to Saigon for transfer to Hong Kong. Although he never admitted outright his involvement in the trade, neither did he seek to cover it up and, when he retired in 1971, he was immensely rich and powerful and proud he had made so much money for his country – which he had – with a commodity which was conveniently not then illegal in Laos.

Ouane Rattikone's ousting of the Corsicans in 1965 caused a minor hiccup in the trade. It produced an air transport shortage which the Laotian government could not entirely redress. A rescuer appeared on the scene in the shape of the CIA and Air America.

Since 1959, the CIA had operated with Hmong guerrillas in Laos, gathering intelligence and monitoring the Laotian Communists. For fourteen years, from 1960, the CIA ran a secret army of 30,000

Hmong guerrillas who fought the Communist Pathet Lao forces close to the North Vietnam border. In order to retain Hmong loyalty, the CIA had to transport Hmong opium, especially from the north-east of the country.

Air America, with Continental Air Service (CAS) and Lao Development Air Service, became the Hmong opium carriers, flying opium to Long Tieng and Vientiane. As Air America and CAS aircraft were not painted with international registration markings, they could move freely between Laos, Vietnam and Thailand, the pilots highly trained and often little short of dare-devil acrobats, landing in the mountains at remote, often steeply sloping, rough earth runways surrounded by forests: pilots landed uphill and took off downhill. They knew what they were carrying when the manifest declared a cargo to be 'miscellaneous', given priority and handled by special personnel. When the cargo reached Long Tieng or Vientiane, it was transferred to Vietnamese or Laotian military aircraft which, as French official aircraft had done, took it to Saigon where associates of Vietnamese political leaders sent it on its way into the national or international market-place.

It is fair to say the CIA probably did not – as the French intelligence services had done – directly profit financially from the opium trade, although some individuals did run a sideline of their own: but, by carrying opium, the CIA did reduce its direct costs and assured the Hmong villages of continued economic survival. The carriage of Hmong opium also allowed the CIA-sponsored Hmong commander in north-eastern Laos, General Vang Pao, to build up his credibility and recruit troops from the villages which also received CIA aid in the form of rice and medical air drops. Vang Pao further came to rely upon the CIA for troop, as well as opium, transportation and for refugee air-lifts of local people under attack: this gave Vang Pao the reputation of being a socially-minded saviour and the CIA of being guardian angels against the Pathet Lao.

Yet it was hypocritical. The CIA used opium as a political lever to sweeten and buy off would-be opponents, to purchase loyalty and to bribe influential local leaders. The type of behaviour they condemned in other countries, and denounced other governments for allowing, they were doing themselves in South-east Asia.

In north-western Laos, the situation was different. The CIA had been present there since 1959, using the Shan opium muleteers to carry equipment and arms to clandestine listening posts on the Chinese border, the political and topographical terrain being too risky for Air America. Shan and Lahu tribesmen, recruited as agents, conducted cross-border intelligence gathering operations in China during the 1960s. A number of arms-related Burmese opium deals were also sanctioned with General Ouane Rattikone, thus starting the Laotian heroin processing industry.

Then, in 1968, Pathet Lao offensives prompted the Americans to bomb their mountain and jungle strongholds. A huge Hmong migration began to escape the bombing, with thousands of opium growers on the move. Opium production fell drastically and opium social customs altered. It was traditionally old men who smoked opium: young men were socially forbidden. Now, young Hmong fighters took the drug to calm their nerves, help them relax and to combat boredom in the jungle.

This social taboo existed throughout Laos where opium was legal and primarily used by the old and sick but, in 1971, opium was outlawed under an American threat to withdraw foreign aid. The American aim was to starve the heroin refineries of stocks but they continued in business whilst the ordinary smoker was hit by the closure of opium dens and retailers. As had happened in Iran in the mid-1950s, addicts changed from opium to the less obvious heroin which was not injected but smoked through a normal cigarette dipped in heroin solution and left to dry or containing heroin powder mixed with the tobacco.

The government of Laos reached a cease-fire agreement with the Pathet Lao in 1973. The following year, Air America withdrew from the country. Without its air support and CIA protection, Vang Pao had to make a run for it. He reached Thailand and was granted a resident's visa to the USA in 1975. With their leader gone, tens of thousands of Hmong refugees headed for Thailand. A Communist government came to control in Laos in 1976 and the problems of addiction were rigorously addressed. Opium production, however, was left untouched for it provided foreign currency and output rose sharply. The new government continued to be heavily engaged in the drugs trade. One important Thai drug trafficker, who worked for the Laotian government selling heroin to the West, travelled with a Laotian diplomatic passport and was named by American agents as the Laotian government's 'Minister of Heroin'.

By 1969, the Golden Triangle region was producing about 1000 metric tonnes of raw opium per annum, some heroin was being made in urban Bangkok and northern Thailand and morphine base was being exported direct to heroin laboratories in Europe or Hong Kong, where heroin was refined for local use and re-exported to the USA. There was, however, another market. It began when the Americans moved in militarily to Vietnam in 1965.

Until 1962, South-east Asian output was in either refined opium or No. 3 heroin, production of this having commenced in 1959 when Thailand banned opium and smokers switched to heroin.

No. 3 heroin is crude being only 20–40 per cent pure, often far lower, and includes adulterants, especially caffeine. It gains its name from being the result of the third stage of processing. Consisting of small dirty grey or brown granules or lumps, it looks somewhat like fish tank gravel, pet litter or unrefined sugar from which it gets the nickname of 'brown sugar'. It is cheap and usually smoked, being unsuitable for injection.

Heroin of purer quality is called No. 4 heroin, deriving its name from a fourth processing phase in which ether and hydrochloric acid are added to heroin base or No. 3 heroin dissolved in alcohol, the heroin forming as tiny soap-like flakes in the solution. These are then filtered and dried. It is highly soluble in water, injectable and normally sold as a white powder although this may vary in colour from pure white through off-white to creamy yellow or even pink. Before being cut, its purity ranges from 80–99 per cent. The making of No. 4 heroin has an inherent risk, but not of addiction such as opium handlers might face. In the final phase, the ether gas can ignite. The resulting explosion can demolish a building.

The first refinery for the making of high purity, injectable No. 4 heroin was erected in a Thai village called Mang Tang Wu in 1963. Its product was sent to Hong Kong. Other primitive refineries were also established but soon closed, the restriction on the expansion of No. 4 heroin production being the dearth of competent drug chemists.

Soldiers are susceptible to drugs and the American military involvement in Vietnam offered a market not to be refused. At the height of the Vietnam War, there were 500,000 American soldiers in the theatre of conflict.

By 1968, Chinese narcotics syndicates in Hong Kong had dispatched skilled chemists to the Golden Triangle to set up laboratories specifically to cater to American GI demand for pure No. 4

heroin. By 1971, twenty-nine refineries were running in the Golden Triangle, fifteen of them producing only No. 4 heroin. Thousands of kilograms were produced and sold to GIs throughout Vietnam. The addiction rate rapidly escalated.

Ban Houei Sai was the centre of heroin production, using Burmese opium. The largest refinery belonged to General Ouane Rattikone and was the source at the time of the infamous Double UOGlobe (sometimes Double Globe) brand of heroin: as with the 999 brand of base morphine, heroin, as it still does, came trademarked. Ironically similar to the first-ever heroin packets devised by Bayer, the Double UOGlobe wrapper has a circle containing two rampant lions holding a globe. It is usually printed in scarlet (a lucky colour for the Chinese) or brown. Across the top are Chinese characters which translate as Double Lion Earth Brand, below which are two statements, also in Chinese – 'Beware of Counterfeits' and 'Pure 100 per cent'. Outside the circle may be printed, in Chinese and Thai, 'Travel safely by sea', a colloquial expression equating to *Bon voyage!*, implying not only that the heroin might reach its destination unmolested by customs officers but that addicts might have a good 'trip' with it.

Not only was this heroin sold in Vietnam but it was also exported direct to the USA with morphine base simultaneously going to heroin manufacturers in Vientiane and Long Tieng. The heroin was mostly flown to Vietnam, primarily via Vientiane, by Laotian and Vietnamese military aircraft. The traffic was controlled by corrupt Laotian and South Vietnamese officials, with some Thais in co-operation or collaboration. Making huge profits out of their allies, these men addicted untold numbers of American personnel. Heroin was available at roadside stalls on every highway out of Saigon, and on the route to the main US army base at Long Binh, as well as from itinerant peddlers, newspaper and ice-cream vendors, restaurant owners, brothel keepers and their whores and domestic servants employed on US bases. No barracks was without a resident dealer.

The heroin was not injected by most GIs but smoked as it was so pure and plentiful, mixed with tobacco or marijuana which was also abundant and grown in Laos and Cambodia. Many GI addicts had their own pipes, often home-made from lengths of bamboo but sometimes purchased. On occasion, bizarre or gruesome examples could be seen, such as pipes made from cartridge cases or human bones. Others removed the end from a cigarette and filled it with heroin. The heroin smoked, being No. 4 heroin and anywhere between 90 and 98 per cent pure, was considerably more addictive than that which would have been injected back home in the USA where it would have been cut to a far lower strength.

So rampant was heroin abuse, questions were asked as to whether or not the Viet Cong were behind the trade but they were not: it was solely run by American allies on the take.

In the summer of 1971, army medical officers reckoned 25,000 to 37,000 (10–15 per cent) serving rank-and-file troops were heroin addicts. In some units, the rate was nearer 20 per cent, with whole combat units made ineffectual by drug usage. It was discovered that 85 per cent of all American personnel, regardless of rank, were offered heroin with 35 per cent accepting and 19 per cent becoming habituated. So overt was drug taking in Vietnam soldiers had their Zippo lighters, a part of the personal kit of every 'grunt' (an ordinary enlisted soldier), engraved with drug-related poems and maxims such as:

> Always ripped
> Or always stoned
> I made a year
> I'm going home

or:

> 'Say Hi! if you're high'.

Many took their habits home with them: in November 1971, there were about 10,000 Vietnam veteran addicts in New York. A third of these were enrolled on detoxification programmes but, generally speaking, treatment for Vietnam veterans was shoddy and many remained addicted, spreading the habit to their home areas and escalating US addiction rates.

It was not only back home the troops spread heroin. They took it with them on R 'n' R (rest and recreation) leaves to Hong Kong, Singapore, Taipei, the Philippines and Australia. Certainly, US troops on week-long R 'n' R in Sydney brought an increase in heroin addiction: an entire street culture of hookers and hustlers grew up around them, sharing their heroin.

Much has been written about the cause of US troop heroin addiction. Theories abound: they turned to it from marijuana to avoid that drug's tell-tale smell or they took it to counteract boredom, fear or from shame at being involved in an unjust, amoral conflict. The truth is less complex. They took it because it was there, as accessible as tobacco and often more acceptable than liquor on which restrictions exist in the US armed forces. It was supplied through a highly sophisticated and organised marketing and distribution system targeted especially at forces personnel. The men behind the trade were untouchable, being highly placed or well protected local civil and military officials, politicians and businessmen who were in a position themselves to safeguard the Chinese syndicates in charge of the day-to-day retailing and smuggling.

One of the most notorious heroin rings was that run by senior officers of the Vietnamese military. Their *modus operandi* show the byzantine workings of the heroin trade and the corruption which accompanied it.

The ring dealt directly with a heroin refinery near Vientiane run by a Chinese called Hu Tim-heng who was himself in business with General Ouane Rattikone. With the son of Souvanna Phouma, the Laotian prime minister, as managing director of a front company, Hu and two Chinese partners siphoned off money from a USAID grant for the building of a Pepsi-Cola bottling plant in Vientiane in 1965. The plant, which was still incomplete in 1970, was used as a cover to purchase heroin processing chemicals and as a laundry for drug income.

The heroin was transported to Pakse or Phnom Penh in Cambodia from where it was smuggled to Saigon on commercial cargo flights or Vietnamese military C-47 transports. The heroin was off-loaded at the Vietnamese air force base at Tan Son Nhut and sold to the Chinese syndicates which distributed it locally or exported it by sea.

As the political situation changed, other military officers under President Nguyen Van Thieu accepted their predecessors' trafficking mantle. One of these was the president's personal intelligence adviser, General Dang Van Quang. He was in charge of the Vietnamese navy which he used to ship heroin into South Vietnam from Cambodia. By 1973, the South Vietnamese armed forces, in alliance with the utterly corrupt customs authorities and Chinese syndicates, were in control of the whole market.

Thieu was, in effect, an American appointee, his authoritarian style of government pleasing to the Americans who were not quick to condemn his drug-dealing minions: when Thieu himself was accused of complicity, no thorough investigations were undertaken even though, in 1972, a US Senate Foreign Operations Appropriations Subcommittee was told there was overwhelming evidence of systematic corruption running through the entire Saigon government.

America was caught in a cleft stick. Congress declared war on drugs on the streets of the nation but the only effective course of action was to eradicate the corrupt generals and officials of South Vietnam who were needed in the crusade against Communism. US aid supported the drug trade and GIs' salaries were spent on it. With the benefit of hindsight, many more American lives were probably destroyed with opium in the cause of fighting Communism than were lost to military action in the paddyfields of South-east Asia. Indo-Chinese loyalties were ultimately paid for with the lives of hundreds of thousands of American addicts.

After being demobilised, some American personnel remained in the region and dealt in narcotics. Syndicates formed. One, run exclusively by black American ex-servicemen, was based in Bangkok and smuggled heroin to the USA using grunts as couriers or mailing supplies to pre-arranged addresses via the US military postal service.

As the war began to turn in favour of the Viet Cong and the US military presence was reduced, the dealers found themselves with a heroin glut. Having learnt of the profitability of heroin and having gained valuable market experience with the GIs, the Chinese syndicates made a calculated decision. They would create mass markets elsewhere.

Their obvious targets were Europe, Australia and, especially, America. Chinese, Corsican and American syndicates began sending No. 4 heroin in bulk to the USA, much of it Double UOGlobe branded. The Golden Triangle, as well as producing 70 per cent of the world's illicit opium, became a mass high grade heroin producer rivalling both Marseilles and Hong Kong in quality and quantity.

When Saigon fell in 1975, the syndicates had to leave Vietnam, abandoning a substantial local heroin addict population. The Communist government quickly instituted a widespread treatment programme although this did not eradicate the problem. As other Communist administrations took to governing the region, in Laos and Cambodia (renamed Kampuchea), the eastward flow of drugs across South-east Asia was mostly brought to a halt.

Meanwhile, in Thailand, the Bangkok corridor was still open. After the Vietnam War, Thailand became throughout the 1970s South-east Asia's main opiate exporter. Heroin from the Golden Triangle arrived in Bangkok by road, rail and air where it was loaded into fishing boats which either transported it around the Malaysian peninsula as far as Hong Kong or passed it to ocean-going vessels. On occasion, it was dropped in waterproof sacks for later interception.

To try to stem the Thai trade, the UN Fund for Drug Abuse Control commenced a long term crop substitution programme in the north of the country. Tropical fruit, coffee and beans were distributed. Agricultural skills were taught but the plan was destined to fail. Although some poppy acreage was lost, the new cash crops were more difficult to grow and get out to market from the remoter areas. All that happened was opium production increased pro rata in the Burmese section of the Golden Triangle.

Another factor working against the international authorities was the degree of corruption in Thailand. Some police and narcotics agents were readily bribed. In 1972, a Thai journalist observed:

> In this country there are no police officers honest or conscientious enough to refuse a bribe or a sweetener. The agents of the Thai Bureau of Narcotics are usually better paid by the traffickers to keep their mouths shut than they are by the government to catch the traffickers.

Senior Thai military officers were integral parts of the heroin trade and, although they lost their positions when a civilian government ruled from 1973, they were back in place after the government was overthrown in a military coup in 1977. General Kriangsak ruled the country for three years: he was deeply involved with the opium trade. Only in 1980, when a coalition led by General Prem replaced Kriangsak, were things to change, for Prem was not connected to opium.

All through this period, the KMT remained active in the Golden Triangle and the opium business. The main figure was General Li Wen-huan, commander of a force of about 1400 men, who was based in a private mansion close to Chiang Mai, the primary centre for finance and dealing in the northern Thailand heroin industry. Li was an astute and manipulative man. In 1972, he collaborated (for a tidy payment) with the CIA and the DEA to appear in a television special attacking drugs. In front of US network cameras, he denounced the opium trade and produced 100 mules loaded down with 26 tons of opium which was burned for the audience. This was, Li stated, the final KMT caravan. However, not all the tonnage was opium. Much of it was opium straw and assorted organic matter: it was also not the last KMT mule train shipment and Li was not retiring although, as the decade rolled on, KMT control of opium faded. Despite this, Taiwan's involvement in the heroin trade continued with not only Taiwanese gangs (including President Chiang Ching-kuo's son, Chiang Hsiao-wu, *aka* Alex Chiang, who was said to be implicated with them) embroiled in trafficking, and heroin being moved through Taiwan, but also with the government remaining actively involved. In 1977, American agents discovered Taiwan was using diplomatic pouches to smuggle heroin into the USA. The discovery was covered up due to American support for Taiwan: this despite huge amounts of drug money pouring into the island.

Others were now moving into the scene. In Burma, the Burmese Communist Party (BCP) became the strongest force in the Shan states, controlling most of it by 1978. At first they were opposed to opium, driving out the warlords, abolishing the opium tax and encouraging the hill tribes to grow other crops. By 1983, however, they started to deal in opium and heroin to gain revenue to make up for Chinese political aid which had been withdrawn: by the end of the decade, the BCP was in decline.

Chaos ruled as ever. The Shan states rebels were breaking into splinter groups, fighting over opium harvests and territory. From 1976, the Burmese army also attacked them, burning opium stocks and spraying weed-killers on poppy fields with the idea of beating them by removing their economic foundation of opium. Heroin refineries were bombed and mule trains attacked. Yet these military operations had limited effect and, as one group declined so another rose, the warlords returned and expanded once more. One returning warlord was to gain pre-eminence. It was Khun Sa.

While he had been imprisoned, Khun Sa's men abducted two Russian doctors from a hospital in Taunggyi. A Western television crew was invited to film them and broadcast the kidnappers' demand of Khun Sa's release in exchange for the doctors. The Burmese government spent some months trying to find the doctors, without success. In the end, they conceded defeat and Khun Sa was handed over to his men in 1974.

He quickly regained his former lands, his 3500-strong Shan United Army (SUA) taking control of half the Shan opium harvest. The Shan states seeking independence from Burma, Khun Sa proclaimed himself spokesman for the nationalist cause, considering himself a nationalist leader, calling international media conferences at which he candidly admitted his opium trading, giving it as an indication of his power. In an interview in 1977, he described himself as 'King of the Golden Triangle', adding with regard to his opium business, 'I know it is a social evil and understand the damage it does, not only in the West, but among my own people. But I don't feel guilty. What we are doing is justified.'

To justify further his role as a statesman, he held meetings with both US congressmen and the Thai media at his base at Ban Hin Taek, just inside Thailand. The government, rather embarrassed at his presence on Thai soil, said he would not be allowed to remain. In response, Khun Sa moved 16 kilometres into Burma, only to return a few months later to Ban Hin Taek.

Having had enough of Khun Sa's political stance, the Thai air force bombed his base in 1980, with no discernible effect, then put a price on his head. Two years later, a full-scale assault was made against Ban Hin Taek which was overrun. The invaders discovered not only seven heroin laboratories but also 300 brick-and-concrete houses with zinc roofs and running water, an electrical generator to power soldiers' accommodation, a substantial modern armoury, a fully equipped 100-bed hospital, basketball courts and a brothel. Khun Sa, it was found, had been living in a comfortable villa with a swimming pool and private videotape library, a few kilometres to the north.

They did not capture Khun Sa who again moved over the border into Burma, gained control of new territory and rebuilt his heroin refining operations. Within four years, he controlled 70 per cent of Burma's opium trade, closed down General Li's mule train routes and demolished Li's private house in Chiang Mai. By 1986, Khun Sa was collecting, transporting and refining 80 per cent of the annual Golden Triangle harvest. He retained this level of activity despite concerted joint Thai – Burmese attacks which only resulted in the enforced re-siting of several heroin refineries in Laos.

In the late 1980s, the Thai economy was in the ascendant. Tourism and legitimate business superseded opium money in the political arena, although they did not entirely remove it. The loose understanding which had existed between government and opium armies was over and opium smuggling was now mainly done by low-ranking corrupt officials rather than with the collusion of their seniors. In 1990, Thailand and Burma signed a trade pact which it was – and still is – hoped will bring about further co-operation over the Golden Triangle problem.

As opium production in South-east Asia increased in the 1960s, international criminals had become more interested in the region. Corsican gangsters in Vientiane acted as brokers between opium producers or heroin manufacturers and Corsican syndicates in France and heroin distributors in America. As Turkey started to cut back on poppy growing, so South-east Asian–Marseilles dealing became more important.

Not only GIs arrived in Vietnam in 1965. So did the American Mafia. Initially, they busied themselves with taking kickbacks from military contracts and running a few escort services in Saigon but they soon entered narcotics smuggling, establishing contacts in Hong Kong and with the Chinese syndicates.

The main distributors of heroin in South-east Asia were – and still are – Chinese criminal syndicates, known colloquially as the Triads. These are criminal fraternities which can trace their semi-mythical roots back two millennia to the Han dynasty but they have been most active since the birth of the Qing dynasty, to the overthrow of which they were dedicated. Only in the last 150 years have they increasingly become involved in criminal activity ranging from prostitution and protection rackets to narcotics and, more recently, white collar crime.

The South-east Asian heroin trade was first infiltrated by Chiu Chau Triads in the 1950s: they have retained it as their fiefdom ever since. The largest autonomous cultural grouping of international Chinese expatriates and the Chinese majority in Thailand, not to mention the second largest Chinese ethnic group in Vietnam, Malaysia and Indonesia, they are more correctly known as the Teochiu people, originating from a rural area near the seaport of Swatow. Their positions of prominence overseas date back a long way. In Thailand, when it was still known as Siam, they gained high profiles in the government, commerce and industry which they have maintained to the present. They have been involved in opium from around 1875 when a cartel of local merchants won the official contract to retail opium in the French concession in Shanghai, since when they have been the Oriental equivalent of the Mafia in Italy or the Corsicans in France. Their international network of contacts includes not just smugglers but chemists, money launderers, skilled managers and businessmen, politicians and lawyers. They have their own banks which are among the world's most prosperous. By law enforcement agencies, the Triads are considered the largest, most efficient and most secretive criminal organisation on earth.

As the Communists grew in political and military power in post-war China, the future looked bleak for the gangsters of Shanghai, many of whom had taken part in the notorious 1927 massacre of Communists. As Mao's victory looked more and more likely, most of the Shanghai, Canton and coastal city underworlds of China moved to Hong Kong. Amongst them were Chiu Chau Triad gangs, the Green Gang and even Big-eared Tu himself, although he died in 1951. Organised crime exploded in the British colony and No. 4 heroin production began, supplanting the local fashion for opium smoking.

The Chiu Chau Sun Yee On Triad Society already had good contacts in Hong Kong. Their influence was well established in the police force which was still riddled by corruption: it was jokingly referred to until the 1970s as the best police force money could buy. Within a short time, the Green Gang's business was destroyed and the Chiu Chau Triads gained complete domination over the importation of Thai opium and morphine base.

Hong Kong was a good place for the Chiu Chau gangs to do business, for reasons other than their contacts and a morally elastic police force. It was only a short time since 1945, when opium had been made illegal and it was still both available and commonplace. The tens of thousands of refugees crowded into Hong Kong to escape Communism existed in atrocious conditions in squatter shack settlements on the hillsides: opiates were often smoked by them to alleviate their squalor. When opium was prohibited, there was scant detoxification provision and many opium addicts switched to heroin because it gave off no obvious scent. New addicts, especially amongst the young, went straight to heroin.

Most smoked it, the slang expression being to 'chase the dragon', a term which gained wider international currency from the 1960s onwards. The smoking variety was usually an uncharacteristically pure No. 3 heroin, nicknamed White Dragon Pearl of between 40 and 50 per cent purity.

'Chasing the dragon' needs little equipment: it is not a luxurious pastime like smoking opium with a jade or ivory pipe. The addict places heroin on a metal surface – a piece of tin can, for example – and heats this over a flame such as a cigarette lighter. As the heroin melts it gives off fumes which are inhaled through a rolled-up paper tube, the 'dragon chased' being the fumes which waft in the air supposedly like a flying dragon's tail. If an open matchbox cover is used instead of a tube, the addict is said not to be chasing the dragon but 'playing the mouth-organ'. Some addicts smoked their heroin mixed with barbiturate and added to a tobacco cigarette: as the heroin came in bursts every few puffs, this method was known as 'shooting the ack-ack gun'.

With mainland Chinese opium supplies drying up in the wake of the Communist take-over, the Chiu Chau expanded their operations and moved into the drug market in Bangkok, operating from within the Chiu Chau community in Thailand. As with most ethnic Chinese groups, there is a strong sense of loyalty amongst expatriate communities. By 1965, they owned a total monopoly over opiates entering and leaving Hong Kong and a virtual monopoly over heroin manufacture, domestic sale and exportation. Since 1972, they have been primarily responsible, with other Triad groups, for most of the South-east Asian heroin reaching Europe and North America: they were, and remain, the force behind the Golden Triangle trade, making them the most powerful players in the market.

Official Hong Kong government figures recorded 80–100,000 drug addicts in the early 1970s from a population of four million: 60,000 were listed as heroin addicts but the estimate is probably conservative. According to DEA statistics in 1972, Hong Kong had 120,000 heroin and 30,000 opium addicts consuming virtually the equivalent amount for all addicts in the USA. It was the highest per capita addiction rate in the world.

So numerous were addicts it was not uncommon to see them.

The author, as a child in Hong Kong in the early 1950s, recalls watching rickshaw coolies smoking opium with a pipe or heroin off a tin spoon held over a small lamp in the alleys off Canton Road, within 100 yards or so of the Peninsula Hotel, then the most extravagant and luxurious in the world. They were gaunt men, their sinews taut and muscles bunched by their employment, their skin like parchment. Virtually every one had a sunken chest and prominent ribs: some had faces like newly-dead skulls. Once they had had their pipe, they lay down on the pavement or between the shafts of their rickshaw and slept like corpses. For many, opium or heroin was the only way by which they could face the pain and effort of pulling a laden rickshaw in the subtropical heat. Most addicts were those involved in heavy physical labour such as working in quarries, on construction sites or at the docks: 60 per cent of dock labourers were addicted and used two-thirds of their wages chasing dragons. Most of the commonly seen addicts were street sleepers who lived in doorways, under bridges, huddled in alleys or on open ground. They were almost all male.

The dragon chasers obtained their supplies quite openly. Dealers were to be seen on the streets and some urban areas of Hong Kong even had their own heroin dens. These were not like the opium dens of old but just meeting places where smokers could buy their heroin and smoke it in the company of peers. Many were attached to tea houses or mahjong gambling clubs, the latter being Triad owned and technically illegal but allowed for their cultural importance. The addiction rate being so high, however, prompted the Hong Kong police to run a concerted drive against narcotics in the mid-1960s. The trade was driven out of sight but not otherwise much affected for the Chiu Chau syndicates had contacts and were wealthy. Police bribery was rampant, reaching even to European officers on the force. The level of corruption was maintained until 1974, when the Hong Kong government organised the Independent Commission Against Corruption (ICAC) which cleaned up first the police then other government departments which were also riddled with sleaze.

The Hong Kong police and customs service were still finding it nigh on impossible to apprehend smugglers, apart from being hampered by corruption. Until around 1968, morphine base and opium shipments from Thailand were brought in hidden in the cargoes of coastal commercial freighters. After that, Thai fishing fleets were used, often showing on US Navy radar watching the Gulf of Siam and the South China Sea as part of the Vietnam War defences, but they could not be stopped. The drugs were landed on tiny islands – Hong Kong contains over 230 islands – or along the coast of China, concealed under rocks, buried in the sand or dropped offshore to be collected later by Chinese inshore fishing and trading junks which took them on to Hong Kong. This route continued until it was closed in 1975 by the new government of Thailand acting under pressure from the DEA and Washington: once more, foreign aid was ransomed.

Flushed by their successes in South-east Asia, the Chiu Chau Triads expanded. Heroin was smuggled into the USA from Hong Kong on scheduled air flights, the couriers often taking roundabout routings to disguise their origin. In 1969, a Filipino network was founded running heroin to the American Mafia via South and Central America: within three years, another was working through the Caribbean. The heroin was flown to Chile on scheduled passenger flights, the country having a sizeable Chinese population. From Santiago, it was taken to isolated landing strips and smuggled into Paraguay by private light aircraft. Paraguay was then the major transit centre for heroin heading north to America, from both the Far East and Europe, whence it arrived by sea through Argentina. About 70 per cent of America's heroin travelled this route, the remaining 30 per cent going by way of Mexico or Panama.

The narcotics traffic was superbly organised and the Triads, their members bound by powerful oaths, were largely beyond infiltration. In 1971, the trade was being headed in Hong Kong by just five Chiu Chau Triad leaders, of whom Ma Sik-yu (aka White Powder Ma), his younger brother, Ma Sik-chun (aka Golden Ma) and Ng Sik-ho (aka Limpy Ho) were considered the most important.

The Ma brothers were to become more than heroin dealers. Ma Sik-yu began in business in 1967, journeying to the Golden Triangle to purchase his heroin supplies at source, having them smuggled to Hong Kong on his behalf. The next year, General Li Wen-huan met him and, taking a personal liking to him and seeing Ma might be of use to the KMT cause, introduced him to several Taiwanese intelligence agents. By 1970, Ma was running a spy network of informants throughout Chinese communities in South-east Asia who reported on Communist activity and any other intelligence Taiwan might use against China. Ma was the linchpin of the organisation, passing collected data on during regular trips to Taiwan: meantime, Ma Sik-chun founded what was to become the most pro-Taiwanese newspaper in Hong Kong. In exchange for this patriotic service, General Li give them a discount on their heroin for which, it is said, the Taiwanese government made up the loss in armaments.

By 1974, the Mas were the biggest drug barons Hong Kong had ever known. They diverted much of their profits into legitimate businesses such as restaurants, property, trading companies, bars and cinemas. Ma Sik-yu was elected a member at the Royal Hong Kong Jockey Club (the pinnacle of respectability) whilst Ma Sik-chun was active in socialite circles. A nephew, Ma Woon-yin, became their third partner and bag-man, carrying money overseas for laundering. With the drop in heroin demand in South-east Asia after the post-Vietnam War departure of the American armed forces, the Mas knew they had to spread their product base so they established an international network for heroin and started liaising with the American Mafia and Japanese organised crime syndicates. With the Hong Kong police closing in, Ma Sik-yu fled to Taiwan in February 1977. Ma Sik-chun and Woon-yin were arrested but subsequently jumped a ridiculously low bail of HK$200,000 each (about £15,000 at the time) and also headed for Taiwan. They reside there to this day, allegedly still controlling a sizeable criminal syndicate although they have not dealt in heroin since 1983 when one of their king-pin traffickers was apprehended by the Hong Kong authorities. Their legitimate businesses continue to flourish in Hong Kong. Taiwan has consistently refused to consider any extradition proceedings.

The only real rival to the Mas was Ng Sik-ho. His criminal career began by his selling No. 3 heroin from a street fruit stall. From this he graduated to a tea house and a rice shop, both fronts for laundering money and selling heroin. His wife was also an experienced dealer. With a flair for business, he set up several heroin partnerships, funding these with loans from other Triad gangsters and legitimate businessmen who saw the chance for a quick and potentially substantial profit. He purchased opium and morphine base from Thailand, converted it into No. 3 heroin for the local market, then re-refined any left over into No. 4, which was exported. By 1970, the profits accruing from the business were estimated to be £15–20 million per annum. He employed over 1000 people, lived in a stylish mansion in Kowloon, owned four restaurants, an illegal gambling casino and numerous street stalls. He had over 150 police officers in his pocket (including at least one senior European officer) and founded the Hong Kong Precious Stone Company which ostensibly imported gemstones from Thailand but, in fact, imported opium as well as gems and acted as a money laundromat.

Ng was the first of the Chinese gangsters to deal directly with the American Mafia whom he met on several occasions in Japan. His arrogance, however, scared them off and they avoided direct contact with him thereafter: it was at this point the Mas more successfully followed his example. Undaunted by this set-back, he built up a heroin network through the Netherlands, distributing his product across Europe and on to the USA, sometimes using as couriers US servicemen in Germany who were themselves dealers.

The end was near, though. In 1972, Ng's empire started to fall apart. Seven hundred kilograms of raw opium and 80 kilograms of morphine base were found in a tunnel connected to a block of flats rented by Ng and on a duck farm owned by a close associate. His casinos were busted. He moved to Taiwan to escape implication in the murder of a double-crosser but, on legal advice, he returned to Hong Kong and was duly arrested for murder, but the charge did not stick. However, after this set-back, he was grassed by another Triad: his arrogance and flashy life-style infuriated other gangsters who preferred to keep their heads down. It is also said the Mas assisted the police in building up their dossier on Ng, passing information through officers whom they owned: like Ng, they had a large number of bent officers at their beck and call. Ng was at last arrested by an untainted, hand-picked police narcotics squad and sentenced to thirty-five years in May, 1975: his wife got sixteen years. In 1992, he was given bail on compassionate grounds, because he was suffering from liver cancer, and died early in 1993.

Not only criminals were in on the game: so were some Hong Kong police officers who were Triad gangsters themselves. In particular five sergeants, actually members of the police Triad Bureau, were involved in receiving massive kickbacks from gambling, vice and narcotics. The central figure of this group was Sergeant Lui Lok who was nicknamed '$600 Million Man'. This was no mere moniker: it was a conservative guess at his wealth for, between them, the five had received hundreds of millions of Hong Kong dollars.

When, in November 1974, the ICAC began to close in on them, they decamped from Hong Kong to Vancouver which already had a substantial Chinese immigrant population and was a conduit for heroin entering Canada. Once settled, they established the Five Dragons Corporation, their most prominent purchase being a Vancouver office block in the heart of the financial centre, for which they paid C$60 million – *in cash*. Such extravagance inevitably aroused suspicion and the corporation folded with the key figures flying to Taiwan. There were by then over forty ex-Hong Kong police officer millionaires in exile on the island: one of their number, a much-admired career policeman called Tang Sang, had escaped there by forfeiting a HK$330,000 bail.

Those who did not make for Canada or run for Taiwan headed for the USA. The most famous was Chan Tse-chiu (*aka* Fast Eddie). He arrived in New York in the winter of 1975, where he joined the On Leong Triad society and invested his money in legitimate businesses, such as a jewellery shop, several restaurants and (ironically) an undertakers. In time, he came to run Chinatown, expanding his tentacles into political circles (including giving donations to election campaigns: one his protégés stabbed himself to death during an anti-corruption investigation), buying off police officers, founding a bank, purchasing a string of cinemas and becoming president of the Continental King Lung Commodities Group, which was a suspected major Triad money-laundering business. By 1983, Chan was allegedly a central figure in the importation of heroin.

In October 1984, Chan was subpoenaed to appear before a commission on organised crime: he did not show up. Testimony put down by the authorities outlined his considerable legal and illegal activities. By November, he was missing although his legitimate businesses were still functioning normally. Guesses as to his whereabouts were legion. The DEA believed he had set up a heroin network in France, the New York Police Department thought he was in the Dominican Republic, the Hong Kong authorities suggested he divided his time between Taiwan and Canada whilst the Dutch claimed he was running a crime syndicate in Malaysia. He remains untraced.

The ICAC purge of police corruption destroyed the syndicates' protection, without which they could not operate effectively. No. 4 heroin entering the USA dropped off for a short while but the syndicates were not beaten: they merely moved their chemists elsewhere. Hong Kong ceased to be a major manufacturing centre for heroin: instead, it became the financial centre for the South-east Asian drugs trade. The considerable affluence of Hong Kong, its huge mercantile base and its array of international and offshore banks made it an ideal money laundering centre – which it remains.

The Chiu Chau syndicates moved to Thailand and Malaysia. Here, they were closer to the opium source of the Golden Triangle, were aided by corruption, could obtain their supplies by land (avoiding well guarded border crossings and airport customs controls) and had the jungle in which to hide their refineries. They also moved to Europe where they based themselves in the large Chinese community in Amsterdam which developed into the main importation and distribution hub, assisted by lenient application of Dutch narcotics laws. By the start of the 1980s, heroin addiction was a major problem in Western Europe.

In part, the Chiu Chau success was unwittingly engineered by the international narcotics agencies. The Hong Kong production of heroin had been largely side-lined, the US Bureau of Narcotics concentrating its attention on the French Connection and ignoring the likes of the Mas and Ng. Despite this, there were some international law enforcement successes against the Chinese. One of these was the taking of the Corset Gang.

Operating out of Hong Kong, the gang was caught in 1967 by international police co-operation. Hired by the Hong Kong Chiu Chau Triads, the gang was masterminded by several retired Australian policemen. The couriers were also predominantly Australian. The heroin was smuggled, as the gang name implies, in specially tailored corsets or vests. Using a set of duplicate passports to disguise their origins, the couriers flew from Sydney to Hong Kong, where they collected the heroin, then flew on via London or other European cities to New York. In six months, they smuggled

$22.5 million worth of heroin which was delivered into the Mafia distribution system.

Even then, it took another successful syndicate bust in 1970 and the horrendous addiction of GIs in Vietnam before the US Bureau of Narcotics turned its attention to the South-east Asian heroin trade and admitted the connection between the American Mafia and the Triad gangs.

Another criminal group was also becoming involved in the distribution of South-east Asian heroin: they were the Yakuza, Japan's equivalent of the Triads. Dating back 300 years, the Yakuza are famous for their tattoos and infamous for slicing off part of a finger as an aspect of their initiation rites or as a punishment to anyone transgressing their code. In the 1920s and 1930s, Yakuza gangs played a part in Japan's opium policy in Manchuria and China. They were also instrumental in importing Japanese morphine – known as 'cotton morphine' on account of its appearance – into the USA early in the 1930s, later supplying drug rings on the west coast with heroin. Pearl Harbour brought to an end that enterprise. During the Second World War, the Yakuza set up supplying illicit amphetamines to Japanese civilians and military personnel. They now monopolise this market, with at least 50 per cent of their income reckoned to be drug-related. After the war, with the American presence in Japan, the CIA employed the Yakuza to spy on left-wing politicians. To this day, the gangsters are a political power to be reckoned with in Japan.

Around 1970, the Yakuza began to expand from being primarily a Japanese domestic criminal fraternity into an international one. They exploited the potential of the Pacific Rim, smuggling and dealing in drugs and arms, and investing heavily in the sex trade. They also linked up with the Triads and are now globally connected wherever there is an ethnic Japanese community. By 1972, they were establishing themselves in the USA. They first set up shop in Hawaii, moved to Los Angeles, then on to San Francisco and New York.

They were not slow in connecting with the Mafia but again it was some years before law enforcement agencies realised what was going on. Yet in May 1979, three Yakuza couriers were to be caught in Honolulu, carrying heroin disguised in duty-free cigarette cartons. It was discovered through passport checks that the couriers had made sixteen trips to Bangkok and twelve journeys to Hawaii, Guam and San Francisco. When Japanese police raided their homes in Tokyo, a curious code of behaviour for smugglers was discovered which, in part, read:

> You should obey whatever you are told to do by your group leader. You have no choice, you cannot refuse or complain of the leader's instructions. The above instructions are given at the request of the financier in order to protect ourselves and to accomplish our work . . . You must pay for your souvenirs yourself. Your leader will pay for your hotel and three meals. He will also pay for your drinks, up to $75.

Faced with the political, geographical and logistical problems of reducing poppy growing and the opium trade within the Golden Triangle, the DEA had decided to attack international trafficking. A large South-east Asian regional force of DEA intelligence gathering agents targeted drug shipments and, by 1975, South-east Asian heroin smuggling to the USA was cut by two-thirds. With the French Connection also severed, addiction rates in the USA fell from an estimated 500,000 addicts in 1971 to 200,000 in 1974. To counteract the heroin shortage on the street, Mexican poppy growers, who had accounted for about 35 per cent of the available heroin in the USA, increased their market share to about 90 per cent by 1975. Poppy fields proliferated in the Sierra Madre Mountains of central Mexico and, to a lesser extent, in Colombia, Nicaragua and Ecuador, but the heroin was of poor quality.

Mexico was easier for the Americans to deal with than the mountains of Indo-China. The DEA was quick to join forces with the Mexican government. Poppy fields were attacked, uprooted by hand or sprayed with weed-killers. The campaign was aided by a severe drought in 1977 which cut Mexican heroin production by half although it picked up again from 1981 to climax in 1986. The lesson was hard learnt: it was one thing to wipe out a harvest but another to keep it suppressed. Farmers merely accepted their loss and waited for the next sowing season.

Overall, the 1970s was a decade with some notable successes in the on-going war against opium. However, when a drought occurred in the Golden Triangle in 1978, opium and heroin production in Afghanistan and Pakistan expanded to fill the sudden deficiency, the heroin from this source being a high quality powder, off-white to mid-brown in colour. At the same time, opium production increased in Iran following the 1979 revolution, leaving more of the Golden Crescent output available for the international market. Then history repeated itself and another lesson was completely ignored.

Until 1973, Afghanistan was a monarchy but this was overthrown by an Islamic republican movement which established a constitution in 1977, vesting all power in the president. A *coup d'état* in 1978 transferred power to a pro-Communist revolutionary council which developed into a Soviet-sponsored Communist government. Internal Muslim anti-communist rebels soon presented the Russians with their own Vietnam-style war which was not to end until 1989.

This was by the way in the eyes of the American government, which saw a Communist Afghanistan bordering pro-Western, but politically temperamental, Pakistan: it was Indo-China all over again. In 1979, the CIA started covert operations in Afghanistan to assist Afghan resistance against Soviet occupation. Acting alongside the Pakistani secret service, Inter-Service Intelligence (ISI), the CIA allied with the Mujaheddin Afghan guerrillas who were already involved in opium growing, particularly supporting Gulbuddin Hekmatyar who employed the CIA to arm his men and provide military back-up to his forces. Opium production soared, doubling between 1982 and 1983. Hekmatyar, later to be Afghanistan's prime minister, was soon the region's most influential drug lord.

Not only the rebels dealt in opium. So too did the Pakistani military and intelligence services. Opium arrived at border posts where it was bought by Pakistani refiners of whom there were about 150 operating in 1986 in the Khyber district of the North-West Frontier Province, protected by the provincial governor. Pakistani military vehicles frequently transported opium made immune to police search by ISI passes.

It has to be said the CIA were not as instrumental or as actively involved in the Golden Crescent as they had been in the Golden Triangle, but their intervention certainly encouraged a considerable increase in opium production. Even when it was known the rebels were dealing in drugs, the CIA would not withdraw support for fear of compromising their political stand. In the Cold War against Communism, the CIA considered drugs the lesser evil and actively gave succour to rebels for whom opium was a currency and who were known opium producers, helping to transform the region into a major world heroin source.

Pakistan suffered from the increase in heroin production. A number of heroin syndicates appeared including well-organised operations run by military officers and civilian officials in the corrupt regime of President Muhammad Zia Ul-Haq. Zia, who was also chief of staff, was almost certainly implicated in the trade, although no concrete proof was ever presented: he was killed in an air crash in 1988. What is certain is he knew of his senior officers' complicity in the heroin trade and of their protection of heroin dealers and the heroin-financed Pakistani criminal organisations which held a degree of political influence. By the time of Zia's death, and the end of his military rule, Pakistan had the largest pro rata addict population in the world.

The civilian government tried to make inroads into the drug trade but with little success for it was so well established in the country's economy. Heroin income in 1989 was in the region of £2.5 billion, substantially more than all the rest of Pakistan's legal exports. The poppy farmers of the North-West Frontier were reluctant to give up a lucrative business whilst over the border, with the Soviet army pulling out of Afghanistan in 1989, foreign aid to the guerrillas halted with opium production increasing to sustain the guerrilla forces who were now engaged in a civil war and with fighting each other for opium supremacy.

By 1979, Golden Crescent heroin had taken over the European market. The Corsican syndicates in Marseilles worked alongside the Sicilian Mafia in starting new heroin laboratories in Europe to handle it. Lebanese smugglers supplied the laboratories and trafficking increased between Europe and the USA where much of the resulting heroin was distributed by the American Mafia through a number of outlets including a chain of pizza parlours, known as the Pizza Connection. Inside twelve months, Golden Crescent originating product made up 60 per cent of the American market, pushing the population of addicts up to equal its previous highest point. When the Golden Triangle drought ended, however, that region began to develop its market share again, eventually becoming the major world heroin source once more.

And so, whilst some optimists might have thought the 1970s were the beginning of the end of the opiate scourge, pessimists took a different view. Since 1960, the global drug trade had become more complex and labyrinthine than ever before. There were more players, more sources, more diversity than there had ever been which meant the problem was all the more difficult to address. The pessimists won the argument for the 1980s saw an unprecedented explosion of addiction across the Western world and especially in the USA where drugs had created an extensive, often alluring and sometimes attractive, subculture. The statistics for world heroin production mirror the problem: between 1982 and 1990, it tripled. Clearly, matters were reaching a crisis point.

15

Warlords, Barons and Laundrymen

Not all the world's opium trade is illicit. There is of course a legal market for opium and its alkaloids for pharmaceutical use. Present day licit production varies with projected sales, stocks and the international supply and demand situation. In line with UN Conventions, only enough crops are grown from one season to the next to meet current demand.

The main producer and only country in which the growing of opium poppies for their actual raw opium gum is still legal today is India. The centres for poppy farming are the states of Rajasthan, Madhya Pradesh and Uttar Pradesh: in all, approximately 13,000 hectares are dedicated to poppies and there are about 100,000 farmers in the licensed opium farming system which is carried out under strict government control. Most processing is carried out at the Government Opium and Alkaloid Factories in Ghazipur, the methods being essentially the same as they were two centuries ago.

Liquid opium is delivered to the factories, weighed, taken into the sunlight and poured into wooden trays, more than 12,000 of which are spread out at any one time under the hot sun during the processing months after the harvest. Each tray is stirred thrice daily to prevent crusting and encourage evaporation which continues until the opium has only a 10 per cent water content when it is formed into cakes on a press, the initials GEO being stamped in them as a quality mark. In this state, as a raw opium gum, it is exported to international pharmaceutical companies for the extraction of morphine or codeine, earning India approximately $15 million annually. An estimated 45 per cent of the world's legitimate morphine requirement comes from Indian opium.

Other countries which grow licit opium poppies produce alkaloids from poppy straw which is less labour intensive and therefore more secure. Tasmania supplies about 40 per cent of world requirement with Turkey, France and Spain also producing alkaloids from poppy straw. The Australian industry was first started during the Second World War, research centring on Janos Kabay's process. A pilot production programme was begun in Tasmania in 1964, the first season of commercial production beginning in 1970. Today, there are on average 600 farmers cultivating about 6000 hectares of poppies annually, the poppies complementing other crops in a rotation cycle. The farmers have developed new sowing techniques and a highly mechanised harvesting process making the Tasmanian industry the most efficient and highest yielding in the world.

Strict controls are maintained. A poppy crop can only be grown by a farmer contracted to one of the two alkaloid manufacturing companies in Tasmania and who must be licensed by the Tasmanian government, the licence being annually renewable and not transferable. Every farmer is security cleared by the police and all fields are regularly inspected before sowing to ensure a minimal security risk. It is even illegal to enter a poppy field.

Where legitimate production is not as highly mechanised, such as in parts of Turkey, poppy farmers leave the pods to desiccate on the stem then harvest them by snapping off each head by hand. These are then sliced horizontally to allow for seed collection for oil extraction or subsequent sowing. Needless to say, this activity is carried out under the supervision of armed guards.

However, the greatest opiate trade today continues to be the illegal one and, during the last thirty years, opiate use has become a global problem, the number of heroin addicts continually increasing, the demand on the street promoting an escalation of poppy growing, heroin manufacture and trafficking, with the political or economic instability of many opium producing countries making effective control measures well nigh impossible.

In May 1995, Giorgio Giacomelli, the Executive Director of the UN International Drug Programme, estimated that there were

40–50 million drug addicts world-wide and that there was an even more worrying distinct trend of addiction spreading from rich to poor nations which are less equipped to tackle the problem.

From the 1930s, illicit world opium production continued to fall steadily, only to rise from around 1970: in 1934, world output stood at 8000 tons, in 1970 it was 1000 tons but by 1993 it was 4200 metric tonnes. Production decreased to 3409 in 1994, due primarily to drought in South-east Asia. The Golden Triangle and Golden Crescent are still the main illicit opium sources although other areas are moving into the trade with higher production targets being expected in the foreseeable future. According to statistics contained in the International Narcotics Control Strategy Report of 1994, Burma produced 2030 tonnes of opium, about 60 per cent of illicit world production, Afghanistan holding 28 per cent of the market at 950 tonnes. Other players were Pakistan with 5 per cent of global output, Laos 2.5 per cent, India 2.4 per cent and Mexico with 2 per cent: output figures for Colombia and Iran, however, are not included and would, if known, greatly alter the statistics. Satellite image-based assessment by the USA of opium poppy fields in Burma put the estimated 1995 harvest at 2500 tonnes. Of course, such figures are to a degree a matter of guesswork, liable to fluctuation from year to year as new areas come into production and growing conditions change.

South-east Asia is, therefore, still the largest illicit producer, a situation unlikely to change in coming years. Furthermore, opium continues to play a part in the traditional way of life throughout the region, as it has done for centuries, being an important medicine as well as a social pastime: up to 400 tonnes of opium are used by hill tribesmen annually although elsewhere heroin is now more common, with drastic results. It is estimated there are over 80,000 heroin addicts in metropolitan Bangkok alone.

Many means of eradication have been tried. Military action has proven unsuccessful. Crop substitution programmes are evaded by the farmers merely shifting their poppy fields. Plants sprayed with herbicide can sometimes be washed clean and fields are camouflaged with other crops which, if effective, not only fool air reconnaissance aircraft but confuse satellite imaging. The arrest of key personnel in the trade is ineffectual because they are soon replaced by others.

Crop eradication can conceal ulterior motives. In 1986, the

Burmese government started using a herbicide, a compound of the controversially dangerous Agent Orange defoliant used by the Americans during the Vietnam War. This was sprayed from aircraft, contaminating water supplies and damaging crops other than poppies, and it was done without warning as to the possible side-effects to health caused by the chemical. The government was using it as a weapon against minority tribes as much as the opium trade, destroying the livelihoods and health of peasant farmers in a form of ethnic social cleansing.

The only way to counter poppy growing is through massive social, political and economic change in the Golden Triangle and surrounding states: the chances of this are slim indeed. The American government was so dismayed by the bloody suppression of the pro-democracy movement in Burma in 1988, it suspended aid, including $7 million for an anti-narcotics programme. Since then, Burma presents Washington with a frustrating dilemma. The Americans want to halt Burmese heroin but do not want to associate with the repressive military junta, known as the State Law and Order Restoration Council (SLORC). The junta jails political opponents, forces peasants into unpaid labour and kept the country's most popular political figure, the Nobel Peace Prize-winning writer, Aung San Suu Kyi, under house arrest from 1989 until her release in July 1995. Yet some US foreign policy experts now question how long Burma can be left to its own devices in the light of its heroin trade.

The UN has started a modest programme in Burma to help build roads and provide alternative crops, but the amount of aid needed to get results is not likely to materialise until there is better political rapprochement between SLORC and the international community. In September 1994, SLORC announced an 11-year Master Plan for the Development of Border Areas and National Races but the US State Department has commented that economic development remains 'largely in the planning stage and there have been no results as yet in the counter-narcotics aspect'.

Burma has over 160,000 hectares of land dedicated to the agriculture of poppies, virtually all of it in the Golden Triangle and much of it under the control of insurgents who buy the harvest for their own heroin factories along the Thai or Chinese borders. The main controllers today are the Wa tribal groups on Burma's border with Yunnan, the ethnic Chinese in the Kokang district of the Shan states and, until very recently, Khun Sa's followers, now referred to as the Mong Tai Army (MTA), a name adopted in 1987, formed by the merger of the SUA and the Tai-Land Revolutionary Army (TRA): Mong Tai Army means the Army of the Tai (or Shan) Land. Such organisations not only manage production but also operate trafficking rings to internationally transport their heroin, even taking an active part in wholesale distribution in the USA. Most, but not all of these rings, are run in collaboration with Chiu Chau Triad groups but some are independent organisations with their own autonomous infrastructure.

In March 1990, the US Attorney-General filed an indictment against Khun Sa for heroin importation into the USA. The indictment accused Khun Sa of being New York City's primary supplier. The filing of the papers was little more than good public relations for, unlike American action against General Noriega in Panama, the capture of Khun Sa would rely upon Burmese government co-operation: Burma has warned it would not tolerate any violation of its sovereignty in an attempt to seize him.

Khun Sa, now in his 60s, has until recently run a mini-state within a state, being regarded by some as a head of government. He established schools and hospitals and built a textile works, a mushroom farm and a gemstone-cutting factory near his base at Ho Mong, thirty kilometres from the Thai border, bringing in street lighting, telephones, hi-fis and electrical goods and beginning a hydro-electric dam project. He did not deny poppies were the main local crop but, in recent years, he preferred to declare he did not produce heroin himself, merely taxing those who did in order to fund the Shan nationalist cause. Other income derived from taxes levied on contraband, jade, precious stones, teak and cattle. Allegedly, personal enrichment was not Khun Sa's aim.

The Mong Tai Army, at its height possibly 20,000 strong and one of Asia's biggest tribal armies, was as well equipped as the Burmese state militia. No doubt aware of the harm opiates can do to an army, Khun Sa dealt mercilessly with addicts in his ranks. A first offence had the offender left in an 18-foot well for 10 days' withdrawal: a second offence was punished with death by a blow to the back of the neck.

A charismatic figure, Khun Sa has over the years invited overseas journalists, even politicians, to Ho Mong where he portrayed himself as a clean-living man who chain-smoked 555 brand cigarettes, had a penchant for a good cognac and declared his only other vice was women. Unlike Big-eared Tu, for example, he has been astute enough not to sample his own wares. He is also a collector of and said to be an authority on rare South-east Asian orchids. At the lunar new year festival in 1993, he performed karaoke songs to his troops, flanked by – it is said – a young woman crooner and a red-lipped transvestite. At a dance later that day his second-in-command, a veteran KMT soldier called General Sao Hpalang, known as General Thunder by the troops, waltzed with the young woman. On the same day, the Shan State Restoration Council declared independence from Burma, electing Khun Sa its president.

Prompted by such declarations, the Burmese government has made some attempt to either militarily crush or politically buy off separatists. In 1989 the Burmese military junta signed peace agreements which effectively allowed some hostile ethnic minorities, particularly the Wa, to trade in narcotics as long as they kept politically inactive and recognised governmental authority. The Burmese provided rice, medical care and money, allowing rebel leaders the freedom to engage in heroin production and trafficking. A main beneficiary of this situation was the warlord, Lo Hsing-han, Khun Sa's long-standing arch-rival for control of the opium trade.

Born in 1934 in Kokang state Lo Hsing-han, with his brother, Lo Hsing-min, was the most powerful opium warlord during the late 1960s and early 1970s especially when Khun Sa was in prison, having also started his opium career in the KKY. Lo's position reduced after the American withdrawal from Vietnam due to his failure to use the boom years of the war to build links with overseas traffickers and extend his distribution network. In the face of this decline, Khun Sa started to become dominant once more. Lo was arrested in Thailand in 1973, extradited to Burma and sentenced to life imprisonment. However, in 1980, his sentence was commuted by Burmese President Ne Win – there were rumours of a substantial pay-off – and he was given troops and arms by the Burmese in the hope he would slow down the expansion of Khun Sa and other groups. With such backing, Lo started to gain power again. Today, as well as his involvement in drugs, he is reported to be substantially investing in several Rangoon hotels.

In response to international criticism SLORC, which promotes compliant narcotics-dealing tribal chiefs as 'national leaders', has insisted its policy is merely giving the tribes – especially the Wa – time to establish other cash crops to replace opium poppies. A SLORC spokesman stated in May 1995, 'the national leaders have given us pledges that they will try to stop (growing poppies) in six to ten years time. They need time to switch to other crops otherwise they will starve'. Experts point out the Wa tribe have probably become the main producers of opium in recent years, also increasing their heroin production along the Chinese border and on the periphery of Khun Sa's territory at his expense, leading to fighting between the Wa and the MTA. Other developments in 1995 had the Karen rebels' headquarters captured with other insurgent groups considering making peace on similarly flexible political and economic terms. The sincerity of their pledges to halt opium growing remains to be seen.

SLORC has argued that if the Americans really wanted to stop Khun Sa's activities, it would have to provide military support: the American response pointed out that of the thirty-two aircraft and helicopters supplied by them in the 1980s for anti-narcotic operations not one had ever been used against Khun Sa. Rumour has it there were occasional deals struck between him and the Burmese government. For example, in October 1988, it was alleged the MTA was offered a free hand in its heroin business in exchange for anti-Communist support and the safe passage of government-felled teak being sold to Thailand. It is also thought that Khun Sa for long bought off local army commanders in exchange for being left alone to get on with his drug trading.

The rise to power again of Lo Hsing-han and his brother led to speculation that the Burmese, in supporting the Los, were becoming willing to capture Khun Sa in exchange for foreign aid and an end to criticism of its human rights record and socio-political policies: from late 1993, the tide started to turn against Khun Sa as Burmese forces began to launch a sustained offensive against him.

Thailand, long censured for its toleration of heroin producers, also began to take steps against Khun Sa who, in 1994, proposed the Shan states become a province of Thailand. This proposition was rejected and Khun Sa rebuffed by the Thai authorities although MTA troops have frequently been permitted to escape into Thailand to avoid Burmese forces. Under heavy American pressure, Thailand finally sent troops to seal off infiltration routes to and from Burma, closing a new road which Khun Sa had been using for supplies, although Thai authorities permitted mule caravans to use jungle paths for, as they put it, humanitarian reasons. Yet the border turned out to be more permeable than expected and Khun Sa's guile under-estimated. To escape the Thai forces, he moved groups of 600 and 800 men through Thailand on chartered tourists buses in March 1995. According to Burmese intelligence sources, Khun Sa's men made substantial cash payments, of $26,000 on one occasion, to Thai border police to ensure passage. However, this situation created trouble for Khun Sa by making him once more reliant upon mountain trails and reports indicated even rice was in short supply amongst his men.

Some DEA/Thai joint operations were successful and many of Khun Sa's traffickers were arrested in northern Thailand including, in 1993, Lin Chien-pang, a close associate of Khun Sa who was captured and extradited to the USA. At the beginning of 1995, ten of Khun Sa's senior aides were apprehended in northern Thailand.

The Burmese authorities knew any attempt to crush Khun Sa generated good publicity: in May 1995, they gave foreign journalists a junket in the Bakyan Mountains, displaying a captured Khun Sa base taken the month before and plugging their anti-narcotics image. In order to impress American public opinion, the Burmese military have reverted to referring to Khun Sa's army as the 'Loimaw bandits', a name by which they were known in their early days in the 1960s.

Khun Sa seems to have fallen victim to a mixture of international pressure, military attack, the growing strength of rivals – especially the Wa faction – and defections from his ranks. Whereas at some times in the past, Khun Sa and his family were to be seen in Bangkok and Chiang Mai, in recent times Khun Sa has hardly dared stray from his jungle headquarters. In June 1995, there was even a mutinous mass departure of several thousand of his fighters led by young Shan nationalists who complained he was more committed to the drug trade than Shan independence.

In November 1995, as the Burmese military inexorably advanced on him, Khun Sa announced his retirement from all positions in the Shan state following the mutiny and other large scale defections, reported to total up to 6000 men: he stated he had lost heart, presumably in the national cause rather than opium production.

He said he wanted to retire to tend his chickens. Observers believe that Khun Sa had few options left other than to reach an agreement with the Burmese government.

At the beginning of January 1996, Khun Sa surrendered to Burmese government forces at Ho Mong. He was said to have welcomed senior Burmese military officers with a party which lasted throughout the night. Burmese troops occupied Ho Mong without a fight and Khun Sa's forces began handing over their bases in the mountains to Burmese troops.

The situation is, as ever, confused and Khun Sa's future uncertain. Many believe he is seeking a deal with the Burmese government to turn his fighters into a government militia. Some disaffected Mong Tai Army members who fled to Thailand say they believe Khun Sa had cut a deal with the authorities before his surrender in return for an amnesty, in which case he might be allowed to 'retire' and live peacefully for the rest of his life.

Whatever happens, it seems unlikely Burma will turn Khun Sa over to the USA which has requested his extradition and announced a $2 million reward for information leading to his arrest and conviction. The Burmese government declare he will be put on trial in Rangoon and dealt with according to their law. This decision for a local trial may not be a mere flexing of political muscle and a statement of sovereignty: many observers believe such a decision has been reached because the Burmese authorities are frightened of what Khun Sa might tell the Americans of their narcotics involvement.

If tried and convicted in Burma, Khun Sa could face a mandatory death sentence but in this predominantly Buddhist nation it would most likely be commuted. With the country's periodic amnesties and further time off for good behaviour, Khun Sa could still end his days a free man. It is even conceivable that the world has not seen the last of Khun Sa: he has been down before and made a comeback against long odds.

Khun Sa's political downfall, therefore, has not affected the flow of opium out of the Golden Triangle. As he predicted to the *Bangkok Post* after his retirement in November 1995, 'Opium production will continue with or without me.' American fears of a deal between Khun Sa and the Burmese government now seem validated and could lead to substantially increased poppy cultivation. Any power vacuum left by Khun Sa will soon be filled for, although as a drug lord, he may have had the highest international profile, there are many other players on the scene. Lo Hsing-han may seize the day. The Kokang group which has allied itself to him, an alliance which dominated the opium market in 1992 when Khun Sa was said to be temporarily starved of cash, is also well positioned to succeed him. Others such as Lin Mingxian, the powerful former Red Guard and one-time Burmese Communist Party commander and the Wei brothers, former colleagues of Khun Sa who operate with the Wa and are now said to be the region's biggest dealers, wait in the wings.

Matters are further complicated because whatever the government of Burma has said, or whichever faction is dominant, it also seems the government itself is substantially connected to the heroin trade and that poppies are now also being grown in areas controlled by the Burmese military. A recent billion dollars' worth of arms purchased from China is alleged to have been paid for from heroin profits. As a spin-off from this deal, Chinese entrepreneurs have been allowed into the country where they are investing heavily in property, the tourist trade and the timber industry.

Whoever is in control, heroin continues to transit through Burma to Thailand which, although it remains the primary route to world markets, is losing some of its trade to India, Bangladesh, Malaysia and, more importantly, China. Heroin is now going overland to Hong Kong or other Chinese seaports whence it goes to Taiwan for onward shipment to the USA, the route begun in 1989 by Lo Hsing-han. The newest routes are through Laos, Cambodia and, once more, Vietnam, partly operating along sections of the legendary Ho Chi Minh trail set up by the Vietcong to supply their troops during the Vietnam War.

The situation in South-east Asia is always, to a greater or lesser degree, in a state of turmoil and change. In Laos, which has a huge area of land under poppies, senior government and military officials remain corrupt and profit substantially from opium despite some reduction in poppy cultivation due to a crop substitution project funded by the US State Department and the United Nations International Drug Control Program: unfavourable weather conditions in 1993–94 somewhat aided the situation by destroying much of the poppy crop. Large scale eradication programmes are, however, side-stepped for fear of political unrest from hill tribes. Since UN troops pulled out from Cambodia in 1993, senior members of the government there are rumoured to have built up strong ties with international drug smugglers, Cambodia developing into such a major drug trafficking centre that law enforcement agents are starting to wryly refer to the country as 'Medellin on the Mekong', a tongue-in-cheek comparison with the Colombian cocaine city of Medellin.

In northern Thailand, although traditional hill tribal poppy farmers have been joined by commercial growers financed by heroin traffickers, there has been a reduction in poppy acreage to half that of the mid-1980s. Yet Thailand remains the key conduit for drugs. It has also become the major destination of 'brat packers' – young, poor, Western travellers, the modern descendants of the Sixties hippies. These itinerants gather around such places as Khao San Road in Bangkok or Haad Rin on the island of Kho Phan Gan off the south coast, where they party, dance, engage in moon raves (night-time naked orgies which have become internationally famous amongst brat *cognoscenti*), snort, smoke and shoot anything from heroin to designer drugs and generally live self-indulgent existences. To finance their life-style, some are tempted to try smuggling. Of the 1200 foreigners in Thailand's gaols, over 900 are held on trafficking charges.

Not only brat packers head for the country. In northern Thailand, mainstream tourism has become established, with hotels and excursions blossoming in what even tourist brochures refer to as the Golden Triangle, using the name for just the small area up against the borders with Laos and Burma which they describe as 'an exotic, colourful region of jungle-clad hills, mighty rivers, magnificent temples and fascinating hill tribe villages with some of the best shopping in Thailand.'

It was hoped Thailand's rapid economic growth in the late 1980s would have discouraged the heroin trade but the new infrastructure has only proved to serve it and some high-level corruption continues. A Thai general, Thanat Phaktiphat, has been accused of being involved in trafficking and plotting to import heroin into the USA in recent years. He was arrested in transit through Kai Tak airport, Hong Kong, in December 1993 with two empty suitcases which, it was alleged, he was using to collect $4 million in narcotics earnings. He lost his third attempt to prevent his extradition from Hong Kong in May 1995.

Another twist occurred in July 1995 when the Chart Thai Party, the largest group in the former opposition, was victorious in the elections and formed a coalition government. The Americans, who have for years been accusing the Thai opposition parties of involvement in the narcotics trade, have found them in power. Members of the new government include Narong Wongwan and Vatana Asavahme, both accused by Washington of having links with drug trafficking.

The use of Vietnam as a transit nation is under way again and it looks as though the country is set once more to become an important route out of the Golden Triangle. It is feared international organised crime syndicates are targeting and exploiting the new open economy and relaxed frontier controls. In northern Vietnam, in the border trading area of Lang Son, just a few kilometres from China, trade in general and contraband in particular have soared since late 1992. Heroin is increasingly moved through the region *en route* from the Golden Triangle and China to ports such as Haiphong and Danang, thence out to international markets.

Along the Sino-Vietnam border, special Vietnamese police teams working with the military and customs officers patrol the all-but impenetrable jungle, often for days at a time, attempting to close supply routes but without any major success: in the environs of Lang Son, heroin addiction is rapidly growing, some addicts being of primary school age.

A report released in March 1995 by the Vietnam National Drug Control Programme, claims a national opiate addict population of 170,000, many long-term users amongst the poppy-growing hill tribes. Officials claim there are no heroin processing plants in Vietnam but that is immaterial. The rise in smuggling alone will feed the growing domestic market in Hanoi and Ho Chi Minh City where, in 1994, 2750 opium den landlords were arrested and where a rise in heroin injection is rapidly spreading AIDS. To combat the mounting threat, death sentences are being handed out to traffickers, customs manning levels are being greatly increased, officers are being trained in Britain with the latest American detection equipment on order: for the first time, Vietnam is to have sniffer dogs.

Not only the Vietnamese are worried: so is the DEA. It has acknowledged all the ingredients are in place for smugglers to take full advantage of the situation to develop new routes. In 1995, the US government placed Vietnam on the list of twenty-nine countries which now serve as major conduits for drugs destined for North America. The DEA also records poppies being grown commercially in the Son La province of Vietnam, between China and Laos, although the quantity of opium produced is unknown.

Developments such as these pose a potential problem for narcotics agencies, for, if they do reduce opium in the Golden Triangle, production may shift to Vietnam or to another, even less approachable country such as North Korea. As long as the Golden Triangle exists, opium and heroin are at least somewhat contained.

Another twist in the story concerns China. When the Communists took over, Mao Zedong wiped out opium and addiction. China was clean for the better part of forty years with only pharmaceutical opium being produced. Now that has changed.

It is estimated illicit poppies are farmed in about sixteen provinces, mainly for domestic consumption but increasingly for export, to such an extent that China is now deemed to be a major producer, perhaps as important as Laos, but its output is unquantifiable. Although the Chinese government refutes it, substantial poppy production is going on and increasing in Yunnan province (the farmers related to the hill tribes of Burma and Laos) whilst, in as diverse an area as Inner Mongolia, the authorities found and destroyed six million poppy plants in 1991. Heroin is readily available in Yunnan and the Beijing government admits it has a problem there: 2.85 tonnes of heroin were seized in Yunnan in 1994. In May 1995, the Chinese government and the UN Drug Control Programme signed an agreement for a $2.9 million project to fight drug trafficking in Yunnan. The three-year plan is to improve the capacity of enforcement authorities by providing specialised training and equipment.

Heroin use is increasing at an alarming rate throughout China. According to the International Narcotics Control Board, Kunming (the capital of Yunnan) has an addict population of around 100,000. Recent economic reforms in China have given peasants money which some have invested in opium, whilst spare cash in the pockets of the young has fuelled the drugs trade, which in turn has caused crime figures to soar. For the infrequently or un-employed – of which China has an estimated 300 million

– drugs are a release from boredom. The state's reaction is draconian. Despite pressures to set up American-style heroin clinics, the government regards addiction as a crime and arrested addicts are forced to withdraw alone, in prison cells. The army is used to attack dealers and even their home villages, with not infrequent success. A raid in the summer of 1994 upon one Yunnan village netted a reputed staggering $500 million's worth of No. 4 heroin. Traffickers, producers or retailers are shot after a show trial, frequently at public executions stage-managed in football stadia or market-places: possession of 50 grams of heroin automatically carries the death penalty.

China executed over 100 drug traffickers in 1993, in recognition of international drug reduction day celebrations. Shenzhen, the special economic zone city just over the border from Hong Kong, is currently a base for Chiu Chau heroin, banking and money laundering operations. Here, 40 per cent of criminals are drug addicts. In the spring of 1995, 126 drug syndicates were discovered in the city: 1910 drug addicts were arrested, those not considered criminals being taken for three-month compulsory rehabilitation, chronic cases being further subjected to re-education camps for up to three years. A three-day crackdown in Guangdong province at the end of April 1995 led to the arrest of 1200 dealers, with 400 drug dens being destroyed and about 10,000 addicts being rounded up. A month later, fifty-one traffickers were publicly denounced at a series of rallies and paraded in front of crowds before being shot by firing squad.

Regardless of these measures, addiction grows unabated, critics of economic reform loud in their condemnation, stating liberalisation has allowed heroin in and quoting a Chinese proverb: if you open the window, sunlight comes in but so do mosquitoes and evil spirits.

Concerned at the South-east Asian situation, Beijing hosted a conference in May 1995 with representatives from China, Thailand, Burma, Laos, Cambodia and Vietnam, to draw up their first co-operative strategy to curb the drug trade. A three-year action plan was tabled, aimed at reducing drug demand, promoting alternative development for drug-producing regions and strengthening law enforcement. In a post-conference declaration, the six nations agreed the situation required immediate attention and acknowledged no country could solve the problem alone. The plan, expected to cost $10 million, including seeking a 75 per cent aid package from international sources.

Despite governmental concern, some official factions in China are involved in their own shady dealings: the PLA, for example, have invested tens of millions of dollars in Hong Kong property, some of it proceeds from foreign arms-for-drugs deals, having used the collapsed Bank for Credit and Commerce International (BCCI) for many of their transactions. They now use other Chinese banks with overseas offices or branches in tax havens around the world, such as the Cayman Islands.

Hong Kong is still a major heroin port, heroin arriving by sea from the Golden Triangle. In March 1994 police, acting on a tip-off, seized 67 kilograms of Double UOGlobe heroin in 96 blocks, wrapped in nylon, waxed paper and plastic and hidden on the sea floor south of Lamma Island: many recent seizures world-wide have been of heavily compressed blocks of powder. In the same year, the Royal Hong Kong Police and Customs and Excise Department discovered a total of 446 kilograms of heroin. Despite maritime smuggling, well over 50 per cent of heroin now comes overland from the Golden Triangle by way of Yunnan and Guangxi provinces and the cities of Guangzhou and Shenzhen. The Hong Kong–Chinese frontier being essentially open, smugglers use the huge daily cross-border traffic of pedestrians, train passengers and vehicles to hide couriers who carry heroin in body belts and baggage from stockpiles maintained in Shenzhen. Rarely, commercial cargo flights are used.

Double UOGlobe heroin is the most common brand brought into Hong Kong but, just as Hong Kong is famous for its fake watches, computer software and designer clothes, so is it for heroin. Some heroin cutting mills and packing houses, often located in the northern New Territories near the Chinese border, have been importing Double UOGlobe product, adulterating it to 50 per cent purity with rice powder, caffeine, antipyrine or talc, recompressing it in hydraulic presses, repackaging it in fake Double UOGlobe labels and sending it on as the genuine 100 per cent pure article. In 1994, twenty heroin manufacturing or cutting centres in Hong Kong were neutralised with thirty-eight drugs syndicates being closed down. Not only traffickers are involved in opium and heroin: as throughout its history, drugs remain an important commodity in Hong Kong's free market-place and it has been suggested that several otherwise legitimate Chinese multimillionaires have substantially invested in narcotics.

Heroin use within Hong Kong has soared since the spring of 1994, purity at street level decreasing from 41.3 per cent in 1993 to 23 per cent in 1994, whilst the street price rose from HK$322 to HK$463 per gram. Over 93 per cent of the addict population consumes heroin, No. 4 heroin the most widely used, with most addicts smoking rather than injecting it: No. 3 smoking heroin is now almost non-existent. Only a very few elderly traditional opium smokers remain: the author was offered a block of fifty-year-old opium with an antique opium pipe in nearby Macau in May 1995, the vendor, a man in his eighties, still referring to it as *nga pin*. In 1994 there was just one arrest in Hong Kong for keeping an opium divan.

A major concern in Hong Kong is the growing number of school-age heroin addicts; 15-year-old girls and even 10-year-old boys are coming to the notice of clinics, one 10-year-old telling a social worker 'I feel happy on heroin.' This 'happiness' may be somewhat dented if, in 1997 when Hong Kong reverts to Chinese sovereignty, the authoritarian measures applied by Beijing are brought to bear.

Hong Kong street dealers and addicts, perhaps because they have such a long history of opiate use, are most artful in their methods of doing business. Heroin is sold either in plastic packets of between 1 gram and 1 ounce, in either powder or rock form, in 2-gram *Po Chai* (Chinese traditional medicine) bottles or as single doses in 'straws'. A 'straw' is a 2-centimetre long piece of plastic drinking straw, filled with heroin and heat sealed at each end. It may be carried either under the tongue, in the cheek or in the hand, held between thumb and middle finger. At the approach of a police officer, it can be flicked up to 10 metres away. Few addicts are caught in possession in the street unless they are exceedingly careless.

Most Golden Triangle heroin is intended for Western markets. Demand in Asia – not including China, which has a huge potential addict population – is not expected to increase significantly. Cultural or economic barriers to drug use exist in some countries, whilst others have reached a peak. In places, heroin is not the preferred drug: for example, in Japan, which has the economic potential to increase heroin use, addicts prefer to use stimulants.

Chiu Chau syndicates still control the majority of the trade but other groups, such as the Hokkien Chinese, also move Golden Triangle drugs, often through Taiwan where there are also excellent money laundering facilities. The Triads, who continue to hold a near-monopoly over international shipments from South-east Asia and control sizeable wholesale distribution networks in the West, are relocating out of Hong Kong in readiness for the 1997 hand-over of sovereignty. As well as moving to London, the European Union and to the USA, they are building up a presence in Australia and Canada. Organised Chinese gangs exist in Sydney, Toronto, Vancouver, San Francisco, Los Angeles, New York, London, Manchester, Amsterdam, Rome, Paris and in places where a Chinese ethnic presence is not traditional, such as the German cities of Frankfurt, Stuttgart, Munich, Cologne and Berlin.

In a potentially alarming development, Chinese gangs have moved to Italy, often using Chinese restaurants as fronts for heroin trafficking. In Rome alone, there are over 400 Chinese restaurants, whereas only a handful existed in 1990. The Italian police are worried about how the Triads and the Mafia may co-exist for, although there has so far been some co-operation between them, the police fear gang warfare if the Triads try to rival Mafia drug interests.

Triad contacts with organised crime syndicates in Australia have existed since the early 1970s when they started importing heroin. By 1994 an evaluation by Australian law enforcement agencies showed 85–90 per cent of heroin entering Australia was owned by Chinese groups associated with organised crime in Hong Kong and China: the same gangs also linked to other groups operating in Vietnam, the Lebanon, Italy, Turkey, Romania and New Zealand. The Chinese are often vital links in the communications network of international organised crime. In Australia, they are allied to motorcycle gangs who are major heroin distributors, thus following a pattern, for Hell's Angels motorcycle gangs, found in seventeen countries, are frequently related to international crime.

Wealthy expatriate Chinese (some of them members of, or related by business to, Triad societies) also run world-wide smuggling networks. On the surface they may be involved in hotels, banks, tourism and manufacturing but a percentage of their profits is invested in trawlers and tramp steamers which carry heroin and illegal immigrants to the West and stolen luxury cars into China. In 1992, more than 100,000 Chinese were smuggled into the USA alone and the trade continues to grow.

Although it is known the Yakuza bankroll bulk shipments of drugs to Western markets, the extent of their involvement in present day international drug trafficking is hard to assess. They are virtually impenetrable and, given their organisational skills and financial prowess, not to say the cover Japanese world trade can afford them, almost impossible to combat.

The Golden Triangle producers and traffickers do not, of course, have it all to themselves. There are other players involved.

Afghanistan is the second largest illicit opium producer and in recent years there has been an increase in the numbers of poppy farmers, refugees returning after the Russian withdrawal growing poppies as a quick and easy cash crop with which to rebuild their country and set themselves up. In some parts of the country the Russians destroyed irrigation systems so poppies have been an ideal crop because they do not need irrigation.

The year 1994 saw a 38 per cent increase over the 1993 production estimate and a bumper harvest of poppies, most of which are grown in Nangarhar Province and the Helmand Valley where poppies have traditionally been raised and poppy head medicine commonly used for stomach ailments. There are approximately 250,000 opium smokers in Afghanistan, with a swelling number of heroin smokers, but most opium is sold for processing into morphine base or heroin over the Pakistan border, or converted into morphine base locally and transported through the Central Asian republics to Europe. Former Mujaheddin fighters and their one-time Communist enemies are now doing a brisk business together by selling arms – either left behind after the Russian withdrawal from Afghanistan or specifically purchased as military surplus from Russia – for drugs which they then market into the international trade.

Neighbouring Pakistan is in some ways the Thailand of western Asia for it is a producer, a processor and a transit country. The price it pays is similar to that of Thailand, too: Pakistan has well over 1.5 million heroin addicts at a minimum estimate. A government ban exists on poppy farming and some crop eradication has occurred, but traffickers have no problem persuading smallholding peasant farmers to break the laws when they can earn ten times as much from poppies as they can from fruit, vegetables or tobacco. Most Golden Crescent heroin is refined in Pakistan in the lawless areas of the North-West Frontier Province where central government rule is still usurped by local tribal chieftains. To attempt to combat the problem, the government offers incentives to compliant chieftains but compliance is usually ignored once the incentive is taken: the drug traders can out-bid and out-bribe the authorities and corruption amongst even senior local officials is rife. There has even been reported a heroin factory inside a United Nations managed refugee camp in the Khyber Pass.

Pakistani drug barons, based in Karachi or Lahore, finance export consignments and act as middlemen for international crime syndicates, their couriers often illiterate Pakistanis who are dispensable. For the courier, who is often ignorant of the penalties he may face, arrest can mean years in a foreign gaol or even the death penalty in certain countries. So brazen are some Pakistani barons, they export heroin or morphine base in loads as large as a ton in weight, shipping through the Suez Canal to Turkey, Turkish-controlled Cyprus and other Mediterranean countries, with some going via Mauritius and Madagascar.

There is another danger from the heroin trade in Pakistan: the country is on the verge of becoming so powerful as a heroin producer, refiner and trader that it threatens to destabilise an already insecure political and geographical region. For this reason, intense international pressure is being put on Pakistan to stamp out the heroin trade and enforce existing laws, seven or eight Pakistani narco-barons allegedly being secretly extradited to the USA over the winter of 1994—95.

Even in India, where the opium industry has for many years been well regulated, licit opium is being diverted into the illegal market and illicit opium produced. According to some estimates, up to 30 per cent of the legal product may be 'disappearing', caused by corruption amongst lower-paid officials who aid poppy farmers in selling to traffickers. The incentives for the farmer are tempting for he can earn up to forty times more from traffickers than from government buyers. Most of the illegal growing is done in the north-eastern state of Arunachal Pradesh and those bordering Burma, where the opium may be taken over the frontier. In the same area of India, pro-independence guerrillas of the National Socialist Council of Nagaland traffic in heroin along the Burmese border: indeed, it seems as if all the separatist groups in India and Sri Lanka are establishing common trafficking networks to raise finance.

Although India clamped down on any domestic use of opium forty years ago, there remain a small number of opium addicts in the rural north who are provided with supplies by the government. They do not pose a problem: what does is the increasing rate of heroin manufacture in India. According to suppressed official reports, India has anything between one and five million heroin addicts. The native product is No. 3 heroin made in primitive, mobile laboratories. Some is exported to Bangladesh and Nepal, where addiction rates are rising, but most exportation is handled by Muslim middlemen in Bombay or New Delhi who deal in heroin from Pakistan, Afghanistan and Burma. Drugs not only pass through in transit but are warehoused in enclaves such as the Muslim quarter of Old Delhi where up to 500 kilograms are held at any one time, waiting to be couriered out.

The last of the Golden Crescent 'opium states' is Iran. Reliable information is hard to come by: the official line is Iran is opium-free. Certainly, poppy farming was officially banned in 1980 but it continues close to the frontiers with Pakistan and Afghanistan and, according to American intelligence, in the Kurdish areas on the Turkish border where morphine base and heroin laboratories exist, the revenue aiding the Kurdish separatist movement. Inside Iran, there are thought to be about two million heroin addicts, the worsening economic and social climate and repressive government policies claimed as underlying reasons. Iran, along with Burma, Afghanistan, Syria and Nigeria, was listed in March 1995 as being 'uncertified' by the USA. This means these countries are not deemed by the USA to be making serious efforts to tackle narcotics, resulting in USA opposition to all but humanitarian aid intended for them from such international agencies as the World Bank. Some believe certification arbitrary. President Hashemi Rafsanjani of Iran has criticised the certification as politically motivated: certainly, Iran has been attempting to halt opiate traffic from the Golden Crescent.

Outside the two 'golden' opium areas, there are also other countries engaged in opiates. In 1991, it was estimated over 3000 hectares of land in Lebanon were used for poppy cultivation, producing 34 tonnes of opium. Lebanon has been cited as the best example of what has become known as 'narco-terrorism', the use of drug trafficking to further the objectives of governments and terrorist organisations. However, from such a definition it is obvious this is not a new phenomena: one is reminded of pre-war Japanese drug involvement in China and CIA use of drugs in South-east Asia, not to mention the Shan states groups who use opium to fund themselves. There have long been connections between international drug traffickers and international terrorists but over the last few decades they have become significantly interdependent.

Heroin has become a terrorist currency and this is especially true in the purchase of arms. Some governments or terror groups also use drugs to undermine their enemies, which for many has often been the USA, accepting they demoralise a nation and introduce criminal activity to society. Terrorists, seeking to cause chaos and disorder, have seen drugs as a powerful strategic weapon.

There had traditionally been a drug trade in the Lebanon: it is famous for growing a particularly potent hashish known by dope-heads as Lebanese Gold, which was marketed especially in the Near East. In the 1960s, some of the religious and political factions in Lebanon began to earn large sums of money from hashish. As internecine tension rose in the 1970s, hashish production mushroomed, the drug farmed in the Bekaa Valley. When the Lebanese civil war commenced in 1975, the country's economy was devastated, drugs becoming its mainstay.

As the fighting escalated hashish, which was sold comparatively cheaply, failed to earn sufficient foreign currency so, in 1982, Turkish poppy growers were brought in to the Bekaa Valley. Under their guidance, poppies were raised and heroin produced. Weight for weight, opiates were at least ten times more profitable than hashish. The trade expanded until it embraced all the fighting factions, much of the conflict centring on the control of narcotics – not just the poppy fields but also the roads, ports and airstrips from which drugs could be shipped.

Heroin (and, to a lesser extent, hashish) also financed troops and armaments. An indication of its relevance to terrorist organisations may be gained from the intelligence that, as early as 1982, it was estimated the Palestine Liberation Organisation (PLO) earned $300 million from the narcotics trade, three times what it was given in political subsidy by friendly Arab regimes.

In 1975, Syrian forces seized the Bekaa Valley and began to extort money from the drug merchants, corruption in the Syrian occupation forces aiding hashish and poppy cultivation and heroin manufacture from which Syria took a large cut of the profits. Ties were established by highly placed Syrian officials with the Sicilian Mafia who, it is believed, administered some Syrian trafficking operations.

There were possibly up to 100 mobile heroin laboratories in the Bekaa Valley in 1991, with more sophisticated, permanent facilities existing over the Syrian border. Although, the next year, production was negligible due to poor weather substantially damaging the poppy crop, it was thought by DEA analysts at the time that it could return to normal in 1993. This did not happen. It now appears most poppy crops have been eradicated, the cultivation of poppies limited and local production considerably reduced. With the ending of the civil war, however, the Lebanon has assumed its traditional role as a trafficking hub, with new dealer networks quickly establishing themselves. Imported morphine is refined into heroin whilst Russian operators and Sicilian *mafiosi* use Lebanese ports to export drugs and launder related earnings. It has also been alleged that several Lebanese parliamentary deputies and government officials are involved in the business.

Future poppy production in the Lebanon relies on how long peace there lasts and how effectively the economy is rebuilt. Yet poppy growing in the region is not restricted to Lebanon for it is going on in the Gaza Strip where Palestinians, displaced by Israeli politics and lacking any substantial form of local industry, regard it as a viable means of income. Palestinian police seized opium to the value of $1.5 million in just a few days of raids in 1994.

It has been suggested narcotics were to blame for the bombing of Pan Am flight 103 in December 1988 over Lockerbie, in Scotland, when 259 passengers and 11 people on the ground were killed. The official view of the American and British governments is that the blame lies with Libya but it is now thought by many observers that the bombing was carried out in retaliation for the shooting down of an Iranian Airbus five months previously by an American warship. It is believed that Iran put out a $10 million contract for the bringing down of an American aircraft and it has been alleged that this was accepted by Ahmed Jibril, head of the Popular Front for the Liberation of Palestine (PFLP).

The suggested scenario is that the CIA was trying to gain influence with Middle East power-brokers, such as PFLP and Hezbollah, to obtain a bargaining advantage in freeing Western hostages in Lebanon. The terrorist groups relied on cash raised through trafficking and they were involved in heroin production in the Bekaa Valley. The DEA and other intelligence agencies were impotent to act against the heroin producers, left merely to monitor the situation. As part of their influence-building strategy, the CIA was covertly permitting – even aiding – specified trafficking shipments (known as 'controlled runs') from the Middle East to the USA. At the same time, it is suggested the CIA was using these controlled runs as part of a 'sting' operation to identify and apprehend big-time, American-based narcotics importers.

Couriers carried heroin through airport security as part of these controlled runs, being allowed through without let or hindrance. It is suggested Ahmed Jibril saw this as a means of not only earning risk-free drugs money but also of getting a bomb on an American aircraft. If a bomb could be placed in a container used on a controlled run, it would go undetected through security checks and on to the aircraft. A young Lebanese courier, Khaled Jaafar, is said to have taken a Toshiba radio-cassette player on board flight 103, thinking it contained heroin: instead, the Toshiba was the bomb.

More recently, drugs are being used in the buying of favours against Iraq which is itself now dealing in heroin to keep its currency afloat in the face of UN sanctions. Western intelligence agencies (particularly the CIA) are reputed to be purchasing Arab anti-Iraqi attitudes either with hard cash or by turning a blind eye to narcotics smuggling. It is even suggested the CIA has reverted to its South-east Asian practices of the 1960s and is itself dealing in heroin as a part of its Middle East strategy.

This stratagem is not restricted to the Americans: drugs featured in the game plan of the former Communist bloc as well. As late as 1979, the Soviet *Military Encyclopaedia* provided a list of measures to be used to promote Soviet foreign policy objectives: it included the use of poisons and narcotics. Reports appeared in 1990 showing how East Germany's premier, Erich Honecker, had encouraged trafficking for twenty years as his contribution towards the Soviet undermining of NATO, his government assisting in the laundering of drug and terrorist money.

Bulgaria was similarly active in the narcotics trade, its geographic position making it an ideal transit centre between Asia and Europe. As early as the 1950s, it had put in place money laundering capabilities, providing a safe haven for criminals who deposited foreign currency in Bulgarian banks. A decade later, Bulgaria was making a profit from imported Turkish morphine base and heroin which was transhipped to the rest of Europe. Then it started to deal in arms. By the early 1970s, the Bulgarian secret service (the KDS) was purchasing drugs from the Palestinians and Middle Eastern terrorists in exchange for weapons. The drugs were sent on to Europe and the USA. Money earned from the transactions was laundered through Swiss banks and subsequently used to buy arms for international – especially Middle Eastern – terrorist organisations.

The transactions were processed by Kintex, a Bulgarian state-owned export company formed in 1968 and fully staffed by KDS operatives. Kintex acted as a middleman, providing cover for criminal associates and linking itself to Lebanese traffickers, the Sicilian Mafia and bent Swiss bankers. By 1980, the trade was worth several billion dollars per annum to Bulgaria.

Kintex also directly financed heroin processing. When Italian police discovered a Mafia-owned heroin laboratory in the Sicilian province of Trapani in the early 1980s, they found it was fitted out with Bulgarian equipment. The annual production of this one plant was said to be 4.5 tonnes of No. 4 heroin. By 1985, another fifteen Bulgarian-backed heroin refineries were unearthed in Italy.

The CIA compiled a dossier on Kintex's activities and, in January 1983, the US government made an official complaint to the Bulgarians, attacking them for their involvement in narcotics and terror. Under US pressure, Kintex was closed down but within months another Bulgarian state-owned company, Globus, took up where Kintex left off: Kintex, today renamed KoKintex (the *o* being shaped like the cross-hairs in a telescopic gunsight) is suspected of being a major illegal arms dealing company.

The passing of Communism has not led to the eradication of the drugs trade in former Eastern bloc nations. There is a new storm blowing over the horizon. The CIS, the former USSR, has been an opium producer for decades but, because of the hermetically sealed Communist borders, the trade was contained. Between 1986 and 1991, Soviet authorities conducted regular poppy field eradication programmes. Thousands of hectares were destroyed with many arrests and the confiscation of drugs, weapons and money but in the political turmoil since the end of Communist rule, inter-republican co-operation has all but ceased whilst former law enforcement agencies have virtually collapsed.

The main CIS poppy-growing regions are the Central Asian republics of Kazakhstan, Kyrgyzstan, Tajikistan, Turkmenistan, Azerbaijan and Uzbekistan where cultivation has been going on for centuries. To date, it seems the opium has not been refined into heroin on a large scale but it surely will be. In January 1992, Kazakhstan declared its intention to legalise poppy farming. Although it later rescinded the decision, Kazakhstan indicated what might happen in such republics which are eager for hard currencies to build up trade or finance separatist armies.

If these republics do start large-scale opium production, much will enter the illicit world market, for Afghanistan heroin travels through the region where local clans and criminal groups are already fighting to control the routes. Central Asian republics also produce large quantities of cannabis which is already smuggled to the West: heroin could easily join this less pernicious drug. In the days of the French Connection, it was Armenian nationals who facilitated the purchase of morphine base from Turkey. They were close at hand for Armenia lies on the borders of Turkey and Iran. Today, Armenians continue to broker and transport morphine and heroin originating in the Middle East and the Golden Crescent out to the West. Morphine base is sent to refineries in Lebanon with heroin going to Turkey and on to the rest of Europe. Within Armenian society, Mafia-style practices have become institutionalised with nationalist fighters using drugs as a finance source. Pessimistic – but realistic – Western intelligence agencies sardonically call all of this region the 'New Colombia.'

During the decades of Communism, whilst alcoholism was of serious social concern in the USSR, drug addiction was not such a problem but now opiate abuse, especially heroin, is on the increase, particularly in Russia where there is a growing problem amongst young adults and in the lower ranks of the armed forces. A massacre in Chechnya in 1995 was reportedly committed by Russian troops high on drugs.

In Russia as elsewhere in the CIS, Mafia-style gangs are pro-liferating and exploiting economic and social instabilities. These hoodlums, commonly referred to as the 'Russian Mafia', mostly exist in ethnically orientated groups dating back to the last century when they operated as either bandit gangs or politically motivated anti-Tsarist partisans. Today, they contain not only hardened criminals but substantial elements of the former KGB, men with expert knowledge of undercover and underworld operations who have turned from being secret policemen into secretive, ruthless and highly organised national and international mobsters.

The hard-core of these gangsters emanate from Chechnya and it is said that as Sicily is to Italy so Chechnya is to the CIS. There is a rumour circulating amongst international drug enforcement officers to the effect that the UN have avoided becoming involved in a humanitarian role in the Chechnya conflict because there is tacit agreement not to criticise Russian military behaviour there because the conflict affords a fine opportunity to hit at the heart of CIS gangsterism.

With links to heroin producers and organised crime in Europe and the USA, these Russian gangs deal in narcotics, distributing throughout Europe and exporting heroin from South-east Asia to North America, using increased tourism and the post-Communist relaxation of travel rules as cover. At their present rate of expansion, Russian gangsters are anticipated to become one of the world's leading drug (and weapons) suppliers by the year 2000, if not before.

Gangsters are not solely involved for heroin in former Eastern bloc countries is not just made in criminal-owned factories. Some pharmaceutical companies, bereft of state subsidies and facing the open market with inefficient or out-dated factories, are thought to have begun their own heroin production.

The political liberation of Eastern Europe, the restructuring of police and security services and political turmoil in the region has been a boon to ethnic organised crime groups who are developing new routes between the old East and the West. It is thought they are encouraging poppy growing in areas such as the Elbasan province of Albania. Indeed, Albanians are following the example of their Bulgarian neighbours, generating foreign currency by transporting heroin through their country whilst also buying morphine base from Afghanistan, Iran, Syria and Turkey and manufacturing heroin in Albania. They also traded arms and fuel to the protagonists in the Yugoslavian civil war, investing the profits in drugs. In the former Yugoslavia, where poppies used to be farmed under licence, warring factions were preparing to use opium as a means of financing their struggles but the conflict ended before the means of income was developed. This is not to say opium may not appear in the future as a source of finance in the war-torn countryside and it follows, as other states slide toward separatism, they too may turn to narcotics for funding. In neighbouring Macedonia, an opium producer in the 1920s and 1930s, poppy cultivation is once more prevalent with heroin laboratories appearing to process the harvest.

Not only post-Communist ethnic nationalist movements deal in drugs in Europe. The Basque separatists (ETA) in Spain, the IRA and Loyalist paramilitary groups in Northern Ireland have all claimed to be engaged in political wars but they have all used drug dealing to finance arms purchases. The IRA have known links to Irish-American gangs and have worked in collaboration with them in drug dealing and other rackets whilst Loyalist units have gained funds from drug dealing despite their quasi-social role as moralists who knee-cap or kill members of their community who are involved in peddling.

The Turkish ban of 1972 ended that country's role as a major opium source but it has since played upon its geographical position to become an important processing and transit centre for Golden Crescent products. Heroin refineries near Istanbul and in south-eastern Turkey receive morphine base from Afghanistan by truck via Tajikistan, Azerbaijan and Georgia, about 65 per cent of the heroin being re-exported by road to Europe, much of it in bonded trucks covered by Transport International Routier (TIR) regulations and not subjected to customs inspection. The TIR system is an international agreement, the signatories to which ease cross-border transportation by removing as much bureaucracy as possible. Once vehicles have been cleared by customs at the start of a journey, they are not inspected again until reaching their destination. This plays into traffickers' hands, especially if the journey commences where controls are lax or officials corrupt.

The trail taken from Turkey is called the Balkan Route which goes to Western Europe by way of Bulgaria, Romania, Hungary and the Czech and Slovak Republics. A southern leg goes through Cyprus (where heroin is also refined), Greece and Albania, thence by sea to Italy from the ports of Durres and Vlore: the seepage of heroin across the Adriatic is extensive. More than 75 per cent of heroin seized in Europe comes along the Balkan Route which is dominated by Turkish and Turkish Cypriot traffickers in league with criminal gangs based in Sofia, Tirana and Bucharest where law and order has broken down.

Italy, Germany and Spain each have an addict population of over 100,000, a per capita rate higher than the USA. In Italy, despite recent successful law enforcement initiatives against them, the Mafia is still active but their involvement in narcotics is reduced, at least as far as the Sicilians are concerned. Other criminal syndicate groups, especially the Calabrian Ndrangheta and the Sacra Corona Unita from Puglia, are becoming more active. The Ndrangheta have expanded internationally, particularly amongst Italian communities in Australia, while the Sacra Corona Unita gains influence in the Balkans where it co-operates with Albanians and Macedonians, trafficking not only in narcotics but also in illegal Eastern European immigrants and arms. As a result of this increased activity, Milan has become a seminal European money laundering centre.

Most of the heroin entering Italy is smuggled by Albanians and Macedonians, street pushing in Italy and surrounding countries being increasingly conducted by black Africans or illegal Chinese immigrants, members of the criminal labour market now existing in Europe. Italy, in particular, is having a huge problem with Chinese illegal immigrants: it is estimated there are over 100,000 in the country, transported in by Albanians from Bucharest, the base of a Triad society which deals in people. Latin American heroin trafficking organisations are also making their presence felt in Europe, especially Colombians in Rome and Madrid: having studied the market in the early 1990s, they are now exporting to Europe in substantial and increasing quantities.

A large percentage of the heroin coming into Germany arrives via the northern Balkan Route and is primarily handled by Chechens. The Netherlands, in particular Amsterdam, is still the drugs centre for Europe and a prime transit point for heroin from both the Golden Triangle and Crescent heading for European and American markets. Many dealers collect their supplies from the Netherlands: in April 1995, 90 kilograms of heroin worth £12 million were found in London under the false floor of a horse-box towed by a Dutch-registered vehicle. Even Switzerland, usually thought of as staid to the point of banality, is not exempt. Parts of Zurich are becoming notorious for attracting large numbers of addicts from all over Europe, catered to by over 100 gun-toting Lebanese and Kosovar Albanian pushers who deal in full view of the police.

France remains a heroin transit nation and is a main consumer with a serious urban addict problem. Distribution is still handled by traditional French organised crime syndicates which continue to process some heroin around Marseilles: as has long been the case, there are still heroin refining laboratories hidden in the rural south of France. Trafficking across the Straits of Gibraltar from Morocco has recently increased with heroin and cocaine beginning to take the place of hashish, drugs shipments entering through Gibraltar and along the adjacent Spanish coast. At least 100 rubber and fibreglass speedboats, costing £30,000 each, with engines capable of 50 knots and berthed at Gibraltar, regularly traverse the straits to Africa: more are harbouring in Spain. In July 1995, the Royal Gibraltar Police confiscated fifty vessels believed to have been used by drug smugglers. Gibraltar, with the rest of Spain, is also becoming a drug-dealing and money laundering centre.

Heroin in Britain mostly originates from the Golden Crescent. In 1993, 52 per cent came via Turkey and Cyprus, 12 per cent from Pakistan, with the remainder arriving via India, the Lebanon, the Netherlands, Nigeria, Ghana and Poland. Only about 1 per cent of heroin was from the Golden Triangle. Today, however, Colombian herion importation would considerably distort this analysis. Turkish and Cypriot dealers play an important role, sending most of their consignments by lorry disguised in general cargo or concealed in the vehicle's body or chassis, often within 'traps' built into the vehicle, those constructed inside fuel tanks being the most reported. Their involvement is central: in London, one of the members of the prominent Turkish Cypriot Arif family has served a nine-year sentence for his role in an £8.5 million drug smuggling operation.

In 1993, 200 kilograms of heroin were found at Dover, hidden in a truck carrying tomatoes whilst a year later, heroin worth £9 million was detected in a lorry carrying a load of Mars bars. The total heroin seizure haul in Britain for 1994 was 620 kilograms but, in 1995, seizures virtually doubled to 1200 kilograms worth £150 million. In September 1995, three heroin hauls were seized in one week, worth a total value of £35 million. It is an indication of the profligacy of heroin in Britain today and makes one wonder how much gets through undetected: official figures state probably only 10 per cent of imported heroin is seized. It seems, furthermore, that smuggling into Britain will increase for heroin is coming through the Channel Tunnel with almost daily seizures, this conduit presumably set to play an increasing part in the future.

The street prices for heroin in Britain in 1995 were about £80 a gram or £10 for a one-twelfth to one-sixteenth of a gram fix but have more recently fallen to as low as £40 a gram in some parts of the country. The profit margin is massive. A kilogram of heroin in Pakistan costs approximately £1500 but the British distributor pays £27,000 per kilogram before cutting. After cutting, it is worth approximately £140,000. Prices are not the only factor to fluctuate. In 1992, British heroin was 45 per cent pure but it is now reduced to 35 per cent which means even greater distributor profits.

Since 1985, there had been some decline in heroin addiction in Britain, perhaps due to government advertising and the AIDS epidemic, but it is beginning to rise again. One place where addiction has soared is Jersey, in the Channel Islands. As an offshore tax haven, Jersey is attractive to dealers for there is more disposable income than in mainland Britain: addicts, therefore, have to pay three times the usual British street price. Addict numbers registered for detoxification have risen from 15 in 1993 to 60 in 1994 whilst there are estimated to be 400 addicts in all on the tiny island. They are supplied from England by either couriers or mail. An interesting aspect of the growth is that it is amongst young professionals not just transient youths. The usual factors claimed to lead to addiction – of social degradation or poverty – are absent: Jersey has no unemployment, no poor housing, no student population and no ethnic groups. The cause of growth in addiction is due to cultural causes rather than traditional need.

Europe has become a trafficker's paradise. With national barriers being opened, not only have easy trade and tourism been facilitated but so too has every crime from the amateur bootlegging of alcohol to computer fraud, terrorism and drug running. Traffickers are making full use of this convenience, as is indicated by the fact that of British heroin seizures made in 1993, over 55 per cent were from EU countries. The figure for 1995 is expected to be around or even above 70 per cent.

Whilst First World countries are the primary destinations of heroin, practically every country is somehow involved in the game. With extensive government corruption and organised crime, Nigeria is notorious as the nerve centre of Africa's drug trade: consequently, it has the highest heroin addiction rate in the continent. Corruption is, in fact, so endemic it has prompted an American Congressman to declare, 'We gave some sniffer dogs to Nigerian customs, but it's a poisoned chalice. Dogs cannot be corrupted. They are a permanent danger for any custom authorities any time a minister's wife walks near them.' Mostly established in Lagos, Nigerian trafficking gangs, which are often tribally based, import from both 'golden' regions, re-exporting to Europe and the USA where Nigerians control a number of urban distribution networks, their methods of smuggling being highly adaptable to prevalent enforcement strategies. Whilst a decade ago, Nigerian nationals were frequently couriers, today they are less likely to be involved as smugglers: the world's anti-narcotics agencies have come to recognise them. Now they employ other black West Africans, white and black South Africans, Europeans and Americans, who usually transport small amounts on intercontinental passenger flights, carrying them by ingestion. Ghana is a particularly popular source of smuggling mules for Nigerian gangs: there is no shortage of volunteers for a trip earns the mule US$2000, forty times the national average monthly wage. Often, the mule/trafficker contract is more than financial by involving a witch-doctor's ceremony in which the mule swears not to disclose his employer who, in turn, guarantees to look after the mule's family if he is caught. The *modus operandum* involves the old trick of flooding flights with couriers, accepting customs officers will be over-stretched, apprehending one or two whilst the rest escape detection. A newer development by Nigerian gangs is the transportation of large amounts concealed in commercial maritime cargoes.

Other African countries which are transit stations include Chad, Zambia, Ethiopia, Ghana, Kenya, Senegal, Egypt and Liberia, enforcement of drug legislation being lax in most because of budgetary restraints and corruption. In some countries, such as Zambia, poor Africans obtain passports which they then sell to Nigerian smugglers. This scam is now on the increase in South Africa where the lifting of post-apartheid sanctions is opening the country up as both a possible transit point and a potential heroin market: the squalid, crowded townships of South Africa, already governed by criminal gangs, is a market almost begging for exploitation. Indeed, heroin is already appearing in the townships where it is nicknamed 'flower': pushers selling it disguise it in small bunches of blossoms displayed on roadside stalls or on offer in the *shebeens* or beer halls.

In most African nations, corruption is rampant with officials deeply involved in the drugs trade: in some instances, even governments have been accused of dealing. A Zambian minister had to resign in 1994 following allegations of drug trafficking whilst substantial South American drug money investments have been placed in Equatorial Guinea, a member of a South American cartel (on the DEA wanted list since 1993) travelling on a diplomatic passport issued by the Guinean government. The son of the president was accused of trafficking and expelled from France in 1990, only to be caught a year later in Miami with a suitcase containing US$10 million.

South America, more often associated with cocaine, also increasingly grows poppies and produces heroin. By 1992, Colombia had 20,000 hectares of land cleared for poppies: the year before, it had less than 2000. This places Colombia third behind Burma and Laos in land acreage available for poppy farming. The Colombian climate is ideal for poppies and it is possible to grow three (even four) crops per annum: in the 'golden' regions, only one can be obtained.

The Colombian opium industry is being run with all the efficiency of the cocaine industry. Traffickers provide peasant farmers with seed and train them to collect opium. When the business began the farmers, unsure of the financial return, grew poppies alongside maize, onions or potatoes: partly, they were hedging their bets and partly they were camouflaging their crops but now many exclusively raise poppies.

Colombian opium gum yields are not yet as good as Asian because, although the plants produce more pods, these are small and the farmers are not yet experienced in scoring and gum collection. In time, of course, this will change and seems immune government intervention. Aerial spraying with herbicides is difficult because of the hilly terrain in which the farmers live, where the weather is frequently too dangerous for flying. When spraying is successful, the farmers merely dig up the crop and replant: they can afford to be so wasteful with three annual harvests. Aircraft also come under fire from traffickers and bandits who extort protection money from poppy farmers, grow their own crops of poppies and, in some places, process opium into morphine base with a percentage of poppy cultivation conducted under the auspices of guerrillas of the Communist Colombian Revolutionary Armed Forces and the National Liberation Army.

The first Colombian heroin laboratory was found in 1992. It was not producing a high quantity of heroin but the operators had been trained by heroin chemists from Asia. Colombian heroin production is now increasing and is starting to impact itself upon world markets.

Many of the Colombian traffickers are small-time operators – there are estimated to be 3000 independent drug trafficking groups operating in Colombia – who have worked with cocaine in the past, but they are being increasingly financed and organised or absorbed by the Cali and, to a much lesser extent, Medellin cartels, consortia of drug barons who, though famous for cocaine, are now heavily involved in the highly lucrative heroin business.

The Medellin cartel – based in the city of Medellin and formerly run by the infamous Pablo Escobar who was killed by the Colombian security police in December 1993 – is in decline but the Cali cartel, which is far more powerful and wealthy than Escobar's organisation ever was, is in the ascendant. The Cali cartel, with brothers Gilberto (who was arrested in June 1995) and Miguel Rodriguez-Orejuela as two of its major figures, 'owns' large numbers of judges, police, military personnel and politicians. Some members of the ruling Liberal Party came under criticism in 1994 for allegedly taking money from the Cali cartel to finance their election campaign and it has been alleged that the Colombian government has secretly negotiated the arrests of certain drug barons to appease the USA, which only 'conditionally certified' Colombia as a combatant nation in the war on drugs in March 1995. A number of drug barons had already stated privately that they were prepared to accept short gaol sentences on the condition, upon release, they could retain their wealth: Gilberto Rodriguez-Orejuela, if convicted, is likely to serve not more than nine years in prison. The Cali cartel handles 80 per cent of the world's cocaine, with strongly established links to the American Mafia and other criminal organisations. One group within the Cali cartel controls large tracts of opium farms. It requires no crystal ball to see how their involvement in heroin will develop. South American heroin is starting to capture a large part of the US and European markets. Cocaine distribution and smuggling networks are already in place to handle heroin and Colombia is set to become a significant world heroin source.

Other South and Central American countries are sure to jump on the heroin bandwagon. Although American government-aided eradication projects wiped the poppy out of Guatemala in 1992, cultivation is underway again in remote, narrow valleys beyond the reach of crop-spraying aircraft, under the guidance of Mexican criminals who are behind the resurgence of Guatemalan culti- vation. Venezuela, Peru, Brazil and Ecuador also seem likely to increase their numbers of opium poppies.

Many countries in Central America and the Caribbean – even those where poppies are not grown – are involved in the trade: there are now so many drugs in the region's countries they are collectively classified by customs agencies as a 'source country' in their own right. Belize was infiltrated by drug dealers within a decade of independence from Britain whilst Puerto Rico has become a major gateway for drugs entering the USA, San Juan having developed into a hub of trafficking, money laundering and dubious South American investments: in April 1995, the FBI busted a ring which had invested US$80 million of drugs-related money primarily in the tourist industry.

Cuba's involvement in drugs (primarily cocaine) goes back many years, originating in the government's ideology. From early on, it was Castro's policy to aid and abet traffickers in order to subvert American society, finance arms and bankroll Latin American revolutionaries. From around 1975 onwards, Cuba commenced the systematic exploitation of any chink it could see in the American armour, narcotics forming a conspicuous part of Cuban policy. An alliance was made in 1975 with the Colombian drug cartels whereby Cuba would turn a blind eye to vessels carrying drugs through her territorial waters, would furnish refuelling services and provide a flag of convenience if required. Aircraft were similarly catered for. Needless to say, these services had to be paid for in hard currency. Instances also occurred where cocaine was refined at Cuban military bases, protected by military security. Today, Cuban trafficking groups are involved in money laundering and drug trafficking in Colombia, the Dominican Republic, Cuba and Haiti, with heroin being discovered in containers of flowers and being run by Dominican nationals.

The Sandinista regime, which took power in Nicaragua in 1979, ran a drugs-for-arms business which also obtained much needed hard currency, particularly US dollars. They were not alone. The CIA used narcotics sales as one means of obtaining financial support for the right-wing, anti-Sandinista Contras, this forming a substantial part of US covert operations in Central America. The part of the CIA in such American overseas policy decisions was more than adequately summed up by one of the world's most successful money launderers who observed in 1987, in respect of the Nicaraguan affair, that drug barons outside the USA were immensely powerful and influential. He stated that if the CIA wanted to meddle in the affairs of foreign nations there was no way they could do so without meeting – and probably associating – with drug dealers and their masters.

Mexico, which at present has a low but growing addict population, is central to much of the region's heroin. This is despite extensive enforcement and crop eradication, the result of which has driven poppy cultivation largely out of the mountains of the Sierra Madre and into the south-west of the country where, due to the weather and new farming methods, more than one annual crop is possible. Most Mexican heroin is 'black tar' heroin which is quick and easy to make, being manufactured directly from raw opium in small, mobile refining units which travel with the farmers as they harvest their crop. The product is on its way to the USA within several days. Such heroin is usually injected and can have a consistency as sticky as roofing tar or be hard like coal. It is most frequently sold by the 'piece' (a Mexican ounce) which weighs 25 grams. It may also be sold in a brown, powdered form known as 'Mexican brown' or 'Bugger'.

In the last decade, Mexico has become *the* major entry point for drugs into the USA. The traffic earns an estimated $30 billion a year in foreign exchange for Mexico: it could not achieve this without help from well-placed officials. Corruption has shifted from local police (who are often accused of trafficking) to the highest echelons of government, with charges of complicity between drug kingpins and top government officials being made nation-wide. The charges and their associated scandals may involve more than money for narcotic connections have been alleged in several high-profile murders. To address this situation, one of the conditions set by Washington on a $20 billion aid package granted to Mexico in 1994 was an improvement in co-operation on anti-narcotics matters.

The drug syndicates in Mexico are a loose amalgamation of drug lords and their families known as 'the Mexican federation' which has, since 1990, gone from being relatively small and unsophisticated to turning Mexico's drug trade into one to rival Colombia's. The federation has liaisons with Colombian cartels who often fly consignments into Mexico with the Mexicans transporting them across the American border.

Mexican smuggling over this long frontier is sometimes conducted in body bags worn by the thousands of illegal immigrants and migrant workers who cross for the bright lights of the USA. Traffickers buy their services with money and work permits or US resident documents.

Yet the main method of smuggling today is by vehicle. The Mexicans usually use quite crude methods, simply stuffing the drugs into the boot of cars then relying on a combination of speed, 'scattershot runs' (the blitzing of border posts, sending eight or ten vehicles through at a time, betting the US customs will search at most one vehicle in the convoy) and sheer bravado for success. So vast is the problem, the DEA maintain a major regional office in El Paso, close to the Mexican border, agents working here calling themselves 'border rats'. They co-ordinate intelligence and monitor the border crossing where the highway from Mexico, US Interstate 25, begins. This is known by enforcement agents as 'Heroin Highway' for it is a major transport route. At Albuquerque, New Mexico, it meets US Interstate 40, the trunk road from Los Angeles to North Carolina, branching at Knoxville, Tennessee, into US 81, which goes to Washington and New York. Inevitably, US 40 is a heroin pipeline. It is also, by co-incidence, part of the old Route 66 and lends some pertinent credence to the blues/rock standard, (Get Your Kicks On) Route 66, written by B. Troup and made famous by the Rolling Stones on one of their early albums, the refrain of which invites the listener to 'get hip', have a kick and take a trip to California on that particular highway.

America remains, at least in the minds of much of the public, the main destination for heroin whatever its source. According to DEA analysis under the Heroin Signature Program, the heroin on the streets of the USA in 1994 came from all over the world: 57% was of Golden Triangle origin, 32% South American, 6% Golden Crescent and 5% Mexican. The relatively high percentage for South American heroin, however, partly arises from the large numbers of seizures made at Miami and New York airports due to the high numbers of couriers apprehended bringing in South American heroin. Average purity in 1994 was 40%, much higher than the figure of 7% prevalent in the early 1980s. Very recent studies suggest 60% of heroin in the USA may now be coming from Burma and that, after years of heroin being second to cocaine as 'the drug of choice', it is now making all the running.

Much heroin is imported by Chinese traffickers, the bulk of their Golden Triangle produce entering the country along the eastern seaboard, where New York City is by far the largest importation and distribution hub, or via the west coast. From ports such as Seattle, San Francisco and Vancouver Chinese societies, their couriers often crew members on container ships, with heroin also being smuggled in imported vehicles, divert the drug through Canada to a distribution hub in Toronto. Golden Crescent heroin is mostly smuggled through north-eastern seaports and distributed down the east coast and in the mid-west. It is primarily brought in by Pakistanis although Afghans, Israelis, Iranians, Albanians, Lebanese and Turks also participate. Mexican heroin is usually only to be found in the west, mid- and south-west.

South American heroin is rapidly increasing in availability, especially in north-eastern cities and along the east coast where it had the highest purity of any source in 1994. Such high purity is essential as the Colombian traffickers seek to build up a clientele and maintain user loyalty in the fiercely competitive market. To establish themselves, Colombian traffickers are known to be using a variety of tactics such as offering free samples to potential distributors, persuading established cocaine distributors to purchase and sell heroin as a condition of doing business and undercutting competitors' prices in some cities in an effort to win over business.

The heroin trade is superbly organised: if such acumen was applied to some legitimate produce, it could increase profits severalfold. The Mafia are no longer dominant in the trade as they were and street peddling is more likely to be conducted by gangs or groups organised on ethnic or racial grounds who cater for their own racial or socio-economic peers.

The smashing of the Mafia was a major law enforcement coup involving the co-operation of a number of state police forces in collaboration with the FBI and the DEA. In 1970, the US government had passed the Racketeer Influenced and Corrupt Organisations legislation, otherwise known as the RICO statute. Originally designed to provide prosecutors with a weapon against organised crime, infiltration of labour unions and businesses, it was realised it could be as effectively used to combat the entire structure of organised crime. To accommodate this, the FBI was remodelled in 1980 to strike at the Mafia. The enforcement agencies targeted, amongst other things, the Mafia heroin distribution system. Thirty-nine *mafiosi* were indicted for narcotics offences and related racketeering crimes. The bugging of the home of Paul Castellano provided more intelligence. Castellano, the notorious godfather of the Gambino Mafia 'family', the most powerful criminal organisation in the USA and the Mafia *capo di tutti i capi* (the Boss of all the Bosses or, literally, head of all heads), had in fact specifically forbidden narcotics dealings in the early 1980s, stating anyone in his family who handled drugs would be 'whacked', a quaint euphemism meaning murdered. He was himself whacked by Mafia opponents in December 1985, certain members of his family having made – and going on to make – enormous profits out of heroin dealing. With successes throughout the 1980s, the 1988 arrest of 200 Mafia traffickers in Sicily and the USA along with Giuseppe (Joe) Gambino, a key player in the Sicilian Connection, and, in 1989, the apprehension of John Gotti, the new Gambino family *capo*, much of the Mafia's infrastructure and power was destroyed.

Created in 1983, the President's Commission on Organised Crime studied the problem of syndicated racketeering in the USA and came to the conclusion it was in a stage of metamorphosis and that the Mafia was not alone: Puerto Rican, Dominican, Mexican and Jamaican criminal syndicates were also at work on the drug scene, in addition to African–American street gangs. And they were, if anything, more dangerous than the Mafia: the Italian Mob was not generally violent outside its own close-knit society but the other ethnic gangsters were and are prone to more widespread violence, particularly in metropolitan environments. Today, the Mafia may be somewhat suppressed but the other groupings continue.

A new development, which has appeared since 1993, is the emergence of independent traffickers using established routes and distribution networks. Some are from ethnic backgrounds already involved – such as Pakistanis or Nigerians – but others are new to the game, such as Russians who are now moving world-wide.

Regardless of who is dealing, the retail structure remains more or less static. Heroin is sold at street level by the gram or fractions of a gram. In both Britain and the USA, a single package is known as a 'deal'. It usually comes in a small paper envelope about the size of a large postage stamp although it may also be sold in cellophane or small plastic bags called 'baggies'. For most of America's estimated 600,000 addicts, intravenous injection is the means of taking a dose although snorting has become more widespread because addicts fear needle contamination and the concomitant risk of hepatitis or AIDS. Snorters tend to use more heroin than 'fixers' (injectors) and a number, in common with fixers, also use cocaine: conversely, crack cocaine users may take heroin to extend cocaine-induced euphoria and lessen the depression caused when the effects of crack start to wear off.

As already indicated, heroin is an immensely profitable enterprise: indeed, it is the most profitable enterprise ever invented. Yet, like any commodity, it has its price fluctuations, supply and demand criteria, market forces, surfeits and paucities. Price controls are affected by dealer profit margins, processing and trafficking costs, losses due to seizure or theft along the distribution chain. An indication of pricing structures may be drawn from the cost in US dollars of Golden Triangle produce in 1993, as published by the DEA in September, 1993:

- raw opium at source in the Shan states: $66–75 per kilogram
- morphine base in Chiang Mai, Thailand: $900–1000 per kilogram
- heroin hydrochloride, Chiang Mai, 70–90 per cent purity: $2900–3200 per kilogram
- heroin in Bangkok, 70–90 per cent purity: $6000–10,000 per kilogram

- heroin, wholesale in the USA, 70–90 per cent purity: $90,000–250,000 per kilogram
- heroin at dealer level in the USA, 30–60 per cent purity (after cutting): $5500–12,000 per ounce (one kilogram when cut and sold by the ounce realised $340,000–745,000)
- heroin at street salesman/pusher level in the USA, 34 per cent purity: $400–600 per gram (one kilogram when cut and sold by the gram realised $940,000–1,400,000).

In the same year in the USA, Golden Crescent heroin (56 per cent pure) fetched $200–500 per gram with Mexican black tar (26 per cent pure) selling for $100–500 per gram.

From whatever source it comes, heroin is cut, which obviously increases profit margins. The list of substances used for cutting today is long and includes glucose powder, chalk dust, icing or powdered sugar, quinine, caffeine, talcum powder, rice powder and flour. The cutting brings about a risk known to early opiate users: the addict cannot judge the purity of his purchase and may be allergic to the cutting substance in his bloodstream. As addicts expect their heroin to be cut, deaths may occur from overdosing: in Britain in 1994, a number of addicts were killed when they purchased only slightly cut supplies.

Such massive profits generate huge sums of illicit money which has to be 'laundered' – that is, passed through legitimate channels so its source becomes disguised. The amount of 'dirty' money circulating in the world is so vast as to be an alternative economy which is the third largest in the world after currency dealing and oil. Just as there are official petro-dollars, so might there be unofficial dope-dollars. Estimates of the annual size of the drugs-related dirty money market vary upwards from $500 *billion*. Over $350 billion was laundered through the USA in 1995.

To the common man, such sums are, as the American axiom puts it, telephone numbers. To set it into context, the global drugs financial market exceeds the gross national product (GNP) of 90 per cent of UN member countries and three of the Cali cartel hierarchy are said to be the wealthiest men in the world apart from King Fahd of Saudi Arabia and the Sultan of Brunei.

Money laundering is essential for a number of reasons. Attention needs to be diverted from the source of the money to place it beyond the reach of asset seizure by enforcement agencies. It needs to be 'washed' so it might be invested in legitimate business ventures and it needs to be hidden so it might be used to fund further illegitimate business, such as reinvestment in drugs.

The laundrymen are highly efficient and expert accountants, bankers, lawyers or businessmen, usually from a professional background or with considerable business experience and usually without a criminal past. These laundrymen contract out their services at a commission rate which varies between 4 and 20 per cent of the gross sum laundered: it is also common for an up-front fee to be levied, of around £25,000 for every £1 million.

The laundromat is a three-phase operation. The first, known as 'placement', is the hardest and involves getting the money into the financial system. Usually, placement is achieved by making comparatively small cash deposits in a wide range of banks, often in a number of different international locations so as not to arouse suspicion, and by purchasing bankers' drafts, bonds, cheques or travellers' cheques with cash. Each operative is known as a 'smurf', a term invented by Florida investigators. The diversification process is known as 'smurfing' because one needs an army of 'little people' to carry it out – like the cartoon characters, the Smurfs.

The drugs trade is cash intensive: most transactions from farmer through to addict are conducted in cash. Some money is 'pre-washed' by passing it through the international art, antiques and antiquities trade, travel agencies, gold dealerships (especially in the Far East and South Africa) and general import/export firms.

Fronts, both legitimate firms and shell companies, are used to transfer money between banks. They are, in effect, underground banks themselves. Dirty money is paid into one and, within hours of it being banked, it is available anywhere else in the world. Although commodity markets are enlisted as laundries, their huge hourly international cash flows providing a very good cover, shell companies are more commonly used, providing imaginary services or selling imaginary merchandise. Ready cash is also transported in bulk by traffickers and there are couriers in the business who never carry heroin but cash. The amount of cash involved can be staggering. In February 1995, a couple was arrested by Spanish police near Marbella following a routine drugs enquiry. Their apartment was found to contain over £50 million's worth of foreign currency in sacks.

The second phase is called 'layering', which creates a confusing banking paper-chase. Once in the world banking system, the small deposits are shifted from bank to bank and country to country, stopping in each only a little while to avoid detection and sometimes being consolidated on the way.

The last phase is 'integration', by which the now heavily disguised money is returned to the legitimate world by investment in legal businesses, property, stocks and bonds. The money is now laundered. The size of the laundry business may be guessed at when one considers it has been estimated that at least 25 per cent of all Hong Kong commercial property investment is based in part or totally upon laundered finance.

Drugs enforcement agencies have long been aware one of the most effective ways to attack traffickers and producers is to hit them in their wallets and a variety of measures have been established.

The US RICO statute, by which courts could confiscate assets acquired through criminal activity, was effective but had a number of loopholes which were addressed in 1986 by the Money Laundering Control Act, which made money laundering a federal offence when carried out in conjunction with other illegal activities. Even this was not legally water-tight so, in 1990, the Depository Institution Money Laundering Amendment Act was ratified, placing the responsibility of reporting laundering transactions on banks' directors. A transaction reporting system was also introduced whereby cash deals exceeding $10,000 have to be notified.

The laws, allied to the DEA Kingpin strategy, produced results. In just one fiscal year (1992), the DEA seized assets within the USA to the value of $857.3 million: overseas, it aided in confiscating another $53.4 million.

In Britain, the Drugs Trafficking Offences Act of 1986 provides for the freezing of assets with confiscation upon conviction. As the act makes it an offence to aid and abet a trafficker, it is also illegal to handle, hold, invest or otherwise dispose of drug-related money. Nevertheless, the law is not as strong as its American equivalent because of the complexities involved in tracing and liquidating drug dealers' assets and the inadequate expertise of British enforcement agencies. There is also a flaw in the system for British bank officials only have to report cash transactions if they are considered 'suspicious' which depends too much on personal integrity and is open to wide interpretation. Of 4500 seizures made to 1994, involving over £42 million, less than £14 million was actually confiscated. Another anomaly is that, in America, all seizures are ploughed back into anti-narcotics work whilst in Britain any money gained is merely added to the general exchequer, reducing law enforcement agents' morale and incentive. The final move in Britain is the Criminal Justice (International Co-operation) Act (1991) which has given customs officers the power to seize cash from travellers suspected of trafficking.

A good many other countries have followed America's example. Australia introduced money laundering and conspiracy legislation in 1987. Hong Kong, the origin of so much heroin and the world's densest banking district, has its Drug Trafficking (Recovery of Proceeds) Ordinance (1989). Since the introduction of this ordinance, assets totalling over HK$16 million have been confiscated from local drug traffickers in Hong Kong, with a further HK$185 million owned by them being sequestered from overseas sources with international co-operation. Thailand, Malaysia, Singapore, South Korea, Japan and most European Union countries have followed suit with similar legislation although the efficacy of it has yet to be thoroughly tested over time and there are sure to be weaknesses.

The Declaration of Basle, signed in 1988, is a commitment by the central banks of a dozen major industrial countries to identify money laundering and laundrymen. The same year, the Vienna Convention organised by the United Nations proposed money laundering become an internationally indictable and extraditable crime. Eighty countries, but less than half the UN member states, agreed in principle but the Convention was a repetition of history. Just as had occurred when international moves were being made against opium, a number refused to sign and, by 1992, only four had actually put their signatures to the paperwork. Countries with interests in particularly secretive or offshore banking chose not to take part. Amongst these were Liechtenstein, the Cayman Islands, Luxembourg and the Dutch Antilles (all offshore banking bases), along with Panama (also filled with offshore banks and an important cocaine and potential future major heroin transit point), Uruguay, Pakistan (a major producer), Russia, Hungary and Bulgaria (all transit route countries or involved in money laundering).

Laundry legislation is easily evaded. When the Colombian authorities put a 10 per cent tax on imported cash, the cartels merely shifted their banking operations to Venezuela: when Venezuela brought in controls, banking was moved to Argentina. As throughout the history of opium, when one door closes, the traffickers open another.

Another means of washing 'dirty' money is to use non-bank-based services, such as money-changers, money transfer organisations like American Express or Western Union, credit-card firms and cheque-encashing companies. The former are much used by traffickers in Mexico, both Mexican and foreign. In every town along the US border there are *casas de cambio* – currency exchange companies. Like Mexican banks, they keep no records, Mexico has no cash transfer controls, no laws aimed at illegal profit-making and no asset seizure legislation. In short, Mexico is a laundryman's paradise. A money laundering scheme uncovered by US Customs agents and the Department of Justice in late 1993 may implicate certain officials in the Mexican Attorney-General's office. The Mexican cartels' influence has spread to the total economy of the nation. Drug barons are using the country's booming tourist industry to launder profits, a development of the laundry business which is growing fast across the world. Billions of dollars are laundered per annum by investing huge sums in beach resorts, financial markets, shopping malls and other commercial enterprises such as Punta Diamante, a resort in the Mexican state of Guerrero which many investigators believe is financed with drug money. The former Dutch colony of Aruba, a Caribbean island resort, is said to be entirely funded and owned by Sicilian mafia interests. Through such legitimate investments, the barons have become integrated into the fabric of society.

A favourite method of cleaning money is by passing it through a casino where it is impossible to prove how much cash a croupier handles during a gaming session. This method was much favoured by the Mafia who had and, to some extent, retain an interest in Las Vegas. Nevada's casinos still being exempt from Federal Currency Transaction reporting makes them very valuable laundries. Although Vegas is still a favourite spot, Macau is even more so. Only 45 miles from Hong Kong and served by high-speed ferries every fifteen minutes, it is an ideal laundromat for over 80 per cent of its revenue comes from a massive gambling monopoly providing superb money-cleaning facilities. It is said up to $2 billion may be laundered monthly. In addition, there is a small but very active Russian gangster element now operating in the enclave. Quite what will happen here in 1997 and 1999, when Hong Kong and Macau respectively revert to Chinese sovereignty, remains to be seen.

Throughout the world, banks claim they have an obligatory client confidentiality responsibility. In truth, they have not. Many countries have removed it. However, lawyer/client confidentiality has not been addressed and civil liberties groups are against the undermining of this right. Therefore, lawyers often hold funds for their trafficker clients, hiding them under the cloak of privileged information.

Laundrymen are always on the look-out for private bankers, secretive financial institutions, countries which turn a blind eye to financial transaction or which might even encourage the importation of 'dirty' money. The former Yugoslavia, for example, contains a number of private banks which offer higher than average interest rates on hard currency deposits. A number of these are secretively owned by prominent Serbian politicians who used profits from laundered heroin money to fund the war against the Bosnian Muslims who, without such financial backing, were comparatively ill-equipped. The private banks laundered their money through shell companies in Austria, regardless of the UN-imposed sanctions against Serbia: with sanctions lifted it will no doubt be business as usual.

Provision exists in Pakistan to hit heroin traders hard. The Forfeiture of Assets Act (1985) allows for confiscation of property and money. However, banks in Pakistan readily take in huge deposits without question, the financial sector protected by a presidential decree (instigated by President Zia) guaranteeing secrecy. Billions of dollars have flowed through Pakistan since the decree with an underground, highly secretive private bank network existing with 'offices' in Kashmir, the Punjab and London which handles heroin finances coming out of Pakistan.

Former Eastern bloc countries, where hard currency is much sought after, are also now awash with 'dirty' money. Banks, ungoverned by restrictions, readily accept foreign currency without demur. Colombian and Turkish drug barons frequently bank in Bucharest and Sofia, though where the latter is concerned, this is of course not new.

American criticism of international banking is loud and pointed. The US State Department has openly attacked the Bahamas for laundering cocaine and marijuana money, Panama for cocaine finances and Hong Kong for being the Pacific Rim centre of Golden Triangle heroin profit washing. Yet, despite their indignation, the USA does not have a squeaky clean record in this field of activity. The CIA has admitted involvement with a money laundry known as the Shakarchi Trading Company which had handled both Kintex and Globus transactions as well as acting for the Mafia in Sicily. The owner of the company, Mohammed Shakarchi, declared his firm had cleaned $25 million for the CIA between 1981 and 1988, which was used to support Mujaheddin insurgents fighting the Russian occupation army in Afghanistan.

The advantage in this terrible global game lies with the criminal. Just as the traffickers and dealers, the drug barons and smugglers manage to stay one step ahead of the enforcement officers chasing them, so do the laundrymen. They will always find a friendly bank, a compliant accountant, an underpaid official or a receptive lawyer to assist them, for their business is driven by greed, the most difficult of the seven deadly sins to exterminate.

16

Bacteria and
The $1,000,000
Bathtub

Illicit drugs are a major global commodity, born in the days of empire-building and mercantile expansion, just as were cotton, tea or coffee. Most Western nations, and Britain in particular, bear the responsibility for the early development of the trade: it was they who addicted China for profit and caused the beginning of the spread of opium smoking. In more recent times, the South-east Asian poppy trade of today was created by colonial opium monopolies which used opium as a revenue source. In post-colonial times, Western political interests have just as readily promoted the trade: without the Americans in South-east Asia and Afghanistan and their rabid fear of Communism it is arguable whether or not the Golden Triangle and Crescent would be the major producers they are today.

Not all the criticism may be levelled at governments. Much of the foundations of opiate addiction were due to ignorance, to medical practice, to the social conditions of the time. With no other potent medicines available, who can blame the sick for dosing on opiates, blame American Civil War doctors for their prescribing, blame mothers for calming children? The latter practice, for which we condemn nineteenth-century mothers, continues: today, a paracetamol-based calming liquid is common. Few parents in developed countries have not heard of Calpol or its equivalent: in 1993, 9.04 million bottles of it were sold in Britain alone.

Just as opium was a global commodity in the nineteenth century so is heroin in the twentieth, the trade governed – as is all trade – by supply and demand, the market fluctuating just as it does for cocoa, sugar or tobacco. Traders speculate in it and re-direct stocks to meet market requirements or overcome local market difficulties whilst producers change their purchasing patterns or move their production base to suit trade climates. The only difference between the heroin dealer and the tobacco dealer is that the former is dealing in an illegal commodity, his market difficulties caused by law enforcement officers not supermarket chain managers or his customer. At the bottom line, both are dealing in an addictive substance grown by Third World farmers: indeed, many millions more people are 'hooked' on nicotine than heroin.

Today, the battle against the international drugs trade is a complex political, economic, social and cultural dilemma riddled with national interests and concerns. As long as the heroin problem exists, there will be those who seek to apportion blame. Are the poppy-growing nations to blame for providing the raw materials or are the consumer nations for not eradicating it?

For the consumer nation, opiate addiction is a major health threat, a socially destructive, crime-orientated problem which can also undermine economic and even political stability. Yet for the poppy-producing nation, opium is often the only sure means of a secure income for a large part of the population and a primary source of foreign currency for the state. The fight against drugs in one country is an attack on the well-being of another and is but a part of the eternal tussle between the developed and the under-developed nations which exists in everything from wild-life conservation strategies to trade. It might be argued the sending of heroin to the USA is basically no different than the sending of Western tobacco goods (with an acknowledged serious health risk) to South America and (ironically) China in order to make up for financial losses in shrinking home markets, or the active encouragement by Western baby milk companies to boost falling home profits by persuading uneducated African mothers to switch from breast- to bottle-feeding.

Since 1945, some opium producing nations have been piqued by the captious attitude of the West over a problem which they see as essentially domestic: the West, they say, should put their house in order. In saying this, the historical tables are turned: do, they imply, as you suggested to the Emperor of China – that if he did not like his people smoking opium then he should prevent them buying it – and leave the producers alone and go after the importers and dealers. Islamic countries have another specific argument. Allah forbids alcohol but not opium whilst the West forbids opium but permits alcohol: opium should not be banned internationally as this would cut across a socio-religious, cultural aspect of Islamic life. If, the argument goes, the West wishes to internationally ban opium then it should also globally ban alcohol.

Masters of opium – call them warlords, drug barons or international criminals – are regarded differently according to who is looking at them. In Western eyes, Khun Sa is considered an evil purveyor of death yet to some Shan state tribes he has been considered a saviour, a politically motivated nationalist leader who has delivered them from Burmese persecution. Khun Sa himself has declared heroin to be a commodity like any other and that he could not stop his people growing poppies for they would then starve. He drew the analogy of asking Americans to stop growing wheat although he was never slow to point out the opium legacy which Asia inherited from Europeans: the whole heroin business, he said, was a matter of karma. Whatever one may think of him, it has to be admitted Khun Sa has made a valid point.

Over the years, Khun Sa made several offers to destroy his opium crop in return for hundreds of millions of dollars. As recently as 1993, he wrote to President Clinton proposing to cease poppy growing altogether in exchange for international aid to establish alternative livelihoods for his people and agricultural redevelopment of the poppy growing areas. The 8 million people in the Shan states, the letter explained, grow poppies because they have no other way of supporting themselves: he added they would destroy the crops as soon as Burma gave them autonomy.

The Americans read the letter with cynicism: to them, Khun Sa is an iron-fisted international criminal and was not the head of a separatist state struggling for independence. As for the Burmese, they take huge foreign currency earnings from the heroin trade. The US State Department's International Narcotics Control Strategy Report of March 1995 stated: '(the) government of Burma continues to treat counter-narcotics efforts as a matter of secondary importance.' It is a Catch-22 situation.

Most opium producing peasants the world over agree with Khun Sa. Opium is their business, their staple, their only viable income with which to feed and clothe their families. They are merely farmers selling their produce: if people do not want it, they should not buy it. Morality is not a part of their agenda and to preach the evils of opium or heroin to them verges on the insulting. They do not make vast profits from opium and many would willingly grow other, perhaps less labour-intensive and police attention-seeking, crops if they could make the same return from them. Asking them not to grow poppies is like asking a bank manager if he would become a teller once more: no one likes to take a cut in salary. The farmers admit they know drugs kill but what is the alternative – an addict dead from an overdose or a farmer's family dead from starvation? What is more, for many, opium is as traditional a crop as grapes are to the French or olives to the Italians: they also use it medicinally and, for them, it is a boon. Most heroin addicts are literally half a world away.

To some peasant cultures, opium is more than just a crop. It is a basic part of cultural as well as agricultural life. A good example of this was to be found in Turkey where, until 1972, approximately 90,000 farming families were dependent on poppies, the opium from which formed an integral part of the daily life of their communities. Opium was a valuable cash crop, all parts of the plant being utilised. Being non-perishable, opium was also a means of accruing wealth: peasant families annually set aside a quantity of opium to go towards a son's bride-price on his marriage whilst other family hoards were used as health insurance, providing a nest-egg against unforeseen hospital bills.

Crop substitution schemes seem an ideal solution but they are fraught with problems. The replacement crops often produce less income: poppies can grow on unfertilised, non-irrigated and often otherwise agriculturally useless terrain: opium is easily transported and does not deteriorate: the opium market is fairly stable: the harvest is assured of a buyer at a reasonably predictable price. There is no other crop in existence to match such criteria.

Eradication schemes also have to take into account the socio-political implications of a prohibition. Remove opium from South-east Asia and a political cauldron will boil over: the Golden Triangle will become a war zone, Burma and Thailand will surely clash over the disputed territory and China may well be drawn into the fracas whilst millions of hill tribesmen will die and the environment will be destroyed.

To eliminate the poppy, massive economic and cultural aid will have to be spent: the price of reducing addiction in the West is the conservation of Third World peasant farmers. The cost is astronomical. An indication of what would be needed on a global scale can be seen in the 1993 US aid package given to Colombia to fight drugs: in just one year, in just one drug-producing country, the USA gave $73 million in cash and technical aid. And, as with any scheme, there is always the difficulty of implementing it, ensuring the money is spent wisely and not lost to corruption. Even then, poppy eradication in one country does not prevent another from starting up.

Another relevant factor working against international eradication is that some national economies are now almost overwhelmed by the drugs trade. This has coined a new noun – *narco-economics*. It is argued, with some validity, traffickers make up the world's most influential special interest group, their economic power such that many poorer countries could not survive without their financial presence. They provide extensive foreign capital income and massive employment opportunities: in Colombia, it is thought 10 per cent of the national work-force is employed in the drugs trade whilst Pablo Escobar was the country's largest single employer. In over a dozen such countries, drug-generated revenue exceeds government revenue with the inevitable result of a good deal of narco-finance entering the political systems. It is not inconceivable for a crime syndicate to buy a major political party and put it in power, this being a natural progression from the present diversification of drugs money into legitimate business.

One way of dealing with the potential which drugs money has for corruption is the rather mundane idea of paying government officials enough so that they would see little attraction in taking bribes: also, they should be promoted only on merit. In Third World countries, poorly paid officials promoted only through a politician's patronage have every incentive to accept bribes. Paying such people more will be a much cheaper course of action than, for example, financing crop eradication programmes.

Today, virtually every nation has a drugs problem. It is perhaps the most significant cultural phenomena of the late twentieth century, affected by such diverse factors as the invention of new alkaloids, war or peace, demographic changes in society, adolescent cultural tastes, poverty, droughts and natural disasters, ethnic traditions, politics and disposable income levels. With such a range of causitory elements, anyone may be susceptible to drugs.

This begs the question: what can be done to counteract the problem? Legislation, crop replacement, informal and formal controls, medical advice and detoxification, advertising and educational campaigns, military campaigns and law enforcement have all failed. Prohibition does not work. Indeed, it promotes demand thereby increasing profit margins exacerbating the situation and encouraging organised crime, social destabilisation, violence and vice.

Perhaps one course of action would have been to follow the findings of the British 1895 Royal Commission on Opium in India, which suggested a society left to its own devices with opium eventually maintained an addict equilibrium which was not detrimental to the society as a whole. Addicts were not criminalised, opium was available, the price remained low and those habituated simply fed their habit and continued with their lives unburdened, as today's addicts are unable to do, by the constant need to search for their next fix and the money to pay for it.

Yet we are now too far along the road to heed this, pressures for strict legislation having irreversibly driven opium onto the wrong side of the law, leading to its replacement by more dangerous and insidious opiates, especially heroin. With opium now beyond the reach of government control and the excise-man, there is no real incentive, other than the moral or political one, to combat the trade. All profits nowadays go to the trafficker and not to the community at large as they did in the days of opium monopolies and taxation. The only money a government sees these days from opium is what is seized in money laundering, the only benefit to the economy at large being what filters through in the corruption of police, customs, military and narcotics bureau officials. This has little actual beneficial effect on the domestic economy for much of the proceeds of corruption finances luxury goods which are usually imported.

International organisations have a vital role to play: on occasion they are successful. Yet more often than not, they are affected by political expediency and treaties are reduced to the lowest common denominator governed by signatories' vested interests.

In the instance of entire administrations being involved in the trade, such as in Laos where it has been suggested military commanders and government officials are involved in opium and where the narcotics trade has become such an integral part of the economy it verges on government policy, international laws and conventions are utterly ineffectual. Even if the government itself is not involved, there have been many examples of individual government officials being involved and, even more, of their families' involvement: the sons of certain government officials seem especially vulnerable. Moreover, more often than not, national anti-narcotic agencies are primarily concerned with competing with each other to keep their own countries free of drugs. It is a self-defeating exercise, like throwing snails into the next door garden: when they have consumed the neighbour's vegetables, they will return. It is better to kill the snails.

Some countries do kill the snails. After the Communist take-over in 1949, China went from the status of a major consumer and producer to being opium-free, but there was a price to pay in the form of a totalitarian government which tightly governed every hour of its citizens' lives. Drugs were eradicated but so too were democracy and civil liberties. Perhaps this is the price the rest of the world must pay to rid itself of heroin and other drugs.

Even this is now unlikely to work for even those countries with draconian narcotics laws have failed to exterminate the problem. Malaysia can pass the death sentence for possession of just 15 grams of heroin. Singapore has the same penalty and 117 people have been executed there since the offence became punishable by death in 1955. All kind and condition of men have been caught: a Nigerian preacher, Sabinus Nkem Okpebie (*aka* Ibbinije Obasa Nepoleon) was arrested at Singapore's Changi airport *en route* from Jakarta to Lagos in 1993 and found to be in possession of two TV sets stuffed with 7.58 kilograms of heroin. He was hanged in May, 1995.

Both Malaysia and Singapore have succeeded in reducing domestic addict numbers but drugs are still smuggled from neighbouring Burma and Thailand. A British man convicted in the Philippines of smuggling 5 kilograms of heroin in 1995 was given a jail sentence of 35 years: he was lucky for the Philippines also execute serious drug offenders. Even Thailand, a producing and major trafficking nation, gives the death penalty for drug offences or at least 25 years' imprisonment, often much more. In 1993 an Australian, Michael Blake, was detained at Bangkok airport with 4.1 kilograms of heroin. His death sentence was commuted to 40 years' incarceration after he entered a guilty plea. Saudi Arabia has in recent years executed a growing number of couriers in transit through Jeddah, publicly beheading them. Indeed, so much heroin is currently coming through Saudi Arabia, virtually all of it carried by Pakistani swallowers that beheadings, usually held on Thursday and Friday afternoons have, since the summer of 1995, also taken place on Saturdays and Sundays.

The imprisonment or even the execution of traffickers does not go far towards solving the problem: others spring up ready to take their place. Placing addicts in gaol is similarly ineffective. It does not even necessarily cut them off from their habit. American prisons are notoriously infiltrated with drugs whilst a survey of British gaols in 1994 showed how urban gangs from London, Manchester and Liverpool had amicably monopolised the prison trade between them, making vast profits from heroin which was so highly cut as to barely register on analysis equipment: the British prison price is five times that of the street. Prison also introduces non-addicts to drugs: 60 per cent of convict addicts reported they acquired their addiction whilst in custody.

Prison budgets might be better spent on rehabilitation and treatment, inner city deprived area infrastructure improvements, job training for the unemployed, after-school recreation programmes to keep youngsters off the streets and summer employment to keep them busy in long school vacations, support for single mothers – the list is endless. Yet where such moves have been made, from Los Angeles to London, from Miami to Madrid, they have not achieved much. The problems are too vast, too complex and too deeply rooted in society to be overcome.

It is not just a matter of addressing deprivation or keeping idle hands at work. What really has to be addressed is an ingrained cultural attitude which may accept drugs as harmful but which sees them as a means of kicking against authority, an exciting alternative to a mundane life, a declaration of ethnic or class individuality. In short, drugs make a statement.

Perhaps it is society which is looking at drugs in the wrong way. Brian Inglis wrote in his 1974 book, *The Forbidden Game: A Social History of Drugs*:

> To punish drug takers is like a drunk striking the bleary face it
> sees in the mirror. Drugs will not be brought under control until
> society itself changes, enabling men to use them as primitive man
> did: welcoming the visions they provided not as fantasies, but as
> intimations of a different, and important, level of reality.

It should also be remembered it is not the drugs themselves but
how they are used which is the important point. As Frank Zappa,
the rock musician, put it: 'A drug is neither moral nor immoral –
it's a chemical compound. The compound itself is not a menace to
society until a human being treats it as if consumption bestowed
a temporary licence to act like an asshole.'

Some believe there is another antiphon. Their response is legalisation, distribution control and taxation. Treat heroin like alcohol:
use decriminalisation to bring down the price, distribution control
to standardise quality and tax revenue to combat the problem.
It is a handsome dream but impractical. One only has to see
under-age British children buying cigarettes in corner stores and
watch cross-Channel shoppers bringing in over-limit supplies of
wine and beer from French supermarkets, or observe American
youngsters dodging the under-21 restrictions in a liquor store, to
know the concept is flawed.

Where legalisation experiments have been tried, problems have
arisen. Amsterdam is an object lesson. All drugs are illegal in
the Netherlands, but the sale of certain amounts of soft drugs
is tolerated. Over 450 coffee shops in Amsterdam (with others
throughout the country) may openly sell cannabis, the idea being
to separate soft drug users from contact with the criminal pushers
of harder drugs. It is a failure. Amsterdam continues to have a
serious and escalating heroin and organised crime problem whilst
the Netherlands now has a registered addict population equal
to Britain's but in a population a fifth the size. This is hardly
surprising for statistics throughout the Western world would
show most addicts start on soft drugs and graduate to worse.
Another unfortunate result of this has been the development in
the Netherlands of a new travel industry, *narco-tourism*, whereby
tourists visit a country specifically to obtain drugs which are more
readily available than they are at home. Narco-tourism is also
increasing elsewhere – for example in Thailand and Vietnam,
especially in Cholon, Ho Chi Minh City's Chinatown – and

is expected to increase as tourism develops in Third World countries.

New initiatives are being suggested. In 1994, the association of British chief constables, admitting they were losing the war on heroin, demanded a radical government policy change. It was suggested registered addicts receive heroin and other required drugs free on the National Health Service, a royal commission be set up on drug control and a DEA-type national task force be implemented.

At the same time General Raymond Kendall, the head of Interpol, suggested drug use (but not trafficking) should be decriminalised with governments addressing themselves to the reduction of consumption. This may work: if demand on the streets of the West falls off, the trade will wither on the vine. Or, in this case, in the pod. The result of such suggestions is leading to increased redirection of resources towards educating the public as a whole against the physical, social and criminal dangers of drug taking. In the long term, this strategy may work, the culture of drug taking being undermined. Modern anti-drugs information and education campaigns, eschewing a patronising tone, avoid censuring drugs and instead suggest an awareness of what the would-be drug taker is embarking upon: facts not finger-wagging admonishments are considered a more effective deterrent. School-based schemes, such as Drug Abuse Resistance Education (DARE), which was begun in America but is being tried in other countries, concentrate on social skills such as how to resist peer group pressure.

There have to be short-term strategies as well. The best is to deprive narco-criminals of their narco-money. Others may include the removal of legal obstacles built into the constitutions of many democratic countries, depriving traffickers not only of their incomes but also their rights. Needless to say, civil liberties groups will complain bitterly but the response to such complaint is to ask for an alternative. All that can be hoped for is a modest improvement in the situation in the medium term. There will be no quick victories in the drugs wars.

The problems also extend beyond the confines of the legal or medical worlds. As has been shown, drugs are well and truly set on the political scene – and political expediency wins more often than enforcement officers. For example, in 1991 the CIA was reported to have warned President Bush the Syrian government was directly involved at every level in opium and hashish production in the Bekaa Valley: the amount earned was said to be nearly $1 billion per annum, or approximately 20 per cent of Syria's GNP. Bush chose to ignore this information in order to retain Syrian support during the Gulf War. This is just one instance of politics dominating overall national and international drug policies.

The only way to stamp out heroin is to eradicate all poppy growing – or would it? Synthetic opiates could one day take heroin's place: codeine has been manufactured artificially although it is not yet commercially viable. An added side to this argument comes from licit poppy growing nations and their pharmaceutical companies: they are quick to point out if all poppies are wiped out and only synthetics are created, this will give a huge protectionist boost to the American pharmaceutical industry which has held the patents for most of the synthetic drugs capable of replacing morphine and codeine registered in the last 25 years.

The development of certain types of poppy may help the situation. Modern commercial production of morphine from poppy straw uses a variation of *Papaver somniferum* with a high oil content but the morphine content of which can only be economically extracted by industrial processing. Another poppy, *Papaver bracteatum*, has been found to be a viable and rich source of thebaine, with up to 26 per cent of the dried latex consisting of this alkaloid: it may be converted into codeine and is the origin of 'Bentley Compounds' which form the basis for the manufacture of a range of powerful analgesics. Perhaps future commercial production could use this poppy for, being low on other alkaloids, *P. bracteatum* is unlikely to be of value to heroin producers.

Whilst research into alternative alkaloid sources grows apace, others are looking into the mechanisms of pain relief and opiate dependence. One recent study into the way the brain works in addiction suggest addictive behaviour is actually quite normal and only becomes problematical when it gets out of hand. The theory revolves around the supposition that humans have evolved a psychological and/or physiological reward system which makes us get hooked on whatever we need to survive. An addict's yearning for his drug, it is argued, is basically similar to the chocaholic's desire for Cadbury or Hershey bars.

Additional work at the cutting edge of pharmacological research, looking into the way the human brain functions, has discovered a system of substrates which are in effect naturally occurring opiate neurotransmitters produced by the brain itself. As chemical messengers, they carry signals between cells, are found to be the primary targets of opium and heroin and, it is suggested by some, may yet prove to be one of the mechanisms of memory. Ongoing psychopharmacological study is hoped to substantiate and explain the link between addiction and the chemical systems operating the brain.

A study by the Karolinska Institute in Stockholm has found that the greater the dose of opium-based painkillers absorbed by the placenta during childbirth, the greater the risk of the infant becoming an addict in later years. This is called *imprinting* – a specific physiological memory created during the highly sensitive period immediately after birth which can affect behaviour in adulthood. This might be why some people are more easily trapped into dependence when trying drugs under peer pressure. It may be we must reconsider the use of opiates as painkillers in childbirth.

Professor Edythe London, of the National Institute of Drug Abuse in Baltimore, is studying brain scans to see what happens when drugs are present in the bloodstream. She has discovered all drugs of abuse act in the same way, reducing the use of glucose over the cortex. Exploring trigger mechanisms for drug craving, she has also found increased activity in the region of the brain concerned with memory: even when detoxified, an addict's brain responds to memories associated with the former habituation. This research may lead to a new means of treating addiction, hopefully with some degree of permanence. Such a treatment could be a major step forward when one considers the impermanence of existing treatments from which only a minority attain lasting abstinence. It may even do away with the fear of withdrawal.

Alongside new pharmaceutical and pure medical research comes innovative applied studies. One such is a detoxification technique developed by a psychologist, Dr Juan Legarda, in Seville. He believes addicts should not and need not suffer during withdrawal, achieving this by accelerating the period of withdrawal by using powerful drugs whilst the addict is anaesthetised. His patients are sedated for about 8 hours during which time they are dosed with powerful opiate antagonists: these are chemicals which, in simple terms, locate themselves in receptors in the brain where they expel opiates. After treatment, the patient maintains a small daily dose of antagonists for six months: Dr Legarda claims a 70 per cent continued abstinence after six months. Although his technique is viewed with some scepticism in medical circles, where the risks of anaesthesia during detoxification are considered too high, some clinics are assessing the methodology of Dr Legarda's approach to see if they might adopt at least certain aspects of his treatment.

Drs Christopher Lowe, Neil Bruce and their team at the Institute of Biotechnology at Cambridge University have made a discovery of considerable potential assistance to law enforcement agents searching for heroin. They have found a bacterium, *Pseudomonas putida M10*, isolated from samples of industrial waste liquors collected from a pharmaceutical factory dealing in opiates, which exclusively utilises morphine as its carbon and energy source – in other words, morphine is its only food source. Possessing unique enzymes, the bacterium breaks down morphine and can at the same time affect certain dyes causing them to change colour. This property forms the basis for a very sensitive and immediate detector of the presence of heroin in minuscule quantities. It could be applied to 'sniff' for heroin much as explosives detectors recognise the presence of plastic explosives. If it was to prove successful, it could revolutionise the drive against the smuggler for postal packages, airline baggage and even vehicles could be quickly and effectively monitored.

A spin-off from the Lowe/Bruce research also contains considerable medical potential. Drugs synthesised from morphine, codeine and thebaine are complicated and expensive to make. They also generate highly toxic waste which has to be treated. The Cambridge team has discovered that when *Pseudomonas putida M10* feeds on morphine, hydromorphone naturally forms. This substance is one of the most powerful painkillers used today. It is six times more potent than morphine and less addictive but it is very costly to produce. If it can be made from a biotechnological process, the cost will be greatly reduced and it will therefore be more readily available. Quite possibly, there are other micro-organisms yet to be discovered which might also serve to provide bio-synthetically produced pharmaceutical products.

Traffickers can also be originative and they are always coming up with inventive ideas. One recent innovation, concerning cocaine trafficking, has yet to be used with heroin but illustrates their success. DEA agents call it 'The $1,000,000 Bathtub'. Cocaine in powder form is mixed into plastic and fibreglass resin which is then shaped into commercial goods such as bathtubs. These are then imported into the target country where the resin is chemically broken down and the cocaine relatively easily recovered. The resin is odourless and there is no way an enforcement agent can deduce the presence of the drug without chemically testing each fibreglass item. The DEA estimate tons of cocaine are currently being smuggled by this method.

Traffickers are also quickly benefiting from advances in technology. In recent years, the proliferation of mobile telephones has played into traffickers' hands by giving them versatile and often untraceable communication. Would-be clients can ring a mobile unit, positioned in empty premises, which is switched to call forwarding: the police may track down the location of the 'phone but not the destination of incoming calls. Stolen telephones can be cloned with a more recent development, masterminded by the Triads, leading to new generation 'smart' 'phone chips being manufactured illegally. This allows for a mobile unit (called a magic 'phone by the law enforcement agencies) to pluck a subscriber number out of the air, use it, discard it and randomly choose another. Unknowing and innocent 'phone owners foot the bill.

Recent cryptographical inventions enable information to be encrypted and sent via e-mail or bulletin boards through the Internet or World-Wide Web. Being encrypted, it can only be read by those for whom it is intended. This provides a fast, global means of secret communication which is a definitive boon to drug dealers as well as anyone else who wishes to conceal their activities from official agencies. In the face of such developments, the time may not be far off when secret service agents do not seek to decipher an enemy's military signals but those of international criminals and terrorists whom they chase not only in fast cars but also by surfing the Internet.

The estimated world annual turnover of the drugs trade is up to $750 billion, a far larger sum than is used by all the terrorist movements on earth put together, not to mention being infinitely greater than the budgets of all the enforcement agencies. Such vast sums of money not only give the drug barons enormous economic and political power but also finance a horrifying amount of crime all over the world.

It may seem an exaggeration yet it is not: the growth and size of the narcotics trade, which ruins the lives of millions of addicts annually, has the potential to be the greatest threat of all to society. Heroin addiction, the legacy of opium which was probably the first medicinal substance used by man, is here to stay, taking its place alongside poverty, racism and war in the sorry catalogue of insoluble human problems.

To every discovery mankind has ever made, from the lighting of the first fire to the splitting of the atom, there has been a good side and a bad side. Opium is no different. It can stop pain and, as Thomas Sydenham observed over 300 years ago, few doctors would be hard-hearted enough to practise medicine without it. Millions have been saved by it: yet it has also destroyed millions of lives, enslaved whole cultures and invidiously corrupted human society to its very core.

Bibliography

Books

Anger, Kenneth *Hollywood Babylon* – Arrow Books (London: 1986)

Ashley, Richard *Heroin: The Myths and the Facts* – St Martin's Press (New York: 1972)

Bard, Solomon *Traders of Hong Kong* – Urban Council, Hong Kong (Hong Kong: 1993)

Beeching, Jack *The Chinese Opium Wars* – Harcourt Brace Jovanovich (New York: 1975)

Berridge, Virginia & Edwards, Griffiths *Opium and the People* – Yale University Press (New Haven: 1987)

Bonavia, David *China's Warlords* – Oxford University Press (Hong Kong: 1995)

Booth, Martin *The Triads* – Grafton Books (London: 1990)

Boucaud, Andre & Louis *Burma's Golden Triangle* – Asia 2000 Ltd (Hong Kong: 1992)

Broomhall, Benjamin *The Truth about Opium Smoking* – Hodder & Stoughton (London: 1882)

Cameron, Nigel *An Illustrated History of Hong Kong* – Oxford University Press (Hong Kong: 1991)

Charters, Ann *Kerouac* – Andre Deutsch (London: 1974)

Coates, Austin *Macao and the British 1637–1842* – Oxford University Press (Hong Kong: 1988)

Cockburn, Leslie *Out of Control* – Bloomsbury (London: 1988)

Cocteau, Jean *Opium* – Peter Owen Ltd (London: 1957)

Collis, Maurice *Foreign Mud* – Faber & Faber (London: 1946)

Courtwright, David T. *Dark Paradise* – Harvard University Press (Cambridge, Massachusetts: 1982)

Criswell, Colin N. *The Taipans* – Oxford University Press (Hong Kong: 1991)

Criswell, Colin & Watson, Mike *The Royal Hong Kong Police (1841–1945)* – Macmillan (Hong Kong: 1982)

Culpeper, Nicholas *Culpeper's Complete Herbal* – Foulsham (London: 1976)

Cummings, John & Volkman, Ernest *Mobster* – Warner Books (London: 1992)

De Grazia, Jessica *DEA: The War Against Drugs* – BCA (London: 1991)

De Quincey, Thomas *The Confessions of an English Opium-Eater* – Bodley Head (London: 1930)

De Quincey, Thomas *Recollections of the Lakes and the Lake Poets* – Penguin (London: 1970)

De Ropp, Robert S. *Drugs and the Mind* – Gollancz (London: 1958)

Detzer, Eric *Monkey on my Back* – Abacus (London: 1990)

Downing, C. Toogood *The Fan-qui in China: 1836–37* – Henry Colburn (London: 1838)

Ehrenfeld, Rachel *Narco-terrorism* – Basic Books (New York: 1990)

Ellmann, Richard *Oscar Wilde* – Hamish Hamilton (London: 1987)

Fuller, Jean Overton *Déricourt: The Chequered Spy* – Michael Russell (Salisbury: 1989)

Gavit, John Palmer *Opium* – Routledge (London: 1925)

Gillingham, Paul *At the Peak* – Macmillan (Hong Kong: 1983)

Goldsmith, Margaret *The Trail of Opium* – Robert Hale (London: 1939)

Green, Timothy *The Smugglers* – Michael Joseph (London: 1969)

Greene, Graham *The Quiet American* – Heinemann (London: 1955)

Greene, Graham *Ways of Escape* – Bodley Head (London: 1980)

Hayter, Aleathea *Opium and the Romantic Imagination* – Faber & Faber (London: 1968)

Hobhouse, Henry *Seeds of Change* – Sidgwick & Jackson (London: 1986)

Hogshire, Jim *Opium for the Masses* – Loompanics Unlimited (Port Townsend, Washington: 1994)

Hunter, William C. *An American in Canton (1825–44)*, published originally as *The 'Fan Kwae' at Canton and Bits of Old China*, Derwent Communications (Hong Kong: 1994)

Inglis, Brian *The Opium War* – Hodder & Stoughton (London: 1976)

Kaplan, David E. & Dubro, Alec *Yakuza* – Futura (London: 1987)

Kemp, E.G. *Chinese Mettle* – Hodder & Stoughton (London: 1921)

Keswick, Maggie (ed) *The Thistle and the Jade* – Octopus Books (London: 1982)

Kohn, Marek *Narcomania: On Heroin* – Faber & Faber (London: 1987)

La Motte, Ellen Newbold *The Ethics of Opium* – Century (New York: 1924)

Lamour, Catherine & Lamberti, Michael R. *The Second Opium War* – Allen Lane (London: 1974)

Laurie, Peter *Drugs* – Penguin (London: 1967)

Lewin, Louis *Phantastica* – Kegan Paul (London: 1931)

Lewis, Eric *Black Opium* – Marshall (London: 1910)

McCoy, Alfred W. *Drug Traffic* – Harper & Row (Sydney: 1980)

McCoy, Alfred W. *The Politics of Heroin* – Lawrence Hill Books (New York: 1991)

Matthews, Peter (ed.) *The Guinness Book of Records: 1994* – Guinness Publishing (Enfield, Middlesex: 1993)

Mills, James *The Underground Empire* – Sidgwick & Jackson (London: 1987)

Morton, James *Gangland* – Little, Brown (London: 1992)

Musto, David S. *The American Disease* – Yale University Press (New Haven: 1973)

O'Brien, Joseph F. & Kurins, Andris *Boss of Bosses* – Simon & Schuster (New York: 1991)

Parssinen, Terry M. *Secret Passions, Secret Remedies* – Manchester University Press (Manchester: 1983)

Posner, Gerald L. *Warlords of Crime* – Macdonald/Queen Anne Press (London: 1988)

Pullinger, Jackie *Crack in the Wall* – Hodder & Stoughton (London: 1989)

Pullinger, Jackie (with Quicke, Andrew) *Chasing the Dragon* – Hodder & Stoughton (London: 1980)

Robinson, Jeffrey *The Laundrymen* – Simon & Schuster (London: 1994)

Robson, Michael *Opium: The Poisoned Poppy* – FormAsia Books Ltd (Hong Kong: 1992)

Rowntree, Joshua *The Opium Habit in the East* – P.S. King (London: 1895)

Schenk, Gustav *The Book of Poisons* – Weidenfeld and Nicolson (London: 1956)

Scott, J.M. *The White Poppy* – Heinemann (London: 1969)

Seagrave, Sterling *The Soong Dynasty* – Sidgwick & Jackson (London: 1985)

Seagrave, Sterling *Lords of the Rim* – Bantam (London: 1995)

Spencer, C.P. & Navaratnam, V. *Drug Abuse in East Asia* – Oxford University Press (Kuala Lumpur: 1981)

Steegmuller, Francis *Cocteau* – Macmillan (London: 1970)

Sterling, Claire *Crime Without Frontiers* – Little Brown (London: 1994)

Stockley, David *Drug Warning* – Optima (London: 1992)

Sultzberger, Hartmann Henry *All about Opium* – Wertheimer, Lea & Co. (London: 1884)

Taylor, Norman *Plant Drugs that Changed the World* – Allen & Unwin (London: 1967)

Terry, Charles E. & Pellens, Mildred *The Opium Problem* – Patterson Smith (New Jersey: 1970)

Thelwall, A.S. *The Iniquities of the Opium Trade with China* – Allen (London: 1839)

Waley, Arthur *The Opium War Through Chinese Eyes* – Allen and Unwin (London: 1958)

Ward, Iain *Sui Geng: The Hong Kong Marine Police 1841–1950* – Hong Kong University Press (Hong Kong: 1991)

Welsh, Frank *A History of Hong Kong* – HarperCollins (London: 1993)

White, Barbara-Sue *Turbans and Traders* – Oxford University Press (Hong Kong: 1994)

White, Edmund & Humphrey, John *Pharmacopedia* – Simpkin, Marshall, Hamilton, Kent & Co. Ltd (London: 1909)

(various) *The War Against Opium International Anti-Opium Association (Peking)* – Tsientsin Press (Tsientsin: 1922)

(various) *Findings and Recommendations of the Opium Investigation Commission appointed by the Philippine Commission: 1904*

(various) *Hong Kong 1995* – The Government Printer/Hong Kong (Hong Kong: 1995)

Booklets/pamphlets

Briefing Book: US Department of Justice Drug Enforcement Administration (September 1992)

Colombian Opiate Assessment: US Department of Justice Drug Enforcement Administration (June 1994)

The Geopolitical Drug Dispatch: (no. 42, April 1995; no. 45, July 1995; no. 46, August 1995)

Illicit Drug Trafficking and Use in the United States: US Department of Justice Drug Enforcement Administration (September 1993)

Money Laundering – Guidance Notes for Insurance Business: Office of the Commissioner of Insurance, Hong Kong Government (1995)

National Narcotics Intelligence Consumers Committee (NNICC) Report 1992: US Department of Justice Drug Enforcement Administration (September 1993)

National Narcotics Intelligence Consumers Committee (NNICC) Report 1994: US Department of Justice Drug Enforcement Administration (August 1995)

Opiate Trafficking in India: US Department of Justice Drug Enforcement Administration (February 1994)

Opium Poppy Cultivation in Southeast Asia: US Department of Justice Drug Enforcement Administration (September 1993)

Pakistan fights Narcotics Menace: Ministry of Information and Broadcasting, Government of Pakistan (1992)

Source to the Street: US Department of Justice Drug Enforcement Administration (September 1993)

Statistics of drugs seizures and offenders dealt with, United Kingdom 1992: The Home Office Statistical Bulletin (Issue 30/9, October 1993)

Worldwide Heroin Situation Report 1992: US Department of Justice Drug Enforcement Administration (March 1994)

Papers

Bruce, Neil C.; Caswell, Deborah A.; French, Christopher E.; Hailes, Anne M.; Long, Marianne T. & Willey, David L. 'Towards Engineering Pathways for the Synthesis of Analgesics and Antitussives' Annals of the New York Academy of Sciences: 2 May 1994

Bruce, Neil C.; Wilmot, Clare J.; Jordan, Keith N.; Stephens, Lauren D. Gray & Lowe, Christopher R. 'Microbial degradation of the morphine alkaloids' Journal of Biochemistry: volume 274, 1991

Bryant, Robert J. 'The manufacture of medicinal alkaloids from the opium poppy – a review of a traditional biotechnology' Chemistry and Industry: 7 March 1988

Lecky, Rhonda Anne 'Biotechnological Evaluation of *Papaver bracteatum* Cell Cultures': a thesis presented to the University of Dublin for the Degree of Doctor of Philosophy in Pharmacognosy (November 1991)

Journalistic sources

Bangkok Post (Thailand); *Eastern Express* (Hong Kong); *Hongkong Standard* (Hong Kong); *Independent on Sunday* (London); *Newsweek* (USA); *Observer* (London); *South China Morning Post* (Hong Kong); *Sunday Telegraph* (London); *Sunday Times* (London); *Time* (USA); *Washington Post* (USA)

Index

abcesses 150
acetic anhydride 77
aconite 60
Acosta, Dr 25
acupuncture 98
addiction
    babies born with addiction or disposition
        to drugs 83, 162, 349–50
    changing attitudes to 191
    child addicts 304, 308
    cures and treatments 91–101, 205–6, 350
    defined by World Health Organisation
        83
    famous addicts of Romantic period
        35–49
    famous addicts of 20th century 163–4,
        204–5, 206, 223–5
    moderage drug use 63, 88
    morphinism 72–6
    origins of heroin addiction 76–9
    physiological mechanisms 349–50
    social effects 340
    symptoms and types 83–91
    tolerance 19, 20–21, 25, 87–8
    withdrawal sickness 95–7
    history
        ancient Greece and Rome 19, 20–21
        Middle Ages 24–5
        Great Britain (1920s) 217–18
        Great Britain (1940s–60s) 220–21
        Great Britain (1970s–90s) 221–5, 322
        USA (1920s–30s) 199–203
        USA (1940s–70s) 203–8
        USA (1980s–90s) 208–9, 291
        see also China, *notably* 103–6, 140,

145, 148–9; Hong Kong, *notably*
    149–51
    present/recent addiction rates
        Afghanistan 310
        China 305–6
        France 321
        Germany 320
        Great Britain 224, 322
        Hong Kong 280, 308
        India 312
        Iran 312
        Italy 320
        Japan 308
        Mexico 327
        Netherlands 347
        Pakistan 310
        Russia 317
        Spain 320
        Thailand 262
        USA 207–9
        Vietnam 304
Addiction Research Centre (Lexington) 95
Adriatic 320
Aesculapeius 17, 28
Afghan (ship) 178
Afghanistan
    see also Golden Crescent, *notably*
        251–4, 288–9
    destinations of opium exports 222, 233,
        317, 318, 319
    and international controls 188–9, 312
    opium production 8, 310
Africa 102, 321, 323–4
African–American street gangs 330
Agent Orange defoliant 296

Agrippina, Empress 20
AIDS 14, 88, 304, 322, 331
Air America/Civil Air Transport (CAT)
    258, 261, 267, 267–8, 269
Air Laos Commerciale 266
'Air Opium' (American) see Air America
'Air Opium' (French) 266
Albania/ns 318, 319–20, 320 (bis), 329
alcohol
    alcoholism 76
    in heroin refining 78
    Prohibition 199
    Islam forbids 341
Aleppo 247
Alexander, Joseph Grundy 153, 156, 157
Algren, Nelson
    The Man With the Golden Arm 193
alkaloids
    definition and formation 4–5, 284
    discovery 67–9
    types 69, 70, 81–2
Albutt, Dr T. Clifford 74–5, 93
Allen and Hanburys 53
Alston, Dr 54
American Civil War 73–4, 102 (bis)-3
American Express 336
American Medical Association
    New and Non-Official Remedies (1906) 78
American War of Independence 191
Amoy 135, 176
amphetamines 88
Amsterdam 286, 309, 320, 347
anaesthetics 72, 98, 350
analgesics 351
Anderson, Winslow 195
anhalonium 216
Anslinger, Harry 204
Anti-Drug Abuse Act (US 1986) 207
Apalachin, 'godfathers' meeting 244
Apothecaries' Company 53
Apollinaire, Guillaume 218
Arabs 21–2, 103, 104 bis, 106
Arderne, John 26
Argentina 282, 336
Arif family 321
Armenia 317
arms dealing 307, 310, 316
'army disease' 73
Arnold, Dr Thomas 136
Arnot, Mr, quoted on poppies 54
Arrow (sailing vessel) 144
'Arrow War' 144–6
art/artists 35, 87, 215
Arunchal Pradesh 311
Asavahme, Vatana 304
aspirin (acetylsalcylic acid) 76
Assam 124, 186
asset-sharing 207

Assyrians 16 bis, 191–2
Asurbanipal, King 16
Atkinson's Infants' Preservative 61
Aubagne 248
Auric, Georges 218
Australia/ns
    Chinese in 177–8
    money laundering legislation 335
    smuggler caught 346
    syndicates 286–7, 309
    US troops in 272
Austria 337
Austro-Hungarians 181–2
Averroes 28
Avicenna 21, 23, 28
Awaji Naru, SS 231
Azerbaijan 317, 319

babies and infants
    born with addiction/disposition to
        drugs 83, 162, 349–50
    opiate-based soothers 61–2, 64, 186,
        192, 339
    used in smuggling 233, 234
baby milk companies 340
Bacon, Robert 94
Bactria 103
Bahamas 338
Baker, Ginger 223
Bakyan Mountains 300
bala goli (opium sweets) 186
Balkans 15
    Balkan Route 319–20, 320 (bis)
Ball, John 54
Baltimore 350
Balzac, Honoré de
    Comedie du Diable 70
Ban Hin Taek (Thailand) 277
Ban Houei Sai (Laos) 264, 271
banditry 161
Bangkok 176, 257, 262, 263, 267, 270, 274,
    275, 287, 295, 303, 331, 346
Bangladesh 302, 312
Bank for Credit and Commerce
    International (BCCI) 307
barbiturates 88, 205
Barbosa, Duarte 103
Barton, Dr 191–2
Basque Separatists (ETA) 319
Batholow, Dr R. 85
Battle of Chuenpi 134
Battle of Fatshan Creek 144
Battle of Hahlam Bay 143
Battle of Kowloon 134
Battley's Drops 46, 59
Baudelaire, Charles 48
Bayer Company 77, 271
Beardsley, Aubrey 215

Beddoes, Dr Thomas 42
Beijing (Peking) 147, 164
Beijing conference (1995) 306
Beirut 247–8
Bekaa Valley 313–14, 348–9
Belize 326
belladonna 94
Belon, Pierre 25
Benares 116
Bengal 8, 111, 115–16, 124
Bentley, Professor 82
'Bentley Compounds' 349
benzedrine 205
Berlin 309
Berlioz, Hector 48
Betsy (sloop) 111
Betts, Dr Thaddeus 191
Bias (Daya) bay 143
Binh Xuyen (syndicate) 266
Birdwood, Sir George 154
black people 200, 204, 220, 249, 274,
    320, 323
Black Sea area 15
Blake, Michael 346
Blandford, Marquis of 223
blood poisoning 150
Boggs, Eli 143
Bogota 236
Bogue forts 125, 126, 134–5, 143, 144
Bolivia 208
Bomanjee Hormusjee (ship) 141
Bombay 116, 151–2, 312
bomoh (Muslim doctors) 98
Boswell, James
    Life of Johnson 33–4
Boy George 223
Boyle, Robert
    The Skeptical Chymist 32
Brade, Professor 59
Brain, Sir Russell/Brain Report 221
'brat packers' 303
Brazil 326
Brent, Bishop Charles Henry 180
Brereton, W.H.
    The Truth About Opium 155
Bridgman, Elijah 132
Bridport 55
Brinks-Mat bullion robbery 225
Bristol 52, 225
Britannicus 20
British Medical Association 65
British Pharmacopoeia (19th century) 11–12
Brontë, Bramwell 48
'Brown Mixture', Dr Barton's 191–2
Browne, Sir Thomas 29
Browning, Elizabeth Barrett 46
Bruce, Dr Neil 350–1
Bruce, Lenny 84

Buchalter, Louis 244
Bucharest 320, 337
Buddhist priests 103
Bulgaria 188, 316, 319, 335
    Bulgarian Secret Service (KDS) 316
buprenorphine 99
Bureau of Drug Abuse Control (US) 206
Bureau of Narcotics and Dangerous Drugs
    (US) 206
Bureau of Prohibition (US) 201
Burma (Union of Myanmar) 259–61, 276–8
    See also Golden Triangle, *notably* 255–7,
        258–61
    Burmans 260
    early trade 103
    and international controls 188, 189,
        306, 312
    Master Plan for the Development of
        Border Areas and National Races 296
    opium smoking technique 13
    output 259, 296–7, 329
    programmes of crop eradication
        295–6, 342
    relations with Shan people *see* Shan
    State Law and Order Restoration
        Council (SLORC) 296, 298–9
Burroughs, William 205
    The Naked Lunch 227
Burton, Robert
    Anatomy of Melancholy 29
Bush, President 208, 348–9
Byron, Lord 48

Cabot, John 22
cadavers used in smuggling 233
caffeine 69, 340
Caine, Hall 47
Calcutta 116, 117
Cali cartel 325, 332
California 177, 191, 193, 197–8, 203, 237
calomel 46
Calpol 339
Cambodia (Kampuchea) 273, 275, 303, 306
Cambridge University Institute of
    Biotechnology 350–1
Canada 177, 220, 238–9, 248, 285, 309, 329
cannabis 42, 60, 104, 177, 189, 317, 347
Canton (Guangzhou)
    17th–18th centuries 107
    19th century 121–2, 125, 126, 129, 130,
        133–4, 135, 144
    20th century 168, 176, 279
Canton Register (newspaper) 142
Carbon Dioxide Therapy (CDT) 95
Carbone, Paul Bonnaventure 247
Caribbean 282, 326
Carleton, Billie 215–16
Caroline (ship) 143

cartels 325-7, 328, 332, 336
casinos 336
Castellano, Paul 330
castor oil 94
Castro, Fidel 326
Cavento, Joseph 69
Cayman Islands 307, 335
'centipedes' (Chinese river craft) 119-20
Central America 282, 326, 327
Central Asian republics 317
Central Commission for the Suppression of Opium, Chinese 162
Central Intelligence Agency see CIA
Ceres (goddess of fertility) 20
Cesari, Joseph 248, 250, 254
Chad 323
champagne 93
Chan Chi-fu see Khun Sa
Chan Tse-chiu ('Fast Eddie') 285
Chang, Brilliant 216, 217
Chang Chien (explorer) 103
Changi airport 345
Changteh (town) 159-60
Channel Tunnel 322
Channon, Olivia 223
charcoal, activated 78
Chart Thai Party 304
Chatterjee, Ramanamdra 186
Chaucer, Geoffrey 28-9
Chechnya 318, 320
Chefoo Convention 146
Chekiang province 147, 165
chemical fingerprinting system 222
Chen k'ou (town) 132
Chen Ping-chun (spy) 134
Chennault, General Claire 258
Chiang Ching-kuo, President 259, 276
Chiang Hsiao-wu (Alex Chiang) 276
Chiang Kai-shek, Generalissimo 165-6, 167, 187, 256, 258, 259
Chiang Mai (town) 275-6, 277, 331
Chicago 197
Ch'ien Lung, Emperor 112
Chien Sha Tsin (village) 133
Chile 282
China
  Imperial China 103-37, 139-58
    early history 103-5
    17th-early 19th centuries 105-27
    First Opium War (1840-42) 134-7
    Second Opium War (1856-60) 144-6
    19th-early 20th centuries 139-58
    traditional opium smoking 11-13, 105-6
    attempts to eradicate opium 109-10, 113, 118, 127-34, 149, 157, 180-81
    (non-drugs) imports and exports listed 108

Chinese Republic 158-73
  Criminal Code 162
  and international controls 183, 187, 258
  Sino-Japanese War (1937) 163-5
  opium exports 204, 230, 240, 244, 302
  production and use of heroin 305-7
  Triads see own heading
Chinese expatriots
  in America 177, 178-9, 193-4, 197-8, 329
  in Asia 239
  in Britain 211-13, 215, 217, 220
  in Burma 302
  in Hong Kong 254, 279
  in Italy 309, 320
  in Shan states 296-7
  in Thailand 280
  world-wide networks 309-10
China Inland Mission 148
China Year Book quoted 185
Chinese Imperial Maritime Customs 145-6
Chinese Passengers Act (UK 1855) 176
Chinese People's Liberation Army (PLA) 263, 307
Chinese Repository, The (journal) 89
Chinchow bay 123
Chiu Chau Triads 278-87, 297, 306, 309
chlorates 68
Chlorodyne 60, 65
chloroform 60, 72, 78
cholera 58, 60
Chowning, Mrs 235-6
Christison, Professor 63
Ch'u Hsien (town) 161
Chui A-pou (pirate) 143
Churchill, Lord Randolph 75
CIA (Central Intelligence Agency)
  and Afghanistan 289
  and French Connection 246-7
  and Middle East 315
  and Nicaragua 327
  and Sicily 245-6
  and Syria 348-9
  and Yakuza 287
  involvement in money laundering 316, 338
cigarettes with heroin 272
CIS see USSR
Clapton, Eric 223
Clarke, Dr Abel 106
Clendenyn (first white opium smoker) 194
Clifton, Captain William 117-18
clinics 200, 202, 205-6, 221
Clinton, President 339
clippers 120, 122, 142, 117-18
Clive, Baron Robert, of India 30, 111

Co-Hong merchants *see* Hong merchants
Cobain, Kurt 223
Coca-Cola 192
coca-leaf chewing 189
cocaine
    in Coca-Cola 192
    Cuba's involvement 326
    legislation 182
    smuggling 209, 351
    used to promote heroin sales 329
    used with heroin 88, 165, 331
Cocteau, Jean 13, 218
codamine 81
codeine 4, 8, 70, 81–2, 229, 349
Coleridge, Samuel Taylor 35–6, 41–5, 46
    Kubla Khan 44, 45
    Lyrical Ballads 36
    The Rime of the Ancient Mariner 44, 45
Collins, Wilkie 46–7
    Armadale 47
    No Name 47
    The Moonstone 47
Collins, William 46
Collis, Maurice 123
Cologne 309
Colombia/ns
    cartels 325–7, 328, 332, 336
    and Cuba 326–7
    in Europe 320
    heroin production 324–5
    and money laundering 336, 337
    quality of heroin 288
    US aid to 208, 343
Colombian National Liberation Army 325
Colombian Revolutionary Armed Forces 325
Columbine HMS 143
Columbus, Christopher 22
Committee on Drug Addiction (US) 201
Commodus 19
Commonplace Book of an Apothecary of Great Dunmow 27
communications 352
Communism
    Burma 276
    China 345
    France 247
    US fear of 245, 257–8, 289–90, 339
computers used to fight smuggling 240–41
concubines 104
condoms used in smuggling 235, 236
Conference on the Limitation of the Manufacture of Narcotic Drugs (Geneva 1931) 184
Conference Shanghai (1909) 196–7
Conference for the Suppression of the Illicit traffic in Dangerous Drugs (1936) 184
Constantinople 10, 52
constipation 63, 74

Continental Air Service (CAS) 268
Continental King Lung Commodities Group 285
Controlled Substance Act (US) 206
Convention Against Illicit Traffic in Narcotic Drugs and Psychotropic Substances (1968) 189
Convention of Chuenpi 134–5
Convention of Peking 145
Convention on Psychotropic Substances (1971) 189
coolies 175–9, 193–4
Cooper, James Fenimore 117
Cornelius Nepos 20
Cornwallis, HMS 135
'Corset Gang' 286–7
Corsicans
    allied with CIA 245
    in France 239
    and French Connection 247–8, 249, 251, 254
    and South-east Asia 265, 266–7, 278
Cottle, William 43
'Count, the' (Hollywood) 201
couriers 238, 323, 333
Coventry 61
Cowley, Dr John 55
Crabbe, George 40–41, 88
    Peter Grimes 40–41
crack cocaine 331
Cream (pop group) 223
Crimean, SS 54
Crimean War 74
Criminal Justice (International Co-operation) Act (UK 1991) 335
crop-substitution *see under* poppies
Crow, Mr (Hong Kong) 150–51
Crowley, Aleister
    Diary of a Drug Fiend 216
Crumpe, Dr Samuel
    Inquiry into the Nature and Properties of Opium 33
Crusaders 22
cryptographical inventions 352
cryptopine 81
Cuba 246, 326–7
Culiacan 203
Culpeper's Complete Herbal 59
Curlew, HMS 118
Cutty Sark (clipper) 117
cyclazocine 95
Cyprus 311, 319–20, 321
Czech republic 319

Daily News 211
Danang (port) 304
Danes 121
Dangerous Drugs Act (UK 1920) 217

Dangerous Drugs Act (UK 1967) 221
database of global opium production
    (1924) 183
Davis, Sir John 136, 141
Davy, Sir Humphrey 42
Day, Horace
    The Opium Habit 74
De Quincey, Thomas 36–40, 48 *bis*, 62–3, 91
    Confessions of an English Opium-eater
        quoted 36, 37, 39
    quoted on Coleridge 43 *bis*
de Ropp, Dr Robert S.
    Drugs and the Mind quoted 96–7
        DEA (Drug Enforcement
            Administration) 206–9
    and Bekaa Valley 314, 315
    and cocaine 351
    Demand Reduction Program 207
    Heroin Signature Program 329
    and Golden Triangle 276, 282, 288
    Kingpin strategy 334
    and Mafia 330
    pricing structures published by 331–2
    and Vietnam 304–5
death penalty for drugs offences
    Burma 301
    China 126–7, 158, 169, 234, 304
    Iran 253
    Mong Tai Army 297
    Saudi Arabia 346
    Thailand 345–6
    USA 203
    Vietnam 304
Declaration of Basle 335
Defence of the Realm Act (DORA) 217
Demand Reduction Program (DEA) 207
Demeter, cult of 17
Deng Xiaoping 215
Dent & Co. 116, 118, 130–31, 142
Dent, John 130–31
dependence *see* addiction
Depository Institution Money Laundering
    Amendment Act (US 1990) 334
Dericourt, Henri 266
Derosne (pharmacist) 67–8
    'Sel narcotique de Derosne' 68
detoxification 350
Detzer, Eric
    Monkey on my Back 87
dextropropoxyphene 82
diacetylmorphine *see* heroin
Diagoras of Melos 17
diarrhoea 58, 60, 73
diascordium 26
Dick, Philip K. 84
Dickens, Charles
    The Mystery of Edwin Drood 213
Dictionary of National Biography, British 137

Dionysius of Syracuse 20
Dioscorides 17, 28
Disraeli, Benjamin
    Sybil 115
Dixon, W.E. 93
Dobell, Captain 113
doctors
    British medical profession 220, 221 *bis*
    'dope doctors' 198
dogs
    addicted to opium 83
    sniffer 241–2, 304, 323
Dole, Vincent 97
dolophine hydrochloride 97
Dominican Republic/Dominicans 326–7, 330
Dover 52, 321
Dover, Thomas 27–8
    Ancient Physician's Legacy to his Country 28
    Dover's Powder 27–8, 60
Downing, Dr C. Toogood 119, 128
Doyle, Sir Arthur Conan
    The Man with the Twisted Lip 214–15
Dreser, Heinrich 77
Drug Abuse Prevention and Control Act
    (US 1970) 206
Drug Abuse Resistance Education
    (DARE) 348
Drug Enforcement Administration *see* DEA
drug barons 239, 327
    see also cartels, Mafia, Triads, Yakuza
drugs
    see also cocaine, hashish, heroin,
        marijuana, morphine, opium
    classification of 221–2, 229–30
    global problem 339–53
        cultural aspects 342
        international drugs control 179–90
        legalisation experiments 347
        use of computers 240–41
        use of military technology 242
        world annual turnover 352
Drugs Supervisory Body (UN) 188
Drugs Trafficking Offences Act (UK 1986)
    222, 334
Dryden, John
    MacFlecknoe 29–30
Dubai 252
Dundee 222
Durres 320
Dutch *see* Netherlands/Dutch
Dutch Antilles 335
dwale (potions) 26
dysentery 58, 60, 104, 135
Dyson, Edward
    story of Mr & Mrs Sin Fat 178

East Germany 315
East India Company 109–17, 124–5

East Indiamen (ships) 117
East Indies 11, 182
Ebers, Georg Moritz 16
Ecstasy 84
Ecuador 288, 326
Edinburgh 55
Egypt/Egyptian opium
    ancient 10, 15, 16, 18
    16th–19th centuries 25, 33, 53–4
    present day 323
Eight Regulations 107, 108
El Paso 328
Elausis 17
Elbasan province (Albana) 318
electro-stimulation 98
Elgin, Lord 144–5
Elliot, Captain Charles 126, 127, 131–7 *passim*
Ely 56, 57
emaciation 74
enemas 71, 94
Enfield 55
'English opium' 56
Epidaurus 17
Equatorial Guinea 324
Erasistratus 17
Escobar, Pablo 325, 343
Ethiopia 323
ethnic cleansing 296
etorphine 82
Europe, Eastern 316, 318, 337
European Union 239, 309, 322, 335

Faithfull, Marianne 223
'Farmers' Bank (China) 167
Federal Bureau of Investigation (FBI) 245, 326, 330
Federal Bureau of Narcotics (FBN) 202–6 *passim*
Federal Narcotics Control Board (US) 201
Fen country 56–8
Feng Yu Hsiang, General 159–60
Ferguson (instrument maker) 72
film industry 197, 200, 216–17
financy *see* prices and profits
Fiori, Etienne 167
Five Dragons Corporation 285
Florida 191
Flynn, Errol
    My Wicked, Wicked Ways 197
Foochow (Fuzhou) 92, 135
Forbes (soldier of fortune) 118–19
Formosa *see* Taiwan
France/French
    see also French Connection
    colonial rule 121, 257, 264–6
    drugs production 244, 294
    heroin consumption 321

Francisi, Bonaventure 'Rock' 266
Franco-Prussian War 74
Frankau, Lady Isabella 221
Frankfurt 309
Franklin, Benjamin 30
Freitag, Dr John 32
French Connection 246–51, 254, 288, 317
French Connection, The (film) 249
French Expeditionary Corps 266
Friend of China, The (magazine) 153
Froggatt, Dr Clive 224–5
Fu Manchu stories/films 216–17
Fukien province 128, 147, 176
Fury, HMS 143

Galen 19, 28
Gambino, Giuseppe (Joe) 330
Gandhi, Mahatma 186, 187
Ganges plain 9
gangsters 243–54
    see also Mafia, Triads, Yakuza
Garcia, Jerry 223–4
Garcias ab Horto 25
Garraway's Coffee House 52
Gay-Lussac, Joseph Louis 69
Gaza Strip 314
General Quiroga (ship) 118
Geneva 188
George III 112
George IV 30
Georgia 319
Germany 52, 182, 320
Ghana 321, 323
Ghazipur 9–10
    Government Opium and Alkaloid Factories 293
Giacomelli, Giorgio 294–5
Gibraltar 52, 321
Gillman, Dr 44
Gladstone 75, 136, 156
Glasgow 225
Globus company 316, 338
glycerides 7
gnoscopine 81
Goa 25, 107, 113
Godfather films 244
Godfrey's Cordial 61
Golden Crescent 251–4, 288–90, 295, 310–12, 319, 320, 321, 329, 332
Golden Triangle 255–88, 290, 295, 296–305, 308–9, 321, 329
    profits and money laundering 331–2, 338
Goldsmith, Margaret
    The Trail of Opium 165
Gordon, Waxey 244
Gotti, John 330
Grateful Dead (pop group) 223

Great Britain
  14th century 26
  Victorian times 51–66
    anti-opium movement 152–8
    attempts to grow British opium 54–6
    colonial opium trade 51–2, 107, 115,
      121, 125–6, 136, 176, 185, 257,
      259–60, 339, 344; see also Hong Kong
    invention of hypodermic syringes 71–2
    morphine manufacture and use 70, 161
  late 19th century to present 211–225
  present day
    heroin addiction 224, 322
    smuggling 237–8
    source countries and prices 321–2
    war against drugs 207, 222, 334–5,
      346, 348
Greece/Greeks
  ancient 16, 19, 21
  modern 121, 188, 244, 246, 319–20
Green Gang 165, 166, 279
Greene, Graham 219–20
  The Quiet American 219–20
  Ways of Escape 219
Gregory, Sandra 235
Guadeloupe 249
Guam 288
Guangdong province 306
Guangxi province 307
Guangzhou see Canton
Guatemala 326
Guerini, Antoine and Barthelemy 247, 249
Guerrero 336
Guinness Book of Records 242
Gujarat state 151–2
Gulf War 349
Gutzlaff, Dr Karl 122–3, 134
Hague Conference (1911) 181–2, 198, 217
Hainan Island 143
Haiphong 304
Haiti 327
Hali 28
Hall, Robert 30
Halliday, Billie 87
Hamburg Codex 27
Han Shao-ch'iung, Rear Admiral 120
Hankow 163, 187
Hannibal 20
Hanoi 304
Hanover 68
Hansen, Juanita 201
Harlem 208, 249
Harper's Magazine 192
Harrison, Francis Burton 198
Harrison Narcotic Act (US 1914) 198,
  201–2, 243
Harvey, William 71
hashish 18–19, 22, 189, 313, 349

Hastings, Warren 111–12
Hau Fook Company 151
Hawaii 287, 288
Hawkins, Dr 57–8
Hekmatyar, Gulbuddin 289
Hell's Angels 309
Helmland Valley (Afghanistan) 310
hemp 106
henbane 24, 42
hepatitis 150, 331
herbal medicine 98
Hero of Alexandria 71
heroin
  see also addiction, smuggling
    and arms 312
  change-over from opium use 197–8, 220,
    262, 269, 279–80
  compared with other drugs/alkaloids
    82, 90–91, 222
  discovery and early development 76–9
  effects 79, 84–5
  manufacture 77–8
    'heroin mills' 249
    substances used for cutting 203, 332
  medicinal use 182
  methods of taking 14, 331
    in 'cocktails' 88, 165
    elixir and pastilles 78
    mixed with marijuana 271
    mixed with tobacco 269, 271
  prices and profits 225, 322, 331–2, 339–40
  supposed cure for morphine addiction
    78, 91
  types and trade names
    Double UOGlobe 271, 274, 307
    'Mexican black tar' 327, 332
    'Mexican brown' or 'Bugger' 327
    No 3 grade 270, 280, 283–4, 308, 312
    No 4 grade 270, 271, 272, 274, 283–4,
      286, 306, 308, 316
Heroin Baby Trial 234
Heroin Highway' (US Interstate 25) 328
Heroin (pop song) 223
Heroin Signature Program (DEA) 207
Hezbollah 315
Hill, Dr John
  Family Herbal 33
Hippocrates 18, 28
hippy trail 252
Hiro Saga (court lady) 163
Hmong tribe 256, 264–9 passim
Ho Chi Minh 265
Ho Chi Minh City 302–3, 345
  see also Saigon
Ho Mong (town) 297, 301
Ho Su-cho (merchant) 169
Hobson, Richard P. 202–3
Hokkien Chinese 309

Holbeach 57
Hollywood *see* film industry
Homer 8–19, 42
Honam 121
Honecker, Erich 315
Hong (Co-Hong) merchants 107–8, 121, 125, 129, 130, 131, 135
Hong Kong
  ceded to Britain 135, 137
  colony from 1842–1945: 139–44, 145, 149–51, 158, 169–73, 230
  during Second World War 173, 187
  since Second World War
    addiction 98, 99–101, 308
    heroin refining 254, 270–71
    money laundering 286, 307, 334, 335
    multinational corporations 122
    police force 281, 285–6, 307
    smuggling and Triad activities 235, 236, 238, 267, 279–86, 307–9
Hong Kong Precious Stone Company 284
Honolulu 287
Hooghly River 117
Hooper's Anodyne 192
House of Commons Home Affairs Commitee 224
Howard, Dr Harvey J.
  Ten Weeks with Chinese Bandits 161
Howison, Dr 55
Howqua (merchant) 108, 127, 130
Hsien Feng, Emperor 145
Hu Tim-heng (businessman) 273
Hua To (surgeon) 104
Huang Yu-pu (official) 106
Hugo of Lucca 26
Human Wreckage (film) 201
Hunan 158
Hungary 319, 335
Hunter, Dr Charles 72
Hunter, Dr Henry Julian 57
Hunter, William C. 127
  The 'Fan Kwae' at Canton 129
Huxley, Aldous 84
  Brave New World 218
hydrocotarnine 81
hydromorphone 351
hyoscyamus 94
hypodermic syringes 71–2, 73, 74–6, 78, 150, 192, 200

Immobilon (M99) 82
imprisonment 346
Independent Commission Against Corruption (Hong Kong) 281, 285–6
India
  opium
    traditional growing and use 7, 8–10, 11
    types and quality 33, 109, 116, 148, 187

    legal production 188, 293–4
    illicit production 295, 311–12
  history of opium trade
    early centuries 22, 103–4
    colonial times 107, 109, 110–13, 115–16, 120–21, 124, 141–2, 151–2, 153, 156, 157–8, 183, 185–7
    Gandhi's anti-opium campaign 186, 187
India Act (UK 1833) 124
Indian Opium Agency 158
  Indo-China 11, 105, 164–5, 180, 247, 248, 254, 262, 266
  Indo-China War, First (1946–54) 265
infant mortality rates 65
Infant's Friend, The (syrup) 192
Inglewood (ship) 177
Inglis, Brian
  The Forbidden Game: A Social History of Drugs 346–7
inhalation 71
Institute de France 68
Inter-Departmental Commission on Drug Addiction (UK 1958) 221
Internal Revenue Service (US) 202
International Anti-Opium Association 160
International Convention (1931) 246
International Narcotics Control Board (INCB) 188–9, 305
  Strategy Report (1994) 295
International Opium Commission (1909) 181
International Opium Conference (1924) 183
Internet 352
Interpol (International Police Commission) 240, 348
IRA 319
Iran
  countries supplied by 222, 228, 258, 318
  opium production – legal 188
  opium production – illicit 251, 252–4, 289, 312
  and terrorism 314
Iraq 315
Ireland 54
Irish-American gangs 319
Isfahan 10, 21
Islam *see* Muslims
isoquinoline alkaloids 81
Israelis 329
Istanbul 319
Italy/Italians 52, 200, 239, 249, 251, 316, 319–20

J. Collis Browne's Mixture 60
Jaafar, Khaled 315
Jamaicans 330
Jamesina (brig) 118

Japan
  drug use 308
  drug smuggling to China 161, 163, 164, 168, 187, 230
  money laundering 335
  in Second World War 173, 258, 261, 287
  and tobacco smoking 105
  Yakuza 283, 287–8, 310
Jardine, William 114–15, 131
Jardine Matheson & Co. 114, 115, 116, 118, 122–3, 141, 142, 151
Java 105 bis, 107
jazz clubs 220
Jeddah 346
Jehan, Jean 249
Jersey 322
Jewish dealers 200, 244–5, 249
Jibril, Ahmed 315
John Biggar (ship) 123
John Calvin (ship) 176
John of Gaddesden 28
Johnson, Dr Samuel 33–4
Johnstone, Revd James 152
Jones, Dr John 30–32, 35
  Mysteries of Opium Reveal'd 30–32
Jones, Thomas 55
Joplin, Janis 223
Jordan, Sir John 159
Journal der Pharmacie 68
Juanita Hansen Foundation 201

Ka Kwei Yei (KKY) militia 261, 264, 298
Kabay, Janos 8, 294
Kabul 252
Kachin tribe 256, 260
  Kachin Independent Army (KIA) 260
  Kachin Liberation Army (KLA) 260
Kai Tak airport 303
K'ang Hsi, Emperor 107
Karachi 311
Karen tribe 260, 299
  Karen National Union (KNU) 260
Karolinska Institute (Stockholm) 349–50
Kazakhstan 317
Keats, John 46
Kemp, E.G. 159–60
Kendall, General Raymond 348
Kenya 323
Kerouac, Jack 204–5
  On the Road 205
Kerr, Dr Norman 76
KGB, former 318
Kho Phan Gan island 303
Khun Sa 263–4, 264, 276–8, 297–302, 341
Khyber pass 311
Kia King, Emperor 110
Kiangsu province 165
King, C.W. 132–3

Kingpin strategy (DEA) 208, 334
Kingsley, Charles
  Alton Locke 57
Kintex/KoKintex 316, 338
Koechlin, Consul-general 167
Kokang district 296–7, 302
Kolb, Dr Lawrence 85
Kong island 135
Koo, Mme Wellington 167
Koreans 164, 165
Kowloon 99–101, 133, 284
Kriangsak, General 275
Kronprinzessin Cecilie (ship) 228–9
Kung, Prince 145 bis
Kunming 305
Kuomintang (KMT) 162, 165, 168, 256–64 passim, 275–6, 282
Kurdish areas 312
Kut Sang, SS 230
Kwangtung province 128, 142, 147, 176
Kweichow 162
Kyi, Aung San Suu 296
Kyrgyzstan 317

La Marr, Barbara 201
La Motte, Ellen
  The Ethics of Opium 185
Ladies' Sanitary Association 64
Lafargue, Dr 71
Lagos 323
Lahore 311
Lahu tribe 256, 260, 269
  Lahu National Liberation Army (LNLA) 260
Laloy, Louis
  Le Livre de la Fumée 218
Lancet, The 75
Lang Son area 304
Lanrick (clipper) 142
Lansky, Meyer 244, 245
lanthopine 81
Lao Development Air Service 268
Laos 13, 83, 188, 237, 295, 302, 306, 345
  see also Golden Triangle, notably 265–9
  Laotian Opium Administration 267
Laredo 236
Larne, HMS (sloop) 131
Las Vegas 336
Lascars 119
Latin America/ns 121, 204, 248, 249, 320
laudanine 81
laudanosine 81
laudanum
  compared with morphine 73
  types
    Battley's drops 46, 59
    Josephi Michaelis 27
    Paracelsus's 23–4, 29

Sydenham's 26–7
users, famous 30, 36, 42, 44, 46, 47, 57–8, 59, 63, 64, 75, 213
LaVerne, Dr Albert A. 95
League of Nations 183, 184, 188, 228
Advisory Committee on . . . Opium 183, 187, 229, 242
Lebanon 247–8, 313–17 passim, 321 bis, 329
'Lebanese Gold' (hashish) 313
Lee, Christopher 216–17
Lee, Harper
To Kill a Mockingbird 192–3
Lee Sing Company 185
Leigh, John
Experimental inquiry into the properties of opium 67
Lester, Muriel 164
Levant Company 51, 52
Levinstein, Dr Edward
Die Morphiumsucht (The Morbid Craving for Morphia) 75, 93
levomethadyl acetate 99
Lewin, Professor Louis
Phantastica 91–2
Li Mah (gangster) 223
Li Ting
The Introduction to Medicine 104
Li Wen-huan, General 275–6, 277, 282–3
Liberia 323
Libya 314
Liechtenstein 335
Lima 179
Lin Chien-pang (gangster) 300
Lin Mingxian (communist leader) 302
Lin Tse-hsu (commissioner) 129–37
Lin Wei-hsi (peasant) 133, 135
Linnaeus 1
linolic acid 7
Lintin Island (Neilingding Dao) 117, 118–20, 125, 126, 139
Lintin (ship) 118
Liquifruita Medica 65
Lisu tribe 256
Little, E.S. 158
Liverpool 52, 346
Lo Hsing-han (warlord) 298, 299, 302
Lo Hsing-min (warlord) 298, 299
Lockerbie bombing 314
'Loimaw bandits' see Mong Tai Army
London 52–3, 215, 217, 225, 309, 346
London Pharmacopoeia (1788) 27
London, Professor Edythe 350
Ling Binh 271
Long Sutton 61
Long Tieng 268, 271
Longfellow, Henry 49
lorchas (sailing vessels) 144

Los Angeles 197, 287, 309
Louisa (cutter) 126
Lowe Countries 52
Lowe, Dr Christopher 350–1
LSD (lysergic acid diethylamide) 88, 95
Luciano, Charles 'Lucky' (Salvatore C. Luciana) 244–5
Ludlow, Fitzhugh 192
Lugard, Sir Frederick 170
Lui Lok, Sergeant 285
Luxembourg 335
Lysis 20–21
Lytton, Bulwer 47, 48

M50/50 (Revivon) 82
M99 (Immobilon) 82
Ma Sik-chun ('Golden Ma') 282–3
Ma Sik-yu ('White Powder Ma') 282–3
Macartney, Lord 112
Macau
foundation of colony 106–7
in colonial times 109, 110, 113, 122, 123, 125, 131, 133, 134, 185
money laundering 336
opium smoking 162–3, 308
opium smuggling 230
McCarthy, Senator 204
McCoy, Alfred W.
The Politics of Heroin in Southeast Asia 245–6, 257
Macedonia 319, 320
Macfarlan Smith & Co. 82
MacKay, Captain 123
Madagascar 311
Madhya Pradesh 293
Madras 116
Madrid 320
Mafia
American 239, 243–51, 278, 290
associates of 254, 282, 283, 284, 287, 325
money laundering by 336
smashing of 330
in Armenia 317
in Australia 309, 320
in Balkans 320
in Russia and CIS 317–18
Italian 249, 251, 309, 320
Ndrangheta 320
Sacra Corona Unita 320
Sicilian 243–4, 290, 314, 316, 320
Sicilian Connection 250
Magellan, Ferdinand 22
Magendie, François 69–70
Formulary for . . . Several New Remedies 69
Mahaban Mountains 251, 255
Maimi 248–9
Malacca 103, 111

malaria 73, 107, 135
Malaya/Malaysia
  addiction cure 98
  coolie immigrants in Malay peninsula
    175–7
  legislation 335, 345
  Malayan in De Quincey's dreams 39
  revenue 185
  Triads in 254, 286
Mallinckrodt Laboratories 97
Malta 52
Malwa 107, 113
Manchester 225 bis, 309, 346
Manchester Guardian 164
Manchu Penal Code 133
Manchuria 161, 163, 230, 287
Mang Tang Wu (village) 270
Manila 180
Mao Zedong, Chairman 165, 256, 279, 305
Maratha states 107
Marcus Aurelius 19
marijuana 205, 271, 272–3
Marseilles 246–8, 249, 250, 266, 278, 290, 321
Martinique 249
Massacre of Innocents, The (tract) 64
Matheson, Donald 115
Matheson, James 114–15, 118, 124, 128,
  131, 141
Mauritius 311
May, Earl of 63
Mayer, Surgeon Major Nathan 73
Mazatlan 203
Mazeppa (clipper) 142
Mecone (city of poppies) 17
meconic acid 4, 68, 69
meconidine 81
meconion 18
Medellin cartel 325
Melbourne 178
Merck (chemist) 70
Merope (ship) 118
mescaline 205
Mesopotamia 15
methadone 82, 97–8, 205
methedrine 88
Mexico
  crop eradication 288, 327
  'Mexican federation' (drug barons) 328
  Mexicans in Guatemala 326
  money laundering 336
  opium output 295
  quality and types of Mexican drugs 203,
    327, 329
  smuggling to USA 231–2, 238, 328,
    330, 336
Miami 197, 324
Middle East 232, 244
Milan 320

missionaries
  Christians linked to opium 145
  Jackie Pullinger 99–101
  Jesuits 105, 107
  Karl Gutzlaff 122–3, 134
  others 123–4, 132, 148–9, 152
Misuse of Drugs Act (UK 1971) 221–2
Mitcham 56
Mithridates 19
mithridatum 19, 26
Mogul Empire 22, 110–11
Mon tribe 260
  Mon National State Army (MNSA) 260
money laundering 332–8
  Britain 334–5
  Bulgaria 316
  Cali cartels 332
  Eastern Europe 337
  'Fast Eddie' 285
  Lebanon 314
  Milan 320
  Pakistan 337
  Puerto Rico 326
  USA 334, 338
  world legislation 334–5
  Yugoslavia, former 337
Mong Tai Army (MTA) 297, 299, 301
Mongolia 305
monopolies 142, 151, 169, 173, 176, 180,
  185, 265, 267, 280
Montauk, SS 231
Moore, Dr William J. 156
Morocco 321
Morpheus (god of sleep) 69
morphine
  999 trademark 267
  addiction 74–6, 161–2
  bacterium that eats it 350–1
  comparisons
    morphine content of types of opium 51
    morphine and other alkaloids 81–2
    morphine and other drugs 90–91, 222
  controls 181–2
  description 4
  discovery 68–70
  heroin preferred to 220
  medicinal use 60, 61, 69–70, 73–4, 81–2, 182
  methods of taking
    in 'cocktails' 165
    injection 150–51, 196
    pills 161–2
  name 69
  poisoning by 70
  preferred to opium 197
  production 8, 349
  products used in cutting 203
  quantities produced 228, 294
  smuggling 180, 234, 247–8

supposed cure for opium addiction 91, 145
Morrison, Robert 124
Moses 18
movies *see* film industry
Mowqua (merchant) 130
Mrs Winslow's Soothing Syrup 61
mui tsai (sale of girls) 177
Mujaheddin 289, 310, 338
mule trains 257, 263, 276
'mules' (people) *see* couriers
Mundelein, Cardinal
    The Danger of Hollywood: A Warning to Young Girls (pamphlet) 201
Munich 248, 309
Muslims/Islam 21, 98, 155, 289, 312, 341
Mussolini, Benito 245
Myanmar *see* Burma

N-methylcyclopropylnorxymorphone 95
naloxone 95
Namoa 122
Nangarhar province 310
Napier, Lord William 125
narceine 70, 81
Narcotic Drugs Import and Export Act (US 1922) 201
narcotine (noscapine) 68, 81, 82
National Anti-Opium Bureau/Opium Suppression Committee (China) 166
National Institute of Drug Abuse (USA) 350
National Narcotics Intelligence Consumers Committee (USA) 208
National Socialist Council of Nagaland 311–12
NATO 315
Ndrangheta (Mafia) 320
Ne Win, President (of Burma) 298
Nembutal 88
Nepal 312
nepenthe 18, 42
Nero 20
Nerval, Gerard de 48
Netherlands/Dutch 105, 107, 121, 182, 239, 284, 286, 320, 321, 347
Nevada 336
New Delhi 312
New Hampshire 191
New York
    addiction 199–200, 208, 209
    Chinese and Japanese gangs 287, 297, 309, 329
    opium dens (1920s) 197, 198
    Pleasant Avenue Connection 249–50
    smuggling into 228–9, 230, 231, 248, 329
New Zealand 309
Newman, Dr J.P. 194

Newsweek (magazine) 209
Ng Sik-ho ('Limpy Ho') 282, 283–4
Ng-a-Choy (speaker against opium) 152
Ngo Dinh Diem, Prime Minister 266
Nicaragua 288, 327
nicotine 69
Nigeria 239, 312, 321, 323, 331
Ningpo 135, 142
nitrous oxide 42
Nixon, President 206, 250, 251
Nonsuch (ship) 111
Noriega, General Manuel 208–9
Normand, Mabel 201
North-West Frontier Province 251, 289, 290, 311
Northern Ireland 319
noscapine (narcotine) 68, 81, 82
Nottingham 61
Nye (merchant) 127
Nyswander, Marie 97

Oakland, California 237
Offences Against the Person Act (UK 1861) 64
Office of Drug Abuse Law Enforcement (USA) 206
Office for Drug Abuse Prevention (USA) 206
Office of National Narcotics Intelligence (USA) 206
Okpebie, Sabinus Knem (Ibbinije Obasa Nepoleon) 345
Old Delhi 312
Old Man of the Mountain (Persian myth) 22
oleic acid 7
Oliphant & Co. 132
Omega (ship) 143
On Leong triad 285
Operation X (French Indo–China) 265–6
opiates 82
    chemically defined 182
    'cocktails' 165
    semi-synthetic 82
    synthetic 82, 99
opioids 82
opium
    see also addiction, poppies
    composition and derivatives 4–5, 81–2
    cultivation and processing 5–10, 293–4
    divans (dens) 142, 149–50, 163, 170–71, 173, 194–5, 196, 211–13, 214–15, 219, 222
    effects
    alters perception 35, 38
    calmness 86–7
    dreams/visions 37–8, 38–9, 87

sexual
  desire/potency allegedly increased
    195, 197
  desire suppressed 177, 219
  orgasmic sensation 31
shortens life expectancy 63
  'soul rubbed down with silk' 48
  wasting away 106
  'white opium night' 219
history
  early use 15–22, 103–4
  15th–18th centuries 22–34
  Romantic period 35–49
  17th–early 19th centuries 105–27
  19th–20th centuries
    Britain 51–66
    China and Hong Kong 127–34,
      139–73
    Opium Wars 134–7, 144–6
    USA 191–8
'Jesus-Opium' 145
means of taking
  early experiments 71
  eating 10–11, 105
  eating vs smoking 186–7
  injection 71
  passive consumption 13–14
  smoking 11–13, 105–6, 195, 308, 310
  smoking with tobacco 105, 106
medicinal uses
  ancient world 16–23 passim
  anaesthetic/pre-surgery 26
  diarrhoea and dysentery 58, 104
  painkiller 70, 103, 104
  patent medicines 51, 59, 60–61, 65
myths 22
the switch to heroin 279–80
Opium Ordinance (Hong Kong) 171
Opium Suppression of Shanghai (aeroplane)
  167–8
Opium War, First 134–7
Opium War, Second 144–6
Oporinus 23–4
Orient Express 246
Ormsby Gore, Alice 223
Osgood, Dr D.W. 92
Osler, Sir William 81
Ottoman Empire 250
oxynarcotine 81

Pacific Rim 287
Paderborn 68
Pakistan/is 251–2, 288–9, 290,
  310–11
  money laundering 335, 337
  opium output 228, 295, 321
  rejects Paris Protocol 188
  in USA 329, 331

Palermo 246
Palestine Liberation Organisation (PLO)
  313
Palestinians 314
Pall Mall Gazette 154
Palmerston, Lord 125–6, 130, 135
palmitic acid 7
Panama 208–9, 282, 335, 338
Papaver bracteatum (poppy) 2, 349
Papaver setigerum (poppy) 1, 15
Papaver somniferum (opium poppy) 1–4, 15,
  55, 349
papaverine 4, 70, 81
Papyrus of Ebers 16
Paracelsus 23–4, 26
paracetamol 339
Paraguay 282
Pardo-Bolland, Salvador 237
paregoric 59
Paris 244, 246, 309
Paris Protocol (1948) 188
Parsees 139
patent medicines 60, 65–6
Pathans 251
Pathet Lao militia 268 bis, 269 bis
Patna 111, 113, 116, 131
Pearl River 107 bis, 110, 116, 121
peasant farmers 6, 8, 53, 157–8, 188, 296,
  341–2
Peking 147, 164
  Beijing Conference 306–7
Peking and Tiensin Times 161
Pelletier, Pierre Joseph 69, 70
Penang 116
Pepsi-Cola 273
Pereira, Dr Jonathan 70
Perkins & Company 116
Permanent Central Opium Board (UN) 188
Persia
  ancient 21, 22, 103
  19th–20th centuries 52, 171, 180, 181,
    182, 183, 230
  quality of Persian opium 10
Persian Gulf 252
Peru 179, 208, 326
pethidine 82
peyote 205
Phaktiphat, General Thanat 303
Phao, General 262
pharmaceutical industry 318, 349
Pharmacy Act (UK 1868) 213
Philippines 139, 180, 272, 282, 345
  Philippines Opium Commission 180
philonium 26
Phnom Penh 273
Phouma, Souvanna, son of 273
Picasso, Pablo 218
Pierce, F.M. 77

pipes
  heroin 271–2
  opium 149, 197–8, 222, 308
piracy 143–4
Pizza Connection 290
Plassey 111
Platerus of Basle 24
Pleasant Avenue Connection 249–50
Pliny the Elder 20
Pneumatic Institution 42
Poe, Edgar Allen 49
poisoning by drugs 60, 62, 63–6, 70
Poisons and Pharmacy Act (UK 1868)
  64–5, 153
Poland 321
police
  British 222
  Gibraltar 321
  Hong Kong 279, 284–5, 307
  USA 249–50
Polo, Marco 106
Pomet (druggist to Louis XIV) 32, 71
poppies
  botanical classification 1–2, 15, 349
  culinary use 7, 11
    poppy-head tea 19, 54, 61
  cultivation
    growing 2–4
    harvesting 5–6, 294
    in Britain 54–6
    in Colombia 324
    in Golden Triangle 255–6, 310
  eradication/crop substitution 342–3, 349
    Burma 295–6, 299
    CIS 316–17
    Laos 302
    Mexico 327
    Mongolia 305
    Thailand 275
    UN projects 189
  legal production 227–8, 253, 293–4,
    309–11
  as symbol 20
poppy acid see meconic acid
Popular Front for the Liberation of
  Palestine (PFLP) 314
Portuguese 22, 105, 106–7, 113, 125,
  182, 185
postal services used in smuggling 233, 274
Pottinger, Sir Henry 136 bis, 140–41
Poulenc, Francis 218
Powhattan, USS 143–4
Pravaz, Charles-Gabriel 71
Prem, General 275
Presidential Commission on Narcotic and
  Drug Abuse (US 1963) 205–6
President's Commission on Organised
  Crime (US) 330

Presley, Elvis 206
prices and profits
  see also money laundering
  Burma 259, 260
  China 146, 159, 161, 229, 305–6
  Far East 176, 185
  French Indo–China 264–5 passim, 121
  Hong Kong 131, 145, 169–70, 171, 308
  India 111, 114, 115
  Japan 163
  Mexico 327–8
  Pakistan 290
  Peru 179
  Philippines 180
  Turkey, compensation paid to 250–51
  USA 121, 228–9, 249
    DEA statistics 331–2
  world 321–2, 343, 352
prickly ash bark 94
Prince de Neufchatel (clipper) 117
prisons 346
Prospero Alpino 25
prostitutes 62, 85, 172, 178, 195
protocols against drugs 188, 189
protopine 81
prussic acid 60
pseudo-morphine 81
Pseudomonas putida M10 (bacterium) 350–51
psychotherapy for addicts 203
Pu Yi, Elizabeth (Empress Wan Jung)
  163–4
Pu Yi, Henry (Emperor Hsuan Tung) 163
Public Health Service (US) 202
Puerto Rico/Ricans 249, 326, 330
Pullinger, Jackie 99–101
Punta Diamante 336
Purchas, Samuel
  Purchas His Pilgrimage 30, 45
Pure Food and Drugs Act (US 1906) 192
pyridine-phenanthrene alkaloids 81

Quakers 132–3, 153
  Joseph Rowntree 105
Quang, General Dang Van 273

racism 178, 195, 198
Racketeer Influenced and Corrupt
  Organisations (RICO) statute 330, 334
Radiguet, Raymond 218
Rafsanjani, President Hashemi 312
Ragged Rag-Time Girls 216
Rajasthan 293
Randolph, John 30
Rangoon 176
Rattikone, General Ouane 264, 267, 269,
  271, 273
Rattler, HMS 143–4

Red Rover (clipper) 117–18
Reed, Lou 223
Reid, Florence 201
Reid, Wallace 201, 217
Revivon (M50/50) 82
Rhazes 21, 28
rhoeadine 81
Richard, Keith 223
RICO statute 330, 334
Rimbaud, Arthur 48
Rio Grande 232
Robinson, Sir George 125–6
Robiquet (chemist) 70
rock musicians 223–4
Rodriguez-Orejuela, Gilberto and Miguel 325
Rohmer, Sax (Arthur Ward) 216
Rolleston, Sir Henry/Rolleston Committee 94–5, 217–18
Rollinat, Maurice 48
Rolling Stones (pop group) 223, 328
Romania/ns 239, 309, 319
Romantic Revival 35–49
Rome
   ancient 19, 21
   modern 309, 320
Roosevelt, President 180
Rosal, Maurice 237
Rossetti, Dante Gabriel 215
Rousseau's Black Drops 27, 67
'Route 66' (song) 328
Rowntree, Joseph 105
Royal Commission on Opium in India (UK 1895) 344
Royal Laotian Army 264
Royal Navy 143–4
Rubens, Alma 201
Russell & Co. 116, 127
Russell, Dr
   History of Aleppo 34
Russia/ns
   see also USSR
   addiction 317
   and Afghanistan 310 *bis*, 338
   and Declaration of Basle 335
   and Lebanon 314
   Mafia-style gangs 317–18
   money laundering 337
   newcomers in drugs trade 239, 331
Rustomjee, Heerjeebhoy and Dadabhoy 116
Rynd, Dr Francis 71

Sacra Corona Unita (Mafia) 320
Saigon
   Chinese in 176
   fall of 257, 274
   government corruption 273–4
   smuggling through 257, 266 *bis*, 267, 273
   as Ho Chi Minh City 304, 347–8
St George's Hospital (London) 72
St Mary's Hospital (London) 77
Sale of Poisons Bill (1857) 59
Salisbury, Lord 153
salt trade 139
Samarang (ship) 118
San Francisco 178, 179, 194–6, 203, 287, 288, 307, 329
San Francisco Evening Post 195
San Juan 326
Sandinista regime 327
Santiago 282
Sao Hpalang, General 298
Saudi Arabia 346
sawbwas (Shan chiefs) 259–60
Schiaparelli Company 246
Schultz, Arthur 'Dutch' 244
Scotland 55
Scott, Sir Walter 35–6, 47–8
   The Bride of Lammermoor 47
Scribonius Largus 16–17
Seattle 329
Sedgemoor 55
Seguin, Armand
   'Sur l'opium' (paper) 68
Selkirk, Alexander 28
Senegal 323
Seppings, Sir Robert 118
Serapion 28
Serbia 337
Serenity Knolls clinic 224
Serturner, Friedrich Wilhelm Adam 68–9
Service de Documentation Exterieure et du Contre-Espionage (SDECE) 247
Severus, Lucius Septimus 19
sex
   effect of drugs on 74, 177, 195, 197, 219
   linked with drugs by press 215–16
   orgasmic effect of opium 31
   use of opium by concubines 104–5
Sex Pistols (pop group) 223
Seymour, Admiral 144
Shadwell, Thomas 29–30
Shaftesbury, Earl of 136, 152, 153
Shah of Iran 253
Shakarchi, Mohammed/Shakarchi Company 338
Shan states/tribe
   Japanese and 261
   Kuomingtang and 258–60, 263
   leadership of Khun Sa 263–4, 276–8, 297–302, 341
   local price of opium 331
   opium smoking 13
   smuggling 268–9
   Shan National Army (SNA) 260

Shan National United Front (SNUF) 260
Shan State Army (SSA) 260
Shan State Restoration Council 298
Shan United Army (SUA) 260, 277, 297
Shanghai
    addiction 94, 150, 168
    foreign concessions 135, 162, 166, 279
    heroin production 171
    International Opium Commission (1909)
        94, 181
    smuggling 165, 230, 244
Shanghai Gazette 185
Shansi railway line 229
Shap Ng-tsai (pirate) 143
Shelley, Percy Bysshe 48
Shelvocke, George 45
Shenzhen 306, 307
Shing May Wong (smuggler) 222-3
Shreveport (Louisiana) 200
Si-chuen see Szechuan province
Siam see Thailand
Siam, King of 261
Sicily/Sicilians 239, 243-4, 245, 246,
    250, 330
    Sicilian Connection 250, 330
Siegel, Benjamin 'Bugs' 244
Sierra Madre mountains 288, 327
Silcock, Sir Rutherford 145, 146-7
silver bullion/coins 103, 112, 114, 122, 128,
    135, 140
Silver Line shipping company 231
Silveryew, SS 231
Simpson, Dr 82
Sinclair, Henry 143
Singapore 222-3, 272, 335, 345
Single Convention on Narcotic Drugs
    (1961) 188-9
Sino-Japanese War (1937) 163, 164, 168
Siraj-ud-Dawlah 111
skin patches 71
slang terms explained
    babania 250
    baggies 331
    Big Harry 86
    bogue 88
    boy 86
    candy 86
    candyman 86
    chasing the dragon 86, 280
    chefs 195
    Chinese needlework 86
    cold turkey 88
    connection 86
    cooks/kitchens 196, 248
    cool 204
    crystal 88
    cutting 86
    deal 86, 331
    deck 86
    dives 194
    downers 88
    elephant 86
    fixers 331
    flower 324
    Frisco speedballs 88
    goof-balls 205
    H 86
    half-lo 86
    hip 86
    hophead 199
    horse 86
    hype 199
    jacket 88
    joints 194
    junkie 199
    key 86
    kick 84
    kicking the habit 96
    kit 14
    lamp habit 86
    long draw 195
    mainlining 14
    monkey on your back 86
    movers 249
    mules 232
    OD 88
    piece 86
    Pig Trade 176
    pipies 197
    playing the mouth-organ 280
    Poison Trade 176
    pusher 86
    rush 84
    schmecker 199
    shanghaied 176
    shit 86
    shoot up 86
    shooting gallery 205
    six and four 86
    skag 84
    skin-popping 14
    smack 86
    smurfs 333
    snorting 14
    speedballs 88
    squeeze 113
    strung out 86
    stuff 86
    tea money 113
    uppers 88
    works 14
    yen/have a yen for 195
SLORC (State Law and Order Restoration
    Council, Burma) 296, 298-9
Slovak Republic 319
Smoking Opium Exclusion Act (US 1909) 197

smuggling 227–42
  see also drugs (*subheading* global
    problem)
  methods and hiding places
    animals 232, 233
    babies and infants 233, 234
    cadavers 233
    chemical trickery 234
    clothing 235, 307
    containerised freight 237
    diplomatic passports 237, 269, 276, 324
    ingenious hiding places 230–31, 232–3
    internal hiding 235–6, 323
    million dollar bathtub 351
    scheduled air flights 282
    vehicles 320–21, 328
  non-drugs smuggling
    arms 267
    gemstones 266
    gold 266, 267
    money 333
  routes 236–7
    Balkan Route 319–20
    French Connection 248–9
    from Golden Crescent 311
    from Golden Triangle 256–7, 262, 271,
      302, 304–5, 307
    old silk and spice routes 52
    US borders 238–9, 328
  Yakuza smugglers' code 288
Smyrna 10, 51, 54, 113
Society of Arts 54–5
Society for . . . the Control and Cure of
  Habitual Drunkards 76
Society for the Study of Inebriety 76
Society for the Suppression of the Opium
  Trade in Britain 115, 153, 156, 157, 213
sodium carbonate 78
Sofia 320, 337
'Soldier's Disease' 73, 94
Sommus (god of sleep) 20
Son La province (Vietnam) 305
Soong, T.V. 166
Sopsaianna, Prince 237
South Africa 177, 323
South America 177, 282, 324, 326, 329 *bis*
South Korea 335
South-east Asia 254, 295, 302, 339, 340
Southey, Robert 43
Soviety Military Encyclopaedia 315
Spain/Spanish 21, 22, 105, 121, 180, 294,
  319, 320, 321
Spalding 57
Spaulding, Captain 201
Special Investigations Unit (NYPD) 249–50
Spirito, Francois 247
spongia somnifera 26
Sri Lanka 312

Staines, Mr (opium grower) 55
State Law and Order Restoration Council
  (SLORC, Burma) 296, 298–9
Staunton, Sir George 136
stearic acid 7
Stockholm 349–50
Strachey, Sir John 152
Street's Infant Quietness 61
strychnine 60, 69, 94
Stuttgart 309
Suez Canal 311
Stultzberger, Hartmann Henry
  All About Opium 179
Sumerians 15–16
Sun Qua, paintings by 89–90
Sun Yat-sen 159, 162, 165
suppositories 71
Surrealists 218
'swallowers' 235–6, 323
Swedish 121
Switzerland 15, 316, 321
Sydenham, Thomas 26–7, 28, 353
Sydney 178, 309
Sylph (barque/clipper) 118, 143
Sylph (brig) 113
Sylvius de la Boe 24
Sym, Mr (East India Company) 124
syndicates *see* cartels, Mafia, Triads,
  Yakuza
Syria 247, 312, 314, 318, 348–9
syringes *see* hypodermic syringes
Szechuan province 148

Tagore, Rabindranath 186
Tai-Land Revolutionary Army (TRA)
  297
Taipei 272
Taiping Rebellion 149, 175
Taiwan
  as Formosa 11, 106, 139
  as Taiwan 237, 254, 259, 263, 276, 282,
    283, 284, 285, 302
Tajikstan 317, 319
Tan Son Nhut (airbase) 273
Tang Sang (policeman) 285
Tao Kwong, Emperor 128
Tartars 22
Tasmania 294
Taunggyi (town) 264, 276
Taylor, Dr Isaac 71
Taylor, Revd J. Hudson 148–9
tea 112, 121, 124, 139
Tehran 252, 253
Teichman, Eric 158
telephones 352
temperance movement 64
Teng Ting-chen (Viceroy of Canton) 126
Teochiu people *see* Chiu Chau

terrorism 312–13, 316
  Lockerbie bombing 314
tetra-ethyl morphine (old name for
  heroin) 77
Thailand (Siam)
  see also Golden Triangle, notably 261–3,
    264, 269, 275, 278
  addiction treatment 98–9
  alleged government corruption 303–4
  centre of opium trade 237, 257
  death penalty for drug offences 345–6
  and international controls 188, 306, 335
  and Shan states 261, 277, 299–300
  syndicates 254
  tourism 303, 347–8
thebaine 4, 8, 16, 70, 81, 82, 349, 351
Thebes 16, 33
Theoderic of Cervia 26
Theophrastus 16, 17
Therapeutic Papyrus of Thebes 16
theriaca 26
Thiboumery 70
Thieu, President Nguyen Van 273–4
Thistle (steamboat) 144
Thomas Coutts (ship) 130
Thomas, Olive 200
Thompson, Francis 48
Thomson, James 48
Tibet 103
Tidder, Thomas 133
Tientsin 163, 164, 165, 231, 244
Tilloy (chemist) 8
Times, The 134, 148, 154, 157
Ting Ling (girl friend of Errol Flynn) 197
Tirana 320
tobacco
  compared with opium smoking 63, 156
  in opiate 'cocktails' 105, 106, 165, 215
tolerance to drugs see under addiction
Tonkin 265
Toronto 309, 329
Total Abstainers of Great Britain and
  Ireland 155
tourism 303, 347–8
Towns, Charles B. 93–4
Townshend, Pete 223
Trafficante, Santo 248–9
Transport International Routier (TIR) 319
Trapani province 316
Treaty of Nanking 135–6, 140, 141, 144, 145
Treaty Ports 135
Treaty of Tientsin 144–5, 146
Treaty of Versailles 183, 217
Triads 193, 278–87, 285, 309, 320, 352
tritopine 81
Truth about Indian Opium (Indian Govt.
  publication) 186
Tsai Chin (film star) 216–17

Tsung Cheng, Emperor 105
Tsung-li-Yamen (diplomat) 146
Tu Yueh-sheng ('Big-eared Tu') 165–8,
  187, 279
Turkey
  early use of poppies and opium 7–8,
    11, 22, 25
  and French Connection 246, 247, 248,
    250–51
  legal production 188, 228, bis, 294
  money laundering 337
  opium trade in 19th–early 20th centuries
    51–2, 53–4, 113, 181 bis, 230
  poppy cultivation banned and resumed
    (1970s) 250–51, 342
  present day smuggling 239, 311,
    316–21 passim
  quality of Turkish opium 10, 33, 51
Turkish Cypriots 320
Turkmenistan 317
Tzu-hsi, Empress 157

U-Nu, Prime Minister 260
Ul-Haq, President Muhammad Zia 290
United Nations 188–90
  and Burma 260, 296
  and Chechnya 317
  Commission on Narcotic Drugs 188
  Fund for Drug Abuse Control 189, 275
  International Drug Control Program 189,
    294–5, 302–3
  Khyber Pass refugee camp 311
  and money laundering 335
'unicorn' 24
United Wa State Army (UWSA) 260
Uruguay 33
USA
  American Mafia see under Mafia
  Chinese immigrants 177, 178–9,
    193–6, 197–8
  history of drugs problem
    heroin 79, 198–209, 291, 329–32
    morphine 70
    opium trade in Far East 113, 121, 339
    opium in US 191–8
    syringes invented 71–2
  internal war against drugs
    anti-drugs organisations prior to
      DEA 206
    clinics 93–4
    computer use 240
    DEA see own heading
    education 348
  international war against drugs 180, 183,
    184, 189, 208–9
  and money laundering 334, 338
  pharmaceutical industry 349
  prisons 346

relations with other countries
Bulgaria 316
Burma 297, 299, 300, 301–2, 341
Canada 238–9
Central America 326
Colombia 325–6, 343
Laos 302
Mexico 231–2, 238–9, 327–8
Middle East 314–15
Nicaragua 327
Puerto Rico 326
Thailand 303–4
'uncertified' countries 312
Vietnam see Vietnam War
and Triads 282, 285
and Yakuza 287–8
US Bureau of Narcotics 255, 286–7
US Coast Guard 208, 242 bis, 336
US Department of Justice 336
US Pharmacopoeia (1851) 27
US Navy 143–4, 242, 246
USSR/CIS 183, 188, 290, 315, 317–18
see also Russia
Uttar Pradesh 293
Uzbekistan 317

Vancouver 285, 309, 329
Vang Pao, General 268, 269
Vasco da Gama 22
Venezuela 326, 336
Venice 22, 52
Vereenigde Oost-Indische Compagnie 105
veronal (diethyl-malonyl-urea) 76
Veterinary and Gynaecological Papyri 16
Vicious, Sid 223
Victoria, Queen 129–30, 137, 145
Vien, Le Van 'Bay' 266
Vienna Convention 335
Vientiane 266, 267, 268, 271, 273, 278
Vietnam
addiction and smuggling 302, 304–5, 306
as French Indo-China 11, 116, 139, 167
partition and after 264–7
tourism 347–8
Vietnam War 233, 257–8, 270–74, 287, 296
Virgil 20
Virginia City 196
Vlore 320
von Helmont ('Dr Opiatus') 24–5

Wa tribe 260, 296, 298, 299, 300, 302
Walston, Catherine 219
Wan Jung, Empress (Elizabeth Pu Yi) 163–4
Wang Hi, Governor 104
Wang Lo-shan (pill-maker) 161–2
Ward, Arthur (Sax Rohmer) 216

Warner, Captain 130
Watts, George 11
Webster, Dr 52
Wedgwood, Thomas 30, 42
Wei brothers 302
Wellington, Duke of 30
West Germany 248
Western Union 336
Whampoa 107, 113, 116, 118, 121, 126
Whittlesea 57, 58
Who, The (pop group) 223
Wilberforce, William 88
Wilde, Oscar 215
The Picture of Dorian Gray 214
Wilson, Sir Henry 156
Winslow 55
withdrawal see under addiction
Wongwan, Narong 304
Wood, Dr Alexander 71–2
Woods, Colonel Arthur 242
Wordsworth, William 25–6, 43
Lyrical Ballads 36
World Health Organisation 83
World War I 158, 182–3
World War II
French influence in Laos 265
Japanese activities 168, 173, 187, 261, 287
smuggling interrupted by 203, 231
US links with Mafia 245–6
Worldwide Web 352
Wren, Sir Christopher 71
Wright, C.R. Alder 77
Wright, Hamilton 181, 196–7, 198
writers and drugs 35–49, 215
Wuchang Uprising 158–9
Wurzburg, Bishop of 23

xanthaline 81

Yakuza 287–8, 310
Yangtze River 135, 141, 145, 165
Yao tribe 256
Yew Peh-ch'uan (censor) 148
Yezd (Persia) 10
Young, George
Treatise on Opium 33
Young, John 55
Yu Te-ch'ang (pimp) 134
Yuan Shi-k'ai, President 159
Yugoslavia 188, 246, 318–19, 337
Yung Cheng, Emperor 109
Yunnan province
addiction 304
poppy farming 147, 160, 255, 305
smuggling 256, 257, 258, 261, 263, 307

Zambia 323, 324
Zappa, Frank 347

Zhou Enlai 215
Zia, President 337
zombies, addicts compared to 202–3
Zurich 321

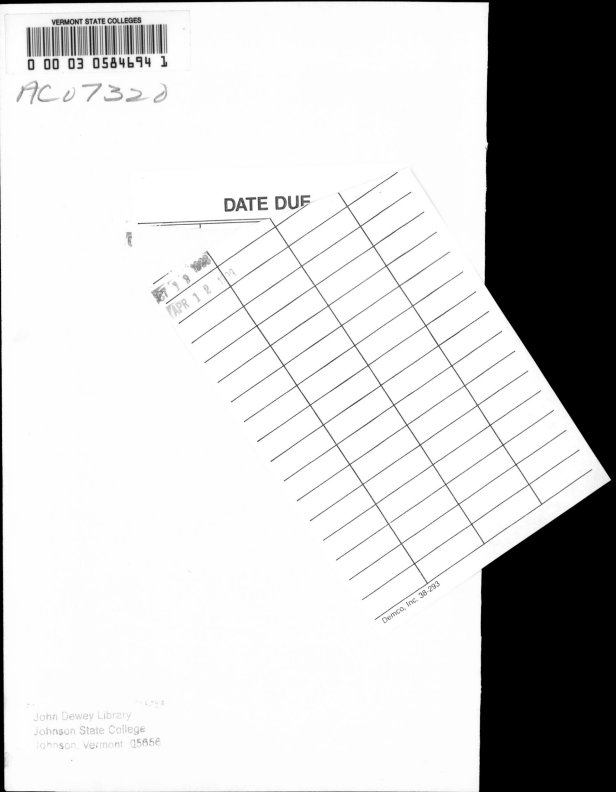

Demco, Inc. 38-293